A volume in the
DOUGLASS SERIES IN EDUCATION,
edited by HARL R. DOUGLASS, Ph.D.,
DIRECTOR OF THE COLLEGE OF EDUCATION,
UNIVERSITY OF COLORADO

VOLUMES IN

DOUGLASS SERIES IN EDUCATION

THE HIGH SCHOOL CURRICULUM—Douglass and others

THE MODERN JUNIOR HIGH SCHOOL—Gruhn and Douglass

AMERICAN PUBLIC EDUCATION—Douglass and Grieder

TEACHING IN HIGH SCHOOL—Douglass and Mills

TEACHING IN ELEMENTARY SCHOOL—Mehl, Mills, and Douglass

EDUCATIONAL PSYCHOLOGY—Guthrie and Powers

EDUCATION FOR LIFE ADJUSTMENT—Douglass and others

EDUCATIONAL PSYCHOLOGY

By

EDWIN R. GUTHRIE

PROFESSOR OF PSYCHOLOGY, DEAN OF THE GRADUATE SCHOOL, AND
EXECUTIVE OFFICER IN CHARGE OF ACADEMIC PERSONNEL,
UNIVERSITY OF WASHINGTON

FRANCIS F. POWERS

PROFESSOR OF EDUCATIONAL PSYCHOLOGY, DEAN OF THE COLLEGE
OF EDUCATION, AND DIRECTOR OF AUDIO-VISUAL ACTIVITIES,
UNIVERSITY OF WASHINGTON

THE RONALD PRESS COMPANY ⟩ NEW YORK

2

PREFACE

This textbook is based on two beliefs shared by the authors: (1) that the heart of educational psychology is the psychology of learning and (2) that for school people the ultimate test of a theory of learning is its influence on the all-round growth of young people when applied in the classroom. The book presents the more important psychological facts and theories that have a clear and direct application to educational practice, and only these. The text is designed for the use of students who are preparing for educational work, regardless of the individual's particular objective in the educational field.

In the selection of subject matter the authors have paid attention not only to the standard topics in educational psychology but also to a considerable number of newly explored areas of the subject. These include such pupil concerns as creative activity and audio-visual learning; the psychological analysis of school levels, of the curriculum, and of teaching procedures; and the psychological study of cocurricular activities and school leadership. Particular attention has also been given to the important subject, so often neglected in school work, of effective methods of study and self-directed learning. The processes of personal and social adjustment of pupils in school life are discussed in terms of the results of psychological research. While the major emphasis has been placed upon the process of classroom teaching and learning, the authors have kept in mind throughout that a balanced growth in emotional and social adjustment is one of the aims of education.

The authors' respective experiences as teachers and administrators have led to a common view of the nature of educational psychology, and it is believed that this book presents a unified and coherent account of the subject. Approximately half of the chapters were written by each author.

To our patient colleagues who have read and criticized the manuscript we offer sincere thanks. Sidney Culbert, Associate in Psychology at the University of Washington, assisted in the preparation of several chapters, particularly those on mental hygiene and school leadership. Harl Douglass, as editor of the series in which this book appears, made friendly and helpful editorial suggestions. Acknowledgment is also due to Helen Nelson for her work on the manuscript.

EDWIN R. GUTHRIE
FRANCIS F. POWERS

March, 1950

CONTENTS

PART I

Introduction

CHAPTER   PAGE

1 THE CHALLENGE OF MODERN EDUCATION TO THE PSYCHOLOGIST 3

2 THE DEFINITION AND MEANING OF EDUCATIONAL PSYCHOLOGY 16

PART II

Foundations of Learning

3 BRIGHTNESS AND DULNESS 25

4 PERCEPTION AND ATTENTION 40

5 EMOTION AND MOTIVATION 52

6 PHYSICAL BASIS OF BEHAVIOR AND LEARNING . . 70

PART III

Learning and Its Measurement

7 LEARNING AS A PROCESS 85

8 VIEWPOINTS ON THE LEARNING PROCESS . . . 100

9 HOW CHILDREN LEARN 117

10 HOW TEACHING GUIDES LEARNING 127

11 HOW TEACHING GUIDES LEARNING—Continued . . 137

12 CREATIVE ACTIVITY IN THE SCHOOL 159

13 PSYCHOLOGY OF AUDIO-VISUAL LEARNING AND TEACHING 170

14 INDIVIDUAL DIFFERENCES 188

15 EVALUATING LEARNING: MEASUREMENT AND STATISTICAL METHODS 202

16 TRANSFER OF TRAINING 240

PART IV

Improving Learning Habits

CHAPTER   PAGE

17 THE PSYCHOLOGY OF REMEDIAL PROCEDURES . . 259

18 TEACHING PUPILS HOW TO STUDY 275

PART V

Psychology of School Levels, Curricula, and Methods

19 PSYCHOLOGICAL ANALYSIS OF SCHOOL LEVELS . . 293

20 PSYCHOLOGICAL INTERPRETATION OF THE CURRICULUM 306

21 PSYCHOLOGY OF TEACHING METHODS 324

PART VI

Social Adjustment Through Learning Experiences

22 THE PSYCHOLOGY OF SOCIAL INSTITUTIONS . . . 349

23 SOCIALIZATION 359

PART VII

Personal Adjustment Through Learning Experiences

24 ORIGIN AND GROWTH OF PERSONALITY 375

25 HOW EDUCATION AFFECTS PERSONALITY . . . 390

26 MENTAL HYGIENE 398

PART VIII

Psychological Factors in School Organization and Administration

27 PSYCHOLOGY OF DISCIPLINE 421

28 PSYCHOLOGY OF THE GUIDANCE PROGRAM . . . 441

29 PSYCHOLOGY OF EXTRACURRICULAR ACTIVITIES . . 455

30 PSYCHOLOGY OF SCHOOL LEADERSHIP 466

31 THE IMPROVEMENT OF TEACHING 477

SELECTED REFERENCES 496

INDEX 525

PART I

INTRODUCTION

Chapter 1

THE CHALLENGE OF MODERN EDUCATION TO THE PSYCHOLOGIST

Learning—The Fundamental Problem of Educational Psychology.—All living creatures learn. This they cannot avoid. Although every animal learns by experience, sharp differences exist between different species of animals in learning skill and the amount learned. Of practical concern to teachers are differences in capacity to learn among members of the same species —in this case, among school children.

Generally speaking, learning may be said to be the modification of behavior through experience; the idea is well expressed by Thorndike [1] when he states that learning is made up of a series of changes in human nature.

Mere modification or change in behavior, however, does not presume that "progress" is being made or that more efficient learning methods are being followed. There is a common notion that we learn only when a useful act is being mastered, such as learning to walk or talk. This interpretation will not stand scrutiny: when we stop to think, it is the same process by which we learn to do useful things and also learn to do things which are detrimental to well-being. For example, both good and bad habits are acquired in the same manner. The widely held misconception of learning as necessarily useful is analyzed by Guthrie,[2] who brings out the fact that learning, like all other evolutionary processes, may be progressive or retrogressive.

---

[1] See Charles E. Skinner (ed.), *Readings in Educational Psychology*, p. 604.
Note: Complete citations for publications mentioned in footnotes will be found in the Selected References.
[2] E. R. Guthrie, *The Psychology of Learning*, pp. 5-6.

When learning is progressing toward goals that have been established in accordance with a philosophy which has been defined for, and is understood by, the learner, it is called "education." If education is to be effective, the learner must be conscious of why he is performing the activity, as Burton [3] emphasizes in discussing this topic.

Not only do all animals profit by experience, but they are also able in one way or another to conserve experiential impressions. The physical structure of animals with nervous systems is such that they retain and, to varying degrees in different animals, select and organize experiences. The selective and integrating function reaches its highest point of development in human beings, who profit by experience in the same way as all other animals but to a greater degree.

Just as human beings conserve their experiences in the complicated storehouse of the nervous system, so the race itself has preserved its records in archives in all corners of the globe. Man began keeping track of himself and his doings on the walls of caves during the Old Stone Age. What urges man to this assiduous guarding of his own discoveries is a little hard to diagnose. Undoubtedly there is often a definitely utilitarian purpose as in the case of the medical profession, which carefully preserves files of case histories on which to base future practice; in other instances, however, much that is reproduced is non-utilitarian or artistic in nature.

From his stupendous collection of data man builds his educational institutions—combining and recombining the materials in an endless series of variations. Indeed, the mass has become so huge and its organization and use have grown so technical that one of the most difficult problems of the educator is the selection and organization of curricular samples from the total fund of knowledge. The excerpts chosen must be woven into a meaningful curriculum representing the sum total of the organized experiences of the child directed toward defined objectives in order to give to the young of the race a balanced and meaningful picture of the shifting panorama of human knowledge.

---

[3] William H. Burton, *The Guidance of Learning Activities*, p. 103.

Psychological Problems of the Curriculum.—As the volume of knowledge in the social heritage increases, the curricular problem increases also, especially in regard to the following :

1. The selection of materials
2. The organization of subject matter
3. The grading of content

Varied considerations must be borne in mind in selecting, organizing, and grading the knowledge which is to be taught to children. What shall children be taught? It is to be remembered that the child starts from virtually nothing as a learning organism. Since the baby comes into the world with only learning potentialities, education's purpose, according to Bobbitt,[4] is to bring this potential to reality, a biological axiom which educationally has tremendous implications and means that the teacher must go back to the raw beginning with every child. Nothing can be taken for granted. The children of a prosperous American family start on a par with the children of the slums or the children of Eskimos who cannot read. Out of the enormous mass of known facts, which no encyclopedia can begin to catalog, and the acquired skills which the Labor Department's list of seventeen thousand occupations only hints at, only a few can be taught in the schools. Public opinion demands that children learn certain elementary skills such as reading, writing, and counting. When the specific list of things to be taught in each grade is compiled, public opinion must be supplemented by more specialized knowledge. The order of subjects depends on the maturing and changing intelligence of children. Certain subjects and skills can be taught to six-year-olds, others to nine-year-olds, etc.

One may wonder what the race would be if the knowledge acquired by each individual in successive generations could be transmitted biologically to his children. Although each child would possess vastly greater quantitative knowledge than at present, there is real doubt as to whether the over-all gain except in the unchanging fundamentals would be made. False knowl-

---

[4] Franklin Bobbitt, *Curriculum of Modern Education*, p. 3.

edge as well as correct would be passed on, and this would
retard new learning. All fathers and all mothers have some
useless knowledge and some wrong beliefs. When new arts
and skills are developed, the old become useless and can well be
forgotten. From the new knowledge comes the new curriculum, and the selection of what is to be taught to the new generation is possibly the most important task men ever face. By that
selection the direction of progress is determined, or progress
may be made to yield to the decay of a civilization.

Contribution of the Psychologist to the Modern School.—
The psychologist who concerns himself with the affairs of the
schoolroom must deal with an infinite variety of puzzling problems. He should be able, for instance, to furnish to the schoolteacher practical experimental findings in learning which have
use both in the classroom and in the administration of the school.
Even though no one these days regards education as trans-
plantation of ideas from one mind to another, the fact remains
that the situation in which the learner finds himself is of determinative importance, and the nature of this situation is set by
the teachers and principal.

The modern psychologist should do still more. He can furnish suggestions to the teacher on ways in which the pupil may
acquire skill in applying knowledge, for theory alone and un-
applied has limited utility. In discussing this objective, Benson [5] has observed that the psychologist not only must give the
teacher information on how to help pupils in gaining knowledge
and skills but also must furnish usable methods of guiding
pupils in social adjustment.

Philosophy of Education and Methods of Teaching.—All
teaching methods are not equally well grounded in experimental
psychological findings. While it is difficult to establish the
complete pre-eminence of any one philosophy and method, consistency of philosophy and method is a paramount necessity.
For example, if one's philosophy of education is that the pupil's
activities should consist primarily of appreciation and aesthetic
experience, the curriculum is far different from one resulting

[5] Charles E. Benson *et al., Psychology for Teachers,* Rev. ed., p. 8.

from a philosophy which lays emphasis upon mastery of facts. It is well to bear in mind the alternate kinds of emphasis. These are:

1. The useful versus the cultural
2. The vocational versus the theoretical
3. The specific versus the general

A word of explanation of the above is in order. It should be noted first that except for limitations of time and energy, forced choices and curricular compromises would not need to be made. For example, no one questions the statement that the ideally educated person would read and understand books, enjoy and appreciate the fine arts, and, besides these things, be able to earn his own living. Psychologically, a complete and balanced education would be ideal because the true psychological foundation of socialization is a wide range of attitudes and information. Practically, the school curriculum is always a compromise, and frequently it is a psychological consideration which determines what shall be left out and what shall remain.

The dilemma of alternate educational objectives presents to the psychologist a serious problem, but not one which is insurmountable or to which reasonably effective compromise solutions cannot be devised. One kind of eclectic education is that suggested by the recent report of the President's Commission on Higher Education,[6] an excellent study which takes the position that a balanced social adjustment and vocational competence must rest not only upon mastery of certain specific skills but also upon a program of general education.

In 1938 the Educational Policies Commission of the National Education Association outlined in detail what were considered to be objectives peculiar to education in a democracy. The list follows in brief form:

Objectives of Self-Realization:
The Inquiring Mind, Speech, Reading, Writing, Number, Sight and Hearing, Health Knowledge, Health Habits, Public Health, Recreation, Intellectual Interests, Aesthetic Interests

---

[6] *Higher Education for American Democracy,* Vol. I, *Establishing the Goals,* p. 63.

Objectives of Human Relationship:
Respect for Humanity, Friendships, Cooperation, Courtesy, Appreciation of the Home, Conservation of the Home, Homemaking, Democracy in the Home

Objectives of Economic Efficiency:
Satisfaction in Good Workmanship, Occupational Choice, Occupational
Efficiency, Occupational Adjustment, Occupational Appreciation,
Personal Economics, Consumer Judgment, Efficiency in Buying, Con-
sumer Protection

Objectives of Civic Responsibility:
Social Justice, Social Activity, Social Understanding, Critical Judgment, Tolerance, Conservation, Social Applications of Science, World
Citizenship, Law Observance, Economic Literacy, Political Citizenship, Devotion to Democracy [7]

A proposal such as the foregoing pictures education as a
lifelong process to be promoted not only by school experience
but by every agency in the culture that contributes to understanding. Any educator who conscientiously uses such a guide
for evaluating the success of his service as a teacher will necessarily view education as a developmental enterprise. Intellectual
growth is then equal in importance to, but no more important
than, physical, social, and emotional development. All educational development is a means by which individual adjustment
and success harmonizes with and furthers the progress of the
cultural group.

Traditionally schools have always been expected to contribute
to the student's facility in clear and concise speech, in compre-
hending printed material, in calculation, and in writing. Not so
widely recognized is the school's responsibility to develop the
"inquiring mind." Schools, then, are obviously not merely to
teach answers, but to stimulate and train the equally important
ability of asking questions. Training in auditory and visual
observation is, in a sense, a newly emphasized function of education. Psychologists and teachers together may well consider
the kind of training given during twelve years of schooling

---

[7] Educational Policies Commission, *The Purposes of Education in American Democracy,* pp. 51-124.

when they, along with others, so frequently encounter the graduate who is allergic to any informational discussion lasting longer than fifteen minutes and who cannot, by any stretch of the imagination, formulate in any tongue a challenging, relevant question! This behavior as an end product is just as surely the outcome of training as any example of improved speed and efficiency of performance.

The "Objectives of Human Relationship" imply an obligation to train students to judge progress in terms of the satisfaction of primary human needs. A fundamental respect for humanity in general as well as for each individual in particular is basic to courteous, friendly, and cooperative interaction among peoples and essential if the much-desired goal of peace is to be gained. Such training should not be an incidental in the school's planning. The psychologist and educator should organize research attempting to understand the stimulus conditions, the past experience, and the attitudes most likely to accelerate the attainment of such objectives. The facts of individual differences, to be dealt with more completely in other sections of this book, are easily understood by junior and senior high school students.

The school has long recognized that it must train students "for life." Particularly important has been the kind of training that would insure greater efficiency and speed of performance "on the job." Do we not have an extended obligation at present to evaluate professions, vocations, skilled and unskilled labor in terms of the contribution each makes to society as a whole and in terms of the job's adequacy in satisfying the worker's basic physiological, psychological and social needs? Consumer education as an obligation of the public school is new and challenging.

That members of a democracy should possess abilities enabling them to accept civic responsibility is without question. Democratic participation by pupils should be encouraged, and every educator should consciously and persistently criticize his day-to-day practices with this objective in mind.

Large social institutions, of which education is one, tend because of their very size to a state of inertia or continuance of the status quo, a condition which presents the greatest difficulty to education. The task of the psychologist and the teacher, therefore, and the challenge to them, are to determine experimentally the kind, amounts, and methods of training requisite to attain changing and progressive objectives which have been established by the philosopher, the sociologist, and the public itself.

Theory and Practice in Learning.—The educated man needs to possess both theoretical and practical knowledge. To illustrate, let us look for a moment at the practical vocation of animal husbandry. This practical art rests primarily on certain biological laws which have been tested by careful experiment and verification. The student who wishes to become an expert in scientific breeding must learn the broad biological principles underlying the development of strains and breeds. The theoretical academic phase of his preparation is general in nature and, to a certain extent, cultural. But other more specific and practical facts and forms of knowledge become indispensable when animal breeding is followed as a vocation. The same biological principles have a different application to horses and pigs, although the basic formula is the same. There are so many variables entering into every situation which the practitioner meets that, in addition to his knowledge of the generalizations in his field and their applications, grounding in scientific method and a generous supply of common sense are indispensable.

Dentistry offers another illustration. A dentist has training in the anatomy of the head and oral cavity, and in the theory and practice of treating and filling cavities, as well as in theoretical and applied pathology, but every new patient presents an entirely new problem technically, to say nothing whatsoever of patient psychology. What can we say then of the schoolteacher whose clients come in groups of thirty, forty, or fifty?

It is difficult to lay down rules on the best combination of theory and practice in making up the curriculum in any branch of knowledge. Areas differ; some require much theory and little practice, others the opposite. The blending is important.

One does not make a better cake by leaving out the flour entirely and making up the difference by adding more baking powder. In disciplinary efforts, one cumulative punishment for three misdemeanors is not the same as three corrective procedures distributed in terms of three offenses. Our world is too complicated ever to hope to write correct teaching equations for every pupil when one teacher has between one hundred and two hundred pupils per day, but a sound mastery of experimentally established behavior trends and an understanding of the genetics of behavior in childhood plus some practice in facility of application mean the difference between master teaching and novice blundering. The teacher must not only have a knowledge of the behavior of children in general but must also know the personalities of her individual pupils in order to supervise learning situations effectively.[8]

The saddest pedagogic partial truth ever uttered is the statement that teachers are born and not made. They are born *and* made. It is no more true of teaching to throw the entire emphasis upon natural aptitudes than it would be of medicine, and yet who would want to be operated upon by a surgeon who had only his natural aptitude and liking for medicine to use for technique? Irreparable damage is done daily by teachers at all levels of the educational system who proceed on the bland assumption that methodology is the automatic by-product of content or an unlearned art resulting from biology's benevolence to the gifted.

Psychological Aims of Education.—There follows a statement of the main purposes of education to which the school devotes itself and in the solution of which psychological data will prove useful:

1. *It is the duty of the school to build in the pupil certain attitudes.* Trabue, in his article on "The Fundamental Purpose in Public Education," [9] asserts that the principal attitude that the schools must try to cultivate in pupils is one of working for, and believing in, the welfare of the society as a whole.

---

[8] See Arthur I. Gates *et al., Educational Psychology,* 1948 ed., p. 716.
[9] *School and Society,* LXVI (1947), pp. 416-18.

Attitudes may rest upon a factual foundation, but they constitute a general orientation which supersedes mere fact. President Conant,[10] in a discussion of the nature of scientific education, advances the thesis that the scientific attitude must be developed in those who study the social sciences as well as in their fellow students in the exact sciences and that this is to be done by setting up courses which portray the "tactics and strategy of science."

2. *The schools should assist the pupil in developing an individualized technique of personal and social adjustment.* In the last analysis, all human beings, except perhaps those congenitally unable to care for themselves, who must be regarded as the wards of society, are responsible for their own personal and social hygiene. We are all familiar with the tragedy of the family where the parents guard too long and too well the conduct of the child. Of course it is true, as was long ago pointed out by Fiske,[11] that the human infant needs and must have a period of sheltering relatively protracted in comparison with that of other animals. Granting this tenet, however, is not to argue that a child cannot be overprotected. Sooner or later in the normal course of development, every one of us must enter society and experience its good and bad features alike. The psychological problem is not whether the child should be exposed to society's impact but how soon and under what conditions. Sex education in the schools, for example, has been woefully retarded by the prudish determination of some parents to guard their children from the facts of life as long as possible. Experimental work in visual sex education by Dr. Lester F. Beck of the University of Oregon, in a state where sex education is compulsory in the schools, has clearly shown how valuable and healthy this type of instruction may be.[12]

The problem of the proper time and method of presentation is encountered in the area of health education, which is just now beginning to come into its own in school curricula. The pedagogical question in health education today is not primarily one

[10] James B. Conant, *On Understanding Science,* pp. 1-28.
[11] John Fiske, *The Meaning of Infancy.*
[12] *Time,* LI (1948), pp. 71-72. Courtesy of *Time,* Copyright Time Inc., 1948.

of facts, but of hitting upon a method which is at once psychologically sound and socially acceptable. Many a bright-eyed
neophyte in the teaching profession has found himself skating
on thin ice because of a brash determination to teach the facts
of life forthwith.

3. *In the course of their education, pupils should develop the
ability to think and to solve problems.* Problem-solving competence is accomplished by teaching the pupil to derive for himself a workable technique of locating the problem, analyzing its
phases, forming a tentative hypothesis, testing the same, and
finally making applications. Karl Pearson,[13] writing a half-
century ago, felt that this problem-solving competence could be
acquired by mastery of a relatively small factual content with
emphasis upon the relationship of the facts to each other and
the laws expressing this relationship. President Conant[14] dis-
agrees and makes a strong case for the thesis that the social
problems of the future will be solved by a specialized social
science and not by hoped-for transfer from physical or biological
science.

4. *Schools should give to the pupil vocational competence,
either in basic or in final form.* Studies of vocational interest,
particularly among high school boys, afford evidence that
childhood interests change and often give little indication of
what future training should be. If the average pupil knew at
the junior high school age what he wanted to do and clung to
his choice, vocational education could be made much more
specific and efficient than it is at present.

The majority of the girls will eventually marry and go into
homemaking. This safe mass prediction justifies a wide offering
of homemaking and allied courses.

5. *The educational process should provide the pupil with
attitudes which will promote his social understanding.* It has
long been recognized that intolerance, the root of misunderstanding and strife, is in reality a form of provincialism. That
which is strange and unknown to us excites our envy and suspicion. The word *hostile* by root is closely related to the word

---

[13] Karl Pearson, *Grammar of Science.*
[14] Conant, *op. cit.,* p. 4.

for *stranger*. The place of intercultural education in promoting understanding and amity, national and international, is explained in detail in *Education for All American Youth*,[15] a painstaking study of the common elements which should permeate educational systems.

6. *Finally, at all levels of the school system there should be an opportunity for the pupil to learn about scientific method.* It is too often assumed that scientific method exists only in physical sciences and that it is comprehensible only at the college level. Neither of these assumptions is correct. As President Conant has shown, scientific method (the ability to locate and analyze problems, gather data bearing upon them, and formulate solutions) may be employed in solving the problems of social science. Furthermore, since the majority of pupils do not go on to college, it is a serious mistake to allow them to enter society without at least an effort being made to acquaint them with the basic tenets of scientific method. We live in an age of science, scientific research, and scientific attainment. Many an American lad tinkering with his first radio, bicycle, or other gadget is striking up a bowing acquaintance with scientific method. No one pretends that a bowing acquaintance is the equivalent of a lifelong friendship, but it is better than no acquaintance at all. A little knowledge is a dangerous thing only when he who has it does not realize how little it is or neglects opportunity to increase it. After all, if studies of the nature of knowledge teach anything, they teach that knowledge is relative. The world cannot be divided into those who know and those who do not know. The ancient Chinese knew enough to boil river water before drinking it although they did not know in a scientific sense why they did so. There is no practical qualitative difference between what the bacteriologist recommends and what the Chinese did. The bacteriologist's knowledge of river water is merely an extension of the knowledge of the ancient Chinese, but both boil contaminated water.

This text will proceed on the assumption that all children of normal intelligence can be taught something about scientific

---

[15] Educational Policies Commission, *Education for All American Youth.*

method in a way which will be useful, practical, and comprehensible.

QUESTIONS

1. What is learning? How does progressive learning differ from retrogressive learning?
2. Give several instances where knowledge of individual differences would aid you as a teacher.
3. Discuss the psychological problems of curriculum-making.
4. What is the role of the psychologist in modern education?
5. What is your definition of a well-educated person?
6. What are some of the characteristics of a good teacher?
7. Why is it so important that pupils be taught the fundamentals of problem-solving?
8. Give some suggestions on how vocational problems in education could be met.
9. Compare the theories of Conant and Pearson on problem-solving.
10. What are the different points of view that you must consider in forming your philosophy of teaching?
11. What are some of the changes that you would like to see take place in the teaching methods used in your major subject?

Chapter 2

THE DEFINITION AND MEANING OF EDUCATIONAL PSYCHOLOGY

Before defining educational psychology, it is logical to examine the nature of psychology itself. Psychology is in all essential aspects a science, using the experimental method, controlling variables, checking and rechecking findings, and stating its results in objective terms which can be understood by anyone familiar with the terms employed.

Historically and genetically, psychology is not a new science. Sandiford [1] brings out the fact that although men have studied psychology for hundreds of years the name was not applied until the sixteenth century. It was compounded of the words *psyche* (which means "soul") and *logos* (which means "talk about" or "science of") by Rudolf Goeckel in 1590 to be used as the title of a book. Brett [2] in writing on the history of psychology says that although the Greeks studied in this field as early as the tenth century B.C. or before, no important work was done until the sixth or fifth century B.C., when it became a part of Greek natural philosophy.

Man has always been interested in himself and his own behavior. Brennan [3] maintains that when men began to take an objective view of the world and to connect its events with natural causes, philosophy was born and for many centuries psychology and philosophy were studied together. The earliest of writings, literary and otherwise, are full of references to human motives. As far back as the time of Aristotle, a statement of some of the principles governing human conduct was

---

[1] Peter Sandiford, *Foundations of Educational Psychology,* p. 2.
[2] George Sidney Brett, "History of Psychology," *Encyclopaedia Britannica* (14th ed.), XVIII, p. 706.
[3] Robert Edward Brennan, *Thomistic Psychology,* p. 17.

made which, with certain modifications, is still valid today. Aristotle noticed that memories of events contiguous in either time or space had a tendency to become associated with each other which foreshadowed modern theories of association and conditioning.[4]

Lacking the wealth of experimental equipment which is at the command of the psychological scientist today, the psychologist of early times was obliged to use observational and intuitive methods. These methods were far from being entirely fruitless. Many significant phases of human conduct can be studied by observation, especially by a careful observer with a little specialized training who keeps a record of his data. Even animals become astonishingly proficient in predicting human behavior on the basis of observed past behavior. Every hunter knows the keen wariness of crows after they have been targets only once. In this particular phenomenon there appears to be more involved than the principle of "once bitten, twice shy," for these birds appear to have so clear a memory of the precursive movements leading up to the actual firing of the gun that the slightest behavior suggestive of reaching for, lifting, or aiming a gun sends them scurrying out of range.

Toward the latter half of the nineteenth century, a considerable change occurred in psychological methods. Sargent[5] in writing of this period credits Wundt with being the father of this new psychology, for it was he who established the first psychological laboratory at Leipzig in 1879. This event was the hinge on which psychology swung in its transformation from a philosophy to a science and was roughly concurrent with the rising development of the sciences of physics, chemistry, and neurology, all of which contribute substantially to modern behavior analysis.

At the turn of the century, psychologists began to make really strenuous efforts to divorce their investigations from philosophy, a trend which has continued and increased until the

---

[4] Aristotle, *Parva Naturalia,* Vol. III, *The Works of Aristotle,* ed. W. D. Ross, pp. 451b-52a.
[5] S. Stansfeld Sargent, *The Basic Teachings of the Great Psychologists,* pp. 4-5.

present time. It should be noted in passing that the interest of the psychologist in freeing himself from philosophy does not indicate a contempt for that field of human thought. In setting up human goals, judgments must be made in the realm of intangibles, but the methods of determining goals and reaching them are different. An analogy might be had from railroad-building. Aside from the natural features of the terrain and engineering considerations, there have usually been several alternative routes over which a railroad could be built. Judgments as to where to establish terminals involve considerations and variables too complicated to subject to exact analysis. Once the points to be linked are established, however, by abstract judgment it becomes the task of the engineering technician to find a way to establish the connection. The philosopher sets goals; the psychologist finds means of reaching them when they are objectively attainable.

What then is psychology? *Psychology may be defined as the planned and organized study of behavior by a method which is appropriate to the type being studied and with the particular aim of prediction.* Benson [6] adds the thought that the study of human behavior enables us to understand the actions and motives of our fellow man so that we will be better equipped to meet the problems which face us in our daily relationships with others. In distinguishing between psychology and educational psychology, he states that the educational psychologist chooses for study those phases of general psychology which deal with learning and teaching.[7] Judd [8] describes educational psychology as a scientific study of the life stages in the development of an individual from the time he is born until he becomes an adult. *Educational psychology may then be defined as the application of established psychological principles to all kinds of educational problems.*

Some psychologists have felt that the behavior of animals, particularly anthropoids, is sufficiently similar to that of human beings to constitute a valid basis for establishing the laws of

---

[6] Charles E. Benson *et al., Psychology for Teachers,* Rev. ed., p. 7.
[7] *Ibid.*
[8] Charles H. Judd, *Educational Psychology,* pp. 3-11.

human conduct by experimentation upon animals. Therefore, in the field of comparative psychology we have many studies upon the behavior and learning of animals, the fundamental objective of which is to shed light on human learning. Many of the studies on which educational psychology is based come under this heading as, for example, the work of Thorndike with cats; Yerkes, Köhler, and others with apes; Pavlov with dogs; Guthrie and Horton with cats; and others.

When all is said and done, however, it must be candidly admitted that psychologists have paid insufficient direct attention to educational problems, and conversely too many educators have had too little of the necessary psychological training. The tendency of the psychologist who regards himself as a "pure" scientist is to look down upon the lowly trial-and-error "blundering" of the teacher. Conversely, the tendency of the teacher, witnessing highly trained and learned men observing the behavior of raccoons on inclined planes or apes looking at themselves in mirrors, is to regard psychology as a weird and theoretical science. This is truly unfortunate. Education must have psychology, and, bizarre as it may seem to some psychologists, they must have "education." Cruze [9] touches this idea in saying that psychology helps the educator by giving him information about the nature of children and secondly by pointing out the methods that would produce the desired end of education most economically.

Psychologists and educators must pool their skill and information in future research as they seek a more reliable and valid understanding of the growing and developing learner. A first step might be a more rigorous check upon the training and skill of researchers who conduct studies. Research should increasingly deal with "real" problems confronting educators. The use of human subjects in investigations will not lend itself to the rigid control of all variables that is often possible in a simple animal study; nevertheless, results of such "imperfect" observation should serve the practical function of pointing the way to more certain success in teaching. Cooperative and integrated

---

[9] Wendell W. Cruze, *Educational Psychology*, p. 19.

research has great possibilities for careful evaluation of alternative methods of subject-matter presentation and of the effectiveness of variable curricular content as a medium through which educational objectives may be achieved. The measurement of any trait or factor is more or less valid depending upon the kind of measuring unit or item used, and valid education is dependent upon a wise sampling of curricular content. Refinement of techniques such as reaction-time studies, interviewing, free association, statistical analysis of results, small-sample methods, test-construction, methods of validation, nondirective therapy, sociometry, and attitude and trait measurement is of paramount concern to the psychologist. Any significant improvement in methodology will be welcomed by the benefiting educator. As clinical psychology is today concerned with the diagnosis and rehabilitation of personality disorders, so the educator possessing psychological insight may serve society in an even more significant manner by furthering the prevention of many personality disorders.

Present trends are on the encouraging side. Much suggestive and thoughtful work has been done on personality and attitudes by psychologists. Since the tendency of the modern curriculum expert is to define educational goals in terms of personality and attitudes as well as academic and vocational competence, in at least this instance both groups are working toward solving a common problem. Interest in child psychology has developed rapidly since the turn of the century, and here again we have a meeting ground for the educator and the psychologist. Institutes of child development commonly have on their governing committees both psychologists and educators. The need and demand for school psychologists have risen tremendously in the last few years, and in the training of these psychoeducational specialists we find another joint field of endeavor.

Conditions are improved, but they are not ideal. Unlimited work remains to be done in the field of pedagogy of school subjects. The work of pioneers in subjects such as reading, arithmetic, and spelling is a creditable beginning and deserves commendation. Continuing school surveys, however, suggest that further experimental work remains to be done, especially in reading. Triggs [10] believes that all educators should be concerned over the lack of efficient reading habits in the schools today. Measurement has made forward strides in both the psychological and educational fields, and it is a reasonable hope that a renewed attack upon improving teaching and learning in the several school subjects can be a joint operation of a combined task force of psychologists and teachers.

Questions

1. What is psychology? What is the popular definition for this term?
2. Give a brief summary of the history of psychology.
3. What is Aristotle's law of contiguity? Do you consider it to be valid?
4. How did Wundt's work influence the growth of psychology as a science?
5. What phases of psychology are of particular interest to the educator?
6. What contributions does psychology make to education? How does education aid psychology?
7. How has the increased interest in child psychology helped promote the association between psychology and education?
8. Why is it necessary for the prospective teacher to develop his skill in observation?
9. What do you consider to be the most desirable outcomes of education?

---

[10] *Educational and Psychological Measurement,* VII (1947), p. 638.

PART II

FOUNDATIONS OF LEARNING

Chapter 3

BRIGHTNESS AND DULNESS

___

1. TESTING INTELLIGENCE

One of the first things that a teacher encounters in the classroom is the fact that some children learn far more readily than others. The annual Science Talents Search brings forty successful contestants to Washington, D. C. The winners are selected from high schools all over the United States for their promise as young scientists. They always include a number of high school boys and girls between fifteen and eighteen who are declared by those in charge of the selection to have as good a grasp of the methods of natural science as will be found in the average graduate student in a university. At the other end of the scale we have children whom all would agree to be incapable of benefiting by the first grade of a public school. In the early grades of the public schools, particularly, there is a wide range of ability. Nearly all children attend the early grades. Exceptionally dull children do not reach high school. Casual observation may often adequately differentiate the bright from the dull child, for the former exhibits a speed in learning new skills, facts, and understandings and takes pleasure in the learning. These differences in speed of learning constitute what is meant by the terms *brightness* and *dulness*. In a very real sense the same concepts may be thought of as describing the behavioral raw material with which the teacher must work. The extensive work that has gone into improving the measurement of brightness and into the search for new methods of teaching which deal effectively with variations in brightness encountered in the classroom represents a considerable achievement in the fields of psychology and education.

Schooling acts as a selective agent in that children of low intelligence tend to drop out of school as they become too large or too old for the simple learning tasks that are required of them, or as the level of abstraction of subject matter becomes too difficult. Counteracting this tendency is the sincere attempt of educators to accept the responsibility of training the dull and dull-normal. A child who has left the American public school for the casual instruction of the streets is looked upon by the professional educator as a lost opportunity. Those who are aware of the contribution education has made to our national progress and of the rather staggering demands our society makes on the citizen are unwilling to shirk the opportunity of doing for dull children what can be done. Education is possible at all levels of ability save the very lowest, but individual differences in children demand differences in training techniques and a flexible set of objectives.

Before we consider in greater detail this challenging aspect of teaching, it will be helpful to review briefly the history of the development of methods of measuring brightness and dulness.

It is only within the last seventy years that psychologists have made an effort to describe difference in ability in terms of measure and quantity. One of the first efforts in this direction was made by Sir Francis Galton.[1] He was particularly interested in the distribution of genius in the population and the possible inheritance of genius. Galton began his studies by using eminence or recognized leadership as the mark of high intelligence or genius. As he continued, the disadvantages of this criterion became obvious, because social position and social recognition depend upon family status and wealth as well as upon individual characteristics.

Galton then made inquiries into the measurement of psychological traits of the individual. He measured the sensitivity of subjects to high-pitched sounds and developed tests which he believed indicated that individuals differ very much in their capacity for visual and auditory imagery.

---

[1] Francis Galton, *Inquiries into Human Faculty and Its Development.*

A technique used by Galton was to ask his subjects to recall a breakfast table. Those who were able to recall the greater number of objects, colors, and relationships in the shorter period of time were judged to be the more intelligent. Galton not only contributed elementary testing techniques but developed and encouraged further improvement of statistical analysis of quantitative differences to determine whether or not such differences were significant. He suggested a graphical method of representing relationships which is basic to our present correlation studies.

Wilhelm Wundt at Leipzig was primarily interested in analyzing consciousness into its elements. He established in 1879 the first psychological laboratory. The studies of reaction time made in his laboratory were interpreted by his student, James McKeen Cattell, as a quantitative measure of individual differences in mental capacity. Cattell used reaction time measures along with other measures as elements of what he called "mental tests." Cattell, like Galton, was searching for an objective measure of mental ability or brightness. Like Galton, he was using the wrong tools. But in spite of this he was responsible for directing interest toward the objective study of intelligence.

In the United States, Cattell wrote an article called "Mental Tests and Measurements" which was published in the British psychological journal *Mind* in 1890, and in 1896 Cattell and Farrand [2] published the results of a large number of mental measurements which they had made on Columbia University students. These early efforts of American psychologists were devoted to collecting measures of all such reactions as were familiar in the psychological laboratories—reaction time, the ability to discriminate between two sounds very near together in pitch, the ability to discriminate colors. This was done on the assumption that intelligence is the product of all the simple mental abilities which can be isolated and measured. Such an attack on the problem of intelligence led strictly nowhere. That it was unsatisfactory soon became evident from the fact that

---

[2] *Psychological Review*, III (1896), pp. 618-48.

the different mental abilities being measured (such as reaction time and pitch discrimination) had no relation to each other and no relation to what common sense expects of an intelligent person. Children with short reaction times do not do better at arithmetic.

It was Clark Wissler [3] in 1901 who used the correlation techniques suggested by Galton to show how chance-like the relationships between physical skills and intelligence were. The need for new tools and better methods was clearly indicated by such indisputable statistical evidence.

The French psychologist, Alfred Binet, started to investigate the matter of intelligence with a radical change in method and point of view. Instead of measuring many simple abilities such as reaction time and pitch discrimination, he examined what might be called the end product of intelligence, namely, the ability to perform what common sense would call intelligent action. His contribution to the science of psychology lay in the fact that he developed simple and objective tests for abilities of the sort children normally develop as they grow older—abilities demanded of them in a social world.

This approach proved much more profitable than reaction time scores. The work of Alfred Binet and his associate, Théophile Simon, set the pattern for the later development of mental tests of all kinds, whether of intelligence, skills, attitudes, personality traits, or school achievement. Binet first drafted a definition of intelligence in terms of attention, adaptation, and capacity for self-criticism. He had been interested in the general problem for some time when, in 1904, he was asked to develop a test that would screen out children who could not benefit from the public education then available. It is said that he asked a number of teachers to judge the intelligence of children previously unknown to them. The method he adopted was derived from the manner in which the teachers attacked the problem, by the use of selected questions and careful note of the performance of the children in answering or failing to answer. Much of the success of Binet's new method lay in the careful selection

---

[3] *Psychological Review,* Monograph No. 16, 1901.

of test items through actual experience with the item. This
selection of items for the tests at various age groups was determined by the following rule: an item was acceptable for a
specific age group (say, the four-year-old group) if from 60 to
75 per cent of children of that age answered it correctly, and if
more than 75 per cent of the children of the next higher group
and less than 60 per cent of the next lower group were able to
answer successfully. Five or six items standardized for a particular age were grouped into a test for that age. A child able
to answer all the items for age four was credited with that
mental age, and correct answers to items from the age five test
would be credited to the child in terms of additional months of
mental age.

Mental age indicates mental development as determined by
tests. William Stern suggested and Lewis Terman introduced
the term *intelligence quotient* to indicate the ratio of mental
age to chronological age. A child of five whose mental age
turned out to be seven would be said to have an intelligence
quotient (I.Q.) of 7/5 or 1.40. This is conventionally multiplied by 100 for the benefit of a public disinclined to read decimal
figures, and would, in the case just cited of the boy of five who
scores a mental age of seven, be stated as an I.Q. of 140, a very
high figure.

Mental age is derived directly from test scores and indicates
level of mental development. The I.Q. is a measure less definite
in its meaning and indicates extent of advancement or retardation in terms which appear to have the same meaning at all ages.
This is an illusion, however, because chronological age continues
to increase indefinitely, while the ability to answer questions of
increasing complexity does not. The term *mental age* becomes
meaningless for adults except when their scores are comparable
with those of children under fourteen. Scores in mental tests
in general increase very little after the age of sixteen or eighteen.

In the United States Binet's tests and mental age scale were
promptly translated and widely used. This led to a number of
revisions and refinements which added to the original items
and established American norms by the use of improved statistical techniques. The most widely accepted revisions of the

Binet tests were constructed by Lewis Terman and Maude Merrill in 1916 and 1937. Since the first translation of the Binet tests there has been a remarkable development and application of similar tests.

In his revision of the Binet tests Terman arranged the individual tests by ages. For each year between the ages of three and ten inclusive he used six tests. For the third year these six tests were:

1. Ability to point to parts of the body
2. Ability to name familiar objects
3. Enumeration of objects in pictures
4. Ability to give sex
5. Ability to give last name
6. Ability to repeat six or seven syllables

For the sixth year the tests were as follows:

1. Ability to distinguish right and left
2. Indication of parts missing from pictures
3. Ability to count thirteen pennies
4. Ability to answer questions
5. Ability to name coins
6. Ability to repeat sixteen to eighteen syllables

Only one subject can be tested at a time. Much of the success of the test depends on the development of elaborate directions for giving the test and for scoring the answers. Only persons who have had training and supervised practice are competent to give tests. In the hands of inexperienced testers results may vary widely for the same child. Testing can become a very serious matter because there is a strong tendency for educators and parents who have not worked extensively with tests and become familiar with their limitations to take test scores too literally or to misinterpret them. Some of the precautions which should surround testing and some of the limitations of interpretation are as follows.

The first and most important precaution is that mentioned above, namely, that untrained persons are not qualified to administer tests and get meaningful results. Test scores mean very little unless the administration of the test conforms very closely to the standard conditions for the test. No innovations, omissions, or additions can be introduced without invalidating the score. A second precaution is that no final judgment concerning a child's brightness or dulness should be based upon the results of a single test. A third precaution is that the fallibility of the test itself should be known by those using the score. The test even when carefully administered by trained persons gives a score which has a probable error, just as a rifle fastened in a vise and fired repeatedly at a target will scatter its shots somewhat. A fourth precaution is that scores obtained from different tests are not necessarily comparable and may even represent the measurement of quite different abilities. A fifth precaution to bear in mind is that mental age or intelligence quotient measures only one of a number of kinds of ability or tendencies to achievement in school, home, community, or occupation. The conventional tests tend to be adjusted to the prediction of success in school subjects rather than in other fields. A child's interests, his habits of work, his methods of attacking problems, his opportunities for learning various skills, and his ability to get along with others are none of them represented adequately in a mental test, but they are undoubtedly factors in success.

A final precaution in interpreting mental test scores is to remember that the notion of mental age assumes opportunities to learn, comparable to the experience of the average child used in the standardization of the test.

Validity and Reliability.—By the *validity* of a test is usually meant the correlation of its scores with some independent measure of the trait measured. One measure of the validity of an "intelligence" test would be the correlation of its scores with the estimates of intelligence made by teachers acquainted with the children tested. Another measure of validity would be the correlation of scores with school grades. All measures of validity are, of course, fallible.

By the *reliability* of a test is meant its consistency or its agreement with itself. This can be determined by giving two comparable forms of the test and correlating the scores obtained. If two performances on a test do not result in scores which have a high correlation, obviously the test does not consistently agree with itself and cannot be expected to measure anything else. No test has a validity higher than its reliability.

No matter how valid or how reliable a test has proved in the hands of skilled workers, unskilled administration will destroy both validity and reliability.

Levels of Intelligence.—Terman defined or accepted an intelligence quotient of 70 as the dividing point between feeble-mindedness and normal intelligence. Approximately 2 per cent of the general population would fall under 70 I.Q. and thus be called feeble-minded. Other levels of intelligence are indicated as follows:

Near genius	I.Q. of 140 or more
Very superior	120 to 140
Superior	110 to 120
Normal	90 to 110
Low normal	80 to 90
Borderline (dull)	70 to 80
Moron	50 to 70
Imbecile	25 to 50
Idiot	0 to 25

It is well to note that while the average I.Q. for large groups is 100, normality is a range which is for convenience of reference defined above as the possession of an I.Q. between 90 and 110. Normal intelligence is not a point but a range on a scale.

The intelligence-testing movement in the United States gained great impetus from the fact that a group of psychologists developed tests for the United States Army in the first World War. Some 1,700,000 soldiers were tested. Mental tests or intelligence tests became familiar to the whole nation and were rapidly applied to civilian uses after the war was over, particularly in the schools.

2. WHAT IS INTELLIGENCE?

The Nature of Intelligence.—The present chapter is concerned with the nature of intelligence and not with the testing movement. It is regrettable that so few of the psychologists engaged in testing have been enough concerned even to speculate concerning the nature of intelligence. They have been content to develop tests which would predict certain types of achievement. The bulk of all intelligence tests was adjusted from the beginning to the prediction of school success. The reason for this is, of course, very simple. School children represent a section of the population that is available for testing and study. The only independent measure of ability readily available for school children is their success in school subjects as judged by their teachers, namely, their school grades. Most so-called intelligence tests are therefore actually tests for the prediction of school grades.

It has become evident that as a criterion school grades gave a view of intelligence or general ability entirely too narrow. In recent years the testing movement has strongly tended to be directed at the prediction of more specific performances and the word "intelligence" occurs much less often in the description of a test.

What do we mean by intelligence? The answer is becoming a little less clear every year. The British psychologist Spearman [4] had in the 'twenties argued that if we test a large variety of abilities or capacities, mathematical, verbal, mechanical, and others, we find that in each case scores depend upon two factors. One of these factors is special to the ability measured, and the other factor, which he called g, may be described as general ability. The score in any test then would be made up of two parts, one of them dependent upon g and the other upon special abilities applying particularly to this test. A good intelligence test would be one in which the score depended mainly on g.

This theory of two factors fits many of the results of measuring human abilities. It is consistent with the very low correspondence between scores in tests of mechanical skill and scores in tests that depend on word skills. On the two-factor theory one or both sets of skills has very little of the general factor g. If both kinds of skills were high in g, there would be a close correlation between them.

---

[4] Charles Edward Spearman, *The Abilities of Man.*

L. L. Thurstone [5] of the University of Chicago, among others, has developed another theory of components of intelligence. By an elaborate statistical method called factor analysis, he calculates the amount contributed to individual test scores not by two factors, the general factor and the specific factor, but by a number of factors. He believes he has evidence that a battery of many tests given to large numbers of children would show that the score in each test depends to a calculable extent upon such factors. These factors have been called verbal comprehension (V), word fluency (W), spatial relations (S), number ability (N), memory (M), reasoning (R), and perceptual ability (P). Separate tests are now being developed for measuring each of these components of intelligence separately. If these factors turn out to be stable and measurable components of performance, the scientific treatment of personality will have made a great advance. In any field the advance of science depends upon finding methods of measuring phenomena.

Both Thurstone and Spearman have written books on the nature of intelligence, and both of them have offered suggestions concerning the actual nature of the processes that enter into thinking. Spearman has suggested that intelligence is a facility in "thinking up" the nature of the relation between two terms when the terms are supplied or in "thinking up" the nature of one of the terms when the other term and the relation are supplied. This was directly tested in a very familiar pattern grouping of items used in intelligence tests almost from the beginning. "The *glove* is to the *hand* as a *shoe* is to *what?* A *power boat* is to a *sail boat* as an *airplane* is to *what?*" Spearman's suggestion has not been accepted by other psychologists. The meaning of intelligence cannot be restricted to the perception of relations.

Thurstone's suggestion is of a very different order. He points out that thinking has a definite relation to action. Such a relationship consists in the fact that thinking originates in action. Thoughts are incomplete or checked action. Thinking a word involves at least a beginning of uttering the word. Thinking of a movement involves having the muscles that would

---

[5] L. L. Thurstone, *The Nature of Intelligence; Primary Mental Abilities; Multiple-Factor Analysis.*

make the movement actually stimulated to very slight contraction or at the least having the motor centers of the central nervous system which supply those muscles activated, even if muscular movement does not actually take place. If thought consists of minimal action in this sense, Thurstone believes that intelligence can be described as the capacity for such minimal action, a capacity for which man may be much better equipped than the domestic hen. A hen, confronted by a handful of corn on the ground with a chicken-wire fence intervening, does not sit down and think the problem through. The hen goes into immediate action, which may consist merely in moving restlessly up and down the wire. Man and apes and occasionally other animals may be observed when held up by an obstacle to pause and then come through with a solution. Described in these terms, thinking is really trial and error in which the trials and the errors are not carried out to completion. The errors are not made in fact. They are merely thought of or postured.

Other psychologists have suggested that intelligence is a capacity for forming associations. It has been proposed that the readiness with which conditioned responses or associative responses to new stimuli are established may measure the degree of intelligence possessed by animal or man. There is little chance that this view, or Thurstone's view, or Spearman's view, will ever be generally accepted by psychologists. The reason for this is that the term *intelligence*, as used by the mental testers, involves notions of value which cannot be described in objective terms.

If our readiness for forming conditioned responses seemed regularly to get a person into trouble, we would not admit it to be a sign of intelligence. Intelligent behavior in common-sense terms means behavior that is successful in achieving certain goals that we all value—a facility for doing the things that we all regard as worth doing. Intelligence cannot turn out to be a quality that acts to a person's disadvantage. The intelligent child will always be the child capable of getting out of his difficulties, of seeing the truth, of solving the problems, and of arriving at solutions which others acknowledge. In other words, the notion of intelligence has packed into it the notion of *good results*. It can never be described in truly objective terms. If Spearman's facility for picking out relations when the terms are given or picking out the terms when the other terms and the relation are given does nothing for the possessor of the ability, it will never be accepted by the public as intelligence. If Thurstone's capacity for checking action does not eventuate in improving the individual's situation, it also will not be accepted as intelligent behavior.

Stoddard,[6] who has objected to the use of the I.Q. as a criterion for genius, defines intelligence as *"the ability to undertake activities that are characterized by (1) difficulty, (2) complexity, (3) abstractness, (4) economy, (5) adaptiveness to a goal, (6) social value, and (7) the emergence of originals, and to maintain such activities under conditions that demand a concentration of energy and a resistance to emotional forces."* In this statement there is a full recognition that good results are to be expected of intelligent behavior.

Definition of Intelligence.—For practical use of the term, *intelligence* may be described as a capacity for arriving at acceptable solutions of problems. When we say one individual is more intelligent than another, we mean that we expect that individual, when he confronts a variety of problems, to be more prompt and more certain than the ordinary man to arrive at a solution which we all grant to be satisfactory.

The term *intelligence,* then, has a limited application. We can use it in describing only general classes of reactions in very general situations. It is useful in describing the behavior of children because with children we are not as a rule interested in specific skills and performances but in the probability that they will come out with satisfactory returns in the problem situations which children in general face. The term will be far less useful in describing the behavior of grownups because what we wish to know about most adults is not general intelligence, but the chances of skilful performance in some limited field.

---

[6] From Stoddard: *The Meaning of Intelligence.* Copyright 1943 by The Macmillan Company & used with their permission.

Will this person make a good stenographer or do well in college courses? Even by the time a pupil has reached high school, the term *general intelligence* has become much less useful, and we can devote ourselves to attempting to predict through tests what he will do in specific studies. The current tendency in general testing programs at the high school level is to discriminate between verbal aptitudes and quantitative aptitudes. It is an attempt to devise tests which will predict how well the high school pupil will work problems that involve number and quantity and to what extent he will exhibit skill in the use of words. As children grow older, the need is for prediction that is even more specific than the prediction of number and verbal skills and aptitudes. Vocational guidance would seem to require that we predict the readiness with which a young man or young woman will acquire a wide variety of occupational skills.

3. INTERPRETATION OF THE I.Q.

Limitations on Test Use.—In placing young people in industry there is one recent development in industry itself which tends to make specific predictions in terms of special aptitudes less important. This is the fact that in American industry, particularly in industry centering in large factories with many employees, jobs tend more and more to be adjusted to the run of applicants and jobs that require special skill are redesigned and changed until they can be filled adequately by an ordinary person. Welding has, for example, been in the past a highly skilled job, but in the press of war production many of the large airplane factories broke up welding operations into a number of different jobs and succeeded in setting up training courses which would make the average applicant able to do one specific operation satisfactorily after training for just a few weeks. The result was that welding was not being done by welders; it was being done by persons who could do only one particular kind of welding or one part of the job—who would be at a total loss if confronted with other welding operations that the old-fashioned welder would undertake as a matter of course. Formerly a welder went through an apprenticeship in which he learned many kinds of welding. This was no longer true in many of the large war plants.

Something very like this tends to occur in the school system where classes are all at capacity size and all courses must be so planned that the great majority of pupils can complete them satisfactorily. The devising of tests for special abilities becomes less important as the needs for special skills are reduced, either in school or in industry.

Perhaps the best realization of the fact that intelligence cannot be reduced to an objective description can be reached by asking the question, "Which are more intelligent, women or men?" The real answer to the question is that there is no possible way of determining which are brighter. If women make better scores on a particular intelligence test than men do, this does not supply an answer. It may mean only that the test gives women an advantage, that it deals with subjects about which women are more likely to be informed, or with skills that, in our culture, women are more likely to have developed. Women are better than men in those respects in which they are better than men, and men are better than women in those aspects in which they are better than women. There is no way of telling whether or not men do men's work better than women do women's work.

The same difficulty applies to attempts to decide between individuals belonging to different cultures. Are the French brighter than the English? Are whites brighter than Negroes? Are Chinese brighter than Kanakas? No way has yet been devised to set up tests which are independent of cultural values and capable of establishing scales on which members of different cultures can be measured. There is no way in which we can really compare the performance of an illiterate West Coast Indian, who earns his living by fishing and trapping, with that of a New York lawyer. Even if the lawyer should go to the West Coast and the Indian's territory and there succeed in catching more fish or taking more skins than did the Indian, this performance would not establish the fact that he is more intelligent. It might only mean that he is equipped better with tricks of the trade, or better instruments and traps, gear, and weapons.

The probable upshot of all this is that we should, if we wish to be accurate, speak more and more of special abilities and capacities and less and less of general intelligence. The older tests of general intelligence, because they were checked continuously with reference to success in American public schools, might better be described as tests of school aptitude.

Education and the I.Q.—The dependence of the I.Q. on training and opportunity is illustrated in the studies reported by Beth L. Wellman of the University of Iowa.[7] Children who were given preschool experience over a two-year period showed a mean gain of ten I.Q. points. These gains were maintained during the first four grades of elementary school. Children in a control group did not show comparable gains. Changes in the I.Q. appear to be associated with many possible causes, including more invigorating or challenging environments, opportunities for the development of language, and the experience of success. The limits of the I.Q. may be set by heredity, but experience can account for wide variations within these limits.

Questions

1. Is there a wider range of ability in elementary grades or in high school? Why?
2. What is methodologically wrong with using eminence or fame as the mark of high intelligence?
3. In what important respect did Binet's method of measuring intelligence differ from most earlier methods?
4. If a child's mental age and chronological age were the same, what would his I.Q. be?
5. In Spearman's analysis of intelligence what did g represent?
6. What is meant by the sentence "Thought consists of minimal action"?
7. Discuss the following statement made by a popular lecturer: "The average American is about twice as intelligent as the aborigine of Central Australia."

[7] *Thirty-Ninth Yearbook,* National Society for the Study of Education (1940), Vol. II, pp. 377-99.

Chapter 4

PERCEPTION AND ATTENTION

---

1. PERCEPTION AND RESPONSES

Origin of Responses.—Every experienced teacher is familiar with the distressing results of occasional substitution of a new teacher in a class that seemed well behaved and well prepared. The pupils are the same pupils that they were before, but in the presence of the substitute disorder and confusion may reign. A naïve person might believe that because the new teacher was so much like the old, and because the stimulus surroundings were so nearly identical with what prevailed before, the expected behavior would be much the same. The answer lies in the fact that behavior is only to a small extent dependent on the situations that surround us. Lines of behavior are in large measure self-sustaining and self-causing.

Behavior is dependent on the stimuli which actually affect sense organs, not on the potential stimuli which happen to be available in the room. Only those light rays that enter our eyes can stimulate us to action. The light rays that fall on the backs of our heads or on our clothing have no such effect. By simply turning his head through an angle, any person can bring about almost a complete change in the visual stimulation that is acting on him. We do not realize it, but we can bring about such changes also in hearing. When we listen, the tension of the eardrum tends to be adjusted to the pitch of the sounds for which we are listening. We tend to hear the sounds and to respond to the sounds for which our ears are adjusted. What we look at and what we listen to are going to have a major effect on our behavior.

One possible explanation of the difference in conduct of the school children under the regular teacher and the substitute may be that the regular teacher has developed devices for holding or directing the children's attention. The substitute teacher is often ignorant of these devices and has not developed effective new ones to take their place. The result is an excessive amount of disorder.

The Selective Nature of Response.—The psychologist, Kurt Lewin,[1] has used the term "life space" to indicate that the effectual environment of human beings is limited to the features of the environment to which they are responding. There are many objects in our own living rooms to which we either have never responded or have ceased to respond. Our "life space" in Lewin's sense would not include these objects. The small boy who is sitting out a penalty at recess time and hears the voices of his companions through the window has a "life space" that is extended to include a considerable outdoor area. The reader who is absorbed in his book may have a "life space" that is limited to his own immediate neighborhood.

Two children may, therefore, sit in the schoolroom and be effectively in two entirely different environments because what they look at is different and what they are responding to is different. The child who is sitting between the two may be to the person on his left a comforting and friendly presence and to the person on his right a disturbing source of hostile teasing. The two children are in the same room but in effectively different environments. They are in the same room, but Lewin would say that they are in two different "life spaces." The playground bully and his small victim may be playing on the same playground in one sense, but for them it is not the same playground. For one of them it contains a large and dangerous tyrant who can be the source of painful cuffs and blows and for the other it contains a small boy whom it is a pleasure to tease and torment.

The meaning of our environment for us and its effect upon us as a stimulus are the result of our own private experiences

---

[1] Kurt Lewin, *Principles of Topological Psychology.*

and our own private history. Every person in a sense lives in his own world. His world is made by his own past.

2. The Effect of Learning on Perceiving

Perception and Experience.—The differential response which we make to a feature of our environment based on our past experiences is called by psychologists our *perception* of that feature of the environment. Children look at the same picture but respond to different features of it and respond to those features in terms of their past associations. Children of well-to-do parents and children of poverty-stricken parents will react differently to the sight of pictures of food or of coins.

Our perceptual response to any situation is affected by the total situation. One part of the total situation would be easy for an observer to forget. This is the internal situation, or stimuli contributed by the child's own attitudes and movements. These have an enormous effect in determining what actual perceptual response will be called out. Food looks more interesting to a hungry person than to one who has just satisfied his hunger. The mountain slope looks longer and steeper to the tired hiker than it does when he is fresh.

The simplest and most typical cases of perception are adequate responses to common objects about us based on our past experience. We say that the chunk of ice in the water glass "looks cold." There is a real sense in which nothing could look cold, because the retina of the eye is not sensitive to temperature. The ice looks cold because we have had previous experience with ice. We have handled it, placed it in our mouths, and had the sense organs for cold stimulated by ice, and our responses to this stimulation have been associated with the sight of ice. The sight of ice now tends to call out the responses previously called out by the stimulation of sense organs in the mouth which are sensitive to cold, and the presence of these responses makes up our perception of the coldness of the ice. The lunch dish looks edible or appetizing. It looks appetizing because in the past this particular visual appearance has been associated with pleasurable eating. What we are looking at may be actually an imitation made of rubber, or it could conceivably be a decoration complete on one side only, like a studio version of a house which has a front but no rear and no interior.

Objects look heavy or light to us because the sight of them has been in the past associated with lifting or moving. Looking at a familiar object tends to call out in us actual muscular preparations for lifting it. Many objects which to a grownup carry much meaning are only vaguely perceived by children because they have had no previous experience of such objects. When an engineer views his drawing instruments, many associations with past experiences are called out. He has learned to pick them up and to use them with caution in performing his task. A small boy coming across them for the first time may pick them up and manipulate them without manifesting any knowledge of their purpose. The same child may react to the books on the shelf only as heavy objects that make a satisfying thump when they are pulled to the floor.

Characteristics of Perception.—One group of modern psychologists has called attention to a number of features of perception which they believe are independent of previous experience and are manifested in our naïve reactions to things. One of these features may be called the phenomenon of *figure and ground*. The importance which these psychologists place upon the fact that perception is a response to a whole pattern or figure and not to the details has given this group the name "Gestalt psychologists" from the German word for "figure" which is *Gestalt*. They point out that in viewing certain patterns, some portions of the pattern appear to stand out as the figure which gets attention, while the rest is reacted to merely as background.

It may be true that this feature of perception is to some extent present before experience. Infants tend to follow a hand moved across their field of vision or the light of a lighted candle or a brightly colored object. At a later age small children begin to reach out for and handle the features of their environment which stand out from the rest. Whether or not this feature of perception is present to any degree before experience has occurred is relatively unimportant because it is so obviously dependent on later training in most of our adult experience. What we see and notice in our environment depends on our experience, upon the total situation, and upon our current behavior.

Another phenomenon of perception pointed out by the Gestalt psychologists is a tendency for certain shapes and patterns to be seen as complete even when the actual visual stimulus is not complete. An elementary illustration would be a circle or triangle in which some small part of the outline is lacking. If such a figure is shown to an observer for a brief time, he is likely to report seeing a complete circle or a complete triangle. This phenomenon is called *closure* for the reason that the person tends to close the incomplete picture. Our failure to notice the wrong letters or missing letters in a word which we see written or printed undoubtedly has the same basis. We react to the general over-all pattern, and our reaction is in terms of our past and familiar experience. Every person has had experience with and has handled circular objects—coins, dishes, rings, and hoops. His responses have been determined by this past experience, and the fact that the object at which he is now looking lacks being a complete circle does not keep it from calling out in him his "circle" response. There is no more mystery in this than there is in the tendency of a child to see a small cube of soap as a bit of candy and to put it in his mouth as a consequence.

The Gestalt psychologists have been particularly insistent on the fact that perception is a reaction to a total stimulus pattern. We do not recognize a friend by first recognizing his nose and then his eyes and then his chin and then his necktie and thus arriving at a recognition that this is John Jones. Very few of us would recognize a model of our best friend's nose. We react to the total visual effect which he has upon us. It was to some extent the influence of the Gestalt movement in psychology that led to changes in the method of teaching children to read. The beginning stages of reading can be actually slowed down when attention is centered upon individual letters. Children can be led to recognize whole words just as they recognize friends' faces. The omission of the old-fashioned training in the letters of the alphabet which always preceded learning to read has without any question made the learning of reading much easier and much more rapid.

Besides figure and ground, and closure, the Gestalt psychologists have suggested another term for a familiar feature of perception. They call it the "aha" phenomenon. By this they mean what takes place in those instances in which we have a delayed perception of something. We hear a friend make a request but do not understand it until we see that he is holding the car door open for us to enter, a sort of retroactive understanding. A pupil hears the teacher's words but they do not "register" until the teacher has made some appropriate gesture. In these cases perception has been delayed until more data were available. We look curiously at the old friend but do not recognize him until he speaks. The child who is daydreaming in the classroom does not understand what is said to him because it does not fit into the picture of his daydreams.

Perception and Language.—A specialized type of experience, language, enters into perception. A study by Carmichael, Walter, and Hogan [2] illustrates this role of language as an organizer of perception. Two groups of subjects were shown similar drawings. When a drawing resembling two circles connected by a short horizontal line was shown to one group, it was labeled "eyeglasses." For the second group the same design was called "dumbbells." Some twenty drawings were presented in this manner. In every case the designs were given different labels when shown to the members of the two groups of subjects. Shortly after the series of pictures had been shown, the subjects were asked to recall and draw as many of the designs as possible. The general tendency was for observers to draw patterns more nearly representative of the respective labels than of the original stimulus patterns. Gestalt psychologists would explain the results by citing the "law of good figure." In other words, the remembered design became more perfectly what it had been labeled. An explanation more in

[2] *Journal of Experimental Psychology,* XIV (1932), pp. 73-86.

line with the position taken in this text points out that memory revives not the stimulus situation but the response made to that situation. This is not at all inconsistent with the Gestalt law of good figure; it is rather an explanation of that law.

3. Individual Differences in Attending and Perceiving

The Relation of Perception and Inner Attitudes.—The strong influence that our own inner behavior has upon perception is well illustrated in the ink-blot tests currently much used among clinical psychologists and psychiatrists. In the ink-blot tests as devised by Hermann Rorschach the person being tested is asked to look at a number of complex ink blots which are essentially nonsense figures of a kind that children often make by dropping a few drops of ink on a piece of paper and then folding and rubbing together the two halves of the paper. The patient is asked what he sees in the ink blot and asked to point out any features of it to which he can give meaning.

Because the shape is vague and irregular, persons looking at an ink blot do not get from it a uniform perception as they would if it were a distinct picture of a child or a familiar object. This leaves the perception free from control by the figure itself or at least sufficiently free from control so that what is perceived will depend largely on processes within the individual looking at the ink blot. What is perceived in that irregular shape has a chance to be determined by the anxieties, attitudes, and thoughts of the person viewing it. At the very least the use of the ink-blot test gives the clinical psychologist or psychiatrist an acquaintanceship with his patient and is likely to betray to the clinician attitudes and tendencies that would be difficult to get at by another method.

The ink-blot test is one of a class of tests which psychologists call *projective techniques* because they lead the patient or subject to project himself into a situation and thus reveal his underlying emotional attitudes. For small children Lewin devised a variation which now has extended use in children's clinics. This variation consists in giving a child the opportunity to play with a number of toys, usually dolls. If one of the larger toys is dressed as a man and another as a woman, and one of the smaller as a boy and the other as a girl, what the child proceeds to do with the toys may prove to be of significance. When the test is conducted with skill, the child often tends to identify these toys with persons who are about him at home— for instance, his father, mother, sister, and the small boy next door. If the child is encouraged to go ahead and have the dolls do something, what he proceeds to do may betray his current attitudes toward his parents and toward other children, his fears, his anxieties, his dislikes, and his loves.

Obviously the child's perception of the dolls as identified with persons depends on his own past experience. The doll constitutes a vague and indeterminate stimulus, and a complete perception depends on factors which lie within the child who is playing with the dolls. One of the dolls may be identifiable with a teacher and a classroom situation is suggested. What the child then proceeds to do with the dolls may throw considerable light on his attitude toward school and teacher. The understanding of some of these prevailing attitudes would undoubtedly contribute to an improvement in teaching. Perceptions, of course, may exhibit subtlety. A teacher's command of the classroom situation may depend on the fact that the children perceive his state of confidence that things will go as he wishes. When he is replaced by a substitute, the children rapidly become aware of the anxieties of the new teacher. We have all learned to respond to details of facial expression which we could not possibly put into words or analyze.

Perception and Past Experience.—The important thing to remember about perception is its complete dependence on past experience. It can almost be said that children can be told only what they already know. Of course if this were literally true, no progress in schooling could ever take place. Children must eventually learn new things; but it is true that we perceive only what we have been already prepared to perceive. The perception of the meanings of words obviously depends entirely upon such previous associations. You may listen to an important secret in Japanese and it will be entirely safe with you. You will not even be able to remember the Japanese words. The Swiss psychologist Piaget made some studies in perception and memory which illustrate this point. He chose certain simple stories which he proceeded to analyze into items. One of the stories was then read to a certain child, who was asked to tell the story to another child. The result is nearly always that many items are omitted and other items are changed and distorted. When the British psychologist Bartlett [3] had short folk tales of the Micmac Indians read to certain Oxford students, written down by one student, and read to a second student, the tale had become typically British and typically Oxford in its nature before it had passed to many hearers. It was no longer an Indian story. Our perception is limited and formed by our past experience and our present attitude. To a frightened child the teacher tends to be perceived as a fearsome object, and to an angry child as an irritating person. When we are depressed, we tend to perceive the depressing features of the situation only. When we are elated, we see only the hopeful and cheerful features of the situation.

At the beginning of this chapter it was suggested that the most important determiner of perception is the direction of attention. Attention may be defined as the orientation of sense organs toward some feature of the situation and, in addition to this orientation, the stopping of movement which would interfere with stimuli from this said feature of the situation, together with a posture of readiness for some line of action. When we listen, we ourselves become quiet. We may even close our eyes to avoid distraction from what we see. It was mentioned before that listening involves behavior within the ears of which most persons are not aware. Listening for a high note involves tensing the muscle which regulates the tension of the eardrum and thereby prepares the ear to respond to high notes. Some persons with defective hearing cup the hand over the ear in order to intensify the force of the air waves which enter the external canal of the ear.

---

[3] F. C. Bartlett, *Remembering,* p. 118 f.

Similarly, when we are looking at something we tend to stop movement and direct the eye toward the object. A teacher's main job is to direct the attention of pupils because what gets attended to is responded to. Nothing else can compete. Textbooks of psychology make a distinction between voluntary attention and involuntary attention, recognizing that to some forms of stimulation an individual must attend in spite of himself. No pupil can continue the study of his history book if someone in the room is blowing a whistle at the top of his lungs. It will be the whistle that gets attention. In general, intense stimuli and rapid change of stimulation naturally demand attention. Attention is also controlled somewhat in terms of the Gestalt "figure and ground" as explained earlier in this chapter. A single phrase in the middle of a blank page of a newspaper will get more attention than the same phrase surrounded by competing patterns.

Although there are primitive tendencies to respond to intense stimuli and rapid change, to loud sounds, bright lights, and the like, there are still more important determiners of attention which are based on past experience and learning. Practice can make us responsive to extremely faint stimuli. Sitting with a company of friends in the evening, the mother of a young infant will hear the child when no other person in the room hears it.

In a college classroom, a dripping sink faucet had very interesting effects on different members of the class. Two members of the class found themselves in a state of acute discomfort listening for the next drop of the faucet, to the exclusion of the teacher's voice. They heard little of what the teacher said. Although they had noticed the faucet vaguely at the beginning of the period, most of the other members of the class came to disregard it entirely. What made the difference?

We do not have any complete answer to this question, but it can be given a partial answer. Those students who, at the beginning of the hour, were sufficiently interested in the lecture to continue to respond to it in spite of the dripping of the faucet became what we might call "drip-proof." The students who happened to be caught by the faucet in a state of not attending to the lecture, and who then gave attention to the faucet, tended strongly to become "lecture-proof," just as the child in the classroom who, with his book open before him, is noticing and responding to the behavior of his neighbor tends strongly to become "book-proof." He develops what has been called negative adaptation toward the open textbook, and it becomes increasingly difficult for him to make himself read it. Another child who finds the book of interest in the beginning will learn to disregard slight sources of confusion around him and to be able to study in spite of distraction. The role of the teacher at this point is obviously to set up a situation which will at the outset intensify interest in the book and lead the pupil to give the book his attention and develop negative adaptation toward what is going on around him.

The experienced teacher never gives directions without first getting attention. If directions or commands are given when school children are in the midst of some activity which continues, the commands and directions lose their effectiveness. An experienced Army officer never gives a command that he does not expect will be obeyed because the command itself then becomes a signal for disobedience. The teacher who raps a pencil for order in a noisy classroom and doesn't get order will soon have the children in a state in which the rapping of the pencil merely adds to the general noise and confusion of the room. Rapping can actually become a signal for confusion when it has been followed often by confusion. The teacher of another generation sometimes had a cruel but effective solution for the problem of getting attention. If he had among his pupils some boy who could be whipped with impunity, he could always reduce the class to a state of close attention by punishing that boy. For the old-fashioned practice of whipping a boy the modern teacher must find his own substitutes.

Questions

1. Give an original example of the "aha" phenomenon.
2. Why do two persons who stood side by side while witnessing a scene later give very different reports of what was there?

3. The phrase "the children perceive his state of confidence" appears in the text. Exactly what factors may enter into this perception?

4. There is an inborn tendency to give attention to certain aspects of the environment. What are some of these?

5. A good teacher stops talking when a parade is going by the window. Aside from the wasted breath, why would talking under such circumstances be poor psychology?

6. What would students do if the following announcement were left on the blackboard? What does this illustrate?

    Schoo   wil   b   dismisse   a   tw   thirt   thi   afternoo

7. "The thief doth fear each bush an officer." What fact about perception was Shakespeare emphasizing in this passage?

Chapter 5

EMOTION AND MOTIVATION

---

1. EMOTION AS BEHAVIOR

The most conspicuous difference between a child and a brick is that the child is active and the brick is passive. What happens to the brick seems to be dictated entirely by what is going on around it. What happens to the child appears to depend very much more on some inner source of action. No child can be understood just in terms of the visible forces acting on his environment.

Because the business of teaching consists first of all in inducing children to be active in certain ways, educational psychology must throw as much light as possible on the springs of human action. At first glance this seems a comparatively simple problem. Action, which must consist always in the contraction of muscles or the secretion of glands, is occasioned by the arrival of nerve impulses at those muscles or glands. The nerve impulses in their turn originate in sense organs. Sense organs are activated by physical stimuli. The word *stimulus* itself is the Latin for "goad." A goad is a pointed stick by which an animal can be prodded in the rear in order to make it go forward. Stimuli do account for action. A cinder in the eye causes blinking, tears, and general uneasiness; presence of food or water in the back of the throat causes swallowing; sudden loud noises startle us, stimulating contraction in muscles all over the body. Slaves are beaten into submission and subservience. A beating is the use of stimuli to incite and direct behavior.

In the civilized classroom the problem of arousing and directing activity is far more difficult. We cannot undertake to un-

derstand it in terms of simple physical stimuli. Physical stimuli
are very nearly adequate for the understanding of the behavior
of a young infant. The infant cries when it is hungry. Carlson
and others have established that hunger is normally coincident
with spasms of the empty stomach and these spasms probably
act as the goad which can eventually change a placid and sleeping infant into a red-faced and active source of a peculiarly
irritating noise.[1] Babies cry when they are too cold, when they
are too hot, or when pins stick into them. The newborn baby
grasps a finger that touches his palm, follows a light with his
eyes, or stops crying at the sound of an unusual noise. In all
these cases stimuli are clearly the goads to action.

General Bodily States Influencing Action.—As children
grow older, we need more than observation of stimuli to understand them. Some of the activities in which they are engaged
are pursued with vigor and persistence and with little outside
encouragement. Other activities are hard to elicit from them.
We recognize that a child is in a state of exaggerated action
when he lies on the floor and screams, or holds his breath until
his face begins to turn blue, or goes into a paroxysm of crying
when the ferry whistle startles him or a strange dog is too
friendly.

The common-sense term for these general states which affect
the energy of action is *emotion*. But common sense is not at
all clear about what is meant by emotion. There are hundreds
of names for such states: for example, love, rage, fear, shame,
humiliation, enthusiasm, disgust, ecstasy. The trouble with
most of these words is that they include in their meaning much
more than a state of the individual. When we describe a person
as being afraid, we are not describing his physical state or the
energy level of his behavior; we mean more than that. We
mean that he is oriented to avoid a certain situation—something
he will try to get away from, something that he will hesitate to
approach. When we describe a person as being angry, we
always mean angry *at* something outside himself. Anger is not
a state which can be described as solely within the individual.

---

[1] *American Journal of Physiology*, XXXI (1912), 441-54.

It involves a relationship to something else. Love likewise involves attitudes toward another person.

Excitement and Depression.—Psychologists have had a difficult time indeed deciding on descriptive terms for the generalized states which reinforce action or diminish action. It is probable that the best description of these generalized states for practical purposes puts them into two classes—excitement and depression. Those dealing with patients in the mental hospital have arrived at this description. Patients are described as excited or as depressed. Excitement and depression are entirely practical descriptions of the general state because they indicate clearly what we may expect of the person. When he is excited we expect his action to be more vigorous than normal. We expect his behavior to be dominated by what he himself is doing and to be less responsive to casual stimuli around him. When he is depressed we expect his responses to be difficult to elicit from him, and responses, when they are obtained, to be executed with little energy.

An analysis of excitement into the observable physical symptoms is complicated. In general, excitement involves the physical processes that favor muscular activity. One of these is, of course, pulse rate. The pulse indicates the rate of circulation of the blood, and an increased circulation means an increased supply of oxygen and glycogen to the muscles and an increased rate of removal of the products of muscular activity. Both of these favor action. In excitement the breathing rate is increased. This is obviously a condition favoring action, because increase in the breathing rate contributes toward an increased rate of oxygen intake from the air. One of the symptoms of excitement is an increase in the general tonus of body muscles. None of the skeletal muscles which move our bodies and their members is, at least in the living organism, completely without residual tension or tonus. The general level of such tonus indicates readiness for action. A child set for quick responses is tense. The child whose muscles are relaxed is not prepared for action.

In the laboratory psychologists have occasionally used what has been called the psychogalvanic reflex as a measure of excite-

ment. When two electrodes are placed in contact with the skin
at different points, a sensitive galvanometer will always show
some flow of current between the two points. The amount of
this current appears to vary with states of excitement, and the
galvanometer reading may then be accepted as an indication of
the level of excitement or at least as an indication of a change in
that level. The behavior symptoms of excitement are familiar.
The excited child is restless, cannot sit still, talks in a loud and
shrill manner, and tends to run rather than walk. In periods of
intense excitement we become capable of physical efforts that
are normally far beyond us.

More recent work by the physiologists shows that the physiology of excitement is not simple. There are many mixed
patterns. The smooth muscles of the viscera may show activity
and tension while the skeletal muscles are relaxed. In anxiety
states some of the symptoms of excitement may be present, but
action is difficult to elicit. The anxious person is restless, un-
easy, tense, but his action will not necessarily be vigorous when
it occurs.

The physiology of depressive states is even less well understood than the physiology of excitement. One of the reasons
for this is that depression is more difficult to induce in animals
and much of the description of the physiology of excitement
rests on experiments with animals.

Conditions That Produce Excitement.—What are the conditions which bring on excitement and reinforcement of action?
Under what circumstances do we act vigorously? Part of the
answer to these questions is rather simple. One of the conditions of excitement is intensity of stimulation. All that would
be needed to guarantee a sharp rise in pulse rate in every person
present in the classroom would be the sudden loud blowing of a
police whistle or a sudden scream. Intense stimuli from any
source tend to activate and energize us—a sudden bright light,
a blow, a dash of cold water, an upset to equilibrium.

States of excitement produced in this way may be cumulative
because excitement tends to prolong itself. When muscles are
tense, stimuli from the sense organs in the muscles themselves
help to maintain and prolong that tension. The effects of

adrenalin in the blood stream do not wear off immediately, and the resulting activation tends to continue. The child who fails to respond to the first aggressive poke from his next neighbor is, by each successive attack, made more excited until finally he has been goaded into energetic reprisal. A series of exciting stimuli may therefore have an accumulated effect.

Besides intense stimulation and recurrent stimulation, there is a third source of excitement. This may be described as interference with or resistance to our own actions. When a contracting muscle meets resistance, the result is a stimulation of the sense organs within the muscle itself which tends to reinforce and energize the contraction. Opposed sets of muscles may thus, if both set into contraction, furnish the conditions for energizing action. Excitement may be readily observed to increase when we are stimulated to two different and incompatible responses. The responses block and interfere with each other. The result is an increase in excitement level.

A great deal of generalized excitement can be attributed to such states of conflict. When confusing directions tend to lead to two different lines of action that cannot both be executed, a conflict situation proves exciting.

2. How Do Motives Originate?

Opposition and Difficulty in Motivation.—The tendency for opposition and interference to produce reinforcing excitement and make action more energetic clearly has its uses. It insures that effort will rapidly be adjusted to the load or task within limits. When the task exceeds these limits, the pain of effort and fatigue tends to lead to the abandonment of the task. When the desk drawer sticks the pull increases and, if the drawer is still obstinate, excitement may result in violent efforts. If we dangle a rope before a puppy and it is seized, the puppy abandons the rope soon if we drop it, but if we keep tugging, the puppy's grip may increase to the point of allowing us to swing it free of the ground.

The fact that human beings can furnish their own opposition when they are stimulated to conflicting lines of action has far-

reaching effects on the way in which our interests develop. One
of the most interesting of these effects is that punishment in a
great many instances, when it is not severe enough to lead to a
radical change in behavior, may do nothing more than reinforce
the behavior that is punished, and the risk of punishment may
introduce just enough conflict in an action, just enough tendency to avoid the action, to cause the act to be performed with
excitement and make the forbidden act an interest. It is this
energizing effect of conflict that accounts for the fascination
which gambling and risk-taking of many kinds offer. It accounts for the strong appeal of big-game hunting where tendencies to pursue and kill the large animal are in conflict with
tendencies to avoid being killed, to behave in a safe manner. It
is those sports that carry some risk of harm which are the most
thrilling, and this is to be explained by the fact that they represent a conflict between the avoidance of injury and the pursuit
of a goal. Uttering forbidden words may carry the same reinforcement. Acts forbidden in the schoolroom can acquire very
strong appeal, an appeal entirely lacking in the act which the
child is urged to perform.

An *interest* may be defined as a line of action usually organized around some goal which has acquired emotional reinforcement and therefore tends to prevail over activities less
reinforced. Development of interest depends to a certain extent
upon opposition and difficulty. No one can be said to have a
real interest in breathing oxygen although that activity is ab-
solutely essential to maintenance of life. The reason that no
one has an interest in oxygen is that air is normally available
in unlimited quantities at all times. If the supplies of oxygen
were restricted to certain places and these places required effort
to reach, air could become one of our strongest interests. We
develop an interest in water only when water is scarce. Food
that is continuously available, as certain foods might be to the
factory operatives engaged in preparing them, tends to lose
all interest as food. The development of an interest requires
that the activity in question be actually called out but that
some difficulty be placed in the way of the completion of the
action.

Development of Interest.—The problem of motivation is largely a problem of developing interests in children. Skilful teaching often resolves itself into transforming an interest in pleasing the teacher into an interest in numbers for their own sake, or an interest in being noticed and praised to an interest in the spelling of words and a strong dissatisfaction with ignorance. We may use the word *interest* to indicate a more complicated and well-organized system of behavior. We speak of an interest in collecting stamps, an interest in competitive games, an interest in girls, an interest in boys, an interest in fishing, or an interest in fiction or history. A temporary hunger or thirst is not an interest in this sense. An interest is distinguished from a passing fancy or from a transient wish or desire.

The interests formed earlier in life tend strongly to guide the formation of later interests because they determine what will be noticed and what will be reacted to and thus control later development. This is called *canalization*. A long generation ago schoolboys were in the habit of purchasing dime novels which were sternly frowned upon by the teachers and by most parents. Their forbidden character gave them an added interest. Children's librarians now realize that the dime novel of fifty years ago may have served a very good purpose in establishing an interest in reading in boys who would not otherwise have developed such an interest. Once their interest in reading is established and reading is indulged in, we can be sure that taste and discrimination will gradually be changed by experience. Where an interest in reading does not develop, a child will remain all his life an outsider to the literary tradition and the extension of experience that reading can offer.

Interests differ enormously in different cultures and in different periods. In the fourteenth century public tortures were enjoyed by large crowds, and merchants sometimes requested the authorities for a burning or a hanging in order to lend interest to a proposed fair. Just what it is that causes one child to develop an absorbing interest in numbers, another in music, another in drawing, another in fighting, and another in teasing cannot be put into simple rules. The understanding

of it in any one case would require a considerable amount of
biographical knowledge of the individual. In the textbook of
psychology there is no room for the biographies of individuals;
textbooks must be content with more or less general accounts of
behavior.

There is no doubt that accident may enter largely into the
direction of development of an interest. We know that experience of success and failure plays a large part and that the
nursery school child who refuses to take part in any of the
activities of the other children can often be led to change his
attitude through forcing upon him some experience of success.
If he is pressed just to try some simple activity in which the
cards are stacked in his favor and the successful outcome is
apparent to himself and others, his attitude may change.

An important feature of interests is the degree to which they
are shared by others within the group. Some of a child's interests are his own exclusively—for example, an interest in
hurting a companion who has offended him, an interest in
teasing one particular girl, or an interest in getting favorable
attention from another. Other interests are so widespread
that we take them for granted in all children. Particularly
noticeable in the classroom are negative interests, such as the
interest in changing posture and activity that makes the end of
the school period welcome to nearly all children, or the interest
in being noticed that accounts for many instances of annoying
behavior in the classroom but accounts also for a considerable
share of the hard work and application that bring distinction to
good students. Attempts have been made to list and classify
these widespread interests, but in the last analysis all interests
are individual and personal. What we really mean by calling
an interest a general interest is that large numbers of private
interests have some features in common. Six children who all
enjoy the period spent in singing may have six different forms
of this interest, depending on six different histories. One may
have formed an interest in getting the favorable attention of the
singing teacher; another may through practice in the home
circle have advanced to an actual interest in music; another
enjoys the period as a relief from reading or the recitation of

subjects in which he attracts unfavorable comment; another thinks of himself as "good at everything" and strives to qualify as a good singer.

Good teaching lies in taking advantage of the interests already present in children to motivate the acquisition of new habits and the development of new interests. The use of short-term incentives like prizes, stars, and honors, or the use of punishments may fail of its purpose in the long run. There is related a story of two volunteer fire departments in the old days of Philadelphia. In order to establish loyalty sufficient to bring the members out to fight fires, a great rivalry between the two departments had been encouraged. As a result, on one occasion when the two departments arrived at the same moment at a bridge across the Schuylkill River, each of the two companies spent the next quarter-hour in a successful attempt to throw its rival's apparatus into the water.

A clear illustration of the inadequate use of interests as incentives is offered by the pupil who cheats in a test or recitation. When great emphasis is put on grades, cheating becomes the natural and logical way for the less bright or the less industrious pupils to respond. Cheating indicates a failure to establish any interest in the activity itself. Few boys will attempt to cheat when practicing for a race.

Successful teachers recognize that good teaching is based on the interests of students. If interests are not already present, it may be necessary to create them. The use of school "projects" can serve that purpose. If an interest in English composition seems difficult to arouse, the school paper may be used to develop that interest. The first rule of successful composition is to have something to express and to wish to express it. For the students who prepare the paper, there is an end of writing just to avoid a low mark or the teacher's displeasure. The student who is composing for *his* paper has an obvious interest in being understood and in being read. A wide variety of news items can be used to touch off active interest in the majority of the members of any English class. If a few less verbal members seem relatively unmoved, they can be depended on to acquire at least some appreciation of the nature of a newspaper.

Interests feed on success. The student who has had an article or an advertisement published in a real paper has probably advanced more than if he had written several papers on conventional topics. Spelling and grammar become important. He has had to choose between different ways of expressing his information and makes his choice not in terms of a resulting grade but in terms of the appreciation of his fellow students.

Incentives.—An incentive may be defined as any reward or punishment other than the natural outcome of learning. A vast array of incentives may be offered as secondary motivation. Special privileges, offices, appointments to committees, prizes, contests, parties, honors, scholarships, badges, buttons, rings, dunce caps, honor rolls, play periods, sarcasm, praise, humiliation, acclaim, corporal punishment, exclusion from the school group, isolation, field trips, vacations with pay, and money are a few items from the list. Some of these incentives are positive and some are negative; but all often achieve only short-term effects. Some of them motivate superficial interests in the appearance of success rather than in the development of real abilities, like an interest in satisfying the teacher with the day's arithmetic assignment in place of an interest in learning to do long division.

Emotional reinforcement may attach to action patterns more simple than interests. We tend toward acceptance or rejection of many transient situations and thus form likes and dislikes. Loves and hates are sufficiently well organized to deserve the name "interest." Likes and dislikes are something less than interests. The history of their formation is, however, very much the same as in the case of interest. Many of them depend upon chance associations. As in the case of interest, a strong emotional reinforcement in likes and dislikes usually implies some conflict.

3. The Problem of Emotional Behavior

Emotion in the Classroom.—Emotion gives classroom behavior its vitality and color. Without emotion, learning would be at a minimum. The sensitive teacher makes use of emotion in developing interests and in inducing participation in class-room activities. Teaching consists largely in directing emotionally reinforced behavior into socially acceptable channels. A modern classroom welcomes the laughter that is typical of active cooperation. A large degree of freedom in behavior is required if the teacher is to be able to select what is worth developing.

A great deal of work has been done in the attempt to understand the expression of what may be called negative emotionality, the emotionally reinforced tendencies to withdrawal, shyness, secretiveness, fear, hostility, hatred, anxiety, jealousy, or the expression of guilt in situations in which it is uncalled for. Most teachers have firsthand experience in dealing with children's fears of failure, of reciting, of dogs, of tests, and an endless collection of things and situations. The emotion in itself is neither bad nor good, but only the emotionally reinforced behavior. A dash of fear regularly enhances the enjoyment of many experiences—a first airplane trip, visiting a strange country, learning to ride a bicycle.

A study by Jersild [2] suggests that children's fears are in large part irrational. From ages five through twelve years, first-named fears were those of the supernatural, corpses, death, mystery, and skeletons. Fear of animals and of the dark were mentioned often. More closely related to school activity were fears of punishment, of being different from others, or of being inferior to others in play or school work. The overuse of competitiveness as an incentive may yield greater speed or larger quantity of work finished, but the final results throw doubt on its ultimate utility. Sarcasm, severe punishment, and overemphasis on grades may result in fears and avoidances.

The conditioning of emotional response is illustrated by an old experiment by Watson. [3] When a nine-month-old child was shown a rat just before hearing a very loud noise, a tendency to be disturbed and cry at the sight of the rat developed. After

---

[2] Arthur T. Jersild, Frances V. Markey, and Catherine L. Jersild, *Children's Fears, Dreams, Wishes, Daydreams, Likes, Dislikes, Pleasant and Unpleasant Memories.*
[3] *Journal of Experimental Psychology,* III (1920), pp. 1-4.

seven "pairings" of noise and rat, the sight of the rat was sufficient to make the baby cry. This is a new mode of response
and obviously one of very little use to the infant.

Similar learnings take place in the classroom. Many an
intelligent student has probably learned to dislike mathematics
because of its close association with the instructor's repeated
sarcasm or derision. Just as the infant's reaction to the rat was
found to be attached to a wide class of new stimuli including
the sight of fur, cotton, and a dog, so the student's dislike may
extend to lessons in English, to the school building, and to the
entire system of public education. This tendency for one associative experience to develop whole classes of new stimuli
as signals for a response is known as *generalization*. Not only
the signal paired with the response but also many signals which
resemble it become effective through association.

Training the Emotions.—Teachers encounter many reactions of fear, anger, or hate in the day-to-day behavior of
students. These reactions may have been acquired in the classroom. The teacher's problem is how to retrain. An important
first step in retraining is to identify the stimulus situation which
is responsible for the emotional reaction. The situation involved in reciting or in taking a test may have become a signal
for fear and panic. Retraining requires that the pupil be led
to face the situation with some other response. The best
method for achieving this result is to train the student to the
necessary degree of skill for meeting the situation and expose
him to the situation by degrees. Arranging for brief examinations of an easy type or for short recitations of well-rehearsed
material under very favorable conditions is effective, because it
substitutes success for failure in the critical situation. The
infant in Watson's experiment on the conditioning of fear was
retrained by associating the sight of the rat with pleasant experiences such as eating a preferred food. The same direct
reconditioning can often be worked out by a resourceful teacher
when a pupil has developed a habit of withdrawal or a tendency
to panic. In many instances the undesirable response is an
attitude toward the teacher.

Nearly all children have ambivalent attitudes toward their teachers—they are both for them and against them. The teacher is the object of both affection and hostility. The teacher's attitude toward pupils is in many instances equally ambivalent. Where emotion is displayed on either side, the noted Swiss psychoanalyst C. G. Jung would contend that this betrays the presence of strong conflicting attitudes, of mixed love and hate, mixed admiration and dislike. The individual himself is at any one time usually unaware that the attitude which he is able to name is mixed with its opposite.

There is a whole new field of social psychology devoted to the measurement of attitudes. The student of physics or chemistry is usually very skeptical when the measurement of an attitude is suggested. The question that occurs to him is what unit can be used. The answer to this is that measurement is not always in terms of units. It may be in terms of comparisons of more and less. If we can compare attitudes with other attitudes, we can arrange them in a scale. All measurement eventually involves such comparisons with a standard. In the measurement of attitudes we can offer choices and determine which of two interests is the stronger in the sense that it will prevail. A dislike for spending twenty cents may be measured against a liking for a malted milk. The case seems a trivial one, but the principle can actually illustrate the beginning of measurement.

4. Differences in Motivational Situations

Motivation of Play.—An interesting light can be thrown on motivation by comparing the activities of children in the classroom and on the playground. Children's play consists in activities which furnish their own motivation. They do not require goading from a teacher in order to play. Children will engage enthusiastically in play until fatigue makes activity painful. Play gets its motivation occasionally from the intensity of the stimuli that it affords. There is no doubt that the yelling and shouting that accompany much play contribute toward the energy with which the play is pursued, but the chief source of the play energy closely resembles the energy enlisted by gambling or dangerous sports. Children's play has the characteristic of exposing them continuously or almost continuously to new situations and situations for which they are not prepared. Familiar and recurring situations are met by routine habit, but there can be no habit adjustment to new situations. New situations always involve conflict. This is one reason why children tend strongly to play together. The solitary game quickly becomes routinized. When the lone player has learned what to expect, the game loses its excitement and interest. But where other children are involved, the unexpected is continuously introduced. The new is exciting because we cannot be ready for it.

The fundamental difference between play and work lies in the fact that work is defined in terms of end results and demands routinized methods. Play is without ulterior purpose. Education can use play as a relief from work, and it can even take advantage of play occasionally to introduce in the form of supervised play certain kinds of training which are not suspected by the children taking part in the games. There is no doubt that certain forms of social skills can be taught through supervised play. The extent to which they can be taught is not yet clear because methods have still to be developed for the objective measurement of such skills as are involved in leadership and cooperation. It might be more correct to acknowledge that some beginnings have been made toward measurement, but very little has been done toward the correlation of results with the methods used in directed play.

Attempts to Classify Motives.—Attempts have been made to describe human motives for as long as men have written about men. A Greek writer of the fifth century B.C. describes his fellow men as impelled to action by three motives: hunger, thirst, and love. There have been thousands of similar descriptions. One of the best known of these was that of William McDougall [4] written in 1908. McDougall held that human

---

[4] William McDougall, *An Introduction to Social Psychology,* chap. 3.

motives can be described in terms of some eleven instincts. His
list included such things as flight or the instinct to flee from
danger, the parental instinct, pugnacity, repulsion, curiosity,
and a number of more vaguely described classes of behavior like
self-abasement, self-assertion, and the instinct of construction.
Such lists of instincts or lists of motives turn out to be of little
actual value in use.   Baldwin [5] claimed, for instance, that human
beings are instinctively imitative. This gives little information
about human beings. Obviously individuals do not ordinarily
imitate each other on all occasions. If they did, all conversations would be duets, and bus drivers as well as incoming
passengers would keep dropping fares into the fare box.
When we ask under what circumstances men imitate each
other, a general principle that men are imitative is of no help
whatever.

    It would be a similar mistake to assert, merely because we
have observed in a number of different persons behavior that
seems to be directed at getting attention, that human beings
have an attention-getting instinct. This would give us no
information at all concerning the sorts of things that men will
do to get attention or the circumstances under which they will
seek attention, for it is obvious that a great many persons under
a great many circumstances avoid attention. We can note in
the case of an individual child that he will continue to do a
variety of things until he gets attention. We may therefore
accept attention-getting as one of his principal forms of motivation. We may find the phrase useful in describing the behavior
of large numbers of school children, but in each individual case
the things a child will do to get attention and whether or not
any particular child has developed an interest in attention *will
be found to depend upon the past history of the individual*. The
widespread occurrence of attention-getting as an interest may
have its foundation in the fact that infants depend on getting
the attention of adults for the relief of most of the forms of
discomfort from which they suffer. A six-months-old baby
must get its mother's attention if it is hungry, if it is cold, if it is

    [5] James Mark Baldwin, *Social and Ethical Interpretations in Mental
Development.*

hot, if a pin is sticking into it, and under many other circumstances that produce discomfort. Relief comes through the aid of the mother, which is procured through what one writer has called the baby's nuisance technique.

Older children must also learn how to get attention or they will suffer from many forms of acute discomfort. One cannot make a purchase at a store without getting the attention of a clerk or take a trip in a bus without getting the attention of the conductor in order that he may make the stop. All persons therefore learn many ways of getting attention. All persons also learn many ways of avoiding attention. School children learn many devices for avoiding the attention of the teacher. A boy on the playground learns to get attention by making a nuisance of himself. Another child learns to get attention by pleasing. An occasional child learns how to get the attention of other children or of grownups by shocking and startling statements about people, by telling lies about prominent persons. *Understanding the motivation of behavior like this demands a knowledge of the individual and the history of the experiences that have developed in him the interests and motives that we can observe.*

The forms of motivation that are common to all human beings, like interests in love or food, are of very little help indeed in understanding any individual human being. If we hope to understand human beings, the first requirement is that we do not look for that understanding in a general textbook on human behavior but in the study of those whom we wish to understand. We make a great step forward in understanding the motivation of individuals when we realize the extent to which habits can explain motives. The description of the way in which habits are formed is left to a later chapter, but we may here accept the word in its ordinary and common-sense meaning, including such things as a habit of eating certain kinds of food, of dressing in a certain way, of going to a certain place for lunch, of seeking out certain companions, of brushing the teeth, of early rising, of smoking, of using profanity, of polite behavior, and of considerate treatment of others. It is a characteristic of all of these habits that when a person confronts a situation that blocks carrying out the habit, this is the occasion for conflict and emotional reinforcement. Under these circumstances the individual tends to learn his way around the obstacle.

In other words, we can depend on people to tend strongly to carry out their familiar habits, even when circumstances put obstacles in the way. If we know these habits, we have a basis for predicting behavior. Habits are motives, and they are motives that will never be adequately described in textbooks because habits are results of individual experience, and no textbook can undertake to describe the individual experiences of all the individuals in a nation.

The realization that the understanding of human motives requires an understanding of the individual and his history we owe, for the most part, to Freud and the psychoanalysts. Freud's interest was centered in the sexual functions and the habits which grow up about those functions. Early experiences direct these habits into one channel or another. This process Freud called *fixation*. In this textbook the process is called *canalization,* following the usage of Gardner Murphy in his book, *Personality.*[6] The details of Freud's account of the development of the forms of sexual motivation have undergone extensive changes in the hands of later psychoanalysts, and they have, for the most part, not received treatment in objective and scientific terms, but the underlying features of Freud's account will undoubtedly stand up under scientific scrutiny. Freud believed that the direction of affection in boys is guided by the responses which have been organized about the mother and that the love interest of girls is strongly influenced by their earlier organization of affection toward the father.

It is unfortunate that Freud, once having arrived at this insight into the dependence of motivation on individual experiences, tended strongly to universalize those experiences and to assert that certain common forms of motivation which he had observed in patients are part of the normal development of all persons. This is getting back to the discarded instinct theories and away from a required road to understanding of

---

[6] Gardner Murphy, *Personality.*

people which lies in an acquaintance with their habits, individual
interests, and background of personal experience.

QUESTIONS

1. Describe the type of behavior known as disgust in completely
   objective terms, that is, without reference to inner feelings.
2. In fear, do the skeletal muscles usually increase or decrease in
   tonus? Can you think of cases in which the reverse is true?
3. Are there occasions in which increase of muscle tonus may make
   learning difficult or impossible?
4. Which of the following experiences is most likely to establish
   an interest: success after hard work, success with no effort,
   failure after hard work? Why?
5. A certain school forbade the reading of comic books on school
   property. Can you think of a good argument against this policy?
6. Why are instinct theories of little or no value in practice?

Chapter 6

PHYSICAL BASIS OF BEHAVIOR AND LEARNING

---

1. The Precise Description of Behavior

There are successful teachers who have not read a textbook of psychology. They learned to teach by teaching. There are also many teachers who have taught for years and have not yet learned how to teach.

It is possible to be a champion swimmer and not know the name of a single muscle used in swimming. The champion has learned to swim by swimming and not by reading books about swimming or by listening to lectures on swimming. But teaching is different from swimming. You can swim alone because the swimming does not necessarily involve other persons. You cannot teach alone. There is always at least one other person involved. While it is true that some teachers become proficient by practice, they have one outstanding disability—inability to tell how they do it—just as the concert violinist cannot put his skill into words that will make his listeners able to play as well as he does. Teachers who have "learned on the job" cannot tell others how they do it because they do not know the words in which the behavior of children is most accurately described. Good teachers may not know the general rules of behavior and learning that have been worked out by specialists in the description of behavior. They can teach but cannot successfully tell others how they teach. Good teachers may not themselves know how they teach. "Knowing how" means being able to put the "how" into words.

In order to teach teaching itself, one must have an acquaintance with the language in which human behavior is most adequately described and an acquaintance with the general principles of behavior.

One can teach without psychology; but one cannot tell others how to teach without making use of psychological terms. The student-teacher can learn to teach without studying psychology; but he cannot learn from the advice of others, and he cannot extend his preparation beyond his own actual experience in teaching unless he understands the language in which behavior must be described.

Behavior as Limited by Physical Structure.—Understanding behavior starts with a knowledge of its physical basis—how the body governs behavior and sets limits on what behavior can be. Some of the limits set by the physical body are so familiar that they are forgotten. One can tell just by looking at a six-year-old child that he will not be able to lift what the average man can lift, or be able to run as fast as a college athlete. No one expects a six-year-old to be as intelligent as the average man—as able to solve new problems or learn new skills.

The body sets other limits on behavior that are not visible at a glance. The shape of a school child's eyeball may make it impossible for him to get a clear view of what is written on the blackboard or a clear view of what is printed in his textbook. The physical structure of his ear may make him seem stupid to his family or to his teacher because he is slow in responding when addressed. These limitations can be understood after the eye defect or the deafness has been discovered by the school nurse.

All behavior, of course, is based on physical structure. No one sees without eyes or hears without ears or thinks without a brain or sheds tears without tear glands or digests a meal without having some portion of the digestive tract in action.

This does not make man a machine. No machine has a structure comparable to man's in its capacity for varied behavior, or for adapting itself to differing climates, different food sources, different conditions for survival.

No blueprint will ever be drawn to show all the connections of the human nervous system. We know only a little about the intricacies of a single muscle cell and what happens when it contracts, but the fact that no machine approaches man's complexity should not lead us to forget that all human behavior and all human thought depend on the physical structure of man.

For the purpose of understanding behavior the physical structures most important are of three kinds : the sense organs through which come signals for behavior, the connecting nerves through which the signals reach the muscles and glands and produce responses, and the effectors or muscles and glands by which we respond to changes in the environment.

2. STIMULI AND THEIR PHYSIOLOGICAL EFFECTS

Receptors or Sense Organs.—The sense organs put limits on action because it is only through them that the signals are provided which eventually cause muscles to contract. There are events about us continually to which we make no response at all. A sensitive radio set would betray the fact that, in the room in which we are sitting, there are rays of radiant energy originating in a thousand broadcasting stations. A new diathermy machine at a laboratory in Seattle had to be remodeled because it was interfering with the police radio in Miami, Florida. Obviously if the police in Miami had no radios they would not have been disturbed. There are no sense organs which are sensitive to the wave length used for radio communication. But there are two forms of sense organs which respond to radiant energy in wave lengths and frequencies quite different from those in radio. The eye is sensitive to a little over an octave of such frequencies, and the sense organs in the skin which respond to warmth are sensitive to radiant heat.

The ear is sensitive to a narrow range of vibrations, usually in the air. The waves that cause hearing may be conducted through other media like water or solids to the sensitive receptor in the ear. When the frequency of air vibrations (the number per second) is increased beyond a certain point, the ears are no longer sensitive to them. Most dogs can, for instance, hear sounds so shrill that human beings are deaf to them. Many insects make noises which are audible to other insects but not to man.   Very few persons can hear vibrations at the rate of less than 20 per second or above 20,000 per second.

This deafness to "supersonic" sounds concerns us not at all because it applies to all people.   Our interest will lie with the special cases of children who through some defect in their hearing apparatus are insensitive to the sounds which other children do hear.   Many educators believe that total deafness or the inability to respond to sounds of any frequency is a far more serious handicap than blindness because it is through the ear that we ordinarily communicate with other persons and the blind person is not deprived of such communication.

Three Classes of Sense Organs.—Man is supplied with sense organs in generous variety.   It is convenient to divide them into three classes: the *exteroceptors* which establish rapport with the outer world, the *interoceptors* which originate responses to what goes on in the digestive tract, and the *proprioceptors* in muscles and joints which originate responses to movements.   Interoceptors are, for instance, responsible for vomiting, for the digestive secretions, for colic pains.   Proprioceptors in the muscles and joints make possible the coordination of movements and make it possible for one movement to be the signal for another.   Without this sensitiveness to movement and posture, even simple actions like walking would be impossible.   The eye, ear, and nose are often called the *distance receptors* because they make it possible for us to react to events which are taking place at some distance.   It is the eye and ear which have the most importance for the classroom, because it is through them that the teacher and the other children influence behavior.   Defects in these two senses are noticeable, and for such defects there are standard tests which can be applied by a nurse or a physician with the proper instruments.   Defects in most of the other sense realms may go unknown either to the individual or his friends throughout a lifetime.   A man may for instance have no means of telling that his sense of smell or taste is a little less acute than that of another person.   Whether we are more or less sensitive than our friends to colic pains originating in our interoceptors we will never know.

Eye defects can handicap learning, and a teacher should be able to recognize quickly the signs of deficient vision. The commonest defects of vision are caused by abnormalities in the shape of the eyeball which interfere with it as an optical system in focusing light on the retina. When the eyeball is not properly spherical but is flattened in one direction or another, it produces a blurred image. This difficulty, called astigmatism, can be corrected by glasses which compensate for the distortion of the eyeball and correct the focusing. When the eyeball is so shaped that it focuses the images of objects in front of the retina, the image falling on the retina is blurred with the effect of making it necessary to bring objects nearer the eyes than normally in order to see clearly. This shortsightedness, like astigmatism, can be compensated for by proper glasses. Farsightedness, in which the images of objects tend to be focused behind the retina, can also be corrected by glasses. Any one of these conditions may make it impossible for a child to see what is written on a blackboard or to recognize persons at a distance. These visual defects may have far-reaching effects on behavior because the child must adapt all his habits to them.

The child himself may be unaware that he has the visual defect and have no notion why he is unable to see what the others see on the blackboard. The result is that he must give the answer "I don't know" when the proper answer would be, "I don't see." And his teacher may in turn treat him as though he were lazy or stupid instead of deficient in vision.

The same remarks apply with even greater force to hearing. It is not unusual to find that a slightly deaf child in a family is not known to be deaf by other members of the family and is treated as if he were stupid or uncooperative.

For the effectiveness of the proprioceptors in muscles and joints, as of the interoceptors in the alimentary tract, we of course have no standards. We realize that they play important roles in influencing behavior, but we can do relatively very little about the situation if they are defective. It must be enough for us to know such facts as that the sense organs in muscles and joints make us sensitive to our own posture and action. There is a disease of the nervous system in which the nerve connections from the proprioceptors cannot act as signals for behavior. A person suffering from such a disease may find it impossible to walk because the movement that he makes next cannot be signaled by the last movement or by the position of his legs. He is just as likely to try to put the leg already forward again forward. He must learn to walk in response to careful watching of what his legs are doing, so that his eyes give the signal for the next movement.

The attitude or posture in which we are at any moment stimulates proprioceptors in muscles and joints and limits our next action. This has important consequences in dealing with children. The proprioceptors in muscles and joints make it possible for most of our actions to become self-maintaining by allowing one movement to become the signal for the next. Walking tends to keep itself up in this fashion. One movement leads to the next. What a child is doing is one of the best indications of what he is about to do. We cannot expect sudden changes in behavior except in extraordinary circumstances or with intense signals. In ordinary behavior, any series of actions or any line of conduct tends to maintain itself because it furnishes the signals for its own continuation.

The foregoing facts have a vital but often unsuspected bearing on the behavior of children. They mean that in order to get a child to obey a command, request, or suggestion, we must ordinarily allow time and furnish signals for a change in behavior. Getting a child's attention requires that we induce him to stop what he is doing, and this often takes time.

In that all too familiar phenomenon, the temper tantrum, a child exhibits behavior dominated by proprioceptors. He is unresponsive to what is going on about him. What the child sees and what he hears have little effect. His own intense activity is so stimulating sense organs in his own body that these stimuli dominate and rule responses. Until the tantrum wears itself out through fatigue or until some striking new attention-getting stimulation breaks in on the current line of activity, nothing reasonable can be expected. When we understand this, we are far better equipped to cope with a situation of this kind.

3. The Connectors

The Nervous System.—Most car drivers would have little use for a wiring diagram of the electrical connections of a car, because when something goes wrong they take the car to the garage and let someone else worry over the details of structure. Similarly most of us have little real concern with the details of the elaborate system of nerve pathways which make possible the infinite variety of human behavior. We grant that the connections exist and assume there is some way in which stimuli cause action. But we never open up a nervous system to try to repair defective brains. Sometimes physicians may operate to sever a nerve connection in certain kinds of acute pain. Neurologists are experimenting with radical surgery of brain pathways in certain serious types of insanity. There may be an occasional operation for the removal of a brain tumor whose presence and location are known by the disturbances of behavior which accompany the growth of the tumor. But aside from measures of this kind, there is little prospect that most of us will have any repairs made on our nervous systems.

The unit of the nervous system is the nerve cell. This is like other body cells in that it has a cell body, which is the center for the maintenance of the cell, and long processes which serve as connections between the points over which the cell will establish communication. The specialty of the nerve cell is the conduction of the nervous impulse. This is a complex reaction which includes both chemical and electrical changes. An impulse travels along the nerve the way combustion travels along a powder fuse. The energy of the impulse is supplied by the nerve itself, just as the energy of combustion is supplied by the materials of the fuse. The difference between the powder fuse and the nerves is that within a fraction of a second after a nerve impulse has traveled along a nerve, the nerve has recovered and is in a condition to transmit a new impulse. It has been established that carbon dioxide is produced by the conduction of a nerve impulse, and presumably many other chemical changes are involved. Since these changes use up energy, we may argue that the energy must eventually be supplied, like muscular energy, from the food we eat. But the energy consumed by nerves in the transmission of impulses is far less than the energy used by muscle fibers in contracting and doing the work. It is probable that nerve fatigue plays far less part in behavior than muscle fatigue. Laboratory experiments in which a muscle with its attached nerve is dissected from a frog leg and the nerves are stimulated repeatedly would indicate that the muscle is exhausted long before the nerve ceases to function.

Nerve impulses travel along nerves at rates up to 400 feet per second. Very little of the delay period between stimulus applied to a sense organ and the appearance of the response is due to nerve conduction. An old-fashioned demonstration of the time required for response consisted in having a circle of individuals join hands and instructing each that when he felt his right hand pressed he was immediately to press the hand of his neighbor on the left with his left hand. The time required for the movement to go around a circle of twenty persons is appreciable. The transmission of nervous impulses from the right hand to the muscles of the left hand accounts for only a small fraction of this delay. A larger portion of the delay is explained by the time required for muscle fibers to contract. Even if the muscle fiber is not attached and is not required to do work, experiments show that it requires time for the muscle fiber to overcome its own viscosity and change its shape.

From the sense organs in muscles, skin, joints, or other places in the body nerve fibers travel to the brain and spinal cord or central nervous system. There the incoming nerve fiber may have many branches and connect in turn with connecting fibers. These in their turn may be branched and connected with numerous other fibers at a second level. Eventually, connections are made with outgoing fibers which extend from the central nervous system to the muscles or glands. These outgoing fibers are called *motor fibers,* and their bundles are called the *motor nerves.* Cutting a motor nerve results in paralysis of a muscle. Cutting an incoming or sensory nerve causes the area served by that nerve to become insensitive to stimulation. When a dentist injects Novocain into a sensory nerve, a definite area of the lips and teeth becomes insensitive. Because the block has been created in a sensory nerve and not a motor nerve, the lip or portion of the tongue is still capable of motion although now insensitive.

The connection of sense organs with response organs is not the most remarkable function of the central nervous system. Physical stimuli activate sense organs. Sense organs initiate nerve impulses which travel over sensory nerves to the central system and over connecting pathways out to motor nerves and so to muscles. We do not really know very much about any of the processes involved, just how the sense organ operates, just how it sets up a nerve impulse, just what the nerve impulse is, or just what the process is by which a muscle contracts. But the general idea seems simple. We could set up a wire system which would do much the same thing and ring bells or start motors as the result of pushing buttons.

The central nervous system, however, has a much more remarkable function than that of serving as a mere connector. It is known that under certain circumstances pathways through the nervous system which would be taken by a nerve impulse are changed as a result of experience. Somehow or other when a response is in action or beginning action, the stimuli which are acting on sense organs at the time channel their impulses into the active muscles. These particular stimuli may before this association have had no tendency to call out this particular response, but after they have once been associated with it temporarily they may become signals for the response. This is a prime foundation of learning. The simplest comparison that we can make with the mechanical effect is probably to compare it with the resetting of the switches in a railroad yard. We can imagine a large railroad yard into which on one side a number of lines lead and from which on another side a number of lines emerge, and the complicated switching arrangement that makes it possible from any incoming track to get to any outgoing track. In human behavior something like this occurs. Switches in the nervous system can be reset through experience. Stimuli which previously had no connection with a response can acquire such connections and become signals.

Pavlov's dogs, whose saliva began to flow at the sound of a bell, demonstrated a resetting of nerve paths which allow nerve impulses from the auditory nerve to start the gland secreting. Even when a housewife asks someone to turn off the oven when the clock strikes five, she has brought about such a resetting and insured that the sound of the striking clock repeated five times can start a series of responses that will end in turning off the stove.

Just how this is accomplished by the nervous system we do not know. When a response is in process, its motor nerves are of course in action. Somehow or other, sensory impulses which had not previously taken the path of these motor outlets do so after one association. Sensory impulses entering the central nervous system must tend to enter active pathways and on future occasions to enter these pathways to the exclusion of the pathways which they had formerly taken.

This chapter has merely sketched in a few lines the high points of the physical basis of behavior and learning. The teacher is not directly concerned with that physical basis except in the few instances like vision and hearing in which something can be done about it, such as providing glasses or a hearing aid. But there is a great advantage in being aware of the physical substratum of behavior because this makes us much more realistic in what we expect of individuals. When we realize that all behavior is dependent on the stimuli received from the outer world and is mediated through sense organs and the nervous system, and that the resultant responses are limited to those which have been on past occasions associated with these stimuli, we should be free of certain highly unreasonable expectations. To expect the impossible of children is to prepare for trouble and failure.

4. RESPONSE AS PHYSIOLOGICAL ACTIVITY

The Effectors.—In a real sense, all that any person can do could be described as the contraction of muscles or the secretion of glands. All the restless behavior of forty children in a classroom—their movements, their talk, and probably even their thoughts—are ultimately achieved through muscular contractions and glandular secretions. All muscles are made up of bundles of small fibers, and it is the contraction of these individual fibers, usually set off by the arrival of a nervous impulse over a nerve to the muscle fiber, which produces movements and ultimately behavior.

In addition to the capacity of muscle fibers to contract, another feature is the fact that when they do contract certain chemical changes take place. The energy of the movement is derived from the burning of sugar in the muscle fibers. This chemical reaction leaves in the fibers the results of that burning. Carbon dioxide and lactic acid make up the bulk of this residue, and until these have been carried away from the muscle by the blood stream and new supplies of oxygen and sugar are provided, the muscle fiber has less ability to contract, and its contraction will be less vigorous. This condition, in which the muscle fiber is less ready to act because of the presence of the chemical products of action and the diminished supply of the fuel that a muscle burns, is called *fatigue*. In a tired child we must deal not only with the impaired ability of the muscle fiber to contract. A state of fatigue makes movement actually painful. There are sense organs in the muscles which respond to fatigue as a signal and tend to make behavior different. We learn to avoid fatigue just as we learn to avoid pain.

The energy of muscular action depends upon several factors, of which the principal one is the oxygen supply brought by the blood stream. This, in turn, is conditioned by the pulse rate and blood pressure because the oxygen must eventually come from the lungs and the rate of circulation determines how much oxygen can be carried from lungs to muscle. The fuel of action, the blood sugar, is derived from food originally, and diminished food intake sets limits on physical performance. It is not pure sympathy that leads us to provide school lunches, since some of the children of a classroom may be inadequately fed otherwise. In many instances the services of the teacher and the facilities of the school would be wasted on an undernourished child.

QUESTIONS

1. Name some effectors which you are now using.
2. Which kind of sense organ would be most important in a child learning to skip rope?
3. What are some of the possible effects of poor sight on a child's personality and social adjustment?
4. Is it possible for a response to be very much more energetic than the stimulus which set it off? Give some examples.
5. How would you describe learning in terms of its physical bases?
6. What is always occurring in the nervous system when a muscle is contracting?
7. Why do we sometimes continue walking even when we can't remember what our errand is?

PART III

LEARNING AND ITS MEASUREMENT

Chapter 7

LEARNING AS A PROCESS

Meaning of Learning.—Children are constantly learning as long as they are awake and active. The reason for bringing them together in a schoolroom is that we wish to try to direct and control learning. If we are going to try to do anything with learning, we should first have some notion of what it is. As soon as we raise that question, we find out that the psychologists are in some difficulty on this very point. They have not agreed on what they mean by *learning*.

Common sense has no difficulty over what "learning" means. For common sense, learning is always a case of improving some performance or gaining some new ability or understanding. We learn to multiply, we learn to skate, we learn the way home, we learn how to drive a car, we learn not to burn our fingers on the stove. If we begin to do something wrong or begin to fail at something at which we formerly succeeded, it is very hard for us to think of that as learning. We are more apt to call it *unlearning*. This common-sense definition of learning as the acquisition of a desirable ability or the improvement of a performance is inadequate for a psychological understanding of learning. It applies learning only to the attainment of good results and we shall find that we acquire bad habits and tendencies to failure in exactly the same way in which we acquire good habits and the tendency to success.

For our purposes, therefore, a more scientific definition of learning is required, and *we shall mean by learning any change in behavior that is the result of past use or experience.* Common sense would call it learning when a child who has in the past known nothing of the multiplication table can after practice repeat the multiplication table or give promptly the product of any two numbers in that table; but common sense does not call

85

it learning if the child who has learned is led by some accident to say that 9×7 equals 64, and on future occasions tends to substitute this for the correct answer. Actually the way in which the child acquires the association "9×7 equals 64" is exactly the same as the way in which it acquired an association "9×7 equals 63." It would, therefore, be absurd to call one of these learning and not the other. The process is the same in the two cases, and we are using learning as the name of the process by which we change for better or for worse.

There are some amendments to make to this definition of learning, because there are some changes which follow and experience which we do not mean to include. One of these has already been mentioned, namely, fatigue. Fatigue is the result of use or exercise, but it is a temporary state and we recover from it by normal physiological processes without any new learning. *Temporary* changes are not called learning. There is one other effect of use which is not included in the definition of learning. This is a process occasionally called *sense-organ adaptation*. An illustration of this phenomenon is the fact that we may enter a kitchen in which cabbage is cooking and be struck by the odor, but within a few minutes after arriving in the kitchen we cease to be aware of the perception. We may notice the contact of our glasses just after we have put them on, but after they have been in place for a short time, we no longer respond to the touch. This sense-organ adaptation is not called learning because it is, like fatigue, another temporary state and we recover from it in a short time when once the stimulus has been removed.

Actually what sense organs respond to is not the constant physical forces but changes in the physical conditions of sense organs. When the forces acting on a sense organ are constant for some time, we normally cease to respond. Water may at first feel cold or hot to the hand. After the hand has been left in the water for a matter of half a minute or so we may no longer notice the coolness or the warmth. A striking illustration of this comes from placing one hand in cold water and the other hand in hot water and, after leaving them there for some time, plunging both hands into water at room temperature.

This water will feel cold to the hand that has been in the hot water and hot to the hand that has been in the cold water. In other words the sense organs in the skin are responding to the sudden shift in temperature and not simply the absolute state of temperature.

1. How Learning Takes Place

Principle of Associative Learning.—If learning is to be defined as behavior change resulting from practice or use, we may well ask how behavior changes with use. The answer to this question may be made in a simple statement. It is not a complete answer, but we will discover that the changes that take place with experience follow an old rule which was familiar even to the writers of ancient Greece. This is the rule of *association.* It used to be thought of in terms of the association of ideas, but modern psychology with its preference for dealing with observable behavior puts it in slightly different terms. The rule is this : *Stimuli or patterns of stimuli acting when a response is made will tend on later occasions to call out that response.*

From the fourth century B.C., when Aristotle wrote about association, up to the time in the first years of this century when Pavlov's experiments began to be widely discussed among psychologists, association was thought of in terms of ideas rather than action. The sight of an automobile accident reminds you of a friend who happened to be riding with you when your own car was in a minor accident. You encounter a name in the morning's newspaper, and this name leads you to recall last night's party, which included some friends with the same last name. Ideas were supposed to be associated under a variety of conditions not limited to their having occurred together in time. It was believed that there is a strong tendency for an idea to suggest its opposite, for white to make you think of black, and hot to make you think of cold. It was also believed that ideas often suggested similar ideas—thinking of John leads you to think of Henry because they are both red-headed.

Aristotle had proposed laws of association as follows : (1) things experienced simultaneously become by that fact associated in the mind, so that thereafter when we think of one, we have a tendency to think of the other; (2) things become associated in the mind because of their similarity; and (3) things become associated in the mind because of their contrasting nature. Thus contiguity, similarity, and contrast were the conditions accounting for association. The law of similarity was reduced to association by contiguity through the process of "redintegration" as proposed by Hamilton and later by Hollingworth. In other words, two things might be associated because they possessed common elements. The perception of the common element in one might serve as a stimulus complex bringing about recall of the second thing.

Research by Ebbinghaus also contributed to the growing concern with learning as a psychological problem. The nonsense syllable was used as material for studying memory. Memory as a psychological process was divided into four components: *learning* (the acquisition of new behavior), and *retention* as revealed by *recall*, and *recognition*. The Ebbinghaus technique for measuring the memory resulted in a more sophisticated understanding of the conditions that make for greater or less efficiency and speed during acquisition.

By the time of William James, psychologists had come to the conclusion that these are all cases of association by contiguity in time. We associate opposites like black and white because we have in the past discussed opposites together. Red hair has been experienced with both John and Henry.

Pavlov's Conditioned Response.—The Russian psychologist Pavlov in the late nineties of the last century had been studying the digestive secretions, and in the course of that study had encountered what first appeared to him to be simply a difficulty in his experimental method. He was searching for the stimuli which caused the flow of gastric juice and saliva. He began to notice that his dogs would on many occasions begin to secrete saliva or gastric juice at the sight of the experimenter or at the sight of the dish. Pavlov had that trait of the real scientist which caused him to recognize that he had encountered something basic and important, and he turned his study from the

study of the digestive secretions to a study of the way in which
such secretion could be brought about by this basic method of
association. For a period of over thirty years after this, Pavlov
and his students investigated the conditions under which responses can be called out by new signals.

Pavlov's work came to the attention of American psychologists at just about the time that John B. Watson's new behaviorism was gaining recognition. Watson preferred to talk
in terms of response rather than in terms of ideas because
responses can be observed by anyone, whereas ideas can be
reported on only by the holder of the ideas and the observing
psychologist has no check on the accuracy of the individual's
report. Between Pavlov and Watson, a new line of experiment
on association has been set up by psychologists. The association is held to take place between a new stimulus and a response.
Pavlov himself thought that the association occurred between
the new stimulus for a response and the old stimulus for a
response.

Reinforcement and Reward.—American psychologists are
not entirely agreed on the circumstances that lead to an association. The majority of the American psychologists who are
working in the field of association or, as it has often been called
since Pavlov, conditioning, believe that something more than
the mere association of the stimulus and the response is required
in order to establish the stimulus as a new signal for the response. In this textbook the position is taken that the mere
fact of association is enough to establish the new stimulus as a
signal. Professor Hull of the Yale University Department of
Psychology is representative of the group of psychologists who
believe that reward or reinforcement following an association
is necessary in order to fix or set the association. Hull would
hold that when a stimulus is followed by a response with which
it formerly had no connection and this association is then followed by what he calls a reinforcing situation, the stimulus then
acquires some capacity to call out the response. The alternative
view is that the mere fact of association is enough to make the
new signal effective.

If this latter view is correct, it may well be asked how it comes about that rewards have the effect that we all recognize in directing behavior. We know very well that rewards tend to establish the rewarded act. We also know that punishment often succeeds in getting rid of an unwanted habit. The schoolroom uses systems of reward and punishment. We have badges of merit to encourage good conduct and light punishments assigned for disturbing the peace. Centuries of experience lie behind the use of such rewards and punishments. How can it be claimed that they are not effective in establishing associations?

Evidence from Puzzle-Box Experiments.—The answer here suggested to this question is that rewards do not somehow mysteriously work backwards to establish an association that has taken place a few seconds or minutes before, but that in general rewards protect associations which have already been made from being unmade. How this can happen can be illustrated by some experiments that Professors Horton and Guthrie [1] performed with some cats in a puzzle box. Even though cats in a puzzle box seem a far cry from children in a schoolroom, there is a basic similarity in the way in which they learn.

By a puzzle box is meant a box in which an animal can be shut up and from which escape can be made only if the animal discovers and uses some lever, string, or other device which will open the door and make it possible to leave the box. The experimenters watched approximately 1,000 escapes of some fifty cats in an effort to discover whether new behavior required reward or reinforcement in order to establish it.

When a cat was placed in a puzzle box, it began to wander about the box and explore. It would claw at the exit door and make a tour of the boundaries of the box; sniff at or paw outstanding features. This particular box was provided with a post so connected with the door by a chain under the floor that whenever the post was moved in any direction the exit door would open and the cat could leave. In its wanderings about the cage, the cat eventually moved this post by one means or

---

[1] E. R. Guthrie and G. P. Horton, *Cats in a Puzzle Box.*

another. Some backed into it, some struck it with the tail in
turning about, some struck it with the shoulder or flank; two
cats lying down moved slightly and touched the post and then
escaped; one cat jumped to the top of the cage and fell on the
post and then escaped.

It was the successful movements in which the experimenters
were deeply interested. It was observed that whenever movement preceded the removal of the cat from the box, that movement was repeated on later occasions. The cat that had backed
into the post continued to back into the post to get out; the cat
that had jumped and fallen on the post did this for a number of
times afterward. The cat that struck the post with its shoulder
continued to strike the post with its shoulder in order to get
out. This rule did not hold always, but the odds were heavily in
favor of the expectation that the cat would escape by the same
movements that it used on the last occasion.

The theory of the experimenters was that the cats continued
to use the successful response not because the escape from the
box was a reward or a reinforcement of the response but because
the successful response took the cat out of the puzzle box. When
the cat was once out of the puzzle box its method of escape could
not be unlearned. The cat cannot associate new responses with
the sight of the interior of the puzzle box when it has once
escaped. To associate new responses with the cues or signals
offered by the puzzle box, the cat must be in the box and be
caused to behave in some new way.

Responses made which do not get the cat out of the puzzle
box leave it inside, where it is confronting the same situation
and doing something different from the unsuccessful response.
This establishes a new response to the situation in the place of
the unsuccessful response. When the cat has opened the box
and left, such new associations cannot be established because the
situation is no longer present.

We may use an illustration from the classroom. Every
teacher is aware of the tremendous predictability of individual
behavior of school children. This is especially noticeable in the
features which are annoying to the teacher. He knows just
what to expect of John, of William, of Harry, and of Patricia.

Their interests in the use of chalk as a projectile, in teasing each other, in "writing notes," in all the crimes and misdemeanors of the old-fashioned classroom can be depended upon from day to day. Changes in such behavior take place only when other behavior can somehow be induced to take its place and become associated with the classroom situation. The boy who had been absorbed in the uses of chalk has been given the responsibility of looking after the goldfish; this behavior we say "makes him forget" what one can do with chalk. It makes him forget because it establishes new responses to the signals and sights and sounds of the classroom.

Forgetting.—Forgetting is itself an interesting accomplishment that can be explained in terms of the simple principle of conditioning. We forget because we have learned something else in response to the stimulus, and the new activity prevents the old. Forgetting does not take place just because time has elapsed. We have some astonishing memories that have survived from early childhood.

This theory was once being explained to a group of teachers and one of them said, "Why have I never forgotten this?" and she quoted in a rather high singsong voice a long rule of German grammar listing the prepositions that take the dative case. "I do not know why I thought of it," she said, "and so far as I know I haven't thought of it for years." A probable reason for the fact that she had not forgotten this rule over a term of fifteen years was that she had had no occasion in the meantime to use the singsong voice in which she had rattled off the rule. There had been no chance for new associations to lead her off the track, nor had the chief words of the rule occurred in ordinary conversation to acquire new associations. Ordinary conversations and ordinary reading tend to be forgotten rapidly because the words that occur in them are used in other contexts and establish other associations. One reason why we remember poems with a catchy rhythm so much better than prose is that the rhythms of poetry are not used in ordinary conversation and this protects the associations of the poem from reassociation or unlearning.

Forgetting is then really the learning of new interfering material. It has been pretty well established that we forget rather little during a period of sleep. We forget more when we are awake because in our waking activities many of the signals acquire new associations.

Action and Learning.—There is one consequence of the theory that learning consists in the association of new signals with active response which is of first importance for teaching. This is the fact that, for learning to occur, the desired active response must somehow or other be brought about. Unless the response is caused to take place, there is no possible chance that it can be associated with proper signals. There is no tendency whatever for children to learn anything simply because they hear it or for them to learn anything simply because they have seen it in a book. The words of the teacher and the sentences of the book can be effective only if they arouse responses in the pupil. What demands so much experience and skill in teaching is that it requires inducing children to do the things to be taught. They learn only what they do—not what the teacher does.

2. The Importance of Response in Learning

Role of Repetition in Learning.—Besides their disagreement on the question of the need for reinforcing associations, American psychologists disagree on another issue. This other disagreement is on the need for repeated pairings of a signal and a response in order to establish an association. Pavlov believed that such repetition is necessary, and this was certainly true in the circumstances under which he experimented. Common sense would hold that the oftener an association occurs the stronger it is, but there are excellent reasons for doubting that this is really true. There are solid grounds for believing that an association can be established in one pairing just as firmly as it can be by a thousand pairings. This seems to violate common sense and all reason. Let us examine it. In watching cats escape from a puzzle box there was little evidence that associations required many practicings. One rehearsal, and the association could be depended on to occur.

Teachers do not expect that children must be told everything forty or fifty times in order that the association shall stick. Teachers know full well that they can expect certain things told to children to be remembered indefinitely from one recognition. You do not have to tell children over and over again that Friday will be a holiday. It may be necessary to tell them over and over again that 9×7 is 63. What is the effect of repetition and why is it in some circumstances necessary? Probably the chief reason is that most of the things we are interested in teaching are things that do not get from the pupil the degree of attention and interested response that is necessary for learning.

Another reason for repetition is that certain things to be learned must be practiced in a variety of circumstances. This requires that they be rehearsed in a variety of circumstances. The small boy who memorizes a short poem at home may not be able to repeat it while standing before the class because the situation of standing before a class causes responses which drive the poem completely from mind. It is an advantage to practice what we wish to learn as nearly as possible in the circumstances in which it is to be performed. It is also an advantage to practice it under a variety of circumstances, because we can then depend on being able to perform in a variety of circumstances. The pupil who learns the multiplication table which includes 9×7 equals 63 has reached that association in a serial response which ran 9×5 is 45, 9×6 is 54, 9×7 is 63. He may be letter-perfect in reciting the table, but a sudden question "What is 9×7?" does not put him back into this serial behavior. He has not practiced responding to that question at all. We may even note that the pupil who can answer correctly 9×7 is 63 goes wrong in his response to the question "What is 7×9?" because this is a different signal. The would-be marksman may learn to make a good score on the target during target practice but find that he does badly in a match. It takes experience in matches to do well in matches.

The reason why repetition and practice are necessary in perfecting so many accomplishments is that what we are trying to learn or what the teacher is trying to teach involves the ability to respond properly to many different situations and to make the response different according to each situation as it arises.

Learning such a thing as how to button a button is no simple association. If you have had an opportunity to observe this learning in a very small child, you may have noted that the ability was first acquired as an ability to button a certain button under distinctly limited circumstances. The child learned to button the button of a certain garment while standing in a certain posture, but this does not make him able to button other buttons. Other buttons require other movements, other positions, and other learning. The ability to button buttons means the child must have acquired a repertoire of hundreds of differing responses which are adjusted to hundreds of differing situations.

Buttoning buttons is a generalized skill, in other words, not a single response. It is only single responses, single movement patterns, that can be established in response signals with one repetition. Skills take persistent practice; they require the unlearning of wrong habits as well as the learning of the correct movements.

3. Learning as an Adaptive Process

General Description of Learning.—Perhaps we are now ready to undertake a general description of the whole process of learning. In the first place learning requires that the learner be actively responding to stimuli. This follows from the fact that learning consists in the association of stimulus with response. Obviously, without active response there is no opportunity for such association.

The typical learning situation, therefore, involves stimulating activity. This stimulation may come from within or from without. Much learning is the result of persistent annoying stimuli of one kind or another. For a cat, being shut up in a puzzle box offers such stimulation. For a small boy who has been used to attention and notice, being unnoticed in the classroom may be such a goad or stimulus.

In response to a persistently annoying situation, activity tends strongly to be varied. One reason for this is that many actions eliminate the possibility of their immediate repetition. We cannot repeat immediately the descending of a stair because we are already at the bottom, or we cannot rise twice without sitting down between risings. We cannot repeat sitting because we are already seated. Having raised a hand, it is impossible to raise it again until it is lowered. When a response leaves the annoyer or the annoying situation present, it thus tends to be succeeded by other behavior, another response, and its association with the situation is lost to the new response.

Eventually something is done that gets us out of the situation, removes the annoyer. When this happens the successful act tends to remain faithful to the annoying situation. It is the thing we do in that particular situation because it got us out of the situation and there was no chance to unlearn the act.

The small boy who is suddenly accused by the teacher of having thrown the chalk is put in such a driving situation. The teacher's presence and questions are embarrassing and annoying. They tend to keep the pupil in a state of active response. If he hits upon a denial of guilt and this turns out to remove him from the annoying situation and turn the teacher's attention elsewhere, such a denial tends in the future to be his way out of that particular kind of trouble. Truth or falsity of the denial will have nothing to do with the situation. He has hit upon denial as his way out of the puzzle box just as one cat hit upon lying down and rolling to get out of its own troubling situation.

Other children have discovered tears as the way out of trouble and tend readily to lapse into tears when they are accused or even when they are blocked by the opposition of elders in the attainment of their wishes and desires. So long as tears tend to be successful and take the child out of trouble, they will remain his method for getting out of trouble. Only when he gets in a situation from which tears do not extricate him will he learn a new method.

One child made angry by another may hit upon the device of "telling on him" and bringing punishment which distracts the tattler from his irritation and rage. A pupil confronts an arithmetic problem. Failure to get an answer will make him the object of highly unwelcome attention and questions. He is made restless and uncomfortable. He may hit upon the device of getting the answer from the pupil to his left. If that gets him out of his puzzle box and stops the unwelcome attention given to failure, peeking at his neighbor's work may well become his method of dealing with such problems. He is not out to learn arithmetic, since few small boys are so inclined. His concern is to avoid the upsetting and annoying state which is created by the teacher for the special benefit of those who do not have the answer. And these odd methods of getting the answer which defeat the intentions of the teacher will remain as habits so long as they are successful. They may readily be established in one case or experience, and once established spread to others.

In describing how people learn, we have another useful notion besides association. In terms of association, when we wish to know what a particular individual will do in a given set of circumstances, we ask ourselves whether we can find out how he last behaved when the more conspicuous features of these circumstances were present. It is in terms of association that we can answer such questions as, "What will Arthur do during the study period?" "Will Miriam join in singing with the others or merely go through the motions?" "Will John really try to answer the arithmetic problem, or will he look about for help?" All these types of behavior can be predicted in terms of what happened on the last exposure to the situation.

Habits.—There is another class of behavior in which prediction is far more certain and easy, namely, habits. A *habit* may be described as a tendency to respond in a specific way under a wide variety of stimulus situations. It is something like a skill in this respect.

Common sense uses the word *habit* for two kinds of behavior pattern. When we talk about the habit of smoking, habits of industry, habits of obedience, habits of complaining, the actions themselves may be quite varied. For example, complaints may be different on different occasions. What we are predicting is that what is said and what is done will fall under the class of actions we call complaint. Such habits can be established only by long practice and are usually the result of being frequently in a situation for which the plan of action described is a solution. Children develop a habit of complaining when they live in households where complaints are effective. If they live in a household in which complaint gets them nowhere, complaint is quickly eradicated as a reaction to situations. Children develop habits of arguing for what they want when they have been in an environment where argument gets them out of difficulties or brings relief.

Many years ago Hartshorne and May in their studies in deceit discovered the interesting fact that whether or not a child cheated in an examination depended more on the last teacher in whose class he was than on his present teacher. In order to influence a child in this respect, the teacher must have influenced the child's conduct and directed it in a wide variety of situations but always consistently in the direction of not cheating—of honest behavior. In this sense, habits are really classes of action which have been established on numerous occasions because the child has been subjected to some sort of consistent direction or guidance or a consistent set of circumstances which tended to favor the development of one type of behavior or another. Children who live in households where truth-telling pays and does not lead to trouble learn to be truth-tellers.

Habits, like truth-telling, exaggeration, careless dressing, friendliness, are very different from another class of behavior patterns, also called habits. A habit of grimacing, blinking, jerking the head, or biting the nails is made up of stereotyped movements. These movement patterns become conditioned on a wide variety of situations so that they occur in fairly stereotyped form in all kinds of inopportune and inappropriate surroundings.

Habits of the second kind are much easier to deal with when they are obnoxious. There are two things that can be done with such a habit. We can discover the stimuli which are responsible for the beginning of the movement and see to it that some other movement is practiced in response to the stimuli.

In this case the habit in a sense remains but is not often exercised because it has been sidetracked. Another device is to break up the habit by establishing other responses to many of the stimuli which occur in the course of the habit.

Habits of the first class ordinarily require long courses of reconditioning and reassociation because they consist in a large variety of responses to a large variety of associative signals. To unlearn the habit of smoking means learning to do something other than light a cigarette at a hundred different signals. The smoker must unlearn smoking as a response to finishing a meal, being offered a cigarette, sitting down at his desk, starting work, finishing a statement to another person, seeing another person take a cigarette, and unlimited other situations which have become signals for smoking.

Questions

1. Why is the common-sense definition of learning in terms of improvement inadequate in a careful treatment of the subject?
2. What are some changes in performance which do not come under the heading of learning?
3. What is meant by saying that "learning and forgetting are opposite sides of the same coin"?
4. Give some examples of sense-organ adaptation.
5. Give some examples of learning in one trial.
6. What is the difference between a skill and a stereotyped movement?
7. Why are dress rehearsals necessary even when everyone knows his lines perfectly?

Chapter 8

VIEWPOINTS ON THE LEARNING PROCESS

In the chapter on the learning process there was some mention of the fact that psychologists are not agreed on learning theory. It will be recalled that two theories of association were mentioned. One theory (straight association theory) assumes that the mere fact of an association of a stimulus and a response is enough to establish that stimulus as a signal for the response, while the other theory (reinforcement theory) holds that association alone is not enough and that some kind of reward or other reinforcement after the association has taken place is necessary in order to establish the stimulus as a signal.

There are still other forms of learning theory. It is of some importance for the student of educational psychology to be familiar with them, because educational psychology is, in the last analysis, concerned primarily with learning.

The fact that there are different theories of learning should not discourage the student and should not be taken as an evidence of incompetence among the psychologists who have devoted their time and attention to the study of learning. Very often different theories reflect different purposes and different uses. It may turn out that the clinical psychologist, who deals with individuals and takes time to go into the history of the patient in whom he is interested, may require a very different theory of learning from the one necessary in the large schoolroom or the one that would interest a social psychologist, whose field is public opinion and the influencing of public opinion, or the advertising psychologist, who wants to know how people can be taught to use one brand of soap rather than another brand of soap. Even the same theory of learning is sometimes restated in different language so that it may fit better into the terminology of a specialized field.

1. Theories in Terms of Stimulus and Response

Hull's Reinforcement Theory.—The learning theory of Clark L. Hull and his students, working in the Yale Laboratory of Psychology, is a reinforcement theory of the kind described in the chapter on the learning process. Hull himself has undertaken to state this theory in the form of some sixteen postulates or general rules which, together with his careful and exact definitions, make his theory the most explicit of those that have yet been offered. The general rules of Hull's theory need not here be described, because their chief use lies in the planning of experiments to be performed in the laboratory. Hull's theory has very few classroom applications.

Hull assumes that activity arises in what he and other psychologists have called *drive*. Drives are conditions of the organism like hunger or thirst, which keep the organism in a state of restlessness or tension until some response is made which relieves the drive. Such a response would be, in the case of hunger, the eating of food; or in the case of thirst, the drinking of water. In the course of its activity the organism encounters many stimuli and of course is making a continuous series of responses. Where these stimuli occur with a response there is a chance for an association, but the association does not take place (that is to say, the stimulus does not become a signal for the response) unless the association is followed by a reward or reinforcement.

Hull means by a *reinforcement,* in the primary sense, a reduction in the drive. If a hungry baby, in the course of restless activity, gets his thumb into his mouth, this might conceivably act as a reduction in the hunger drive. It has all the appearance of quieting the baby. This would account in Hull's theory for the baby's tendency to learn this particular habit. The response of putting the thumb in the mouth would have become associated with the restlessness of hunger and the stimuli that accompany hunger, and the drive reduction would insure that these stimuli became signals for inserting the thumb in the mouth. The hungry dog, rewarded by a morsel of food by his master when on some occasion he has sat up on his hind legs for a brief moment, learns to do this in the situation which combines hunger with the presence of his master, because that situation has become a signal for the response due to the drive reduction offered by the morsel of food.

Hull allows for certain types of reinforcement or reward which are not, strictly speaking, drive reduction, but are what he calls *secondary reward*. These represent states which are not in themselves rewarding, but which have been associated with reward. After a child has, on numerous occasions, purchased an ice-cream cone for a coin, the coin itself may serve as a reward, and the child learns to do the things that get him a coin. The coin would then be a secondary reward, because there is no interest in the coin for its own sake and the coin does not of itself produce drive reduction.

Hull's general description of learning is as follows: Some drive produces restless activity in the animal. In the course of that activity a response is eventually hit upon which reduces the drive, and this establishes an association between the stimulus situation present with the response and the response itself. The animal learns to do what reduced the drive in the situation in which it found itself at the time.

One other essential feature of Hull's theory should be noted. He has, more than any other American psychologist, sought to describe the phenomena of learning in quantitative terms. He has insisted on being able to measure learning. One of Hull's measures of learning is what may be called *latency of response*. By this is meant the length of the interval between a signal and the response to it. Sometimes this interval is very short, sometimes it is much longer. Hull assumes that a short interval is a measure of learning. Knight Dunlap, many years ago, published a study of a very unusual form of examination. He examined his students by having them, one at a time, sit across the table from the examiner and listen to a question which could be answered in a word or short phrase. The examiner used a stop watch to measure the time between the end of the question and the student's response. Dunlap found a very high correspondence or correlation between the promptness of the response and its tendency to be correct. Students who knew the answer, in other words, could give it very quickly. A long latency was usually associated with a high probability of error. This, of course, does not surprise anyone. We are all familiar with the fact that when we ask anyone "How much is 7 times 9?" and he requires a long time to think, we can have very little confidence in his ability to give the correct answer.

Another measure of learning which Hull used is the certainty of a response. The response which can be depended on to follow its signal fifty times in 100 is better learned than the response which can be depended upon to follow its signal only three or four times in 100. Another common measure of learning used by Pavlov as well as by Hull is the vigor of a response. The response which is made with more energy is judged to be better learned.

Still another measure of learning on which Hull depends is the resistance of a response to extinction. This will require some explaining. It is a fact familiar to all that in a great many cases repeating a signal over and over again "wears out" the response. The old proverb which suggests that "A new broom sweeps clean" has reference to something like this. In experiments on the conditioned response in animals, it is a familiar observation that repeating the signal over and over again without any reward or reinforcement gradually reduces the response until the response will no longer take place when the signal is presented. If Pavlov had trained a dog so that saliva would flow at the sound of a bell, ringing the bell over and over again without giving the dog any food would reduce the amount of saliva until there was no response of that sort to the bell.

Hull's insistence on quantitative measures of learning in the forms of reduced latency, increased resistance to extinction, increased vigor, and so forth makes his theory of far less direct use in educational psychology. The experiments to which his theories apply consist in presenting, usually to animals, some signal and causing the animal to react with some response, and doing this over and over again, in some cases for many hundreds of trials or pairings. This is not in any sense the procedure of the classroom, although there are some classroom achievements which can be described in quantitative terms like these. Such tasks as the memorizing of a poem, the spelling of a word, or repetition of the multiplication table may follow Hull's quantitative descriptions, but in general the teacher is not confronted with a child who can be put through certain behavior fifty times on the assumption that one fiftieth will be learned on each occasion.

Thorndike's Theory of Effect.—Another form of association theory, older than Hull's, was that described by E. L. Thorndike of Columbia University. Thorndike's theory, perhaps because it originated in a college of education, has been by far the most popular theory of learning in the textbooks of educational psychology. It is less behavioristic than Hull's theory in the sense that it is harder to tell whether Thorndike is talking about actual movement or ideas. His language does not commit him to the notion that behavior must be described in terms of stimulus and response.

Thorndike's general doctrine is, like Hull's, that when a stimulus or signal is presented to an organism and some response is made, an association will occur or the stimulus will become a signal for the response if, and only if, this event is followed by what Thorndike calls a *satisfying state of affairs*. When no satisfying state of affairs occurs, there is no tendency for the signal to acquire any ability to call out the response. Bonds, he said, are stamped in or out according to the effect of the action. When the effect is satisfying, the bond is stamped in. When the effect is not satisfying, there is a tendency for the bond to be stamped out, although Thorndike in his later writings said that punishment weakened bonds little or not at all. Thorndike's "law of effect" did, however, point to motivation as an important variable in the learning situation. As the influence of reward and punishment upon animal learning became understood more fully, the question arose whether there was the same effect in human learning. There followed a tremendous amount of research and speculation regarding the impact of promotion, failure, school grades, prizes, approval, disapproval, gold stars, honor rolls, and Phi Beta Kappa keys on learning as "satisfiers" or "annoyers." Today wide ac-

ceptance is given the law as restated by McGeoch who wrote:
"Other things being equal, acts leading to consequences which
satisfy a motivating condition are selected and strengthened,
while those leading to consequences which do not satisfy a
motivating condition are eliminated." [1] The law does not apply
to recall; often unpleasant experiences are recalled vividly many
years later.

Closely related to the law of effect is the law of readiness.
Readiness was seen by Thorndike as a physiological prerequisite
for the law of effect. While the "readiness" proposed by
Thorndike was not a developmental or maturational readiness,
it seems to anticipate the present concern of the educator regarding "reading readiness," "spelling readiness," etc. Evidence supports the idea held today that the child must have
reached a certain developmental level or readiness before training can be of benefit to him. Effects are neither satisfying nor
annoying if there is no readiness for that satisfaction or the
lack of it.

If a learner repeats a long list of sentences in which each
sentence has nothing to do with the one before, it will be found
that within the sentence associations have been formed so that
one phrase suggests the next; but the last phrase of each sentence
is less effective in suggesting the first phrase of the sentence
following. The association has been practiced the same number
of times in each case. In 1931 this discovery led Thorndike to
propose a *law of belonging*. He understood "belonging" in the
sense of an understanding of relationships between the elements
of the sentence. A close examination of the notion of belonging
will show that it includes features of set and attitude, and also
long-standing associations. The effect of belonging is open to
interpretation in terms of the association of response with
situation. A single sentence has a topic, and the perception of
the meaning of a sentence involves an integrated response. To
proceed from the sentence, "John loves Mary," to the sentence,
"Whales suffer from rheumatism" involves a great shift of
attitude. The word "whales" may have been read just follow-

---

[1] J. A. McGeoch, *The Psychology of Human Learning—An Introduction*,
New York: Longmans, Green & Co., 1942, p. 574.

ing the word "Mary" just as often as "Mary" has followed "loves," but Thorndike's belongingness here is obviously connected with the fact that "loves-Mary" is a familiar component of perception, while "Mary-whales" is not. The validity of Thorndike's suggestion that belonging helps determine association is not to be questioned.

In his early writings, Thorndike emphasized also the *law of practice.* He assumed that repeating a connection tended to make it stronger and more certain. In his later writings, because of experiments of his own, he tended to discard this principle of practice and to recognize that effect was the main determiner of what happened. The learner as pictured by Thorndike is an active agent, coming to the learning situation with needs, desires, attitudes, sets, problems, and value judgments which determine what rewards and punishments (deprivations) will be effective—for him.

It will be recalled that the theory presented in this book is in terms of straight association. Both Hull and Thorndike believe that the association must be followed by some confirmation or reward. It has been the contention of the writers of this book that confirmation or reward is effective, not because it is a reward, but because most rewards take the animal out of the situation and protect him from unlearning the response.

These three theories, therefore, do not differ in any very important practical respects. Thorndike and Hull both believe that there is something about a reward which sets or fixes an association. The authors believe that if we examine the nature of rewards we will find that they protect associations from being replaced by other associations. This is actually an unimportant difference from the practical point of view. The authors believe that their form of theory conveys a little more exact information than the other, that it explains why rewards have their effects.

The original experiments on which Thorndike bases most of his learning theories were experiments with the cat in the puzzle box. Thorndike had described what he saw the cat do in terms of restless activity, trial and error, and eventual success. He called attention to the fact that the success appeared to be somehow or other "stamped in" in a way that errors were not "stamped in." The cat could be depended upon to preserve the successful movement as its method of escape and gradually to eliminate all the useless responses.

2. The Gestalt Viewpoint

Criticisms by Gestalt Psychologists.—This description of learning in terms of trial and error was the object of a very strong attack made by the Gestalt psychologists (notably Köhler and Koffka) on Thorndike and American views of learning in general. Köhler based his criticism on a long series of observations which he had made on the behavior of chimpanzees while on the island of Teneriffe during the first World War. The chimpanzee is a creature notably different from the cat, and there is small wonder that theories based on the behavior of chimpanzees turned out to be somewhat different from theories based on the behavior of cats in a puzzle box. Chimpanzees are so like persons that we tend to be interested in their perceptions, in their experience. In cats our interest is in motor behavior. It was Köhler's argument that experiments performed by the American psychologists, which had consisted very largely in putting animals in mazes or in puzzle boxes and taking note of the time that they required for escape, did not give the animal a chance to show what it could do. Chimpanzees are notably more intelligent than cats. They can be depended on to solve many problems which leave cats helpless. Among the better-known experiments of Köhler was the simple one in which he left a banana out of reach of the chimpanzee beyond the bars of his cage, and in the cage a stick. Under these circumstances, the chimpanzee does not, according to Köhler, waste his time in vain trial and error. A careful observer would note that the animal, after a number of futile efforts to reach, suddenly pauses and then picks up the stick and rakes in the banana.

Chimpanzees placed in a cage in which a banana is suspended out of reach from the top would eventually "suddenly see" an available box in a corner of the cage, drag the box over under the banana, climb up on it, and reach the goal. In some cases the animal was capable of piling one box on another in order to reach the banana.

Köhler's point is that the chimpanzees did not merely set out on what he called blind trial and error when they were made restive by the sight of a banana hanging from the ceiling of the cage. Somehow or other their trials were good trials, that is, trials calculated to achieve the goal, not blind trials or random behavior, and on a large number of occasions the animal suddenly came through with a correct and successful response without previous fumbling or previous trial and error of any sort.

Now it is to be noted that this phenomenon of sudden solution, which Köhler called *insight,* is not a theory of learning. It makes no attempt to describe how learning occurs. It describes an end result of learning, not the process of learning. Köhler showed no interest in investigating how insight came about. There is, therefore, no contradiction between this doctrine of insight and the other theories of learning. It seems entirely reasonable that insight such as that displayed by the chimpanzees can be developed by previous trial and error. Investigation might show that only those apes which had had a long trial-and-error experience playing with sticks were capable of the sudden use of the stick to retrieve an object.

A very similar situation has been observed in a small child confined in a crib on the floor. His glance having fallen upon a stick lying outside the crib, he reached through the bars and grasped the stick by the middle and tugged. The stick, of course, would not go through the bars. The child showed mounting excitement and activity. His tugs grew harder, but continued to be unsuccessful. He eventually let go and grasped the bars of the crib. The behavior had its natural completion when the child finally took hold of the stick by one end and pulled, whereupon it came readily into the crib and he began contentedly to play with it. It is quite possible that any later insight that this particular child showed in the handling of the stick through bars would be dependent on trial-and-error learning, such as had occurred in this particular case.

The Gestalt psychologists were unwilling to relegate perception to a second place in psychological research, and it was in the field of perception that they were most successful. Perception as a process was assumed to operate lawfully. A basic principle was the law of *Prägnanz,* which proposed that psychological organization will tend toward the formation of a "good" configuration possessing the optimum wholeness, simplicity, regularity, and stability possible in its context. This "good" Gestalt (configuration) is achieved by the operation of other laws including:

1. *Law of nearness or proximity.*
   Those elements in any situation perceived closer in time or in space tend to be grouped or structured together.

2. *Law of similarity.*
   Grouping is influenced by identity of parts or by likenesses between elements.

3. *Law of closure.*
   An incompleteness in perceptual organization makes for instability; therefore, the perceptual process tends to fill in missing parts, i.e., to perceive the elements as completely structured.

4. *Law of good continuation.*
   A structured perception will tend to maintain its typical configuration. A shirt known to be white in color is perceived as white even though it is actually gray under shade or reduced illumination.

These laws of perceptual organization are regarded as important in the learning process; in fact, it is claimed that the laws of learning and perception are alike. The chief contribution has been the emphasis upon the role of organization, meaningfulness, and understanding as conditions making for better learning, improved retention, and increased transfer, and a denial that learning is basically a trial-and-error process as opposed to insightful activity.

One feature of insight as described by Köhler is that, once achieved, it is retained and is readily repeated. This, of course, offers no difficulty to the theories of learning above described.

The next theory of learning is so radically different from those we have described and so thoroughly committed to descriptions in terms of purpose instead of in terms of process that it will require some discussion of the nature of purposive explanations.

Tolman's Theory in Terms of Purpose.—Automobile manufacturers issue two kinds of books to go with new cars. One of these books is written for the owner-driver. It tells how to operate the car, where the starter button is, what to manipulate in order to start the car, the points at which the car should be greased. In general it tells what the various parts of the car are for. This information is important and necessary.

But suppose on some occasion the owner, by this time thoroughly familiar with his car, pushes the starter button and nothing happens. It will do him no good to read his book because what he will find in his book is just the statement that if you wish to start the car, push the button. He has already done that without effect. He may then call up his garage and have the car towed in. In the garage the mechanic has another kind of book. This book shows the wiring diagram. With this mechanic's manual in hand, the repairman can trace the wiring system for possible defects. The shop book that goes with the new car tells how the car works, not what it will do.

Perhaps it is unfortunate that children do not come into the world accompanied by two kinds of books like these, one which would show parents and teachers what buttons to push in order to get the behavior they wish out of the child, and the other which would show doctors and nurses the child's wiring diagram and physical structure and indicate what makes him tick.

The theory of Edward C. Tolman, University of California psychologist, is frankly in terms of purpose. It is an attempt, not to describe how learning takes place, but to describe what we can expect to get learned. Tolman's fundamental position is that all behavior is goal-directed. When we look at a child in action, we may assume that he is doing something, aiming at something. There is some end result in terms of which we can understand the child's behavior. His goal is to tease the boy in the next seat, to learn a lesson, to avoid the teacher's eye, to escape being kept after school, or to get noticed by the other children or by the teacher. Tolman makes these end products of activity the real basis of explanation of the activity. Action is explained by what it leads to, not by what led to the action. Notice that this is a radical difference from the three theories first described. Hull, Thorndike, and the authors of this volume describe behavior in terms of stimulus and response and find that the occasion for action is in stimuli which act as goads or inciters of response. Tolman finds the occasions for action not in stimuli, but in the end products of the action. A child gets up and leaves the room when the teacher dismisses the class, not as a conditioned or associative response to the signal given by the teacher, but in order to go out and play, or in order to attain some other goal.

Descriptions of behavior in terms of goal and purpose are in many cases convenient and enlightening. Common sense and ordinary speech use such descriptions regularly. The boy who makes faces at the other pupils when the teacher's back is turned is readily described as doing it in order to get attention. Description of the behavior in terms of stimulus and response is difficult because the stimulus is not easily determined. The boy who draws a ridiculous picture of the teacher on the blackboard might be described as doing this in order to annoy the teacher. Here again a description in stimulus-response terms would be quite difficult.

But there is one strong disadvantage in purposive descriptions. When we say that the boy drew the offensive picture on the blackboard in order to annoy the teacher, this explanation leaves it a complete mystery why the boy should have chosen this particular means instead of some other means of annoying. There are a thousand other ways of getting attention besides making faces at the class. Why does this particular little boy at this particular time choose to make faces?

Tolman's purposive system improves on most purposive descriptions of behavior by adopting a form of association doctrine in order to remedy this lack. Experience, according to Tolman, establishes certain responses as means-objects towards goals. We learn through association to attain a goal in a particular way after having had experience with that way. In describing the behavior of the cat in the puzzle box, Tolman would say that touching the post has become a recognized means of getting out of the puzzle box. This establishes the motion of touching the post as a goal, a minor goal. Touching the post has become a sign that escape will follow and has the sort of secondary goal character that explains why the animal behaves as he does. Tolman considers behavior adequately explained when it can be shown that there is a goal for the behavior.

Tolman uses the term "docility" for the change of behavior toward reduced effort and time in reaching a goal. Docility shows itself in two ways: in the establishment of expectations as the result of experience and in the tendency to select short and easy devices instead of long and difficult ones. A child who has gotten something that he wanted learns to expect the reward to follow whatever it was that he did or was doing when rewarded. He learns that certain acts are the ways to get certain results.

Notice that Tolman's theory has certain resemblances to the first three theories in spite of its statement in terms of purpose —in spite of the fact that he explains behavior in terms of its results instead of in terms of its antecedents or causes. Tolman invokes association as a result of experience. This gives his theory a certain resemblance to the theory of Hull, who holds that associations are established when they are reinforced.

Where Tolman makes the reduction of effort with practice a general principle of behavior, the theoretical position taken in the chapter on learning in this textbook would allow for the reduction of effort not as a law of behavior but as an occasional or frequent result of painful stimulation of fatigue, which tends to break up habit, or a tendency for prolonged efforts to favor new learning because they leave the animal in a situation where new associations can be established.

From the point of view of a practical educational psychology, all four theories, Thorndike's, Hull's, Tolman's, and the one described in this textbook, amount to much the same thing. All of them predict that rewarded behavior generally gets established as the child's response to a situation. The theories differ only in the fact that they attribute this to different principles.

Hull states that reward has this effect because reward has this effect. In other words, it is one of his foundation principles and needs no reason. Thorndike would agree with Hull on this point. The theory of this textbook would say that reward has this effect because it removes the animal from the situation to which the animal has reacted. The result is to protect this particular association from unlearning. Tolman would say that reward tends to establish the behavior which led to the reward because the animal has associated the situation with the reward. The fact that children and animals seek certain kinds of goals he regards as a fundamental principle of behavior just as Hull regards it as basic that rewards have a reinforcing effect on the association.

Lewin's Description of Behavior.—In most accounts of learning the theories of Kurt Lewin are included. In the strict sense, Lewin does not have any theory of learning and is not interested in the process of learning. Lewin is interested in the general principles of behavior and not in the manner in which behavior is modified by experience. Lewin's descriptions are, like the descriptions of Tolman and the Gestalt psychologists, stated in terms of goal and purpose. He believes that behavior is best understood by understanding what the outcome of behavior will be rather than by understanding the conditions that give rise to behavior. His notion of life space has already been referred to. This, it will be remembered, means the surroundings of the child to which the child is responsive.

Some of the features of the child's surroundings stir the child to approach or avoid them. They give direction to the child's behavior. Lewin describes this in terms borrowed from mathematics, using the word *vector* to indicate that the child's interest is drawn in a certain direction and with a certain force or repelled in the opposite direction and with a certain force. Vectors can be represented by arrows, whose lengths indicate the strength of the impulse. Behavior is stimulated by goal objects. A child in his play-pen, for instance, might see a brightly colored toy lying outside and be strongly stimulated to propel himself to the toy. The walls of the pen represent what Lewin calls the *obstacle* or *barrier*. It can be predicted that the child will spend his time at the barrier looking toward the goal object.

Lewin further describes behavior in terms of tensions, which have been aroused in the child. These tensions operate to direct behavior until they are relieved by carrying out a line of action or by reaching a goal.

Lewin's descriptions apply much more readily to elementary situations in which a child is trying to reach some goal object across a barrier. Goal descriptions have certain inherent ambiguities and difficulties, however. A child with a stomach-ache is hard to describe in Lewinian terms. It is difficult to say just what is the goal and what is the barrier. It is hard to diagram a goal, which consists in the absence of the stomach-ache, as lying on one side of a barrier, on the other side of which we find the child.

It is evident that this system is not an attempt to describe the circumstances under which learning takes place, or even to describe the nature of learning. Lewin's system is very close to Tolman's in that its chief interest lies in describing what is going to get learned without concerning itself about how that learning will take place.

A brief overview of the various viewpoints on learning reveals a great deal of similarity. Associationist, trial-and-error, purposive, and Gestalt approaches all recognize that learning as a process includes both *acquisition* and *retention,* as well as *forgetting* or failure to retain. Furthermore, acquisition and retention are mutually interdependent, i.e., there is no progressive acquisition such as improved speed and efficiency or gradual increase in understanding without retention of previous acquisition. Conversely, a loss in retention (forgetting) is shown to be the result of new learning. In other words, forgetting one thing is, or at least *may* be, a function of learning other things.

All approaches have directly or indirectly been concerned with the problem of the learning potential, or capacity of the learner. Thorndike proposes a physiological explanation for differences in capacity in his connectionist theory of intelligence. The number of neural connections in a given organism would therefore determine the capacity for learning. The position of this text is that capacity is limited only by the receptor, connector, and effector efficiency of an organism. Important limits are also set by previous habits. Any response of which the organism is capable can be associated, under proper conditions, to any stimulus condition to which it is sensitive. Capacity is seen by the Gestaltist as limited by primitive perceptual organization which determines the patterning and restructuring of elements in any situation, and also by the conditions of the situation itself. In other words, insightful learning is possible only when all relevant factors can be and are perceived. Tolman's purposive approach has been most directly concerned with capacity. *Capacity* laws form an important part of his theory by which he accounts for variations in ability in animal learning.

The various approaches have likewise emphasized motivation as a significant variable in any learning situation. Hull's reinforcement theory recognizes the importance of drive and tension-reduction through learned response. Tolman's "latent learning" studies cast some doubt on the simple reinforcement explanation of learning, as does the work on secondary reinforcement. Thorndike first brought the question to the front by his theory of satisfiers and annoyers. A more satisfactory understanding of motivation is probably dependent upon understanding the motives "existing" at the time in the learner. But all would agree upon the inclusion of motivation in any learning theory.

The role of repetition in learning is viewed differently by the approaches presented in this chapter. Thorndike's connectionist explanation holds that while repetition increases the strength of associations when rewards are forthcoming, repetition alone does not itself insure learning. For example, Thorndike once wrote, "The repetition of a situation may change a man as little as the repetition of a message over a wire changes the wire." [2]

Our position is that a response may be learned at full strength in a single repetition, but that habits and skills represent learn-

---

[2] E. L. Thorndike, *Human Learning,* New York: Appleton-Century-Crofts, Inc., 1931, p. 14.

ing in many situations and therefore are dependent upon repetition or practice. Repetition without reinforcement or reward actually contributes to an active inhibition of the response in Hull's analysis. Gestalt psychologists deny that repetition, as such, is necessary for acquisition, though repetition may clarify relationships so that elements may be perceptually restructured. Insightful learning is an "aha" experience accomplished in a single situation and retained for future application without practice—as an essential determinant. Tolman supports the idea that repetition or practice tends to fix the learned response but that satisfaction of the purpose is alone necessary for the "learning" of the response.

The problem of transfer or the application of past learning in new situations is considered by Thorndike to be a function of identical elements in the old and new situations. Our position is similar to that of Thorndike. Transfer for Hull is either a generalization of behavior or a generalization of stimulus cues for evoked behavior. Tolman's sign-Gestalt expectations are cognitions which facilitate transfer.

QUESTIONS

1. What does "reinforcement" mean in learning theory?
2. What are some of the quantitative measurements of learning used by Hull?
3. What is the significance of "a satisfying state of affairs" in Thorndike's theory?
4. What is the principal difference between the theories of Hull and Thorndike and that preferred by the writers of this text?
5. What does Köhler mean by "insight"?
6. What is a practical disadvantage of purposive descriptions of learning?
7. What is the use of learning theories which are not known to be true?

Chapter 9

HOW CHILDREN LEARN

The business of learning is in one sense the same in children and in chipmunks. All we mean by that is that associative learning in all creatures that learn consists in establishing new signals for responses. But there are enough characteristic differences about the details of such learning to make it worthwhile to give special attention to learning in children. Between the learning of animals and infants and the learning of grown persons there is one very important practical difference. This lies in the fact that adult human beings can be directed by words and can use words as signals for complicated behavior. This makes the problem of teaching a man to do something very different from the problem of teaching a chimpanzee to accomplish the same thing.

1. Trial and Error in Children's Learning

Children represent a between-stage. Our commonest mistake is to overestimate the extent to which they are amenable to influence in terms of words. We do not realize the fact that nearly all that a young child learns he must learn with only slight help from verbal direction. One reason for this is that in the case of most simple performances there are no directions. Could you put down in a letter to a friend directions for buttoning a button, or for tying a shoe, or for drinking a glass of milk? Most of these things we all learned before we had acquired any ability to follow verbal directions, and these basic abilities, the ability to walk, to stand up, to sit down, to run, to climb, to pick up an object, to set it down, are all taken for granted in any later directions for performing anything. Very few carpenters learn, through word direction, where to hold the handle of a hammer when driving a nail. They learn this as they have learned other basic abilities through what may be called trial and error.

Trial and error is not too good a name for the process that we go through in acquiring abilities of this sort. It has sometimes been suggested that a better phrase would be *trial and success*. A child learns to drive a nail by somehow being kept busy and active with the hammer until the nail is successfully driven. He works at an activity until some result is attained. When he holds the hammer in the right place and moves it in the correct way the nail enters the wood as he has seen it enter the wood. Even a grownup may not have perfected himself at this activity. Not long ago a university professor, having occasion to drive a nail in a board and seeing nothing about on which to rest the board, put it against his stomach and drove the nail through the board and into his watch. Many grownups have never learned how to drive a nail or to use a screwdriver with any success.

Gates and Taylor have made an investigation that illustrates rather clearly the possible facilitation of learning by trial-and-error solution.[1] The specific problem was to determine whether motor control in writing is aided by "putting the child through" the various movements to be made. One group of twenty-one kindergarten children practiced writing the letters *a b c d e* by tracing them. A comparable group of fourteen children practiced the same letters by the visual free-hand copying procedure and was thus free to make many mistakes. Both groups practiced five minutes per day for five successive days. On the sixth day a copying test was given the two groups with the following results :

MEAN STROKES ON LETTERS

Group	Day 1	Day 2	Day 3	Day 4	Day 5	Day 6-Test
Tracing	11.4	20.6	20.8	24.2	29.8	8.2
Copying	3.7	7.2	13.5	17.6	19.5	21.1

[1] *Teachers College Record,* XXIV (November 1923) 459-68.

Copying skill, similar to that called for in daily experience, was more than twice as good for the "free to try and err" group (copying) as the performance of the group who were given little chance of making errors.

Further training revealed transfer advantages favoring the "copying" group. When tested with a task of copying previously unpracticed letters, both groups had low scores. However, while the mean score for the tracing group was 0.77, the mean of the copying group was 4.6.

Of particular significance is the fact that those children who were "busiest" in terms of work output each practice period were making the least true progress. Such concrete evidence as this calls up the criticism rightly leveled at excessive drill in which it is referred to as "squirrel-cage activity—all movement and no progress."

Learning in childhood is a slow process from the viewpoint of the adult and impatient observer. Most certain progress comes when motivation is *within* the child and when his action is largely *self-directed*. Only very gradually are we able to supplement actual doing and discovery by means of using verbal symbols. The "pull" which the child feels to respond in order to satisfy his needs and the "push" to avoid deprivation, disapproval, or punishment are the pincer-like forces which activate the learner.

Trial-and-error behavior arrives at the successful mastery of various activities in very much the same way in which the cat learns to get out of the puzzle box. What is required at first is some situation which will activate the child, make him restless, keep him in movement. Very often his annoyance and activity derive from the fact that some response he has made is blocked or interfered with. He has grasped something which will not come loose. He has started to open a door which sticks. He has spilled his milk in starting to drink it. Interruptions of this sort are annoying and exciting; they result in heightened activity. The normal effect of such interruptions is to lead to some change of movement which allows the act to proceed or does away with the annoyance.

When a child enters school he confronts an enormous number of new skills which must be acquired by trial and error—holding a pencil or a crayon in his hand; holding a book, opening a book, putting on or taking off his overshoes when there is snow underfoot, removing his outer garments in the cloakroom. It takes a high degree of skill to avoid getting unfavorable attention from the teacher. He must learn how to sit relatively still, how to remain relatively quiet. A generation ago in some strict European schoolrooms children sat for protracted periods with their hands clasped behind them. In a large number of these skills, the motivating agent is the teacher. She is the goad that keeps prodding the child into activity until he achieves the required result.

That is the natural development of a skill. Something incites the child to be active and keeps him restless, or something interferes sufficiently with activity already aroused to produce the same restless annoyance. In this restless and active state new behavior is developed. The new behavior normally and eventually does away with the goad, and the successful behavior thus remains the last association with the inciting stimulation. Some very odd skills result as well as some which are planned and are part of the educational scheme. There are children who by the time they reach college age have developed a facility for sitting in the classroom looking alert when in reality their attention has wandered far afield. They have learned to preserve this look because on the occasions when their appearance betrayed the fact that their attention was wandering they have had rude awakenings by embarrassing questions. There are even occasional college students who have learned to nod approvingly when a lecturer has made an emphatic point and to do this without having heard what was said.

One interesting feature of learning in children is the ease with which they develop ritual. All parents are familiar with this tendency and the rituals of rising in the morning and going to bed at night are often highly stereotyped. It is a wise parent who falls in with such ritual, because children are much more easily managed with regular routines than they are with new behavior and fresh ways. It was the French physician Pinel who discovered a century and a half ago that the insane could be managed in terms of ritual and routine. It is perhaps even a bit easier with children than with the insane.

Responses to annoyances which leave the annoyance present are quickly unlearned and replaced by new responses. The reason is that the annoying stimuli are still present, and some other response therefore replaces the unsuccessful response. The other response becomes associated with the annoying stimuli and this "unlearns" or "dissociates" the first unsuccessful response from the annoyer. The second response in turn is replaced by still another unless it takes the child out of the situation. In that case his successful response remains even for days or months or years his last association with that particular pattern of annoyance.

Even where words begin to enter into an activity, this does not do away with the trial-and-error character of the learning. For the words themselves, children do not ordinarily have to go through the same trial-and-error process. By the time that they have learned to imitate sounds (which does require trial and error) the resulting tendency to make the sound in the presence of a situation directly establishes the sound as an associative signal for the behavior appropriate to the situation. It remains true, however, that children must discover by trial and error the extent to which other persons will respond adequately to their own speech. The use of language alters the nature of trial-and-error learning.

The function of verbal guidance in learning was investigated by Goodenough and Brian [2] in a study of four-year-old children. All children were motivated by praise and colorful stickers when they were successful in making "ringers" in a ring-toss activity. The children were divided into three groups. Group A was given the standard instructions and no criticism or verbal guidance. Group B was shown (as was Group A) how to throw the ring and then given critical verbal guidance such as "Not

[2] *Journal of Experimental Psychology*, XII (1929), pp. 127-55.

so far next time" or "A little higher next time, so it won't hit the post." Group C was required to adhere to a single method of holding and throwing the ring and was also given verbal criticism and guidance like that given Group B. Each child was given twenty trials per day for fifty days. The number of "ringers" for each twenty trials was the score.

In this experiment, although defective in its use of too few subjects in each group, the restricted and guided Group C showed greatest improvement, Group B the next greatest, and the free unguided Group A the least. An evaluation of the individual learning data cited the following conditions as significant in bringing about success or failure: overconfidence, undue caution, stereotyped undesirable reactions, false association of cause and effect, peculiar meanings assigned to the verbal guidance, incorrect focusing of attention, and many changes in procedure.

The use of language always makes possible either increased understanding or confusion. In any case, what was once trial and error in discovering right and wrong responses may well become trial and error in assigning right and wrong meanings when language is introduced into the situation. The early uses of language by parents and teachers are to point out errors or to goad the child into the acquisition of new habits. A large proportion of the questions asked children have had the character of goads. "Didn't you know any better than to do that?" is just meant to make the child restless and unhappy and to insure that he will try something else in the situation and possibly establish a new mode of dealing with it. In its most elementary form, language may be used toward children much as the bark of a sheep dog is used to stop the sheep from running off in the wrong direction and keep them on the right path. The word "don't" may startle and so interrupt what is being done.

Even in an activity so verbal as beginning arithmetic a certain amount of trial-and-error behavior is still involved. Through trial and error the pupil learns what kinds of responses are tolerated, what kinds of responses will relieve his situation.

2. Problem Situations in Learning

At first it is usually the teacher, unfortunately, who must supply the stimulation that causes a child to search for an answer to an arithmetic problem. The real goal of the mathematics teacher, and incidentally a goal which is often attained, is so to guide the child's behavior that the situation of being confronted with an unsolved problem is in itself disturbing and offers sufficient motivation to drive the child to search for the answer. Obviously the ability to make problems stimulating is one of the real arts of teaching.

What constitutes a problem? There is no general answer to that question, because whether or not any situation is a problem depends on the individual who confronts it. The less intelligent the person is, the fewer problems the world puts to him. A problem is a situation which strongly stimulates an individual to respond but either offers two conflicting responses which cannot both take place at the same time and so block each other, or leaves indeterminate some essential of the response so that no response can be carried out.

One of the simplest problems is to be required to answer a question. The questioner engages our attention. We are in the habit of replying to questions. The questioner looks at us expectantly. All these things keep us from wandering off about our business. They keep us standing there unhappily until we hit upon something in the way of an answer. In working on a problem, there is one feature besides language in which there are important differences between children and animals. Most animals in using trial and error must actually make the trial, that is, they must make an effort that brings them up against a blind alley or failure before that particular line of behavior is eliminated. With human beings this is not necessary. Human beings are capable of thought. We do not have to decide the issue at this point whether or not thought always involves some motor activity. It is very probable that thought, even if it does not involve movement, does at least involve the activity of nerve pathways which were established in the course of movement and that in a great many cases thought does involve light or

minimal movement.   Children can make responses of this hidden
type to a situation and have such responses furnish signs which
cause the action to be abandoned and another course to take
its place.

As an illustration of what is meant here the reader is asked
to consider a formal problem.   Draw a circle which will represent a fence around a residential area.   Within the circle locate
three houses, A, B, and C, none of them adjacent to the fence.
If the houses A, B, and C stand in a line and are named from
left to right, then indicate at the bottom of the circle three gate-
ways, C, B, and A, in that order, from left to right.   The problem is: Can driveways connect each house with its appropriate
gate without crossing each other?   Notice what you do in
trying to solve this problem.   Many persons will make tentative
movements with a pencil, but if this is impossible, as it would
be if the diagram were on a blackboard and the listeners were
sitting in seats in the classroom, many students will make passes
at the board as they trace the possible lines of driveways.   Students who make no observable movements with their hands in
nearly all cases follow pathways with their eyes from house A
to gate A and from house B to gate B and from house C to gate
C, giving up one arrangement after another when they discover
that it crosses the place where one of the other driveways would
be situated.

This behavior can rightly be called minimal trial and error.
Such trial and error is the manner in which a student attacks a
great many problems.   He is dependent on his repertoire of responses already acquired.   Certain of these responses have features which lead them to be associated with the problem itself.
Others, which might have proved excellent solutions, are never
thought of because the association does not occur.

There is some evidence for believing that the difference
between bright and dull pupils in confronting a problem is that
the bright pupil more readily abandons unsuccessful lines of
attack.   The dull pupil will try over and over again a line which
leads nowhere and leaves the problem unsolved.

Experimental evidence indicates that overt trial and error in
the solution of such problems as these decreases with increase

in the age of the learner, past experience, and increase in intelligence. Overt trial-and-error problem solution is also a function of the problem situation itself. If all relevant details are apparent, less trial and error usually is necessary. If all relevant details *can* be perceived, the greater are the chances that implicit trial and error through symbolic processes such as speech will successfully solve the problem. The challenge to the educator is that of setting up the right degree of "apparentness" so that optimum trial and error of either the overt or implicit variety must be engaged in by the learner for the best retention and transfer. This the teacher and the parent accomplish with widely varying success and by using trial-and-error techniques of their own. Truly, a most important purpose of this text is to increase the "apparentness" of some of the relevant factors that function importantly in the learning process.

3. Negative Practice

Knight Dunlap [3] noted many years ago that one method of eliminating certain types of mistakes was through what he called *negative practice,* that is, through practicing the mistake itself. This seemed to violate all common sense and reason. How can one get over tending to write "hte" on the typewriter instead of "the" by practicing the wrong movement? Dunlap found, astonishingly enough, that such was actually the case and that writing over and over again "hte" eliminated this particular error entirely. He also used this for the cure of certain out-of-place movements which are called tics. A tic is something in the nature of a useless or embarrassing movement which occurs on numerous occasions without being under the individual's control. Most tics were once movements which on some occasion or other actually were normal responses to a situation. A cough, a shrug of the shoulders, a movement of the hand, a grimace of dislike, a shake of the head, a nod, a wink—such movements occasionally, if they have been established under excitement, become associated with signals of which the indi-

---

[3] Knight Dunlap, *Habits, Their Making and Unmaking.*

vidual is unaware. The individual, once the movement is started, can by setting himself tensely against it postpone making the movement, but this condition gradually increases tension until the movement occurs as the only possible relief. Most habits have this self-maintaining character in that when once the habit is initiated, interference tends to produce a state of tension which furnishes the conditions for learning a way around the obstacle.

Dunlap found in many cases that by inducing the patient to repeat his grimace time and again until he had reached a point of great unwillingness to continue would remove the tic. Here again he had succeeded in eliminating a movement habit by repeating the habit. What Dunlap had probably succeeded in doing by the repetition of the unwanted act was to enable the patient at some point in the movement series to substitute a different set of movements for the unwanted habit. In the case of the typist, the substituted set of movements is, of course, the correctly spelled word.

QUESTIONS

1. Should ritual ways of doing regular routines be broken up as a matter of principle? What are the disadvantages of ritual behavior?
2. What is the essential function of a question like "Can't you do better than that?"
3. Why is thinking sometimes called "vicarious trial and error"?
4. What possible danger is there in the use of Dunlap's method of negative practice?
5. What is the main difference between learning in humans and in lower animals?
6. Why can we refer to successfully evading doing lessons as a "skill"?
7. How can a situation be a problem for one child but not for another?

Chapter 10

HOW TEACHING GUIDES LEARNING

———

1. FROM THE PUPIL'S VIEWPOINT

No one ever has any trouble getting children to learn. They are learning all the time that they are awake. The real problem is to get them to learn what you want them to be able to do, and the teacher's job is somehow or other to bring it about that the children will do what they are supposed to learn to do. Learning is essentially the attachment of responses to new signals, and this cannot possibly happen without the response. The teacher's job is to use all his possible knowledge of children, and his skill from experience, to get his pupils to do the thing that he wants them to learn.

It may throw some light on the teacher's problem to point out some popular misconceptions of the way in which animals are taught animal acts for the vaudeville stage or the circus. Many persons labor under the great misconception that the trainer first writes a scenario of an act that he thinks will amuse the public and then buys his animal and trains it to do what is required in the act. Nothing faintly resembling this happens. What the animal trainer does, actually, is to notice something interesting or unusual that his animals do and to figure out a way in which this particular act could, if he could arrange for it to be done on a signal or under the right circumstances, be dressed up to attract popular attention. No animal trainer decided first that it would be a wonderful stunt to have sea lions balance balls on their noses and toss them back and forth. What really happened was that men observed sea lions doing skilful tossing and catching with their noses and worked until they had succeeded in getting them to repeat the act in captivity and under conditions which would cause an audience to applaud. Many dogs learn to sit up without any training at all, but it would be a waste of time to try to teach a cow to sit up.

A number of rules are followed by the skilled animal trainer which it would be well for any teacher to observe. For instance, one of the best dog trainers of our acquaintance never works with the dog on a particular stunt or trick more than ten minutes at a time. At the end of such a period the dog's attention begins to flag. Children's attention can be held for longer periods under some circumstances, but it is well to bear in mind that attention quickly fatigues and that we notice what is new and changing to the exclusion of what has become familiar. It is probably impossible to fix the eyes on a dot on a piece of paper for more than a fraction of a second except in very unusual circumstances. There are inborn tendencies to keep the direction of our gaze shifting unless the object at which we are looking is in continuous change. At an institution for the feeble-minded the superintendent discovered that by mistake a section which had no relevance to the rest had been spliced into a film. There was a sudden and complete change of actors, scene, and action. This change did not in the least disturb the feeble-minded children, who continued to gaze at the screen with rapt attention. The flames in a fireplace can hold us for long periods by their continual flux and change. If they remained motionless we could not fixate them for more than a very brief time. Either the observer or the object must keep changing if attention is to be maintained.

The animal trainer sees to it that he always has the animal's attention before giving the animal a command or a signal. One skilled trainer of dogs was observed, when inattention on the dog's part caused by a sudden movement among the spectators several times made the dog disregard a command, to abandon his series of commands, get the dog's attention, and start all over again. The trainer was aware that his giving the command and the dog's failure to respond had established a certain degree of negative adaptation or associative inhibition. The command had to some extent lost its power to call out the appropriate

action in the dog, because the command had been followed by
doing something irrelevant.

The skilled animal trainer never gives a command that he
does not expect to be obeyed.   In this he is like the Army officer
and the experienced teacher.   If a teacher makes a request for
silence in the room and it is disregarded, the request actually
becomes a signal for disturbance.

Freedom.—George Washington is reported to have been
very much disappointed on a visit to Philadelphia to discover
that free brick masons could in a day's labor lay six times as
many bricks as his own slave masons.   Why is it that free labor
is generally able to accomplish a great deal more than slave
labor? What is after all the difference between being a slave and
being a free man?   The free man is often less well fed.   He may
be less well clothed and housed, and he may have more worries.
But the real difference is that the free man is carrying out
actions which are his own plans—actions for which he has
called the tune, whereas the slave is compelled by the discipline
of training to do what he is told and in the way told him.

A class of forty children cannot be given complete freedom
of action.   Such freedom has been attempted in certain varieties
of the progressive education movement in recent years, but
where the freedom is actual the result is normally confusion and
aimlessness.   In the ordinary classroom the teacher must attempt a compromise.   What the pupil does must in some sense
be chosen by himself and directed by himself, must be in some
sense his own action.   His reply to questions should be his own
discovery.

Current psychological writing makes considerable use of the
word "permissive" to describe situations which do not surround
an individual with cues for repression.   Perhaps "freedom of
responsible action" would describe what is often meant by "permissive."   The ideal school environment undoubtedly has this
quality.   In a "permissive" atmosphere individual differences
can be appreciated, not just tolerated or repressed.   Study
achievement is more satisfying to the student because the social
climate in the classroom has made possible an optimum amount

of self-direction. In such an atmosphere pupils tend to act according to their own plans and wishes, but these plans take into account the wishes and interests of others.

2. THE USE OF EXISTING MOTIVES

Using Children's Roles.—One characteristic of children of which skilled teachers take full advantage is children's tendency to play a role or a part. These roles are usually organized around names, sometimes of persons but much more often around names of classes of persons like cowboys, soldiers, nurses, doctors, policemen, mothers, and fathers. A trip through a toy store demonstrates that most children's toys are merely stage properties for roles. There are cowboy and Indian suits, toy guns, toy bows and arrows, toy trucks. It is not as a rule necessary for the toy to work like the real thing. It is more important for the toy gun to look like a gun than it is for it to shoot. The possession of a truck makes the small boy a truck-driver, and this is the idea, not the moving of dirt. Dirt is not moved for the sake of moving dirt, but in order to play truck-driver. The mud pie need not be edible. Its service is performed in making the little girl appear more like a cook or a housewife.

It is largely through role-taking that children develop a notion of self as compared to "not-self." It is through play and a variety of roles that breadth of understanding—seeing the other fellow's point of view—is made possible. Often a very temporary childhood experience of assuming some responsibility for the teacher will result in a much improved teacher-pupil rapport. A recent study on experiences that influenced college students to select teaching as their profession revealed that a short experience as a substitute teacher or in "helping out" in the classroom was the most frequently noted deciding factor. Consequences of role-taking are far-reaching and represent a promising approach for both constructive and practical development.

The Experience of Success.—The teacher is continuously concerned with the roles of pupils. What they think of themselves is going to determine the pattern of what they will do, how they will behave in the classroom and out. One serious concern of the teacher is to see to it that pupils incorporate into their notions of themselves the capacities which he is going to demand of them. This often requires that a teacher take special pains to see that a boy or girl has an experience of success and that the success is noticed by other persons. It is often fatal to introduce children to work beyond their capacity. Repeated failure makes individuals think of themselves as failures. The task given the child by the teacher must be from the beginning something that most children can accomplish with encouragement. The accomplishment should be publicly acknowledged by the teacher and companions in order to have its full effect. The child should see that others recognize his success.

If a child is led by certain experiences of failure or by adverse comments of the teacher or of other pupils to think of himself as a person who cannot spell, this as a rule is fatal to any real effort at spelling. He enters all activities which are going to demand spelling with a sense of defeat. He goes through the motions but does not exert himself.

Group Loyalties.—A study of any child's use of the word "we" will throw great light on his relations to family, playmates, and school. It will betray the extent to which group loyalties have been established toward the more permanent and the less permanent groupings into which school children enter—the cliques, the clubs, the crowds, the gangs, the neighborhoods, the grades and classes, the teams into which they are associated. It is very rare indeed that a teacher can succeed in being accepted into one of these "we" groupings. "We" does not include the teacher. The experienced teacher has learned the extent to which titles and offices tend to direct behavior. The grownup who has been made program chairman for the club can hardly avoid going out and getting up a program, whether anyone wants to listen to a program or not. Just so the monitor, the group leader, tends to take responsibility along with the acceptance of the name. The whole social order is maintained and preserved partially in terms of such roles. If there were more differentiation possible in the classroom, individual roles might account for the order and discipline.

3. Benefits of Experience

Study for Use.—There is a continuous adjustment of behavior by experience. Hard work and effort that lead nowhere tend to disappear. The rule that is not enforced or checked upon gets forgotten. Every experience that children have of a study assignment which leads to nothing tends to bring deterioration of study habits. Only where children are, after study, called upon to recite, to apply, to exercise what they may have learned, do the habits of attention and the activities that are required for study and reading get preserved. Our skills degenerate when they are no longer regularly tested. Wheeler, Tolman, and others call this rule the "law of least effort."

There is no such thing as just simple study. All real study is an activity directed by some demand or purpose. There is no advantage whatever in a habit of just reading. It is what we read in order to tell about it later, what we read in order to confute an opponent in an argument, what we read in order to impress the teacher with what we can do that maintains reading as a skill. Even when we read just to prove someone else wrong, that knowledge stays with us.

The rule for the teacher to bear in mind is that study must always be directed at a specific achievement. The goal achievement may be nothing better than to be able to answer questions about material that is read. When children read a chapter of a book in order to find out something, reading is directed rather than aimless. The child is busy formulating an answer. What is read is far more likely to be remembered. It was said previously that the teacher's job is to induce activity in the pupil. This is not the whole story. Nearly every schoolroom is likely to be more active without the influence of a teacher than with it. The teacher's full job is to establish *aimed activity, activity directed at goals.* A goal may be described as anything of which the lack is disturbing. Children's goals are things children are unhappy without.

As class procedures and activity become more "goal-directed," there is a shift from drive from external sources to drive from *within* the pupil. Subject matter more closely related to the affairs of everyday living—economic, social, recreational, political, and civic problems of current importance—puts flesh and blood into the curricular structure. The artificialness, repressiveness, and deadliness of routine are eliminated. The real challenge offered by physical education, home economics, music, agriculture, dramatics, and journalism is often found to be a function of the purposeful activity permitted and encouraged in those courses as compared with mathematics, English, and language training taught in conventional material, i.e., with artificial incentives in terms of imposed goals. Any imaginative and enterprising teacher can correlate the subject matter with contemporary realities and will benefit from self-generated enthusiasm as a by-product.

Of necessity in the classroom the teacher is the original source of much of the child's unhappiness and uneasiness. The teacher's job is a problem of transfer. He must furnish the original stimuli that induce action and activity in the children. His next problem is to see to it that the same restiveness for which he was originally responsible is now conditioned on problems, questions, contradictions, and difficulties in the subjects themselves. The boy who has been made curious and restive in the presence of an unsolved arithmetic problem has acquired an interest in arithmetic and a chance to become skilled in that subject. With many children any spelling would do. It is the teacher who is annoyed by misspelled words, not the pupil. But this form of discontent can be transferred to students by virtue of the fact that the teacher makes them uncomfortable. The curiosity of the mature scholar that drives him to years of hard study has its beginnings in the dissatisfaction that teachers and other persons have expressed and communicated in the presence of unanswered or wrongly answered questions. There are of course other motivations eventually.

The potential teacher may well recall the school activities from which he gained most greatly, asking himself, "What aspects of this learning situation make it a highlight in my educational experience?" Very likely the answer will be something like this: "This exceptional lesson was one in which I felt responsible for my own progress, though I was constantly aware of willing teacher aid and guidance available to me every step of the way. I was fully aware of the goal desired and found myself and my fellows planning, evaluating, progressing, and criticizing in satisfying cooperative action. Mastery of certain skills and need for relevant information were recognized not as ends in themselves, but as means to an end."

From the Familiar to the New.—The rule that teaching means stimulating children to goal activities has many corollaries. The most important corollary of the rule is a saying that has been quoted in writing about education for over a century: *Teaching must proceed from the known to the unknown.* Stimulating children to activity requires that the stimuli used be stimuli which have already through associative learning been established as signals for behavior. No one is stimulated by strangeness alone. If strange events and strange places prove exciting, it is because they have familiar elements that call out conflicting responses and therefore produce excitement and emotional reinforcement. In order to make children responsive to their studies, the appeal must be made to interests they already possess and to knowledge they already have. The materials with which the teacher can work consist of the habits and interests which children have already acquired. Out of these the teacher can induce activities which will lead to the mastery of new subjects and new skills.

The requirement that education must use the familiar in order to introduce the new helps to determine the sequence of the curriculum, the order of studies pursued in grade school and high school. Recourse is had naturally to the growing knowledge and skills which children acquire outside the schoolroom. Children become different each year. The grade-school teacher finds that she can chat easily with children of the age group to which she is accustomed—for instance with seventh grade pupils. The same teacher may find herself at a loss in talking to high school children. The successful high school teacher often finds college students dull and uninteresting, and many college teachers are hopelessly inept in carrying on a conversation with high school students.

Effects of Maturing Intelligence.—Developing habits and interests are paralleled as children grow older by a development in capacity or intelligence. If there is such a thing as the "native intelligence" of which psychologists talked a great deal a generation ago, it has proved thus far almost impossible to separate it from the development of habit and interest and knowledge. It has been observed a number of times that children who from birth on were unable to see because cataracts interfered with vision never established full and complete use of vision if the relieving operation was performed much after the seventh year. If the operation is performed many years later, the visual mechanism may be perfect but the individual will, if he has been blind from birth, never learn to use his eyes as an ordinary person does. This is undoubtedly because the development of the nerve structures that are concerned in vision is affected by the exercise of those structures in the early years and the development simply does not occur when this exercise is prevented.

The development of intelligence and interest and habit and skills in school children has one important consequence for teaching. This consequence is that teachers and parents must both be on guard against underestimating the capacity of children if the parents and teachers are habituated to children of a younger age. This is necessarily true of parents because all children are three years old before they are four years old, and they are five before they are six. During the third year parents have of necessity adjusted themselves to the three-year-old and to three-year-old intelligence and three-year-old skills and information—to three-year-old helplessness. Once this adjustment has been made, parents tend strongly to lag behind the actual development of the child. When the child is five years old, the parent and some teachers may still tend to treat him as if he were three, because that treatment is a function of parental and teaching habits. There is a general and continuous tendency for parents to underestimate the capacities for responsibility of developing children. The mother who knows that she cannot trust her four-year-old to keep out of puddles or to execute an errand at the grocery or to come home when he promises or to observe ordinary safety precautions in the use of matches develops habits of looking after all these situations herself. These habits are in many cases still present one or two years later or even four or five years later when some of the mother's precautions could be relaxed and children given more responsibility. The current practice of having teachers remain with the grade rather than with the advancing children is probably well justified by these facts. The teacher of the seventh grade becomes highly skilled in knowing what to expect of children at that age. She learns what will appeal to seventh graders—how much responsibility seventh graders can be given. A large proportion of this knowledge would become useless if the teachers were assigned to the fifth grade or the senior high school.

Questions

1. Why is it dangerous to tell a child that he is a "nonreader"?
2. Why should school rules be kept to an absolute minimum?
3. Why should a child recite answers that he and all the rest of the pupils already know?
4. Why is it usually a poor idea to have a teacher teach a grade several years older or younger than that to which he is accustomed?
5. Mention some roles that the careful teacher will avoid giving to his students.
6. A teacher who lets his pupils laugh for some time after a funny incident usually has a more orderly class. Why is this?
7. What is the basic reason why complete freedom in the classroom is not practicable?

Chapter 11

HOW TEACHING GUIDES LEARNING—*Continued*

---

1. SOME FACTORS AFFECTING LEARNING

The relation between what a learner does and what gets learned can be readily illustrated by a very simple experiment. Learn to tie one of the simpler knots such as a bowline. Then try to teach a number of other persons to tie the same knot. A teacher could lecture for a long time on how to tie this knot without imparting skill in tying the knot to any pupils. The teacher's real job here is to induce the student himself to tie the knot and to put in an occasional word of direction at the right place. Learning to tie the knot does not depend on learning these directions. The series of movements can be acquired without words. The learning will take place only if the learner ties a few knots. The learning will be more certain to stick the more knots the learner ties, because this will make it possible to tie the knot from a number of different initial positions of the rope and in varying circumstances. It would be quite possible to tie the knot but have the ability limited to successful performance only when the line is placed before the learner in just a certain position and no other.

Learning a song, learning a poem, learning arithmetic, learning history require active participation just as much as learning to tie a knot, but the participation may be a different sort of thing. A great deal of verbal material may be learned. We can learn rules and principles. We can learn to talk about certain things without actually going through the full performance of speech. The activity may be confined to inner speech. There are singers who can sing a new song in a concert with no more practice than is involved in sitting down and reading the song over a number of times. The song has been sung, but in a kind of inner singing that makes no sound. Teaching many students at a time requires that these minimal responses, this inner behavior, be used for all it is worth. When a student recites, the recitation may serve to give point and purpose to previous study. It also consists in an active performance that leaves learning effects behind it. The beneficial effects of recitation are well known. The teacher should so manage recitation that it is not only the children who speak who actually recite. The other children should be reciting to themselves. This is not a thing to be achieved by demanding it or by talking about it. It can only be achieved by so managing the general situation that all the children are stirred to speak but all except one inhibit that speech or restrict it to inner speech. When in a large class one pupil is reciting, others must be forming sentences, rehearsing statements, and answering objections.

Negativism.—Of particular importance to teachers is the fact that in attempting to induce children to work arithmetic problems, to study a lesson, to sing, to carry on any one of the multiple activities of the classroom, the pressure methods on which the teacher must often depend result in reinforcing resistance and evasion, and resistance and evasion are what get learned.

Gesell [1] proposes the interesting idea that negativism is often properly viewed as developmental. For example, at two and a half years most children are expert in declining, in saying "No" emphatically, and in resisting highly attractive and interesting events. This negativism is of a temporary nature, for at three the child exhibits an equally noticeable tendency to conform and to assent in order to secure approval. Intensive use of "No" at two and a half may actually increase the child's understanding of "Yes" and all its implications. In this sense, negativism may be expected, welcomed, and valued as a developmental process.

---

[1] Arnold L. Gesell *et al., Infant and Child in the Culture of Today.*

If we were to place a small kitten on the table and pull backward on its tail, it would dig in its claws and pull forward. On the other hand, to a push from behind, the kitten will brace itself against the push, and push backward. Tendencies to opposition and negativism are learned early. Persons who have formed no habits of resistance to the commands and directions and requests of others are helpless and become involved in much trouble. We learn many devices for resisting others, devices which range from open, violent resistance to pretended compliance.

Where children have studied only under what might be described as pressure conditions from parents or teachers, they can be depended upon not to study when these pressures are relieved. The real job of the teacher is to establish interests in all children which will operate in the absence of the teachers. What the teacher must do is to bring it about that the subjects themselves demand attention and elicit activity and response. Many persons have never realized that in arguing with a friend or member of the family or with a pupil in the classroom, what actually is being done is to give the opponent practice in taking the opposition and to establish habits of contradiction. Prohibitions often tend to increase the interest in an activity. Perhaps the reasons for this increased interest deserve some examination.

There are many restrictions on what the muscles of the body can do. One of these restrictions is the pattern of contraction prevailing at the moment. Muscles are so arranged that they control the movements of our limbs in opposition. One set of muscles bends and another set straightens the elbow. One set raises and another set lowers the arm. The muscles that turn the head to the right oppose the muscles that turn the head to the left. Controlled movement demands that muscles be thus arranged to balance each other.

Two different movement patterns may involve opposing sets of muscles so that two different movements may be impossible to execute at the same time. One of them may be physically impossible to combine with the other, like raising and lowering the arm. In some cases the combination is not physically impossible but is neurologically impossible. One movement stimulates receptors which inhibit or prevent the other movement.

We may be stimulated to conflicting action, to both a movement and the opposed movement. The normal result of conflict is to call out certain physiological reinforcers of action in the body, to speed up the pulse, to increase the general tension of body muscles. The result is heightened activity, and the result of heightened activity is in its turn an acceleration of learning.

One of the results of this is that punishment or the threat of punishment often does nothing but increase the interest and excitement with which an action is performed. The fact that the action is forbidden, that there is a certain risk of punishment, produces some conflict. The action is undertaken with a mixture of cautionary behavior, and this mixture serves to speed up behavior and produce what may be called an emotional reinforcement of behavior. The forbidden act therefore tends to have an added interest of its own.

There are many illustrations of this in ordinary life. The thrill that we get out of gambling and the dogged persistence with which many persons insist on spending all their savings on horse racing or cards can be explained by the exciting nature of gambling. Gambling is exciting because it offers an ideal balance of conflict. Whether to put your money on the horse or not—there is no clear indication of the outcome. As a consequence, every person is strongly motivated both to bet and to abstain from betting. It is the fear of losing that makes betting so attractive, the fear of being injured that makes elephant hunting exciting and sought after, the fear of being punished that lends a real thrill to breaking classroom rules.

The father of an eighth grade boy found his son in great difficulties with his arithmetic. He suggested certain short cuts, using letter symbols as algebra does. These were represented by the father to be a method of which the teacher would probably disapprove, a method slightly questionable in ethical value, but a remarkable short cut to the correct answer. The boy developed an astonishing interest in the use of letters in the solution of his eighth grade arithmetic problems and became highly skilled at it. This interest carried over into high school and eventually developed into a mathematics major in college with great scholastic success.

Sir Walter Scott attributed the fact that the English gentry of his day displayed an active hostility toward reading to the fact that the reading they had done in school had been motivated very largely by the use of switches. The British country squires had acquired a strong negativism toward books in the schoolroom.

There can be no doubt that the motivation of children in the classroom is much more important in determining whether or not they will learn than is the detail of learning methods, and that the direction of interest is the teacher's primary job. A number of years ago, at a large state university, classes were offered freshmen in how to study. These classes were eventually discontinued because it was discovered that students who became really interested in study picked up good methods without much direction. The same thing is true of children in the classroom. If an absorbing interest is established in a subject, and if the child is not dependent on pressure from his parents or teacher, he tends to hit upon effective methods for learning by his own efforts.

Role of Language in Classroom Learning.—So far as learning is concerned, the situation in the classroom imposes some very formidable restrictions. Children's activity in the classroom is very largely limited to talk, so that classroom learning is going to be confined very largely to speech habits. Driving an automobile, arts and crafts, good table manners, and morals cannot be directly learned in the classroom. They require the full activities of life outside that restricting situation.

What sort of learning does go on in a classroom? Classroom learning will, like all learning, be limited to what is being done. Our real question is: "What goes on in a classroom?" because children are learning what they are doing. Any teacher knows that a great deal more than talk takes place in a classroom, but probably the activities of most interest in education center about speech and the establishment of new verbal habits. This is not intended to minimize the contribution to a child's education made by singing, by drawing, by the habits of give and take in his relations to other children, and by the discipline of the classroom.

If the learning organized about language and its use were limited to words which are actually spoken, classroom instruction would have to be abandoned. It is because we can depend upon establishing habits of inner speech or thought that the classroom recitation can be made effective in teaching large groups of children. The classroom depends for its value on the extent to which the teacher can arouse and control thought or the inner speech of his pupils. If, when a question is asked of a class, the only pupil to frame the answer were the pupil of whom the question is asked, the procedure would not be worthwhile. It is because the question provokes active verbal behavior in the other pupils listening that the question becomes profitable.

The fact that classroom activities center very largely about the control of language, the establishment of language habits and language patterns, and the use of language does not for one moment decrease the importance of classroom instruction. On language depends the whole structure of civilization and culture, morals, science, and tradition. On language depends the existence of a nation as a nation. There exists a French nation only when there exist millions of persons who recognize themselves as Frenchmen and acknowledge France as the symbol of their country. Man's control over nature and his control over himself are both dependent on linguistic habits. Raoul de Roussy de Sales suggests that it is absurd to make a virtue out of loving one's country.[2] It is inevitable for most men because their inward voices speak their native tongue.

In their first use of language, children experience language symbols always in connection with other persons. They learn to control the behavior of those about them through language by expressing their wants and desires. Language is not at first used for understanding or controlling natural events or the physical world about us. It is a means of dealing with people.

---

[2] See *Atlantic Monthly,* June, 1949.

One of the things that a child learns in the classroom is to use language for purposes other than dealing with people. He learns the use of language for multiplying and adding and subtracting. He learns the use of language for describing the behavior of physical objects. He learns the use of language for expressing the nature of relationships between things as well as between persons, and he learns to extend his use of language to written symbols and printed symbols, as well as to sound and voice. Much of this training is available to him only in the classroom. He would not be exposed at home to situations which would induce such learning.

Profitable learning in the classroom tends strongly to center around word activities, and it is the teacher's job to incite and guide inner speech and the spoken word. Many classroom activities do not involve inner speech— drawing, marking up a book, teasing another child, idly looking at pictures, folding bits of paper, or manufacturing paper wads. There are a thousand such activities that do not require either inner speech or overt speech.

The child who is beginning to read may delay in acquiring that ability for a long time by acquiring a habit of looking at pictures and not at the printed word, or looking at the printed word without forming it in inner speech. The devices for teaching late readers or nonreaders to read, when they are successful, always involve a method which will guarantee that the child must look at and utter the word at the same time. When the child has learned to read, the teacher's next concern is to incite him to an activity that involves a great deal more than merely forming the words which he sees. His problem is to make these words the signals for speech of his own, which does more than merely reproduce the seen word. He must learn to ask questions of the text, and he is incited to do this by being asked questions by the teacher. The sight of the text itself must become the stimulus which stirs him to inquiry and sensing problems. Active reading is far more than following the words of the text. Active reading involves noticing, comparing, questioning, recapitulating, preparing for questions and speech to others.

Under natural circumstances, this tremendous verbal activity of the child does not require any special motivation. Anyone who has lived through the interminable accounts that small children give of their first motion pictures will realize this. The words in which the picture is described are not furnished by the picture itself. The small boy has his own descriptive vocabulary, which is often poverty-stricken and repetitive, and crammed with statements about what "this guy" did and what "the other guy" did. It is this interest in telling about, in arguing about, in finding fault with, and sometimes in improving on that the teacher must arouse in the child. Active listening, like active reading, requires a great deal more than a mere following of the heard words. It involves comments, contradictions, assent, and in some cases a rehearsal for a future telling. Children will do all these things for an interested audience. The problem of the classroom teacher is to manage forty children at once in such activities. Often a single child would represent no problem at all.

Types of Learning Outcomes.—Effective guidance of learning is much more likely to result when teachers are clearly aware of the many *types* of lessons learned by students. Traditionally, knowledge consisting of information, facts, concepts, and understanding is recognized as necessary to educational growth. But not so commonly understood, and certainly not commonly practiced, is the developmental method of increasing a child's store of these essential components. The very nature of factual, conceptual, and informational material becomes a factor tending toward the use of authoritative rehearsal, recitation, drill, and memorization, leaving the child or student intellectually stunned if not actually "cold and numb." Understanding which is most likely to have transfer value is much less painfully achieved by developmental, socialized methods of instruction.

The teaching of factual information can become an obsession, and when it does, many other valuable educational objectives are often lost. Facts can be taught in a relatively short time in a very logical or systematic manner by less able and unimaginative teachers. The size and location of cities, the repetition of definitions, and the listing of courses or of results are items easy to test, to score, and to grade. The busy teacher is attracted by such simple, routine, and expedient busy work. The innumerable workbooks used testify to such attractiveness. But the encouragement of initiative, independent study habits, creativity, and the development of useful techniques of problem solving are left wanting. For these gains, teaching must be supplemented by student discussion, activity, illustrations, audio-visual aids, projects, field trips, and concrete applications.

Skills and habits are also learned. Using the telephone efficiently and courteously, making introductions, typing, skating, writing, and speaking are all skills. Repetition of the desired behavior is essential for the development of a skill, but there must also be a knowledge of the results of performance. The master teacher must be able to point out just what is lacking in an English composition that makes it less than acceptable. The penmanship instructor must have concrete ways of indicating what characteristics make for illegible writing and a definite technique of evaluating such deficiencies : objectivity of evaluations is just as essential as in standardized measurement. For the teacher to show concretely that letters are poorly and not uniformly written, that letter height is uneven, that slanting is very irregular, or that *t*'s are not crossed and *i*'s are not dotted gives the child a set of specific and attainable goals for which to strive. Success experiences are thereby increased. The drill periods should not be long and exhaustive, but of relatively brief duration and of sufficient frequency. In the early learning stages, drill or practice periods should be more closely spaced. As the learning becomes mastered, the time interval between drill periods may be increased. Every time a child is expected to develop a certain habit, he is automatically expected to *unlearn* something else. If he is to develop the ability to speak in clearly enunciated language, he must somehow unlearn careless expression. To learn to be self-sufficient in preparing his assignments he must unlearn dependence upon his teachers, his parents, or a friend. No abrupt change should be expected but only a gradual, yet progressive, appearance of the new way of behaving. Skills and habits once developed become relatively permanent acquisitions and hence form an extremely important portion of educational development. Skills and habits are knowledge in action.

Students also acquire ideals and attitudes. By comparison, skills, habits, facts, and information seem very tangible and are much more easily arranged for. Most effective for this kind of training is some type of indirection. The teacher's behavior in contact with students—friendliness, patience, fairness, honesty, tact, enthusiasm, and efficiency—is usually very important in establishing the accepted pattern of behavior in a classroom society. A fundamental appreciation of differences, expressed in actions rather than in words, does much to preserve the integrity of each individual in the society and becomes a most helpful attitude.

Ideals may be thought of as high-level goals that determine what young people will try to accomplish and often what they will become. As a prerequisite step, students should be interested in this goal. It must be, at least in some degree, attainable. Ideals must necessarily arouse strong emotions, so that decisions regarding them can be made. A final guiding principle would be that opportunities for practice should be provided. The teacher herself should show informed and rational loyalty to the ideal in her thought and action.

Perhaps the attempt to develop serviceable attitudes, ideals, interests, and tastes (as a first objective) *by means of subject matter* would be an improved approach in methods of education.

Many studies have been aimed at discovering the most effective and economical methods of learning rather than the basic nature of learning. Some of the results of these studies have been interesting and important and of practical use.

Usually studies of learning efficiency select some useful skill like sending or receiving Morse code, typing, shooting at a target, memorizing a poem, or mastering the ideas of a section in a book. Other studies have used learning materials that have no practical use but offer as compensation the fact that most learners have no antecedent experience with them and all start "from scratch." Nonsense syllables have some of this advantage. Learning the series *"nem-geg-tok-cos-dez-wob"* offers no one of the would-be learners the advantage of previous familiarity. In a motor performance, tracing a figure which is seen only in a mirror has the same advantage.

2. EFFICIENT LEARNING

Whole-Part Learning.—Is it more economical for a person who undertakes to memorize a poem to practice by reading the poem through on each occasion of practice, or to repeat over and over single stanzas until each of these is learned? Is a lesson best acquired by reading the chapter of the history text through each time, or by reading over sections until the section is clearly in mind and can be reported?

A whole generation of experiment in this field gave results which are not easily summarized because they differed with the nature of the material being learned or studied. In such material as a poem of moderate length there appears to be an advantage in learning the material by reading it through on each trial, and not by repeating each stanza until that is memorized. We can speculate upon the reason for this. The person who repeats each stanza until it is learned has tended to establish as an association with the final phrases of each stanza the beginning of the same stanza rather than the beginning of the next. At each such point there is therefore a tendency to the wrong association, and this leads to confusion.

Massed or Distributed Practice.—Is it more economical to practice what is to be learned in long or in short practice periods? How long should be the intervals between practice periods? These questions have been attacked with a wide variety of practice materials, including typing, target practice, memorizing nonsense syllables, learning lists of paired words, memorizing poems or prose, and many other learning tasks.

The questions just asked are very practical. When a student undertakes to learn to type, should the duration of each practice period be a matter of minutes or of hours? Should he practice morning and afternoon or once a day? Many experiments with both animals and persons appear to give the advantage to distributed practice periods with intervals as long as twenty-four hours between.[3]

As in the case of studies of whole versus part learning, results depend on the nature of the task being learned. It is fairly safe to make the practical generalization that fatigue is effective in setting the limits of a single practice period. When a period spent at practice on the typewriter is so prolonged as to cause fatigue to interfere with the efficiency of movements, it can be predicted that the learning will be less efficient than when each period stops before fatigue has set in. In the practice of many skills there appears to be a law of diminishing returns. The rate of improvement is higher at the beginning of practice and diminishes as practice is continued, until in a protracted session a point is reached beyond which no improvement takes place.

Retroactive Inhibition.—Another of the practical conditions affecting the economy or efficiency of learning concerns the way in which the learner's time is spent between learning sessions. Some activities can be shown to interfere with learning. It has been mentioned that one activity, namely sleep, has a minimum adverse effect on retention. In other words, we forget very little during sleep. This fact may throw light on the way in which intervening activities favor or interfere with progress in learning. The inference is that the between-periods have an unfavorable effect on the progress of learning of a particular task when they include activities which attach irrelevant or conflicting responses to some of the associative signals involved in learning.

McGeoch defined retroactive inhibition as *"a decrement in retention resulting from activity, usually a learning activity, interpolated between an original learning and a later measurement of retention."* [4] McGeoch pointed out that the word "retroactive" is not to be taken in the literal sense of meaning that the activity works backward on the previous learning, but only in the sense that it reduces the amount of the learning which is retained.

---

[3] See *British Journal of Psychology,* XXVII (1937), pp. 303-12.
[4] John A. McGeoch, *The Psychology of Human Learning,* New York: Longmans, Green and Co., 1942, p. 458.

Certain cases of retroactive inhibition are so obviously founded on learning conflicting associations that experiment would appear unnecessary. Our skill in the use of the emergency brake of a car or of the clutch pedal is interfered with when we have practiced for a time with another car in which these instruments are differently placed. The new habit destroys the old. It would take little to persuade us that when a child is learning the multiplication table, spending the time between lessons in learning a new table with wrong answers would seriously interfere with the retention of the correct table. Retroactive inhibition could, in fact, be inferred from our basic principle of associative learning. A corollary of that principle is that it is the last association that prevails. All that is required for retroactive inhibition is that some of the associative cues involved in a skill be associated with new responses which are irrelevant to the skill or act as sources of interference.

Recitation.—Another of the practical conditions affecting learning which has been the subject of considerable experimental investigation is the use or nonuse of recitation in learning verbal material. Gates [5] tried out the effect of reading plus various amounts of recitation on the learning of both nonsense syllables and meaningful material. The nonsense syllable task consisted in learning to repeat a list of sixteen syllables. The meaningful material consisted of five short biographies of about 170 words each. In learning nonsense syllables when all the time was spent in reading and none given to recitation, 35 per cent remembered immediately after nine minutes. When one-fifth of the time was spent in recitation, this percentage reached 50. Two-fifths produced 54 per cent, three-fifths 57 per cent, and four-fifths of the period spent in recitation resulted in a recall of 74 per cent of the syllables. For the meaningful material the percentages remembered were 35, 37, 41, 42, and 42 under the same conditions. Increasing the percentage of recitation gave better remembering. The same relative effects

---

[5] "Recitation as a Factor in Memorizing," *Archives of Psychology,* American Psychological Association, 1917, No. 40, pp. 1-104.

were evident after four hours as well as immediately following practice.

The explanation of the value of recitation in terms of the theory of learning suggested in this text is that, since all learning is limited to the attachment of responses to new stimuli, the practice of overt responses demanded in recitation is more sure to establish associations than is silent reading in which adequate responses may or may not have occurred, and the acts of recitation offer far more opportunities for the establishment of the necessary associations. Recitation stimulates the learner's sense organs, his own ears, his proprioceptors in speech muscles. These stimuli, which are not present in silent reading, become associative cues which help to integrate the action of recitation and to insure that what is studied will be re-established if the proper cue occurs. Recitation insures attention and eliminates distractions which will confuse learning.

Reward and Punishment.—Thorndike,[6] who described learning in terms of the law of effect, reports numerous experiments in which reward and punishment consisted in saying to the learner who was acting as the subject of the experiment the word "right" or "wrong." The word "right" was assumed to act as a reward and the word "wrong" was supposed to act as a punishment.

We may take it for granted that both these words depend for their effect not on the mere fact that they are intended as reward or punishment but on what they, as stimuli, cause the listener to do. What does a person who has volunteered an answer do as a result of hearing the word "wrong"? Thorndike showed that the response which evoked this comment tends to be abandoned. How does the word "wrong" cause a response to be abandoned?

We may safely assume that this word causes the listener to do something which results in a conditioned inhibition of the wrong response. Hearing the word "wrong" he actually practices, if only in inner speech, another response to the situation. To the word "right" the listener may rehearse the right re-

---

[6] E. L. Thorndike, *Human Learning.*

sponse. In the first case the response tends to be eliminated, and in the second case the response tends to be preserved. In themselves these two words are neither reward nor punishment. *Their effect is solely dependent on the behavior that they induce.*

Actual rewards and punishments operate in much the same way. A child punished for writing on the wall with a crayon may or may not learn to avoid this offense in the future. All depends on what the punishment made him do in the presence of the situation. If a child were punished while facing the damaged wall with the crayon in his hand, there might be substituted for the tendency to mark on the wall the response induced by the punishment, a strong effort to escape from the situation. Punishments are effective in breaking up undesired habits when they induce in the presence of the motivating situation other and less objectionable behavior.

The role of an instructor in golf or an instructor in typing is to stand by and observe in order to interfere when undesirable methods appear. The instructor's corrections are not necessarily punishments, but they serve to break up awkward efforts and bad habits. In some instances the instructor does very little more than this and the correct movements appear only through trial and error following correction. When the movement has once been performed correctly, it is allowed to stand.

Punishment and reward involve complex personal relationships and their chief effects often lie in their alterations of these relationships rather than in the direction of the immediate task. The punished child may establish attitudes toward the punisher which interfere with any proper relation of parent to child or of teacher to child.

3. Skills and Habits

Learning Skills.—Acquiring skill in writing, in sports, or in arithmetic operations involves practice. There is evidence that the acquiring of a single associative connection between a response and a specific stimulus does not require repeated association but can be established on one occasion. We remember many facts with one repetition. Why do skills require practice and repetition when associations can be established on one occasion?

The answer is that skills require much more than a few associations between stimuli and responses. Skills require the adjustment of many response variations to variations in the situation. Learning to catch a ball involves learning not one response but an indefinite variety of responses all nicely adjusted to the sight of the approaching ball and the cues for judging its speed and trajectory. Even so simple an act as sitting down at his school desk is not a stereotyped response for a child because the movements must be adjusted to his distance and direction from the desk and the way he has approached it.

We define a skill as *an ability to achieve some end result,* not as a tendency to respond in a specific way to a specific stimulus. Learning skills involves learning thousands of associative responses and unlearning thousands of others. It is for this reason that practice is necessary to the acquisition of skills. Every skilled achievement is accomplished by definite movements, and each of these movements must have been associated with the stimuli that evoke it. In arithmetic skills, Thorndike has suggested plausibly that the associations may be as specific as a response of "63" to the question "What is 7×9?" A response of "63" to the question: "What is 9×7?" is another association and requires its own practice. The algebra student who has used only x and y as symbols for the unknowns in solving equations may have no idea of what to do when confronted with an equation in which s is used as the unknown.

Motor Skills.—Teaching a motor skill involves a number of activities which can be roughly distinguished as follows:

1. Establishing interest: this covers the general task of getting the child's attention, getting him to notice the goal, and take an interest in it.
2. Demonstrating performance or, in some instances, describing performance when that will suffice.
3. Inducing the learner himself to try.
4. Correcting faulty execution by breaking up bad habits and allowing trial and error to discover new correct ones if these

are not available in habit responses already established to directions.

5. Promoting performance under the conditions in which the skill must be practiced.

Continued practice in itself tends strongly to eliminate awkward movements and unnecessary effort, because fatigue serves as the corrective which breaks up unnecessary components. But it has been demonstrated that, even after a long life-occupation at such a skill as bricklaying, most artisans have preserved bad methods and unnecessary motions to a surprising extent. All through training, motivation must be maintained. One of the best devices for maintaining interest is to have performance noticed and appreciated. A powerful component in learning any kind of skill is self-confidence, which may be more accurately described as the habit of success. Children who are led to attempt tasks in which success will be long delayed can easily acquire the habit of failure. The reaction to failure is thus easily attached to the beginning of a new activity, so that the child starts work with the preparation for withdrawal interfering with the performance itself. A discouraged performance or a half-hearted performance is a performance in which the actual behavior of failure is mixed with attempts to succeed.

Numerous psychologists use the phrase "aspiration level" to indicate the goal which a child is setting himself in attempting a performance. There is no doubt that aspiration level influences performance. This can be illustrated by placing on a table two similar castings, one of lead and the other of aluminum. If the subject of the experiment first picks up and handles the aluminum, he may not succeed later in lifting the lead, which is many pounds heavier. He will perceive it as fastened to the table. If the first object lifted is the lead, the initial muscular effort is usually adjusted in a few quick stages until a point is reached at which the effort is sufficient to pick up the heavy mass.

Motor skills enter into a child's adjustment to his surroundings to an extent sometimes not realized. The coordination that results from physical games and sports—the ability to walk, run, jump, all with minimum effort and awkwardness, may enter into the determination of many attitudes toward persons and toward activities. Many avenues of development and expanding interests may be shut off by poorly developed physical coordination.

Making and Breaking Habits.—Certain drugs are correctly called *habit-forming*. So are certain practices like thumb-sucking. What makes these drugs or these practices habit-forming? The answer is probably to be found in considering the fact that all activity is driven by stimuli and that the normal effect of those persistent stimuli which constitute drives or motives is to bring about eventually some response that removes the goad. This response tends to remain the habit adjustment to the situation that caused the original restlessness.

Opiates and thumb-sucking do not remove the motivating stimuli. They quiet the activity, and this has much the same effect. A man in chronic pain who has begun to take morphine is freed from the restlessness occasioned by his pain, and the act of taking morphine tends to remain his last association with pain. The baby, restless from any cause, is quieted by the presence of his thumb in his mouth, which stimulates the movements of nursing and inhibits the general restlessness which had preceded. The drug and the act (thumb-sucking) are both habit-forming because they relieve restlessness and discomfort and therefore tend to remain associated with the restlessness and discomfort. To become dissociated from distress it would be necessary to cause distress and prevent morphine or thumb-sucking from relieving it.

Smoking has, of course, a very close resemblance to thumb-sucking. In fact it might be described as a somewhat more adult form of that activity. When it has been practiced for a considerable time, it becomes associated with so many situations that it is difficult to stop because unlearning such a habit requires that all the cues which have become established be present with some response other than smoking. This takes time and practice.

The breaking of any habit involves establishing at some point in the performance of the habit a new associative response

which is incompatible with the bad habit. The habit of responding to a situation can be changed only by presenting the situation
under circumstances which compel some different and incompatible response. There may be said to be three practical ways
in which this can be brought about. The stimulus for the unwanted response may be presented along with the stimuli which
elicit an inhibiting response. The inhibiting response can be
either a response to punishment or to distraction. The mother
may induce her child to stop pointing at the stranger either by
slapping the child or by calling his attention to something more
interesting. The second method consists in presenting the
stimulus but in such slight intensity that the response does not
prevail over competing responses. A book on the training of
hunting dogs suggests that a gun-shy dog can be cured by
habituating him to the sound of the explosion through discharg-
ing a cap pistol at a great distance at first and then nearer and
nearer, and by repeating the process with the shot-gun of which
the dog was afraid. Children can be habituated to situations
which would cause excited revolt if at first long continued and
of some severity, provided that the exposure is short to begin
with and of mild intensity. The third method is to expose the
child to the situation and continue until the response is exhausted and no longer given. All these amount to the same
thing. The three methods all provide that the situation shall
be present and the response not occur. The first method inhibits
the response by stimulating conflicting responses; the second
prevents the response by keeping the stimulus below its threshold; the third method insures a period of stimulus present and
response absent by first exhausting the response.

4. INFORMATION AND ATTITUDES

Acquiring Information.—It would obviously be difficult to
explain the impending arrival of daylight-saving time to the
family cat. Information can be imparted only to those who
already possess the elements of the information. There are
persons to whom it is almost equally hopeless to try to explain
the change. We become capable of acquiring information only

by having built up a large repertoire of symbolized meanings. The arithmetic problem can be explained only to one who has already acquired the basic arithmetic skills. Many children in school have never acquired these skills and are condemned from now on to attempt arithmetic and algebra as fearful tasks in rote memorizing of rules which are fundamentally meaningless. If subtraction has never been identified as a search for what must be added to one number to get another, it is never fully understood. Most persons learn to subtract in order to make change; but many children have never been led to see this in their arithmetic. That multiplication is repetitive addition must be appreciated or multiplication tends to become just another mysterious contest with the teacher.

If a teacher reads off the letters: *m-s-g-w-t-b-c-n-r-i-l-z-a-y*, very few pupils could repeat. If, instead, the teacher reads "There will be no final examination in this course," many pupils will be able to repeat. The difference is that one combination of sounds is in an unfamiliar order and an order that has no association and hence provokes no specific perceptual response. The second series of syllables is already familiar, or there are at most only one or two unfamiliar sequences in the series. It evokes interest and approval and, most important for future reproduction, it evokes repetition.

There has been some complaint in educational circles that in our zeal to make elementary textbooks conform to the abilities of pupils to understand we have deprived pupils of the opportunity to encounter new words and to enlarge their vocabularies. We cannot press the acquisition of vocabulary just for its own sake without running the danger of introducing words that are detached from their connections with appropriate behavior. The child who wrote "Liza grapeman allry minus" instead of "Lives of great men all remind us," was not much worse off than the child who can spell "sublime" correctly but has never made the word part of his behavior and associated it with an attitude somewhere between awe and admiration.

Learning Attitudes.—By an attitude is meant a tendency to respond to a class of stimuli (as for example children, symphony concerts, fishing trips) and to the cues associated with these, by withdrawal or approach, disapproval or approval, as for or as against. We form attitudes toward persons, projects, activities, things, places.

The psychoanalyst Carl Jung pointed out that an emotional reaction toward any of these persons, etc., can betray a conflict of attitudes, a mixture of favor and disfavor, of tendency to approach and tendency to avoid.

The presence of such conflict is an original cause for emotional excitement.

An illustration of this emotional betrayal of conflicting attitudes would be the excitement of stage fright which often betrays a strong interest in being seen and noticed together with an interest in avoiding notice—a fear of being noticed. Extreme shyness often betrays a similar interest in being noticed. We are not shy in the presence of persons we dislike or toward whom we are indifferent.

Because strong emotion tends to establish and fix habits, many attitudes are established more firmly by opposition and difficulty. The child who has unlimited access to candy soon loses all interest in it. Membership in an exclusive group is more desirable than membership in a group that attempts to recruit.

We have not yet discovered the whole explanation of the formation of interests like painting, music, sports, science. The part played by the example of others is hard to assess. It is obvious that enthusiastic interest tends to be catching. We tend to form interests in what will interest our companions. Bored teachers spread boredom among their pupils.

It is interesting to note that this communicability of both enthusiasm and boredom has a clear explanation in terms of associative learning. Every person is occasionally in a situation which enlists general interest, and the sight of other interested persons therefore tends to evoke the attitude in us. Being bored in the presence of others makes the sight of bored persons a cue for boredom.

Children must be noticed by their parents to get fed, caressed, and relieved from pain and discomfort. All persons therefore form some interest in being noticed. The attention of other persons remains important as children grow up. It is required in order to make a purchase at the store, to get the bus to stop, to give a message, or to make a request.

Questions

1. If learning can occur in one trial, why practice doing something many times?
2. What is the value of asking listeners to repeat important points made by the pupil who has just recited?
3. Why is a certain degree of negativism useful in daily life?
4. Why is forcing children to study under considerable external pressure a poor idea?
5. Does conflict usually heighten or decrease tension?
6. If people gamble mainly for excitement, why do they sometimes gamble on a "sure thing"?
7. Which theory considers learning to be an association between two stimuli rather than between a stimulus and a response?

Chapter 12

CREATIVE ACTIVITY IN THE SCHOOL

1. The Education of the Whole Child

Unity of the Child as an Organism.—The child is a whole and entire organism. He exists in a world of situations which are complex stimulus patterns. To these situations he responds as an entire organism. Burton puts it this way:

The learner reacts to whole situations or total patterns and not to isolated or abstracted parts thereof.

The learner reacts as a whole. He reacts all over, intellectual, emotional, and physical reactions being simultaneous.[1]

This is our basic point of departure.

Specialization of Function and Education.—Although the human body is a mechanical unit, integrated to varying degrees of efficiency in different persons, it has specialized parts just as does an automobile. These parts have particular functions as does the carburetor in the car, and they respond to selected and particular items in the complicated pattern of environment. But each specialized response has its reverberations throughout the organism and in subtle ways and in varying degrees affects the functioning of other parts of the body or is in turn affected thereby.

The education of the past (the Greeks with a sophisticated view of balanced development being a notable exception) was primarily "education of the mind," especially during the Middle Ages. The education of the recent past has had a vocational

---

[1] William H. Burton, *The Guidance of Learning Activities,* copyright 1944, with permission of Appleton-Century-Crofts, Inc., p. 212.

and athletic emphasis. At present, attention is being given to the education of the emotions. Butler writes:

> No chain is stronger than its weakest link; the chain of learning should have no weak links; the chain should not be weakened by the links of emotional learning. Teachers need to be more concerned with the personal development of young adolescents, everlastingly and untiringly concerned.[2]

The trend toward education of the emotions is a fortunate development. When one attends to education in the abstract or thinking, education of the muscles or skills, and education of the emotions or creative aptitudes, he has gone a long way toward formulating a balanced program and toward the education of the whole child through the development of all his specialized aptitudes. The emotions, as is indicated at length in another chapter, rest upon a physical foundation; they respond to stimuli; and they can be conditioned in precisely the same way that muscular actions can be conditioned. In *Foundations of Educational Psychology,* Sandiford states:

> Pavlov and his school have shown how easily certain reflexes can be conditioned. Watson and his school have shown that emotions can be conditioned with equal ease.[3]

2. FORMS OF AESTHETIC EXPERIENCE

Education for Appreciation.—Appreciation is a process of evaluating, of judging, and of appraising. Blackhurst[4] qualifies this idea to include principally those values which satisfy a desire. One can learn to appreciate a wide variety of experiences. Witherington states:

> To enumerate the various fields of appreciation is to mention all the fields of human learning and culture, not merely the fine arts. Perhaps it is incorrect to speak of appreciation subjects or even fields of appre-

---

[2] Frank A. Butler, *The Improvement of Teaching in Secondary Schools,* Rev. ed., Chicago: University of Chicago Press, 1946, p. 121.
[3] Peter Sandiford, *Foundations of Educational Psychology,* New York: Longmans, Green & Co., 1938, p. 280.
[4] J. Herbert Blackhurst, *Principles of Methods,* p. 213.

ciation. Value or worth is revealed in all aspects of educational endeavor.[5]

Appreciation rests upon both knowledge and emotion. The person who appreciates a "hot-rod" car is always the lad who wants one or has one. Desire for ownership is often a factor in appreciation—witness art and stamp collectors. Appreciation has a wide sensory basis, although the eye and ear probably predominate. The sense of touch, however, can be regarded as just as valid a creative or appreciational channel as the sense of sight. One long skilled in handling textiles can tell by the touch of a fabric much about its qualities, i.e., he appreciates it. Appreciation of the beauty of a superb and subtle chess position is not primarily a matter of the eye but of the cerebral cortex.

A balanced and complete creative and appreciational life in the pupil is not developed through any one subject or any small group of subjects but by means of all subjects and by extracurricular activities as well. Yet any teacher who offered a course in the appreciation of mathematics would more than likely be viewed askance. Still, the master of mathematics knows that some of the most lyric accomplishments of the race are to be found in the field of mathematical discovery and that only the ability to understand is necessary to the appreciation of these superlative attainments.

Aesthetic pursuits which are of indispensable importance to character or personality cannot be taught easily or directly. According to Strayer:

It is a mistake to think that appreciation is mainly taught in classes set up solely for that purpose. It should be taught wherever there is something that can add beauty or happiness to life.[6]

As in all conditioned behavior, we learn only what we do and not what we read or are told about. Classroom courses in sunset appreciation would be a poor substitute for reacting to sunsets. The person who "appreciates" a steelhead trout story

[5] H. Carl Witherington, *Educational Psychology,* Boston: Ginn & Co., 1946, p. 303.
[6] George Drayton Strayer *et al., Principles of Teaching,* New York: American Book Co., 1936, p. 145.

is another fisherman who has caught a steelhead. His data for appreciation are derived from his own muscles and glands and the story that he is told serves as the cue—a stimulus substituted for the stream and the steelhead—to evoke the old exciting reaction and the appreciative thrill to the surge of a fighting fish. Basically, the behavior is in many ways simple enough, but the appreciational products themselves are a complicated fusion of reactions, emotional, muscular, and mental.

Leading pupils to appreciate is indeed a task for the expert teacher, combining sound fundamentals and inspiration in one nicely balanced performance. If in the future you desire to test yourself upon how good a teacher you have become, ask yourself how many pupils you have led truly to value the subject in which you are guiding their development.

Creative Activity in the School.—Creative activity is closely related to appreciation, and both are a form of aesthetic experience. All creative work need not bear the stamp of genius. The genius is probably no different qualitatively from other men, although as Hartmann points out, a common opinion is that "creative acts are said to be possible only for persons of high genius." [7] Many "geniuses" have said that an unusual amount of hard work constituted the basis of their productiveness. Basically, creative activity, even in the hands of the master, is usually a combination and recombination of more or less familiar behavior elements. The inventor and musical composer are both fitting familiar elements into new patterns.

Early observational analyses of the developmental stages of creative thought noted the following stages: (1) the stage of preparation, (2) the stage of incubation, and (3) the stage of illumination. More recently observers have added a fourth stage, that of revision.

The first, or preparatory stage, is one familiar to students and teachers. It is the time of focusing one's attention, organizing the data at hand, defining the problem or the end product desired, and producing relevant ideas or parts toward that end. It is a period of study, of learning, and of attempting.

---

[7] George W. Hartmann, *Educational Psychology,* p. 349.

The second stage of incubation is a period of organization and reorganization, of acceptance and rejection, of temporary testing out and perhaps then of starting anew. Incubation may involve vicarious experiencing. It is likely to be a persevering, interfering experience demanding attention for a long time now, a moment then. Gradually, things begin to fit; interrelationships begin to "jell."

Illumination is the "Eureka" experience that comes suddenly, a moment when the theme is perceived, the relationships are clearly observed, or when just these touches add the desired and significant difference. Only necessary are the preparatory and assimilative stages and the tenacity to persist toward the goal.

Revision is the final stage of reflection when the work or method is evaluated and submitted to critical appraisal.

Catherine Patrick [8] has conducted a study of the stages of mental activity in creative work. Autobiographical accounts by creative artists report four steps: (1) The urge to create—a vague desire, restlessness, state, or impulse to action, an identification of the problem; (2) flashes of insight and trial judgments—fragmentary, illusive and built up in a haphazard manner; (3) an attempt to express the "dream" with the materials, techniques, and skills of the creator; and (4) the will to persist in order to see the job through.

All pupils can be helped to become creative by being placed in an environment which is conducive to the kind of behavior which creation requires. Furthermore, any subject in the curriculum can open the door to the educational world of creative opportunity. It may be said, therefore, that both appreciational and creative activity of appropriate sorts and in reasonable amounts should permeate the entire curriculum and constitute a vital part of the educational adjustment of the child.

In working creative activity into the curriculum, pupils must be encouraged to experience beauty as well as to recognize it intellectually; experiencing precedes creation. The showing of movies and slides, visits to art galleries or to scenes abounding in natural beauty will build up a sensory basis for creative expression. There might then follow the attempt to imitate a model, to recall and to express. Johnson in a recent article argues for the value of art as a way of thinking and of understanding life:

> The concept of "art for everybody" is so relatively new that an adjustment to it has not as yet been made in the art-teaching techniques of the average liberal arts school. The idea that the production of art is a way of thinking and of understanding life, which should be as much a part of a well-trained student's mental equipment as are logic and science, is new. It is opposed to the older notion that art is for the artist and that training in art is for the selection of the specially gifted persons who are to produce art objects for others to enjoy.[9]

In both creative activity and appreciation there are a combination and recombination of more or less familiar imaginative elements. To quote Garth:

> Imagination is variously called mental play, manipulation, and invention, but actually it is merely a process of changing the form of some experience. It is putting old things together in new ways, as a piece-quilt is made by putting together, in new patterns, little scraps of cloth which had former uses.[10]

There is a possibility worthy of further exploration that the manner in which the child expresses himself creatively may offer illuminating clues to his personality and emotional patterns. Johnson says on this point:

> Enough work has already been done in art analysis to convince us that the individual artist not only can express himself associatively regarding his subject matter but does so almost automatically as far as his technique is concerned. For example, Alschuler and Hattwick [11] made a careful analysis of personality traits and the emotional problems of children at the primary-grade level. It was discovered that there was a direct relation between the way a child painted and his emotional

---

[9] *School Review,* LVI (1948), p. 223.

[10] Thomas R. Garth, *Educational Psychology,* New York: Prentice-Hall, Inc., 1937, p. 176.

[11] Rose H. Alschuler and LaBerta Weiss Hattwick, *Painting and Personality: A Study of Young Children.* Chicago: University of Chicago Press, 1947.

problems. The type of stroke used, the choice of color, the kind of form chosen—these technical operations—were unconsciously associative and symbolic in nature and were directly related as symbols to the child's special emotional character.[12]

3. The Development of Aesthetic Activity

Optimum Conditions for Aesthetic Activity.—It is now appropriate to describe some of the conditions which encourage aesthetic activity. These are:

1. Opportunity for free expression
2. Knowledge of fundamentals
3. Guidance and correction
4. A feeling of success

These points merit a word of separate explanation and elaboration.

1. *Opportunity for free expression.* One of the essential elements in inducing aesthetic activity is that the pupil be accorded the opportunity for free self-expression. Struck[13] claims that creative learning is fostered by an environment that is free of preconceived ideas and teacher-made requirements. Memorization could never be expected to lead to either creation or appreciation in literature. The pupil must have the opportunity to try things out and to see for himself what happens. Thomas Edison was of the opinion that the essence of creative invention was trial and error and hard work. Given the urge, therefore, whether it be natural or developed, the pupil must do some experimenting on his own.

2. *Knowledge of fundamentals.* Aesthetic activity presupposes a knowledge of fundamental techniques. It is not to be expected that creative productions will spring full-blown from the minds of those untutored in the fundamentals of a subject. The world's enduring artifacts in all fields have come from the hands and minds of those who, far from being technical novices, were masters of the basic skills.

---

[12] *School Review, op. cit.,* p. 227.
[13] F. Theodore Struck, *Creative Teaching,* p. 575.

3. *Guidance and correction.* The student may well ask what place guidance and correction should have in the curriculum of aesthetics. Why should something which by its very nature probably represents satisfaction to the pupil be changed or his attention called to the fact that it can be improved? This is a reasonable question, and its answer is in terms of practical expediency.

First of all, it must be borne in mind that many of the creative efforts of pupils are attempts to improve something—to invent. More often than not, however, society has already discovered a method which is better than that which the pupil is likely himself to discover. The pedagogical trick is to acquaint the student with this fact without discouraging him or destroying his urge to try still further. Panton [14] urges the teacher of creative activities such as music and art to be careful in techniques of guidance so that the "spontaneity and freshness" of work will not be lost. It is in the ceaseless effort to improve, both on the part of the individual and the race, that the best hope of social improvement itself finally lies. If we dwelt in an Elysian field of easy bounty and with no problems of time and space, aesthetic urges of imaginative appreciation or free creativeness could be allowed to express themselves with complete casualness. Since our lot is not so easy, a practical school program for the encouragement of aesthetic activity needs some provision for its direction toward channels of practical competence. Thus, we get commercial artists, boogie-woogie musical compositions, and improved baby carriages.

4. *A feeling of success.* The pupil should be made to feel a sense of success with his individual aesthetic efforts even though his appreciation consists of saying, "Gee, that's swell," or his creation is a miniature plane that will not fly. Increased sophistication and more ability at self-analysis will produce a feeling of success on a higher level. Harriman believes that a pupil's creative work is stimulated by others who are engaged in the same activity.[15] The approbation and good wishes of one's

---

[14] J. H. Panton, *Modern Teaching Practice and Technique,* p. 198.
[15] See Charles E. Skinner (ed.), *Elementary Educational Psychology,* p. 252.

colleagues are powerful stimulants not only to pupils but to mature artists. Even Handel found difficulty in putting his genius to practical use in the face of an unappreciative society, but given a resurgence of self-confidence rooted in renewed public approval of his efforts, he made the gigantic effort necessary to produce *The Messiah* in the face of titanic odds and physical limitations. He was at one time creating and appreciating.

Aesthetics in Education.—We turn now to a consideration of the psychological essence of the aesthetic process and its place in the school program. Let us at once disavow any subscription to the palpitation theory of aesthetics. The dilettantes at concerts and art exhibits are not necessarily evaluating anything. They are often merely repeating stereotypes, the meaning of which is frequently unknown to them.

The appreciational phase of aesthetics must involve judgments. By root, "to appreciate" means to place a value upon something. Value implies a set of standards, and standards imply a systematic and deliberative contemplation of the affairs of the world and an arrangement in some hierarchy of worth. Some of these values, such as religious concepts, are usually taught categorically at an early age. The thoughtful individual may later question or examine critically for himself what he learned early by rote. The liberal education in which alone appreciation is possible can exist just as well at the high school as at the college level, and at the secondary level the process of maturing can begin.

The educated man in his thoughtful contemplation of the universe continually arranges and rearranges his set of values to a personal system which at full maturity should approximate a reasonably consistent frame of reference. Then, and not until then, is he in a position to classify the ceaseless flow of his sensations and experiences according to a fairly static pattern of critical reference. Far from being a happy-go-lucky, easy, casual sort of thing, aesthetic experiences and judgments are rather the end result of much thought and intellectual labor.

What then is the kind of school organization in which appreciation and creative activity flourish? First of all, the teachers and administrators must understand the kind of environment in which creative activity can appear and appreciational judgments can be formed. In addition to this, there must be carefully thought out provisions in the program of the day that evoke aesthetic activity from the pupil. Forced it cannot be; encouraged it must be. Appreciation and creation do not develop according to formula, but when the teacher understands the psychological essence of creating and appreciating, he can be counted upon to devise ways of stimulating them through his own subject.

Far too little attention is given to aesthetics in teacher-training programs. There should be many more discussions in music departments of how classic compositions came to be written along with the ceaseless hours of practice, practice, practice—the psychological history of music, so to speak. The same is true of all other subjects, for in all fields there have been master creators. Nothing can be more fruitful than the study of the conditions from which artistic masterpieces emerge. Such a genetic study reveals astonishing parallels and similarities of circumstance and is the best training for the teacher who himself would like to develop the creative urge and appreciational desire in pupils. Further than that, research going much deeper than the mere perusal of textbooks is necessary, and he who undertakes this type of research receives dividends not only in pedagogical method but in a rich store of the illustrative and anecdotal material useful in teaching.

QUESTIONS

1. What is meant by "the education of the whole child"? Why is it important that we keep this phrase in mind when we teach?
2. Give some examples of education that emphasize the development of a single part of the child only.
3. What is appreciation? How does it affect us in our daily lives?
4. Point out the fallacies in the theory that only geniuses are able to create.

5. How is creative work related to appreciation?
6. What constitutes "creation"?
7. Under what conditions does creative work prosper?
8. Why must a person have a thorough knowledge of techniques in order to produce effectively?
9. Do you believe that a child should be praised for producing creative work even though his work is not up to the standard of his ability?
10. Give some methods that could be used in guiding pupils to appreciate the famous works of your major field.

Chapter 13

PSYCHOLOGY OF AUDIO-VISUAL LEARNING AND TEACHING

1. Audio-Visual Education Defined

A modern program of education calls for rich and varied learning experiences for every child, and provision of these experiences involves the intelligent use of a variety of instructional materials, a term not easily defined because of the difficulty in separating instructional materials from other aspects of a child's learning environment. Dale, in *Audio-Visual Methods in Teaching,*[1] and Olsen, in *School and Community,*[2] have summarized the interrelationships of the various types of instructional materials.

It is recognized that all types of instructional materials should be carefully studied and evaluated as to possible contribution to instruction and that a wise combination of a variety of educational tools will provide psychological balance and interest. Audio-visual materials are treated specifically because of their general and widespread use. Further, the best utilization of audio-visual materials requires the application of certain basic psychological principles.

But what are audio-visual materials? There is diversity in the expressions which have been used to describe these materials. One of the earlier terms was simply visual education. Other designations are visual instruction, audio-visual aids, audio-visual instruction, instructional materials, and multisensory aids. Perhaps the definition most commonly employed

---

[1] Edgar Dale, *Audio-Visual Methods in Teaching.*
[2] Edward G. Olsen, *School and Community.*

in the audio-visual field is that given by McKown and Roberts [3] which states:

These aids are supplementary devices by which the teacher, through the utilization of more than one sensory channel, helps to clarify, establish, and correlate accurate concepts, interpretations, and appreciations.

Audio-visual materials have been variously classified. The classification given by McKown and Roberts [4] is cited here to give the reader an idea of the extensiveness of the scope usually covered and to present the more commonly used types of audio-visual materials:

Blackboard and bulletin board.
Charts: table, stream and tree, and organization or flow.
Dramatics: pantomime, playlet, pageant, puppet show, shadow play.
Flat pictures: photographs, prints, and post cards.
Graphs: pictorial statistics, bar, area, line, diagram.
Maps: flat, relief, projection, electric, globe.
Models, objects, and specimens.
Motion pictures: silent and sound.
Phonographs, records and transcriptions.
Posters, cartoons, and clippings.
Radio, dictaphone and loud-speaker (classroom), public-address and
   inter-communicating systems.
Stereoscopes: hand and telebinocular, and stereographs.
Still pictures: flat—photographs and prints.
   Projected: opaque and daylight, positive transparencies.
   Slides: glass, Cellophane, film strip, ceramic.
Trips, journeys, tours, and visits.

It will readily be seen from the above listing that the majority of the devices and materials included are not new. Audio-visual instruction then is not a new fad, it is not entertainment, and it is not a separate field of education. This idea is well

---

[3] By permission from *Audio-Visual Aids to Instruction*, 1st ed., by Harry C. McKown and Alvin B. Roberts, p. 6. Copyrighted, 1940. McGraw-Hill Book Co., Inc.
[4] *Ibid.*, pp. 7-8.

expressed by Paul G. Chancellor in a recent article in which he says:

> Let us not consider all this matter of audio-visual programs anything strange or new-fangled. It is old wine in new bottles. For centuries the world was largely illiterate, and still is. After all, literacy is the new-fangled notion.[5]

2. Types and Uses of Audio-Visual Materials

Four types of audio-visual aids will be described. These are:

1. Pictorial materials
2. Other visual aids
3. Auditory materials
4. Direct experiences

A survey of the listing of types of aids included in audio-visual materials will readily reveal that the large majority of them fall in the category of pictorial aids.

1. *Pictorial materials.* No matter what type of method or material the teacher uses in the classroom, a careful evaluation of the information presented should be a part of the regular teaching procedure. There have been many general and specific evaluative criteria presented for helping the teacher to judge these materials for use in the classroom. The following criteria for pictorial aids are given as a guide and are intended to help the teacher in the selection and utilization of pictorial materials:

Standards for the Selection of Pictorial Aids

A. *Presentation and content:*

1. Is the material relevant to the topic being studied?
2. Is the material suitable for the grade level at which it is to be used?
3. Is the number of concepts kept to a minimum?
4. Are concepts clearly developed with logical continuity?
5. Is there printed information to interpret the pictorial material? Is this information suited to the vocabulary or the grade level at which the material is to be used?

_____
[5] *Independent School Bulletin*, May, 1948, p. 15.

   6. Is motion necessary to the effective presentation of the subject?

   7. Will the presentation of the pictorial material involve more than a third of the class time for any given period?

B. *Technical quality:*

   1. Is the picture simple in composition?

   2. Is the picture artistic and interesting?

   3. Is the picture excellent photographically—clear and definite?

   4. Is the picture free from blemishes, such as dust, scratches, stains, and glows?

   5. Is color necessary to the effective presentation of the subject matter?

   6. If color is used, is the color true?

   7. Is the picture realistic, authentic, and up to date?

   8. Is the size of the picture appropriate to the use to which it will be put?

There are two main categories of pictorial materials—*still pictures* and *motion pictures.* The term "still picture" refers to flat pictures and to projected pictures which do not give the optical illusion of motion. A still picture stops motion and captures and portrays an experience the moment it occurs, thus providing opportunity for detailed observation, study, analysis, and interpretation of the elements in the picture. One picture may preserve only a part of a whole experience so comprehensive that a number of pictures may be necessary to tell the entire story pictured. Pictures help to make vicarious experiences vivid. They have long been used as vital factors in communication and education. The motion picture actually is a series of still pictures which are presented in such rapid succession that the psychological illusion of motion is created. Motion pictures are further subdivided into silent motion pictures and sound motion pictures. These pictures are always projected.

Another type of picture is the *stereograph,* which presents a realistic impression of depth and perspective. The stereograph is a double photograph of an object or a scene. Such photographs are taken with a stereoscopic camera, which has two lenses so arranged that one lens photographs the object or scene from an angle slightly to the left while the other lens photographs it from an angle slightly to the right, just as a person would view that which is being photographed. When the stereograph is seen through an individual optical instrument called a stereoscope, realism through the illusion of depth is created.

Many times it is not possible to supply individual pictures for a whole class, and sometimes a picture the teacher wishes to show is not sufficiently large for the whole group to see it well enough to distinguish certain details which should be analyzed. In such cases it is highly desirable to project the picture to be studied on a screen so all the students can see it. When projected pictures are used properly, the attention of the entire class can be focused on the specific thing the teacher wishes to call to the attention of the group. This helps to heighten interest and to stimulate participation in discussion.

To be psychologically effective, good educational pictures of any type should be realistic, social, historical, and technical documents. They should record facts accurately and express them directly.

Flat pictures are not meant for purposes of group instruction unless they are used in an opaque projector. It would be impractical from the photographic standpoint to make a picture large enough for a whole class to study its details at one time. The function of the flat picture in the classroom is to aid in individual study and research. Carefully organized units of pictures mounted on panels have proved to be of functional value when they are used for individual study. Pictures may be used singly or in groups according to the needs of the class. They should be brought together in portfolios, file collections, or visual texts for purposes of presentation, preservation, and organization. A picture which is worth preserving is worth mounting. Mounting helps to display pictures attractively, to preserve them, to make them more useful and functional, and to facilitate storage and filing. Pictures should be readily accessible and should be mounted in such a way as to protect them from dirt and careless handling.

By means of projection, the still picture is enlarged on the screen so it may be studied by a group rather than individually.

Projected still pictures include : flat pictures shown in an opaque projector, 2- $\times$ 2-inch slides, 3¼- $\times$ 4-inch slides or standard lantern slides, and 35-mm. single- or double-frame filmstrips shown in appropriate projectors. The main function of a projected still picture is to present on the screen an enlarged image which may be seen clearly by each individual in the room. The group discussion or socialized lesson with teacher and pupil participation takes place during the presentation of slides or photographs.

There are several important points to be considered in presenting projected pictures to a class. The following are physical requirements which should be met :

1. An adequate projector for the specific type of aids to be shown must be available.
2. A projection table will be necessary for the placement of the projector.
3. Adequate extension cords must be available in order to carry the power from the outlet to the machine.
4. Proper room-darkening devices, such as opaque shades or drapes, are necessary to eliminate light. Good pictures show to poor advantage when they are projected in a room which is not well darkened.
5. A suitable screen should be available for projection.

Whenever possible the projector and screen should be set up in advance of a showing, in order to avoid confusion and delay in the presence of the group. The slides should be clean and should be in logical sequence. The projector should be checked in advance to make sure that it is ready for use and that there is power at the machine. The projected image should fit the screen, whether horizontal or vertical pictures are being used. The distance from the projector to the screen should be adjusted so there will be a minimum of waste of screen; however, there should be no overlapping. The projected picture should be neither too large nor too small for the screen. The lower edge of the screen should be just above the eye level of the pupils. The projector should be in focus in order that the first picture of the presentation may be seen instead of the brilliant glare from the blank screen.

It is important to have a projector in best working condition and to keep its lenses and condensers clean. Vivid images cannot be formed in the student's mind from blurred, dirty, or vague projections caused by the inferior quality of the transparency or by poor projection conditions.

Smooth presentation is facilitated by careful preparation, which includes previewing the aids to be shown and eliminating distractions and interferences. It is a wise precaution to have extra lamps, fuses, outlet plugs, and extension cords readily available.

Whenever possible, it is desirable to preserve the classroom situation in projecting pictures. Showing pictures in the regular classroom has many advantages over showing pictures in the auditorium. The effectiveness of utilizing still pictures depends in large measure on the way in which these aids are presented. The showing of pictures can be made interesting and instructional by knowing how to catch and hold the interest of the audience.

A number of factors are involved in the selection of pictures for classroom use, and it would be wise for the teacher to familiarize himself with specific evaluative criteria for the selection of the different types of pictures ordinarily utilized in the classroom. There is a practical discussion of criteria for the selection of filmstrips contained in a recent book by Vera M. Falconer [6] on filmstrips. A teacher should consider the role pictures are to play in teaching the particular lesson to be presented. Each picture used should help to fulfil a significant need or objective. The teacher should consider how the pictures used are going to enrich, clarify, or motivate learning in connection with the subject being studied; only thus can the psychological objectives be attained.

The number of pictures to be used in teaching a particular lesson will vary according to the number available, the objective to be accomplished, and the level of the class group. Three or more pictures are frequently needed to present a complete phase

---

[6] Vera M. Falconer, *Filmstrips: A Descriptive Index and Users' Guide,* p. 27.

of some topics. The tendency on the part of the less experienced is to show too many rather than too few pictures to obtain the proper psychological learning reinforcement. If students have had training in how to interpret pictures and if teachers present them in such a way as to utilize their full teaching value, it is not likely that too many pictures will be used. Of course, the teacher will find it necessary to organize the pictures in such a way as to develop the lesson in its logical and meaningful sequence. This necessitates careful study and arrangement on the part of the teacher previous to the showing of the pictures to the students.

If teachers keep in mind that pictures must be taught and not merely displayed, they will soon learn to judge and to select pictures on the basis of contribution to the lesson being studied. Pictures should be evaluated just as carefully as other supplementary materials in relation to the part they play in the improvement of classroom instruction. The elements of a picture may help to bring reality into a classroom by providing vicarious, concrete experiences with places, activities, people, events, and objects. In order to get a full understanding of the significance of a picture, it is necessary to analyze such qualities as size, distance, depth, weight, color, temperature, and tactility.

Smooth presentation of pictures is also necessary to their effective use in the classroom. Pictures should be shown in such a way as to make clear to the student what is being represented. Flat pictures should be attractively arranged and should have captions so located that the student will not apply a caption intended for one picture to another picture to which it does not relate. The rules of efficient projection should be applied in showing pictures on a screen, for a poorly projected picture will distract student interest and detract from the value of a picture.

Students should be psychologically "ready" to learn from the pictures which are to be presented. They should be prepared through previous classwork and background assignments to interpret the pictures which are to be studied. Each picture may be introduced. If the picture has a title, students should see the relationship of the caption to the picture. Ordinarily, it is sound psychologically to have the class consider the whole picture before the teacher attempts to focus student attention on specific details. Students should be encouraged to express their interpretation of the picture in terms of their individual backgrounds. If students have been given time to look at the whole picture before they are requested to seek out certain elements, they are much more likely to concentrate on the detail being studied because they have already satisfied their curiosity and desire to see the things which might distract their attention from the specific detail.

After an overview has been given, the teacher may wish to bring out a number of points which will help the student obtain correct and clear concepts. In order to give a correct impression of the size of objects, comparisons must be made with things within the realm of the experience of the group. A scene which represents a number of different aspects is one which must be used wisely. A landscape, for example, may present different appearances depending upon the season of the year when it is used. A child from one of the prairie states might think of an ocean as being always calm or always tempestuous depending upon the impressions he got from a single photograph. Every attempt must be made through the use of pictures and other supplementary materials to give students accurate information. Frequently it may be necessary to show several pictures of the same thing—taken at different times or at different angles and distances—to help students obtain correct impressions.

Some teachers employ pictures satisfactorily for review purposes. In this case, pictures may be used as the culmination of a unit or for tying together many different types of classroom work and study experiences. Pictures on foreign countries or resources may be used to advantage in this manner.

There are many instances in which a motion picture depicting change and movement has advantages over a series of still pictures. Through such media as animation, time-lapse photography, microphotography, close-ups, slow-motion photography, and high-speed photography the motion picture is able to bring reality to the screen.

The use of the motion picture as a vital tool for in-school and out-of-school mass communication and education has been recognized the world over. It is a versatile and adaptable medium which may be used equally advantageously for the education of children and of adults. Ruth Inglis in her recent book on *Freedom of the Movies* says:

The demands of the second World War tested the medium as never before and demonstrated its great potentialities. As a result, both inside and outside the motion picture industry there is increasing recognition that the movies have an essential role to play in social life and that the freedom of the screen is important because of what the film can do. Freedom finds its meaning not only in liberty but in responsibility, as the leaders in the motion picture industry have publicly acknowledged many times.[7]

The armed forces, industry, and the schools have found that the motion picture has a number of advantages over some of the other types of instructional materials. The most important of these are: (1) the medium is time-saving in that it presents materials in a short period of time; (2) the motion picture is motivating and interesting because it presents information in a realistic and concrete form; (3) the motion picture is a valuable tool for mass instruction because it provides a medium for obtaining uniformity in the way in which material is presented and in the type of concepts which are represented.

In many schools, programs have been set up to help teachers help themselves by providing information relative to materials or equipment available, by suggesting criteria for the selection and evaluation of different types of materials, and by offering instruction on the operation of new equipment.

The points listed under the summary of the utilization of still pictures will apply also to the utilization of motion pictures in the classroom. The survey of motion pictures available and the selection of the most appropriate motion pictures to fit the needs and purposes of a particular situation are, of course, the first things which should be taken into consideration in connection with motion picture utilization. The teacher should

[7] Ruth A. Inglis, *Freedom of the Movies,* Chicago: University of Chicago Press, 1947, p. 1.

early determine the purpose for which the film is to be used. Films may be used advantageously in a number of different ways. For example, some films serve better as an overview; other films are designed for direct teaching; and still other films might better be used as a medium of review. After the instructor has determined the purpose the film is to serve, he should make his lesson plan and consider the other activities and materials which will be used in the presentation of that particular unit. It will, of course, be necessary to make plans also for the projection of the motion picture and for the follow-up activities which will be part of the lesson.

It should be pointed out that there is an increasing tendency to supplement one kind of audio-visual aid with another. In other words, it is not uncommon to find filmstrips as an auxiliary to motion pictures. The filmstrips may be used advantageously after the motion picture has been shown in order to give students an opportunity to study in more detail certain elements of the motion picture which were presented in continuity by the motion picture itself. Flat pictures, too, may be used as part of the sequence of materials for the teaching of a particular lesson. Printed materials such as textbooks, manuals, and carefully selected tests may be combined with audio-visual materials, particularly motion pictures, to cover all the different phases and purposes of a particular assignment. By these supplementary devices, psychological reinforcement is added.

2. Other visual aids. Not all visual aids are pictorial aids. Many different types of visual materials may be presented on the blackboard or display board, although these represent media which are so commonplace and traditional that teachers take them for granted. It should be recognized that their effective psychological use depends upon careful preparation and proper technique of presentation. For example, let us consider the utilization of the blackboard. Preparatory steps for using the blackboard are:

1. Be sure the blackboard is clean.
2. Be sure the proper materials are handy for making the best use of the blackboard.

    a. Have clean erasers.

    b. Have a straightedge or some device for drawing lines.

    c. Have compasses, triangles, etc., if you are teaching mathematics or other subjects where you are using figures.

    d. Have different colors of chalk for purposes of differentiation.

    e. Have a pointer to direct and focus attention.

3. Sharpen chalk for special purposes.
4. Practice printing, drawing, and shading so you develop proficiency in the use of the blackboard.
5. Organize and prepare materials so they may be placed on the blackboard with the least inconvenience to you and to the class.
6. Place written and drawn material on the blackboard before the class meets whenever possible.

When using the blackboard in class :

1. Make your material neat and legible.
2. Incline the chalk in the direction of the stroke in drawing or printing.
3. Use aids (tracing, figures, etc.) to make work more accurate and effective.
4. Draw according to scale. Indicate the scale used.
5. Include legends for maps and graph interpretations.
6. Be sure all drawings can be seen by all students in the room.
7. Use successive drawings if necessary. Explain the drawing step by step as the drawing proceeds to indicate relationship.
8. Limit blackboard writing to essentials during class time.
9. Use correct spelling and grammatical construction.
10. Make every mark on the blackboard meaningful.
11. Don't forget the class—talk to the class and not to the blackboard.
12. Assume a position to the side of the blackboard material during presentation—use a pointer to direct and focus attention.
13. Erase supplementary or other material as soon as it has served its purpose in order to prevent its distracting attention from the material being presented.

14. Provide sufficient time for students to take notes.
15. Encourage students to use the blackboard for drawings, reports, solutions of problems, presentation of new vocabulary, etc.
16. Evaluate your own use of the blackboard.

The use of objects, specimens, and models provides firsthand information about our environment. The resourceful teacher can ordinarily stimulate his students to find and collect many different kinds of material for the study of science, social science, and other fields. Student interest in realia which they have discovered for themselves is usually higher than in materials which are a regular part of the classroom environment. School journeys may also provide an opportunity for direct contact with objects, specimens, and models. In some cases it is possible to obtain through various sources traveling exhibits that include materials which can be brought into the classroom and studied by the group. Such traveling exhibits are available from museums and from certain of the industrial concerns which provide inexpensive or free materials to schools.

Industry and the armed forces have also found this type of visual aid to be extremely useful. In a number of cases working models have been a valuable means of training students in the operation of complex machines. Mounted working models called *mock-ups* are extremely valuable in providing a thorough understanding of the parts, functions, and operation of different types of machines. Such mock-ups are being used to excellent advantage in many of our schools today.

3. *Auditory materials.* Psychological research and experimentation in the field of auditory aids have shown that these devices, which include radio, records, transcriptions, sound systems, and sound track on film, may be used to convey useful knowledge and information to listeners, to sharpen discernment of social significance, to fortify socially desirable attitudes, to enhance aesthetics of appreciation, to stimulate systematic inquiry, and to implement convictions with an impelling urge to action. Although the above uses may be made of auditory aids, it cannot be assumed that listening automatically results in

educational outcomes.   The selection and proper use of auditory aids are as necessary and as important as the selection and proper use of visual materials.   A few useful tests of auditory aids are indicated in the following questions:

1. Is the commentary suited, as to both vocabulary and accent, to the level at which the material will be used?
2. Is the information accurate?
3. Is the information presented interestingly?
4. Are concepts clearly developed with logical continuity?
5. Is the volume adjusted to the room size and conditions?

Evaluation with regard to technical excellence would include consideration of the following points:

1. Is the music or enunciation sharply defined?
2. Is there a high fidelity in the recording?
3. Will the material be capable of clear reproduction?
4. Is the tone quality acceptable?

These criteria for the evaluation of auditory aids may be applied to any of the aids which the teacher wishes to consider for use in the classroom.   There are, of course, more specific criteria which might be applied to each of the different types of auditory aids.

Careful preparation for the use of auditory aids is important. Both the teacher and the pupils must be prepared for the presentation of auditory aids in the classroom.   With certain types of auditory aids this preparation may sometimes be difficult, but every effort is being made to provide advance information relative to all types of materials which may serve educational objectives.   Records and transcriptions should of course be auditioned in advance of the time when they are to be used in the classroom.   A number of newer records and transcriptions are now being prepared so that the lesson is presented on one side of the disc and suggestions to the teacher for the utilization and presentation of the material are given on the other side.   Manuals, too, are now available with certain records and transcriptions intended and designed for classroom use.

Radio stations and educational organizations have done much to furnish free information on educational broadcasts.

This information is extremely useful to teachers in preparing themselves and their classes for the use of live broadcasts in the teaching process.

The listening program will require careful correlation and integration of the program with the classroom work. It is as necessary for the student to understand the relationship of the auditory program to the material being studied as it is for him to understand the relationship of the visual program. It is well also to insure close attention to any listening programs. Plans must be made so that there will be as little disturbance and interruption as possible when a listening program is in session.

Training in listening is an essential part of the auditory aids program. One of the significant outcomes of listening assignments is the development of discrimination in the selection of programs. It should be recognized that students devote considerable leisure time to such activities as listening to the radio. This medium is an important tool for education, communication, and propaganda.

Recordings are of several different types—discs, tapes, and wire. It is becoming increasingly less expensive and easier to make recordings for school use. Recordings and transcriptions have a number of advantages which are not inherent in live radio broadcasts—free choice of time, multiple usage, and pre-audition.

A number of suggestions may be useful to the teacher in insuring psychologically sound results when auditory aids are used in the classroom. For convenience, these suggestions are broken down under several main headings:

1. *Preparation for the use of auditory aids:*
    a) Have proper equipment for the use of these materials and be sure the equipment is in working condition.
    b) Select the auditory aid to be used in accordance with the grade level and objectives to be taught.
    c) Audition the material to be presented.
    d) Determine what supplementary materials may be used to best advantage in the presentation of the unit.
    e) Establish relationship between the auditory aids and the subject matter being presented.

  f) List items for preliminary discussion.

  g) Adjust the sound as nearly as possible before the class-work begins.

2. *During the listening activity:*

  a) Be sure that everyone listens comfortably.

  b) Avoid interruption.

  c) Set an example to the students to listen attentively.

  d.) Do not insist that students shall take full notes. Note-taking frequently detracts from the listening activity and may cause the student to lose continuity.

3. *After utilizing the auditory aid:*

  a) Keep the reasons for utilizing the aid in mind. Do not let the discussion wander away from the main purpose.

  b) With the students, evaluate the program presented.

  c) With the students, determine what follow-up activities would make the lesson more purposeful and more meaningful.

4. *Direct experiences.* The value of active participation in the learning process is recognized by educational psychologists. The field trip or school journey has long been used as such an educational device and is an excellent means of providing a realistic and concrete experience in which the students may participate as planners. The planning process is one of the most important steps in the direct experience of the school journey, for it provides an opportunity to capitalize on the anticipation of the student. Much instructional work can be accomplished in the period when student interest is at its height and when the curiosity of the group has been aroused.

  The field trip or school journey need not be expensive; some of the finest field trips are the least expensive and are in the immediate vicinity of the school. Perhaps one of the greatest values of the field trip is to acquaint the student with his own immediate environment and to make him alert to and aware of its attractive and educational features.

  The more extended field trip requires special scheduling and careful attention to legal liability, which must be taken into account in order to protect the student and the school. In a school district which makes regular use of field trips there is usually a well-planned program which the teacher may follow in requesting that students be permitted to go on a particular school journey. Forms to be signed by parents are prepared in order to release the school from its obligations, and bonded carriers are arranged for as transportation.

Other types of direct experiences are of value in the educational process and may be utilized to excellent advantage if they are well planned. Community surveys, for example, when carried on by a whole school, have created interest in the community and stimulated cordial public relationships for the school. All such programs, however, must be carefully planned and executed in order to achieve desirable objectives for the individual student and for the entire school.

3. Psychological Values in Audio-Visual Education

In conclusion, attention is called to the basic psychological principle governing the use of the various forms of audio-visual materials. This basic principle is that learning which is reinforced through several sensory channels is more meaningful, more persistent, and more motivated. Just as the stereograph gives a better idea of a landscape than a flat picture, so does multisensory impression give a better concept of the environment which surrounds us than does unisensory. A picture of an apple is superior to a mere verbal description, but picking apples and eating them add a whole new world of sensory meaning. It is for this reason that emphasis has been laid in the foregoing discussion upon the mutual supplementary value of aids one to another. Naturally, the old problem of limitations of time and space applies in the use of audio-visual materials. Pupils who can pick and eat apples may not be able to pick and eat pineapples, but the principle of extended experience should be carried as far as practical circumstances permit.

Questions

1. Give several definitions of audio-visual aids and illustrate each.
2. Discuss the standards for selection and presentation of pictorial aids.
3. What are the two types of pictorial aids? Give examples of each.
4. List the points that must be kept in mind when preparing to use pictorial aids.
5. Name other visual aids and tell how they are used.
6. What are auditory aids and what requirements must they meet in order to be acceptable for use?
7. What preparation must be made for using auditory aids?
8. How do direct experiences supplement regular classroom work? List several types of these experiences that are appropriate for use.
9. What are the psychological values of audio-visual education?

Chapter 14

INDIVIDUAL DIFFERENCES

1. The Importance of Individual Differences

Traditionally, five-year-oldness has been the entrance requirement for kindergarten enrollment, as six-year-oldness has been for first grade entrance. The child thus entered is expected to progress regularly thereafter in a perfectly positive relationship that is almost unknown under actual school conditions; i.e., for each additional year in age we predict success in mastering the curriculum of the following school grade. With improved measuring instruments such as mental, reading readiness, achievement, and social adjustment tests and many others, and with their extended use, educators have become aware of the tremendous range of ability in any group of equal chronological age. For example, among first graders six years of age chronologically, mental age may vary from an I.Q. of 80 to an I.Q. of 180. Reading readiness tests would show comparable diversity. Social adjustment scales reveal that some six-year-old children are unable to button and unbutton clothing and are not up to the adjustment problems that confront a member of a group of six children in a free-play situation. On the other hand, others in the same group may thrive on the stimulation of a twenty-five member group and behave in a self-sufficient and independent manner. Variation of a range as wide would likewise be revealed in such physical characteristics as height, weight, visual acuity, strength of grip, dentition, skeletal development, muscular coordination, and others.

Homogeneity in chronological age, then, brings with it all manner of important diversity. Homogeneity in mental age or in reading readiness likewise does not factor out the many other differences that significantly influence teaching methods seeking to promote the physical, mental, social, and emotional development of the whole child. Individual differences must be considered as one of the realities in classroom management.

The Problem of Individual Differences.—The problem of individual differences among pupils is one of the most deceptive and baffling with which the teacher has to deal. Cruze says :

> The problem of providing for the needs of *all pupils* of school age is becoming more acute, with the tendency to raise the age limit for compulsory school attendance and the development of a universal recognition of the necessity for more education.[1]

Kandel emphasizes the need for more attention to individual differences in the following quotation :

> The great task ahead in American education is to interpret the meaning of individual differences in such a way that "the gates of excellence" will stand open for all, that each will receive the maximum of education from which he can derive the greatest profit, and that the welfare of society will be considered as well as the interests of each of its members.[2]

Every methodological solution to the question of how to deal in the classroom with individual differences has had to be a psychological compromise. Many of the defects of our present educational system—defects which are often noted critically by the lay public—arise from the desperate efforts of schools to be all things to all children, i.e., to furnish everything to all ability groups.

The bedevilment awaiting teachers who conscientiously try to give as much help as possible to pupils of varying ability levels is a by-product of our system of mass education. Kandel writes :

> Mass education promises to be one of the greatest achievements of the United States; its success, however, may be endangered if talent and ability are allowed to be submerged by it.[3]

---

[1] Wendell W. Cruze, *Educational Psychology*, p. 553. Copyright, 1942, by The Ronald Press Company.
[2] *School and Society*, LXIV (1936), 375.
[3] *Ibid.*, p. 375.

If it were possible to have one teacher for every child or to assign one teacher to a small group of children, the problem of individual differences from the standpoint of methodology would be negligible. The differences would still exist, but with more attention to individuals these problems could be conquered. The teacher's task in a tutorial or semitutorial situation is relatively simple.

2. Approaches to the Problem of Individual Differences

Extremes in Methodology in Handling Individual Differences.—The problem of coping with individual differences is not one which can be avoided by the realistic teacher. A compromise solution can be avoided in only one way : by subscription to a philosophy of education holding that some particular stratum of the school population deserves more attention than the others. The educational philosophy supporting this approach is sophistry, but it is found in a sufficient number of places to warrant the following brief epitome of this line of thought : "Bright children learn more rapidly and in greater amount. Therefore, they get the most out of the process of education and return the most to society. This being the case, what can be more logical than to direct teaching to the brightest in the class, perhaps the upper 10 per cent in intelligence, and let the rest get what they can?" Or, conversely, the argument may run something like this : "There are more ordinary children than there are brilliant children. Democracy in education means service to the majority. Therefore, teachers should aim their instruction at the level of the normal or slightly subnormal. Let brilliant children in one way or another get the extra for which their ability equips them." It is entirely possible to organize an actual school system according to one or the other of these two theories, but any teacher or administrator can tell you about the terrific headaches that result in either case. For example, suppose we organize according to the second alternative. In this type of setup, the brightest children shortly have nothing to do except cause trouble, which they promptly proceed to do. Experienced teachers know that the idle hands and minds of the superior group constitute a prime disciplinary hazard. Well then, let us organize according to the first alternative and teach to these brilliant children so they will not become troublemakers. The fallacy in this approach is that children of ordinary mentality can be troublemakers also!

The hypothetical alternatives just given are not the only possibilities, of course. Hundreds of pure or combined forms actually have been tried under one or another fancy name in order to solve all the learning, disciplinary and social problems which arise inescapably in a mass system of education. Our illustrations have been oversimplified for the sake of emphasis; actual classroom situations tend to be more, not less, complicated than the instances given. Later on in this chapter some attention will be given to the various kinds of psychological approach that can be employed and to a psychological analysis of certain current methods of handling this problem.

The only realistic approach is an acceptance of individual differences and an actual appreciation of them, rather than the oft-prescribed toleration of differences. The biologist sees diversity as an asset. The agriculturist recognizes it as a source of "hybrid vigor." The social scientist recognizes that in diversity we are most likely to develop improved ways of meeting human needs. The educator can also capitalize on the variability in any classroom. A training in human relationships and interaction *sans* diversity would be an "out of this world" event completely unrelated to practical day-to-day experience. Differences in socioeconomic status, in intelligence, in skin color, in vocabulary and dialect, in customs and mores, in artistic, musical, and mechanical ability, in height, weight, race, nationality, and in religion are not merely to be tolerated but are to be *appreciated*. Developing these differences can be a real challenge to the most skilful teacher and can be a source of enjoyment and benefit to everyone in the classroom society. Diversity in ability must be dealt with by flexible methods and by variation in curricular content.

Stroud supports the same view when he states:

. . . we may infer that the presence in a school system of vast individual differences does not constitute an indictment of that system. It is not a sign of poor teaching. Only the absence of such differences should be disturbing. If by good teaching is meant the developing of each student at a rate commensurate with his ability, then we may infer that the better the teaching the larger are the differences in progress likely to be.[4]

Classification of Individual Differences.—We turn now to a consideration of the kinds of individual differences and their classification. No kind of difference is of more determinative force in schoolteaching than the environmental background, home and community, of the individual pupil. Jordan[5] is of the belief that both heredity and environment are of importance in the formation of individual differences.

Every means which the school can employ, including cumulative permanent records, to keep a systematic account of both family and environmental background is a contribution to the improvement of method. Along this line, Jaggers feels that the teacher must know his pupils well in order to understand their needs and interests. To help teachers in this work, the Western Kentucky Teachers College Training School keeps cumulative records of all students for teacher reference.

These records include such information as intelligence test scores, achievement test scores, personality tests, health records, special ability tests, vocational preferences, and socioeconomic background.[6]

There have been many kinds of classification of individual differences, some of which go into exhaustive detail. For example, it is possible to derive elaborate statistics and charts on all manner of differences—age, sex, race, rate of muscular growth, neurological development, etc. It is not the purpose of this discussion, intended primarily to give the elementary psychological considerations involved in school provision for indi-

---

[4] James B. Stroud, *Psychology in Education,* New York: Longmans, Green & Co., 1946, p. 403.
[5] A. M. Jordan, *Educational Psychology,* Rev. ed., p. 385.
[6] *Peabody Journal of Education,* XXIV (1947), 322.

vidual differences, to go into such minutiae. We are primarily concerned with a description of individual differences which possesses some functional significance for school organization and administration. Viewed from this standpoint, the following clearly must be taken into consideration:

1. Physical differences
2. Mental differences
3. Social differences
4. Emotional differences

1. *Physical differences.* There are many kinds of physical differences. Mention has already been made in other chapters of those who have physical handicaps which retard learning. Among children otherwise normal, differences in mere physical size may offhand seem to have no pedagogical significance, but actually size as such has been shown to be related to social adjustment, which in turn is related to learning. According to Pressey and Robinson:

Childhood and youth are rough-and-tumble periods, and a youngster's position among his fellows is determined in large part by his physical size, strength, and vigor. In proportion as a child can associate and compete physically, he will achieve confidence and ability to get along with others and will have a happy or a miserable childhood.[7]

2. *Mental differences.* Differences in mental ability naturally weigh heavily in school work, which of necessity involves concept formation and abstract thinking. Differences in mental ability are scattered according to the normal distribution curve principle, which means that there are relatively few very bright or very dull at each end of the distribution, with the largest group of average intelligence in the central range. As Griffith points out:

An average school is almost sure to include a few pupils with a very low and a few with a very high rating. Of almost any group of one hundred typical ten-year-old children, there would be some with a men-

---

[7] Sidney L. Pressey and Francis P. Robinson, *Psychology and the New Education.* Rev. ed., New York: Harper & Bros., 1944, pp. 14-15.

tal age of about eight and some with a mental age of about twelve. A large number would cluster around the middle point.[8]

3. *Social differences.* A limited number of physical and mental traits are predetermined by heredity and are beyond the control of the child, his parents, or his teachers. Social differences between pupils, however, are likely to be the result of experience and conditioning. Because of this happy circumstance, social education may be made a focal point for minimizing differences and developing a common core of understanding and adjustment. In this connection, Trow says:

Since the school has nothing to say about the heredity of the children who come to its doors, it must concern itself with the task of setting up those environmental conditions which are most conducive to individual growth and development.[9]

4. *Emotional differences.* Emotional patterns bear an intimate relationship to learning efficiency. Prescott says:

Mental hygiene clinics are finding out continually that personal relationships actually are damaging the mental health of some children in public schools and suggest that much more attention to this aspect of curriculum cannot be put off indefinitely.[10]

Likewise, the emotional disturbances that arise from difficulties in learning are sometimes highly determinative of the direction of pupil development. For this reason, increased attention is being given to education of the emotions and the place that emotional differences play in education.

Compensation vs. Correlation of Abilities.—Let us digress for a moment at this point to examine a widely held concept which influences school practice, namely, the theory that there is a sort of compensation at work in the field of individual differ-

[8] Coleman R. Griffith, *Psychology Applied to Teaching and Learning,* New York: Rinehart & Co., 1939, p. 602.
[9] William Clark Trow, *Introduction to Educational Psychology,* Boston: Houghton Mifflin Co., 1937, p. 138.
[10] Daniel Alfred Prescott, *Emotion and the Educative Process,* Washington, D. C.: American Council on Education, 1938, p. 290.

ences and that if a child has low arithmetic aptitude he is likely to possess high aptitude in some other school subject.

Investigations tend to show correlation of ability rather than compensation, particularly in academic subjects. It is possible, however, that the investigators themselves are guilty of a bit of prejudice and premature generalizing or perhaps too narrow a view of the spread of psychological traits. If *all* good things are correlated, for example, the brightest people in the world would always be the happiest, assuming that it is desirable to be both bright and happy. Patently, there is no such general correlation. Furthermore, the data are not entirely conclusive even in the performance areas. There is still something to be said, therefore, for a belief in compensation in education, especially when education is viewed in the larger sense. It has been shown that the correlation between intelligence and grades is low, which probably means that many pupils have learned to compensate for low intelligence by better attitudes, increased efforts, etc. Even in the realm of physical capacity, it is probably yet too early to write off for certain the possibility of compensatory endowment.

"Exceptional" Children.—Passing reference should be made to a habit which has grown up in the field of education of calling all forms of sharp psychological deviation "exceptional." According to this practice, both handicapped and gifted children are described as "exceptional" statistically, although their traits are antithetical. This general use of the term with reference to opposite types of departure from statistical norms differs from the ordinary usage, in which an "exceptional" pupil is an unusually gifted one. Nine out of ten mothers, on being told that their children were "exceptional" in arithmetic, would think that their performance was superior. In the authors' opinion, nothing whatsoever is gained either scientifically or socially by terming subnormal performance or aptitude "exceptional," and no such usage will be resorted to in this volume. When reference is made herein to general categories of deviation either above or below the established norm, the term "atypical" will be used. Performance above the norm will be termed "superior," and performance which does not reach the norm will be referred to as "subnormal."

3. Methods of Dealing with Individual Differences

Diagnosis of Individual Differences.—Several psychological devices are being used in school systems to diagnose individual differences and to serve as the basis for determining the methodological provision to be made in taking care of them. The principal ones are:

1. Tests
2. Clinics
3. Conferences
4. Classroom contacts

1. *Tests.* As the student will note from the chapter on evaluating learning, substantial progress has been made during past years in the development of tests of all sorts. Intelligence and survey tests predominated in the early days of the development of the testing movement. Witherington defines what we mean by intelligence tests as follows:

Actually we do try to measure the general level of intellectual maturity by what we call intelligence tests. But the object of such tests is to be able to estimate the original capacity to learn, or to do school-work, in order that we may be able to decide what to do next. Testing of intelligence is analogous to the diagnostic work of a physician who makes tests to determine what to do next.[11]

As the need for remedial instruction grew and was recognized, the diagnostic test came to play its part. Scott and French state:

The purpose of diagnostic tests is to single out skills which need special attention during instruction. If a choice is to be made in materials taught, test results may furnish evidence for that choice. Whenever there is opportunity for any individualized instruction and practice, the diagnostic test is a prerequisite.[12]

---

[11] H. Carl Witherington, *Educational Psychology,* Boston: Ginn & Co., 1946, p. 135.
[12] From *Better Teaching Through Testing* by M. Gladys Scott and Esther French, published by A. S. Barnes & Co., Inc., New York, 1945, p. 3.

As guidance became more and more prominent, aptitude and prognostic tests in turn developed and reached a relatively high point of excellence. Ross [13] credits America with leading in the development of these aptitude or prognostic tests which predict performance in specialized fields.

Of late years, education of the emotions and the development of attitudes have been recognized as cardinal aims of education. In discussing this phase of testing Ross writes:

The development of wholesome attitudes has been recognized in recent years as an important objective of education. Since about 1920 much attention has been devoted to the measurement of attitudes of various kinds.[14]

As is usual when interest in a field is widespread, tests of emotional adjustment and attitudes have advanced accordingly. Highly gratifying progress has also been made in the area of personality assessment and character testing.

2. *Clinics.* Psychological and child research clinics have been introduced into an increasing number of school systems. Clinics conduct a variety of research to assist teachers and administrators. On the nature of these clinical studies Gray says:

Clinical study consists of getting all the incidental information about the individual by direct and indirect questioning of anyone who can supply it.[15]

Unfortunately, even today clinics tend to be confined to the larger districts because of the expense and personnel required. There is no valid reason why clinics or their essential counterpart should not be found in school systems of practically all sizes. Even part-time attention from one teacher who has had specialized work in psychology and casework is of value.

The development of a training curriculum for school psychologists, which is growing rapidly as the mutual understanding

[13] C. C. Ross, *Measurement in Today's Schools,* 2d ed., New York: Prentice-Hall, Inc., 1947, p. 41.

[14] *Ibid.,* p. 56.

[15] J. Stanley Gray, *Psychological Foundations of Education,* New York: American Book Co., 1935, p. 477.

between those in teacher training and psychology has grown, is due for augmented attention.

3. *Conferences.* The conference-case method is an old social-work standby which has been brought to a fairly high point of objectivity and standardization and which has educational usefulness. As interview techniques have been improved and made more objective and as record-keeping has been developed to a higher point of efficiency, the conference method has begun to pay dividends. As found now in the better school systems, it is more than "going down to the office and having a talk with the principal."

4. *Classroom contact.* Although much can be said for the scientific techniques which have already been mentioned, it is after all in the classrooms day after day that the pupils are under the constant observation of the teachers. It is here too that their individual behavior patterns, their little emotional blockages, and their typical difficulties in orientation come to light. These insights are of immense significance in making adequate provision for individual differences. After all, even the physician, who makes extensive use of all manner of scientifically exact measurements, has to make his final diagnosis on the basis not only of these objective tests but upon his observation and subjective judgment as well. The overworked cult of decrying all subjective evaluation is based upon a false conception of the nature of scientific procedure. There is no need to guess at blood pressure when it can be measured. But there is no instrument to make the decision as to whether or not to operate upon a patient when there are complicating and deterrent factors. Nor has any machine ever been invented to make judgments on the mass psychology of a classroom. These things are matters for human judgment, which in the last analysis is a rare and wonderful calculating device in its own right.

Specific Provisions for Individual Differences.—In addition to devices and techniques for the diagnosis and measurement of individual differences, there are established and widely used methodological patterns which serve as a complement. These are:

1. Track systems
2. Remedial education
3. Automatic promotion
4. Differential teaching

1. *Track systems.* In the track-system form of setup there are various ways in which segregation is accomplished. A typical example is segregation by ability grouping based on intelligence tests. The idea in this type of organization is to secure homogeneity of pupil population which will enable the teacher to pitch methodology at one level.

2. *Remedial education.* Remedial education will be discussed in Chapter 17. It is sufficient to say at this point that the best school organization under this plan should keep all the pupils together and take care of individual differences by intraclass devices; when these fail, special classes are organized.

3. *Automatic promotion.* Obviously, it is a matter of no particular concern what differences between pupils exist if promotions are made regardless of the quality of performance. Automatic, nonperformance promotion has the theoretical advantage of keeping a child in his own social group and possibly avoiding the emotional complexes arising from failure, but its weakness is clearly shown by Foley, who says:

> It is no real kindness to a pupil to cover up his real failure to do what the job requires by a comfortable statement that he is "working to capacity." Encouragement is not something to be handed out right and left without discrimination.[16]

4. *Differential teaching.* Genuine differential teaching, which requires a mature and superior person, compels the teacher to know the pupils as individuals and to adjust teaching techniques to these differences. All the varied devices by which differences are diagnosed are brought into play. Not the least of the difficulties encountered is that of keeping pupils unaware of what is occurring.

---

[16] *School and Society,* LIX (1944), 354.

Various Provisions for Individual Differences.—It will be remembered that any method which attempts to take care of individual differences in large groups has some drawbacks. The four methods which have just been briefly discussed definitely fall in this category. The track system may produce homogeneity, but it is artificial and unlike anything actually found in society. The danger involved in the system is explained by Krug and Anderson as follows:

> Attempts to organize homogeneous groups on the basis of one characteristic alone fail not only to produce homogeneity, but may result in forming groups who differ more widely in other characteristics.[17]

The remedial approach has a fair chance of success if all teachers can be trained in remedial education. Automatic promotion avoids difficulty for several years, but the eventual stymie is inevitable. All things considered, differential teaching under competent supervision is probably the best answer to the challenging problem of individual differences.

QUESTIONS

1. Why is the study of individual differences so important for the prospective teacher?
2. Why has the problem of individual differences become more acute during recent times?
3. Under what conditions could the problem of individual differences be eliminated?
4. What are the dangers involved in the classification of pupils according to one characteristic only?
5. How may individual differences be classified? List several not appearing in the text that you would include in a list of your construction.
6. Give the importance of the present-day trend toward education of emotions. Do you consider this phase of education to be as important as mastery of the academic curriculum?

---

[17] Edward Krug and G. Lester Anderson (eds.), "Adapting Instruction in the Social Studies to Individual Differences," *Fifteenth Yearbook,* National Council for Social Studies, Washington, D. C.: National Education Association, 1944, pp. 15-16.

7. Why is it improper to classify all types of deviation as exceptional? What are some of the difficulties that arise from this classification?

8. What are several of the devices now in use to diagnose and remedy problems arising from individual differences?

9. How has the development of special tests helped the cause of education?

10. What are some of the distinct advantages of conferences for solving problems due to individual differences?

11. What are some of the methodological patterns now in use in the schools for solving the problem of individual differences?

Chapter 15

EVALUATING LEARNING: MEASUREMENT AND STATISTICAL METHODS

I. MEASUREMENT

1. CAN LEARNING BE MEASURED?

Although the treatment in this chapter is primarily of educational tests, it is recognized that evaluating the products of learning cannot be reduced entirely to a discussion of tests only, since evidences of learning are apparent on every hand provided we are alert to their presence and significance. William A. Brownell points out that:

> Some of this evidence is susceptible to measurement by means of paper-and-pencil tests. Other evidences of learning are best assessed in other ways, for example, by examining pupils' work products, by questioning pupils in the classroom and in conferences, and by observing their behavior in and out of school. Such opportunities to evaluate learning are too important to be neglected.[1]

The point of view that the appraisal or assessment of the individual must include factors other than those which can be measured directly or indirectly is expressed again in a recent book entitled *Assessment of Men:*

> Fortune—call the old hag or beauty what you will—can never be eliminated from the universe of human interactions. And this being forever true, prophetic infallibility is beyond the reach of social scientists.

---

[1] William A. Brownell, "The Measurement of Understanding," *Forty-Fifth Yearbook,* National Society for the Study of Education, Part I, Chicago, University of Chicago Press, 1946, p. 1.

Furthermore, we would guess that no matter how substantial are the advances of scientific psychology, the best series of predictions of *individual* careers— apperception operating as it does—will involve the play of experienced intuitions, the clinical hunch, products of unconsciously perceived and integrated symptomatic signs. The assessment of men—we trust that Samuel Butler would agree—is the scientific art of arriving at sufficient conclusions from insufficient data.[2]

Although recognizing the limitations of tests in the measurement of human development and behavior, we must admit that they usually provide a much better basis for making judgments and predictions than unsupported subjective opinions. Tests also offer a means of comparing individuals in a group and of comparing groups.

The field of scientific measurement as applied to the social sciences is still in its developmental stage. The measurement movement, as it is sometimes called, dates back to Binet's work which culminated in 1905 in the first crude form of an intelligence test, and to J. M. Rice, who, between 1894 and 1896, administered the same spelling test to many different school children.

Binet's work was followed by a flood of individual and group tests of general intelligence. The first World War gave strong impetus to the testing field, particularly in connection with the refinement of an intelligence test. These tests were followed by special aptitude tests and later by personality and interest tests, scales, and questionnaires. Almost concurrently came the achievement tests, first for basic subjects in the elementary school and later in the various subjects of the secondary school.[3]

Progress in measurement in recent years has been almost phenomenal. Every effort is being made to eliminate the sources of error in testing. Study and research[4] have contributed much to the improvement and refinement of tests and measuring instruments. Errors introduced in the administration and interpretation of tests are being reduced through the

---

[2] The OSS Assessment Staff, *Assessment of Men,* New York: Rinehart & Co., Inc., 1948, p. 8.

[3] See *School and Society,* LX (1944), 276.

[4] See *Journal of Educational Research,* XXXIX (1946), 321-400.

careful training of teachers and test administrators in the utilization of measuring instruments. There is every reason to believe that tests and other measuring devices will become increasingly useful and dependable in the measurement of human performance.

Purpose of Evaluation in Education.—The primary purpose of evaluation, measurement, assessment, or appraisal in education is to provide a better understanding of the pupil. The individual child and his development and behavior must be appraised with reference to the values of society as these have been or can be formulated. If the schools are to fulfil their obligations, they must somehow bridge the gap which now exists between the aspirations of and for children as expressed in our social philosophy of education and actual pupil accomplishment. Evaluation is not an end in itself—it is just a phase, but an essential one, of the integrated learning-teaching-testing-guidance process which constitutes functioning whole-child education.

The skilled teacher will use a variety of methods, devices, and tools to gain a better understanding of his classes and the individuals who compose them. Tests are one of the modern teacher's professional tools. Through their use the teacher can obtain an understanding of the needs, abilities, achievement status, interests, and personality characteristics of pupils as well as appraise the outcomes of learning and measure the efficiency of instruction. Some students read two to three times as fast as others; and some students have vocabularies three to five times as large as their·fellows. All these and other interesting facts have been and can be discovered about any group of students through the use of simple tests.

With tests as tools the teacher can identify learning difficulties, diagnose causes of failure, and plan educational programs designed to meet the student's needs just as accurately as the physician diagnoses health difficulties and plans for treatment. The old argument that schools formerly got along without tests does not mean that we should go back to the methods used half a century ago. We know that physicians "got along" without

X rays and penicillin, but physicians do better today because of
new instruments and new medicines, and patients live longer
and are healthier. Pupils, too, are understood and guided better
today because educational measuring instruments have been
refined and have been used as professional tools.

2. Tests

Uses of Tests.—Too frequently we associate tests only with
school, forgetting that tests are used extensively by other agencies too. The most elaborate testing program in the history of
the world was developed in connection with the second World
War when the armed services of many nations were attempting
to make the best possible utilization of their available manpower.
In the United States alone, nearly ten million men were given
certain tests in this program.[5] Results are still being analyzed
and reported. This testing experiment enabled the armed services to obtain information quickly about individuals and groups.
Further, we learned from the program many things about our
total population, its educational background, mental abilities,
and aptitudes. The testing program carried on by the armed
services in wartime gave impetus to the study and construction
of tests, and many of the things learned from the work are
already being applied generally in the field of measurement.
The first World War helped to define the field in its early
period, but the recent war provided opportunities for the use
and study of many more types of tests on larger populations.

Governments use tests in peacetime too. Federal, state, and
local government positions are part of our regular civil service
system and usually are secured by competitive examination.

Industry is a major user of tests. Here, too, knowledge of
the individual's abilities, attitudes, aptitudes, achievements, interests, and personal characteristics is of value in making placements that are satisfactory both to the firm and to the applicant
for the position.

---

[5] John Arthur Stewart, "A Study of the Army Testing Program During
World War II at the Induction Station and Reception Center, Fort Lewis,
Washington," p. 9.

Our main concern, however, is with the uses of tests in schools, where tests are used for a variety of purposes. The purposes which are universally accepted are:

1. Motivation
2. Organization and expression
3. Diagnosis
4. Prognosis
5. Measurement
    a) Pupil achievement
    b) Pupil classification
    c) Ability sectioning
    d) Efficiency of method
    e) Efficiency of teachers
    f) Guidance
    g) Instructional purposes
    h) Public relations
    i) Research

It should be noted that no one test can possibly serve all purposes. As a matter of fact, it may require several tests or types of appraisal to provide complete evaluation of a particular objective. Moreover, since there are so many things to be desired from tests, it is essential that the measuring instruments be as carefully constructed and as refined as possible.

Another way of determining school uses of tests is to study the values of tests to certain groups, such as administrators, teachers, and students. A brief statement of the values to each of the above groups will indicate further uses of tests.

1. *Administrative uses of tests.* Administrators may use tests for a wide variety of purposes such as:
    a) To show pupil growth and progress
    b) To provide a basis for reports to parents
    c) To provide bases for reports of school progress to the community
    d.) To provide objective, cumulative records of student work when the pupil is to be transferred to another school
    e) To provide a basis for guidance and optimum placement both in the classroom and in outside positions

   f) To provide information which will enable the administrator to help teachers improve instruction

2. *Teacher uses of tests.* There are again numerous reasons
   why teachers find results of tests of value. Some of these
   reasons are:
   a) To determine educational needs of pupils
   b) To determine the progress of each pupil in relation to
   his ability
   c) To analyze and diagnose individual problems
   d) To determine the efficiency of teaching methods
   e) To provide motivation for study and review
   f) To determine special student aptitudes as a basis for
   guidance
   g) To provide objective information for helping the student
   to understand his own strengths and weaknesses
   h) To provide a good medium for instruction

3. *Student uses of tests.* Students also find test results very
   enlightening and helpful in understanding their own progress. Students find that tests:
   a) Provide motivation for study and review
   b) Show special strengths and weaknesses
   c) Help to indicate special interests and aptitudes which
   may be useful in the selection of careers
   d) Reveal abilities of the student
   e) Provide a record for transfer or basis for admission to
   advanced schools and also for recommendations regarding job placement

Classification of Tests.—There are many possible classifications of tests. They may, for example, be classified according
to purpose, as achievement tests, aptitude tests, attitude tests,
etc. They may also be classified according to type—oral examinations, essay or discussion examinations, teacher-made objective tests, and standardized tests.

No matter what classification is used, it is necessary to have
a number of subdivisions under each main division. For example, under objective tests we list such specific types as recall,
completion, alternate response, matching, and multiple choice.

These might be further expanded by indicating a number of modifications of basic types.

More important than the classification of tests is a basic understanding of the characteristics of a scientific measuring instrument, no matter what its type. Teachers particularly should be well informed relative to the qualities of a valid and reliable test. This information is valuable whether a teacher is constructing or selecting tests to be used in any phase of the educational program.

3. How to Use Tests

Characteristics of an Effective Test.—There are three principal characteristics of a measuring instrument which should be considered as criteria for the evaluation of tests. These criteria should be thoroughly understood before a teacher attempts to construct or to select examinations. The first and most important characteristic of an examination is its *validity*. This term expresses how well an examination measures what it purports or claims to measure. Validity is the most difficult characteristic to attain with certainty. It is largely specific rather than general in its nature. A test which may be valid in one situation may be quite lacking in validity when used for some other purpose. Nor is it always easy to define exactly the particular thing which one is attempting to measure. For example, if one seeks definitions of intelligence or personality in books on general or educational psychology, he is likely to find a divergence of opinion as to what should be included in these definitions. It is therefore highly important that a person determine specifically what the author of a test claims to measure before he considers whether or not the test is valid. Some tests, even in the same area, do not yield comparable measures because, as their authors admit, their objectives are at variance. Test constructors need to determine, at least in their own minds, what constitutes intelligence, personality, aptitude, attitudes, appreciation, or whatever they desire to measure before they attempt to construct tests measuring these qualities. The fact that test-makers are not always agreed on their definitions or on their testing procedures does not mean that these tests have no value. Even in the exact sciences there are measurements which are valuable but which are complicated by difficulty of definition or by the necessity for indirect rather than direct measurement. The measurement of rare gases in the higher aerial strata represents indirect measurement just as the measurement of intelligence is indirect. However, in spite of these limitations, the measurements are exact and useful.

In the field of education there are two kinds of validity—*statistical validity* and *curricular validity*. Statistical validity may be determined on any type of test, but when one is dealing with achievement tests it is also necessary to determine curricular validity, which is the extent to which the content of the test is representative of the content of the course. A test should include a representative sampling of the essential materials employed in instruction. It should also measure the understanding and development of the individual pupils. Statistical validity refers to the mathematical process for determining the degree to which the test agrees with, or correlates with, some assumed criterion.

Many different methods of validating tests have been used, and there has been wide diversity of practice reported, showing that no one technique has been accepted as distinctly better than any other.

Specialists in test construction not only attempt to validate the test as a whole against an outside criterion, but also to validate the individual items; item validity is usually based on an inside criterion. Although many of the processes of item validation are technical and complex, the essential purpose is to determine the discriminating value of each item. Obviously, those items answered correctly by everybody or those items missed by everybody are of no value in discrimination. Test manuals available with standardized tests should give adequate information relative to the purpose which the test claims to serve and the way in which the test was validated.

The second principal characteristic of a scientific measuring instrument is its *reliability*. Reliability is the ability of a test to measure consistently whatever it measures. Manifestly then, an examination might be reliable but not valid. The ideal test possesses both validity and reliability; reliability by itself is of doubtful value.

Reliability is much easier to determine than is validity, which may account for the fact that test-makers have given more attention to determining the reliability of tests than to establishing their validity. Reliability is a purely statistical concept determined after a test has been given, and little can be told about the reliability of a test from an examination of the test itself. It can, of course, be observed that a test which can be objectively scored is more likely to be reliable than one the scoring of which is subjective; but the degree of reliability cannot be determined by objectivity alone. It is also possible to estimate to a certain degree the reliability of a test by its length, for a long test has a greater likelihood of being reliable than has a short test. However, the final check of reliability is in trying out the test. Reliability, like validity, is usually discussed in test manuals accompanying standardized tests.

Three rather distinct techniques are used to establish the reliability of a test. One method commonly used by test-makers is to give two equivalent forms of a test to a large number of individuals with only a short interval between the tests. If there is a close agreement between the scores on the two forms, the test is said to be reliable. There are two other methods of computing reliability in which only one test form is used. In one, self-correlations are obtained by using correlated scores in chance halves of the test. This is the reliability of the half-test. The second method which has been used with one form of a test is to present the test at a later time and to determine the extent of agreement by computing the coefficient of correlation between the two series of scores.

It has been indicated that objectivity is a factor in the reliability of a test. By *objectivity* is meant the degree to which equally competent users get the same results or the same scores. If an adequate key is provided with an objective test, it should be possible for a teacher or his helper or the students to obtain the same total scores on the tests. Objectivity is extremely important and helpful in scoring.

The third characteristic of a satisfactory measuring instrument is its usability, and a number of subpoints should be considered under this main heading. C. C. Ross in his book, *Measurement in Today's Schools,* lists the following factors determining usability:

1. Ease of administration
2. Ease of scoring
3. Ease of interpretation and application
4. Low cost
5. Proper mechanical make-up [6]

Practical Suggestions on Test Construction.—In addition to, or as a part of, the principal characteristics of a measuring instrument, a number of factors should be especially considered in the production or selection of a test. Some of these are:

1. The teacher should plan his test or select the test which will best serve all the learning or growth objectives to be measured with appropriate weighting in harmony with the relative importance of the various objectives.

2. The more tangible the goals of instruction and the more definite the objectives, the greater likelihood there is that the objectives may be adequately measured.

3. The test should be adapted to the level of the group to which it will be given.

4. Tests should represent an adequate sampling of the factors or of the material to be measured. The more comprehensive the sampling, the greater likelihood there is that the test will possess both validity and reliability.

5. The measuring instrument should be one likely to yield a range of scores large enough to provide differential measures of all the individuals in the group.

6. The teacher should plan carefully to determine the type or types of test which are going to serve his purposes best. It may be that the teacher will wish to use a combination of different types of tests given over a period of time in order to measure different phases of instruction or different qualities of the in-

---

[6] C. C. Ross, *Measurement in Today's Schools,* 2d ed., New York: Prentice-Hall, Inc., 1947, p. 90.

dividual's work. The teacher should experiment with different types of tests in order to determine which type serves specific purposes most advantageously. A variety of tests will lend interest to classroom work and will be more likely to meet the approval of the students than will the repetition of the same type of test. Each type of test has its particular merits and limitations. These should be carefully studied and understood by the teacher and should be used as the basis for the planning of the testing program.

7. The teacher should have a larger number of items in the preliminary draft of a test than he will expect to use in the final draft of the examination. This will permit the elimination of items which on further study seem to be ambiguous or irrelevant. The first draft of the test should be prepared early in order to allow time for evaluation of items.

8. An adequate key should be prepared as test items are formulated.

9. It is advisable to avoid the use of "catch questions." The inclusion of catch questions makes the student suspicious and complicates the examination.

10. The teacher should avoid using verbatim statements from the text. Application of knowledge is much more important than mere possession of knowledge. It is possible for students to repeat statements of the text without having the slightest idea as to the meaning of the content.

11. A good test avoids giving clues to the answers.

12. The content and not the form of the item should determine the answer.

13. Usually, a single word in a statement should not determine whether an answer is correct or incorrect.

14. Items of the same type should be grouped together.

15. In speed tests—those in which the object is to determine the rate at which the individual can react to certain items or exercises—the items should be of equal difficulty.

16. In power tests—those in which the object is to determine how far a person can go—the items should be arranged in order of difficulty. There are both timed and untimed power tests.

17. The test should eliminate in so far as possible the measurement of secondary characteristics. In other words, the measurement of factors other than the primary factors should be kept to an absolute minimum. It is recognized, of course, that the ability of the student to read and to interpret examinations is inherent in all written tests.

18. Directions for taking a test should be clear and well stated. Examples indicating how the directions are to be carried out should be included with types of tests which are unfamiliar to students.

19. The way in which the test is to be scored should be determined before the test is given. In informal teacher-made tests this information should also be given to the students.

20. The individual items of the test should be carefully and clearly stated in order to avoid ambiguity.

21. The test should be fair.

22. The test should be interesting.

23. The format of a test should be attractive and should help to facilitate test-taking.

24. Space should be provided for student answers. A definite arrangement and placement of responses will greatly facilitate scoring.

25. Scoring may be facilitated by avoiding the use of minus scores and fractions.

26. If a teacher wishes to evaluate his own test, he will receive many interesting suggestions and interpretations from his classes. It is sometimes a desirable technique to ask students to prepare questions covering materials which have been studied. Teachers should be acutely aware of the fact that their testing methods in large measure determine the manner in which students study. If the purpose of the examination is to measure understanding, it is necessary to keep this objective foremost in mind in test construction. Measurement of understanding is more difficult in most cases than the measurement of factual information, but it is important to emphasize in the test those things which one expects students to accomplish. If tests are detailed and trivial, students are likely to study any way which will help them to answer the test questions, but in a way which

may not enable them to see the over-all relationships and the most important outcomes of the material presented. It should be borne in mind then that tests may serve a teaching purpose in the improvement of study habits and in the improvement of instruction. There is no reason why teacher-made tests should not be used for instructional purposes more frequently than they have been in the past.

Utilization and Interpretation of Tests.—Points to be remembered in giving tests and interpreting results are as follows:

1. All the information and materials necessary for giving a test should be available. If a machine-scored test is to be used, it will be necessary to have proper answer sheets and the proper marking pencils. Separate booklets of instruction are also sometimes necessary. It is, of course, well at all times to keep in mind the purpose or purposes which the test is to serve and to construct the test or select the test in accordance with the objectives. It is entirely too expensive in time, effort, and money to give tests unless they are to serve a definite purpose. When a test is given, it should be scored as soon after administration as possible and the results should be used according to a previously drawn plan.

2. If a standardized test is being used, one which has two forms is ordinarily considered preferable. By two forms of a test is meant two examinations covering the same field or unit with the same number of equally difficult but different questions, so well paired that, if both forms are given to the same group, the same mean scores and the same approximate spread of the group will result and the correlation of the scores will be high.

3. It should be kept in mind that all measurement is subject to error.[7] This fact must be taken into account, and allowances should be made for error in the interpretation of examination results and in the application of their results.

4. Whenever a new type of test is introduced, it will be necessary for the teacher to give more adequate instructions for

---

[7] See William A. McCall, *Measurement,* p. 17.

taking the test than he might give for a type more familiar to the students.

5. If students are to perform well, it is necessary for them to have the right psychological attitude toward tests. Teachers can influence the psychological attitude of students toward all types of examinations. Examinations should never be used for disciplinary measures, and students should be able to enter upon the examination without fear or reluctance.

6. Teachers will do well to have a general understanding with the students as to the plan of the over-all testing program. If tests are to be given without notice, students should be advised of this fact early in the course.

7. Students should be given some instructions in test-taking and should have special instructions in following directions.

8. Teacher and student alike should be on time for tests. It may help to reduce disturbance to discuss in class some of the points regarding courtesy during the testing period in order to avoid unnecessary disturbance.

9. The teacher should see to it that the room conditions are as comfortable as possible for test-taking. The ventilation and lighting should be checked. Noise should be reduced to an absolute minimum. Wherever possible students should be given sufficient room so as to reduce any temptation to look at other papers and to permit greater ease and comfort.

10. The teacher should select with care the time when examinations are to be given. Consideration should be given to be sure that there will be no interruptions for announcements, assemblies, or fire drills. It is also inadvisable to give a test at a time when students' interests are absorbed elsewhere, such as during football games or school plays.

11. The best learning period is that which immediately follows the test period. At no other time will student interest be as high as it is immediately following the examination. This has several implications: first, that we may give shorter tests and allow time for discussion of the test immediately following the examination; second, that the test should be scored and returned to the student as early as possible. The latter is espe-

cially true of teacher-made tests. Discussion will usually help to clear up points in question.

12. It is easy for most students to understand why and how they got the scores which they received if the teacher will take a little time to explain the method of scoring to the student. At most levels students are capable of understanding such terms as *range* (the difference between the highest and the lowest score), the *mean* (the average score), the *median* (the middle score), and the *mode* (the most frequently occurring score).

13. Last but not least is the point that sound interpretation of tests depends upon the application of judgment. Tests should serve the teacher's needs and the students' needs. At no time should the teacher become a slave to tests. In the interpretation of test scores, the guiding point should always be to favor the student and not the statistics, for the student is much more important than mere test results.

Questions

1. Give a brief summary of the history of the testing movement.
2. Discuss the functions of tests in the school from the standpoint of the administrator, the teacher, and the pupil.
3. Name the three characteristics of a good measuring instrument and explain each characteristic fully.
4. What is *objectivity*?
5. List the ten most important suggestions on test construction.
6. What are six important factors to consider when applying tests?
7. Construct a sample test covering this chapter that will meet the requirements of a good test as nearly as you can determine.

II. STATISTICAL METHODS

Statistical methods in education would require two complete books for their exposition—an introductory textbook and an advanced text to cover the current statistical devices being used in research.

There are, however, certain basic concepts and principles about which any student of educational psychology should know something. These include the concept of measurement as used in education and psychology, the concept of probability applied to the accuracy or trustworthiness of measures, the frequency distribution of measures and its implications, and the concept of central tendency.

The Concept of Measurement.—At first glance the grades assigned to a number of test papers by a teacher in terms of letters, e. g., *A, B, C, D,* or *E,* would seem to have no resemblance at all to a set of physical measures like the heights or weights of the same students. These physical measures are given in units of feet or inches and there would be high agreement among a number of persons in measuring the heights of a class or their weights. The pupils' heights can be compared with the units marked on a tape measure or weights read from the dial of a scale. There would be less agreement on whether a certain test paper is to be marked *A* or *B*. There is no physical yardstick for determining high or low quality.

The difference between measures of a physical dimension like height and the measurement of the quality of a test paper is, however, not as great as would appear at first sight. In the end both depend on a comparison and a judgment that one of two things being compared is greater than or not greater than another. A pupil is as high as, or higher than, a certain point on the tape which is marked 40 inches. Or the same pupil's test paper is judged equal to or better than another's. The difference between the two kinds of measures lies in the fact that the aid of a physical rule makes the judgment of relative height somewhat easier to agree on than the judgment of relative merit. Rulers and tape measures are widely accepted and easily compared with heights. In other words, they are relatively public and objective. Judgments of merit tend to be more affected by the private views of the measurer and to be, therefore, subjective. If they were entirely subjective there would be no point in making the comparison. But a high degree of agreement can be reached by teachers even on such items as the quality of a test paper, or a reply to one question of a test. This chapter will describe ways of measuring that agreement.

1. Central Tendency and Dispersion

The Mean.—To return to the measures of height, it will be noticed that the strong agreement between different observers is a relative matter and if we call for measurements to the sixty-fourth of an inch we may find that no two of ten observers report the same height.

Suppose the ten persons report the following measures of the same individual pupil: 40 and 17 sixty-fourths inches, 40 and 21 sixty-fourths inches, 40 and 30 sixty-fourths inches, 40 and 23 sixty-fourths inches, 40 and 26 sixty-fourths inches, 40 and 22 sixty-fourths inches, 40 and 25 sixty-fourths inches, 40 and 23 sixty-fourths inches, 40 and 23 sixty-fourths inches, 40 and 20 sixty-fourths inches. What is our best estimate of the pupil's height? The answer to this question is the average or mean of the measures. We find this mean by adding up the measures and dividing by the number of measures. In the above case the sum of the measures would be 400 inches plus 230 sixty-fourths of an inch. One tenth of this would give us a mean of 40 and 23 sixty-fourths inches. This is the mean of the ten measures of the pupil's height and is our best value of that height.

Suppose we wish to compare the grades of boys and girls in a test in which marks of A, B, C, D, or E are assigned by the teacher. Here there is no unit like the inch which can be marked on a tape and used by anyone. We must assume that the teacher has some sort of quality standard in mind and that she can judge certain papers to be of outstanding quality as compared with the rest, others slightly inferior to these but better than average, and so on, and has assigned these grades of A to E. We can make a direct comparison of the grades made by the girls and by the boys by assigning number values to the letters and using these as measures. We can make $A=4$, $B=3$, $C=2$, $D=1$, $E=0$. This is a common practice of high schools and colleges in getting grade averages. We can get the mean value of the boys' grades and the mean value of the girls' grades and compare them.

Suppose 19 boys and 23 girls have received grades as follows:

Grade	Boys	Girls
A	2	3
B	6	6
C	7	9
D	4	4
E	0	1

The sum of the boys' grades would be:

> 2 A grades at 4 points each, 8
> 6 B grades at 3 points each, 18
> 7 C grades at 2 points each, 14
> 4 D grades at 1 point each,   4
>   Total, 44

The mean grade of the boys is therefore 44 divided by 19, or 2.31+.

For the girls the total is:

> 3 A grades at 4 points each, 12
> 6 B grades at 3 points each, 18
> 9 C grades at 2 points each, 18
> 4 D grades at 1 point each,   4
> 1 E grade at 0 points each,   0
>   Total, 52

The mean grade of the girls is therefore 52 divided by 23, or 2.26+.

It would appear that the boys have done better than the girls. How much confidence we can place in this difference is another matter and involves the question of the reliability of these averages.

The Average Deviation.—When sets of measures do not agree—and this is usual and expected—it becomes necessary to measure the amount of agreement, or the extent of their dispersion. If we asked two persons each to measure the height of a pupil and one person reported a height of 41 inches and the other a height of 39.5 inches, we would suspect that one has made a serious error in measurement, but we would not know which measurement was wrong. From a single measure we have no way of estimating how far our measure may be from the real value.

If we then ask the two observers to make ten measures each, they might report as follows:

> Observer A: 40.5; 40.0; 40.5; 41.0; 40.5;
> 40.0; 40.5; 40.0; 40.5; 40.5.
>
> Observer B: 39.5; 41.0; 40.0; 40.5; 41.5;
> 41.0; 40.5; 42.5; 39.5; 40.0.

The mean of A's measures is 40.4. The mean of B's measures is 40.6. In which mean can we place the most confidence?

We answer this by using a measure of the variability or dispersion of the measures. The observer whose measures cluster nearer the mean value is presumably more accurate than the other. How do we measure this "cluster"? The measure used at first appears unnecessarily complicated. We could find how far each measure is from the mean and find the mean of these distances. Observer A's measures have the following deviations from the mean: $+0.1$; -0.4; $+0.1$; $+0.6$; $+0.1$; -0.4; $+0.1$; -0.4; $+0.1$; $+0.1$. Observer B's measures have these deviations from the mean: -1.1; $+0.4$; -0.6; -0.1; $+0.9$; $+0.4$; -0.1; $+1.9$; -1.1; -0.6.

First, it may be noticed in passing that the deviations from the mean add up to zero. This is a property of the mean and could be used as its definition. The mean of an array of numbers is a value such that the sum of the deviations of the numbers from the mean is zero.

The sum of A's deviations, if we disregard signs, is 2.4, and the average deviation is therefore 0.24. The sum of B's deviations, if we disregard signs, is 7.2, and their mean is therefore 7.2 divided by 10, or 0.72. This is three times the average deviation of A's observations from their mean and A is to be regarded as by that much the more consistent observer.

The Standard Deviation.—There are reasons for selecting a more complicated average of the deviations. This more complicated average is the square root of the average of the squares of the deviations. First square the deviations. A's squares: 0.01; 0.16; 0.01; 0.36; 0.01; 0.16; 0.01; 0.16; 0.01; 0.01. The sum of these squares is 0.90 and their mean is 0.09. The square root of this mean of the squares is 0.3. This square root of the mean of the squares of the deviations is called the standard deviation. The lower case Greek letter σ is the commonly accepted abbreviation for standard deviation, though the letters SD are sometimes used.

The squares of B's deviations are: 1.21; 0.16; 0.36; 0.01; 0.81; 0.16; 0.01; 3.61; 1.21; 0.36. The sum of these is 7.90. The mean of these is 7.9. The square root of 7.9 is 2.81+. This is more than nine times as large as the standard deviation of A's measures. A is more accurate.

The mathematical expression for the standard deviation, like many formidable looking mathematical symbols, is really a remarkably convenient shorthand for defining the concept. It is:

$$\sigma = \sqrt{\frac{\Sigma x^2}{n}}$$

This is read: The standard deviation is the square root of the sum of (Σ is a Greek S to indicate "sum of") the squares of the deviations (x^2) divided by the number of measures.

The practical use of the standard deviation requires the understanding of another statistical concept, the normal frequency curve.

2. The Normal Curve

In the earlier part of this chapter there were two frequency tables. They showed how many boys and how many girls received various letter grades. The boys' table could have been pictured as in Figure 1.

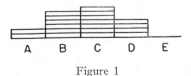

Figure 1

Another example of a frequency distribution could be formed by tossing ten pennies and tallying the number of times they fell all heads, nine heads, eight heads, and so on to no heads.

No. of Heads	Frequency
10	0
9	13
8	41
7	125
6	221
5	247
4	203
3	124
2	40
1	8
0	2

This frequency table can be represented by Figure 2.

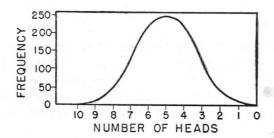

Figure 2

The shape of this diagram begins to be interesting and important. It approximates the theoretical shape that we would get by calculating the chances of getting 10 heads in one throw, 9 heads, 8 heads, and so on. Such a calculation is not too difficult. The probability that the first penny shall be heads must equal the probability that it shall be tails. It is therefore one-half or 0.5. The probability that the second penny will be heads is also 0.5 and the probability that both will be heads is 0.5 times 0.5. The probability that all will be heads is one-half to the tenth power or 1/1,024.

The probability that the first penny will be tails is 0.5 and the combined probability that the first will be tails and all the rest heads is $(0.5)^{10}$ or $1/1{,}024$. This would produce nine heads, but there are ten ways this could happen. The tails penny could be first, second, third, or in any position of the ten. The probability of nine heads is therefore ten times $(0.5)^{10}$. The probability that the first two pennies will be tails and the rest heads is also $(0.5)^{10}$ or $1/1{,}024$. But there are forty-five ways of arranging two tails and eight heads. The probability of eight heads is therefore 45 times $(0.5)^{10}$.

Calculated thus, the frequency distribution for the incidence of 10, 9, 8, etc., heads is:

No. of Heads	Frequency
10	$1 \times (\frac{1}{2})^{10}$
9	$10 \times (\frac{1}{2})^{10}$
8	$45 \times (\frac{1}{2})^{10}$
7	$120 \times (\frac{1}{2})^{10}$
6	$210 \times (\frac{1}{2})^{10}$
5	$252 \times (\frac{1}{2})^{10}$
4	$210 \times (\frac{1}{2})^{10}$
3	$120 \times (\frac{1}{2})^{10}$
2	$45 \times (\frac{1}{2})^{10}$
1	$10 \times (\frac{1}{2})^{10}$
0	$1 \times (\frac{1}{2})^{10}$

A graph of this table is shown in Figure 3.

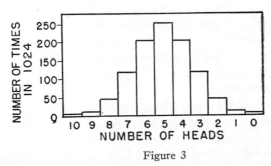

Figure 3

A smooth curve drawn through the tops of these columns would look like the curve of Figure 4.

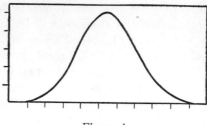

Figure 4

If we increase *n* indefinitely, this curve becomes the normal probability curve (Figure 5).

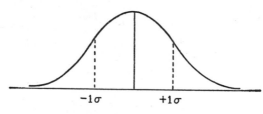

Figure 5

This curve has interesting properties. Its dimensions are known in terms of the standard deviation. Beyond a point one σ to the right (or left) of the mean will be found approximately 16 per cent of the measures.

Given the mean of a set of measures and the standard deviation, the theoretical curve can be drawn for the distribution as it would be if the variation of the measures were due to an indefinitely large number of independent factors. It is remarkable how closely most measures in psychology and education fit this theoretical curve.

There are available in textbooks tables of statistics which show the areas or per cents of the normal distribution to be found between the mean and any given fraction of the standard deviation. A condensed table of this kind is given on page 229.

We know that the mean height of college men at a given institution is 68 inches and the standard deviation of heights is 2 inches. We could, consulting the table, know that we should

expect 34.13 per cent of the men to be between 68 and 70 inches,
and 15.87 per cent to be over 70 inches.

The table tells us not only the per cent of the area to be
found between the mean and 1σ, but also the percents between
the mean and values of χ/σ less than and greater than 1σ.

For instance, if we ask what per cent of the men will be found
to be under 65 inches, we note that this is 3 inches below the
mean and is 3/2 standard deviations below the mean. The
table shows that 43.32 per cent of the population will be between
the mean and 1.5 σ below the mean. The remainder of the
lower half, or 50—43.32=6.68 per cent will be below that figure.
This is 6.68 in each hundred or 66.8 in a thousand. Given
similar figures, a six-foot girl can find how many men six feet
or over she may expect in the college population. An imposing
amount of information about a population or a collection of
measures is packed into these two statistics, the *mean* and the
standard deviation.

3. Means Have Standard Deviations

If we were concerned to know how well sixth grade boys
from a given school system can read and devised a reading test
on which reading ability could be scored, it would obviously not
do just to give the test to one sixth grade boy. We know that
boys vary considerably. We would do better to give the test to
a number of boys and find the mean score. How many boys?

The answer to this question can be made once we have given
the test to a sample group of sixth grade boys and found the
mean and standard deviation of the group. From the variability of the group as measured by the standard deviation can
be calculated the standard deviation of means of samples of a
given size. Obviously the larger the groups, the less will be
the variability of the means. This relationship can be expressed
exactly. The σ of a mean of a number of measures is the σ of
the measures divided by the square root of their number. In
convenient mathematical shorthand:

$$\sigma_m = \frac{\sigma}{\sqrt{n}}$$

When we know the standard deviation of a mean, we can place bets on what new determinations of the mean will give. If in the case of the men students the mean of 68 inches is determined by measuring 100 men, the σ of that mean is 2/10 or the σ of the measures divided by the square root of the number of men measured. A σ of 0.2 inches assures us that the odds are overwhelming (9987 to 13) that another sample of 100 will show a mean not over 0.6 inches or 3 σ's away from 68 inches. Look in the table for the percentage of the area under the normal curve that is more than 3 standard deviations from the mean.

If we had measured only nine men and found the same mean and σ, the σ_m would be 2/3 or 0.67, and the chance that another sample would give M greater than 68.6 would be approximately 18.41 in one hundred or almost one in five. In other words, we could not trust our sample of nine cases to give us a reliable mean.

The number we take in a sample depends on how accurately we wish to estimate the mean of the group, or in other words, within what limits we wish to be fairly certain what the real mean actually is. These limits are often expressed by saying, for instance, that the mean height of the men in the college group is 68 ± 0.2 if we had measured a sample of 100 men, and 68 ± 0.7 if we had measured only nine. The chances are about two out of three that the real mean is within one σ of the obtained mean of the sample.

The reader will encounter the phrase "standard error" as well as the phrase "standard deviation." They are the same statistic but the term "standard error" is used for the σ of the means of *samples* because in this case the means of samples are thought of as approximations of the means of whole populations and their deviations from population means are errors.

4. Comparable Scales

The normal frequency distribution makes possible the use of scales and scores which do not require elaborate tables of equivalents.

In order not to evoke conventional answers which may obscure the point, let us ask a question which is essentially without precedent and which may sound like nonsense. Does John Wilson play ball better than Walter Holmes plays the piano?

How can ball-playing and piano-playing be compared? There is one obvious method which is the one used in the schools when we say that a given pupil is better at arithmetic than he is in spelling. There would be no point in having John and Walter exercise their skills for our benefit. There is no common measure that can be applied directly to comparing their performances. A comparison is possible, nevertheless. We can examine the ball-playing of John's sixth grade companions and discover what is average performance of sixth graders and what is their standard deviation on their performance. We can locate John's score on this scale and say that at playing ball John is one standard deviation better than the average sixth grader. We can do the same for Walter and discover that Walter is two standard deviations below the average of sixth grade boys at performance on the piano. John is therefore in a sense a better ball-player than Walter is a piano-player, though this has a certain air of absurdity when we put it this way. It has, however, definite statistical meaning.

There has recently arisen in a Western state some question over the accreditation of students from a certain college when they apply for admission elsewhere. The argument turns on the fact that this college has recently abandoned the prevalent A-B-C-D-E grading system for a system of Honors-Pass-Fail. The other schools are confronted with a problem. Is a Pass grade, as the college claims, the equivalent of a C grade? What the other colleges are actually doing is to assess 50 hours of Pass as the equivalent of 40 hours of C and 10 hours of D on the ground that there is no basis for direct comparison of grades in different institutions and the only fair assumption is that achievement is equivalent and that if 8 per cent of the students in the first college receive D grades, 8 per cent of the students in the second college would have received D grades if the grading standards had been the same (Figure 6).

FIRST COLLEGE

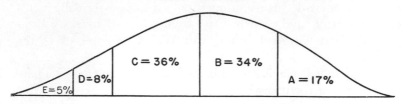

SECOND COLLEGE

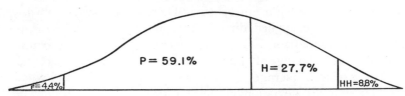

Figure 6

With the above distributions of grades, how can one college evaluate in its own system grades from the other? Each point in the second distribution represents a *z*-score, and the equivalent *z*-score in the first distribution will fall in one of the areas *A, B, C, D,* or *E.*

z-Scores.—At the University of Washington numerous teachers take advantage of a service which surveys the student opinion of their teaching. Many are also judged by their fellow teachers. The two scales are not directly comparable. But when both are reduced to the deviations from the mean in standard deviations, they become comparable. Scores in these terms are sometimes referred to as *z*-scores:

$$z = (\text{score} - \text{mean})/\sigma$$

To know that an instructor's *z*-score in student ratings is +0.3 and in fellow-teacher ratings is +1.5 is to know (1) that he is above the mean in both ratings and (2) that the teachers have a higher opinion of him than his students and place him in the upper 7 per cent, whereas the students place him 38 per cent from the top of the distribution. (Confirm this by an examination of the accompanying table.)

THE NORMAL CURVE: AREA BETWEEN MEAN AND VARIOUS z-SCORES

$z = (\text{Score} - \text{Mean})/\sigma$	Area Between Mean and z-Score (Given in Per Cent of Total Area of Normal Curve)
0.00	00.00
0.10	3.98
0.20	7.93
0.30	11.79
0.40	15.54
0.50	19.15
0.60	22.57
0.70	25.80
0.80	28.81
0.90	31.59
1.00	34.13
1.10	36.43
1.20	38.49
1.30	40.32
1.40	41.92
1.50	43.32
1.60	44.52
1.70	45.54
1.80	46.41
1.90	47.13
2.00	47.72
2.10	48.21
2.20	48.61
2.30	48.93
2.40	49.18
2.50	49.38
2.60	49.53
2.70	49.65
2.80	49.74
2.90	49.81
3.00	49.87

The use of the normal frequency curve as a scale is typical of measurements in biology, social science, and psychology. One system of units of length in terms of inches, feet, yards, miles, or light years can be used to measure an indefinitely large variety of things. But it should be noted that in biological or psychological measurement even such simple dimensions as the height of six-year-old boys are significant or the weights of newborn infants are significant only when we translate inches and pounds into a standard deviation scale and know where the boy or the infant falls with reference to age classmates. Told that an eleven-year-old boy is 50 inches in height, we do not know whether he is tall or short until we know the distribution scale of eleven-year-old boys. Told that his z-score for height is 2.0, we would know that he is so tall that only 23 eleven-year-olds in a thousand equal his height. (This can be confirmed by the table on page 229.)

5. Correlation

One of the questions most often raised in educational research concerns the extent to which two measures are associated or the accuracy with which one measure can be predicted from another.

If we have the grades of a class in a test of reading ability and the grades of the same pupils in a more general "intelligence test," the extent of association between these can be measured. We can measure the association between high school grade point average and first year college grade point average, or between the grades of freshmen and the grades of the same persons as seniors. None of these is strikingly high in the extent of their association.

At the University of Washington 93 teachers were rated by their students in 1932. The same teachers were rated again in 1948-49 in a rather different rating plan. Do teachers change materially in student opinion? Our answer is not just yes or no but in the form of a definite measure of the association or correlation between the two sets of ratings.

Following a technique first used by the British psychologist Galton, we can plot the ratings of the Washington teachers in 1932 on one axis and those of 1948-49 on the other and get a picture of the association. In the diagram it is evident that there is some general tendency for teachers who were rated high in 1932 to be rated high in 1948-49 and the same may be noted of the low and middle ratings. There are comparatively few rated high on one occasion and low on the other.

CORRELATION OF 1932 STUDENT RATING WITH AVERAGE OF RECENT STUDENT RATINGS

AVERAGE OF RECENT RATINGS	1.6	1.8	2.0	2.2	2.4	2.6	2.8	3.0	3.2	3.4	3.6	3.8	4.0	4.2	4.4	4.6
1.0																
1.2																
1.4									11	1	11		1			
1.6				1			1		11							
1.8							11	1	1	1	11					
2.0								1	1	1						
2.2				1						11	1					
2.4					1	1			1	1		1				
2.6				1				1	1		1					
2.8						1										
3.0		1		1				1	1	11						
3.2								1								
3.4					1											
3.6					1											
3.8					1	1										
4.0																

1932 RATING

How do we measure this? The answer is comparatively simple. If ratings are reduced to z-scores, a convenient measure of association, the Pearson coefficient of correlation (named after the British statistician, Karl Pearson) is formed by multiplying the z-score of each individual in one measure by his z-score in the other measure, summing, and dividing by n, the number of individuals.

$$r = \frac{\Sigma z_1 z_2}{n}$$

The z-score, it will be remembered, is the deviation from the mean divided by the standard error. If we call the 1932 scores X scores and the 1948-49 scores Y scores, and let:

Σ = "the sum of"
X = 1932 rating
Y = 1948-49 rating
M_X = mean of X ratings
M_Y = mean of Y ratings
x $= X - M_X$
y $= Y - M_Y$
r_{xy} = correlation between X and Y
σ_x = standard deviation of X
σ_y = standard deviation of Y

we can write the formula for the coefficient of correlation thus:

$$r_{xy} = \frac{\Sigma z_x \cdot z_y}{n}$$

$$= \frac{\Sigma \dfrac{x}{\sigma_x} \cdot \dfrac{y}{\sigma_y}}{n} = \frac{\Sigma xy}{n\sigma_x\sigma_y}$$

This correlation coefficient varies from a maximum value of 1.0 when the association is perfect, through zero when there is no association, to —1.0 when the two measures are negatively related and the larger the first is, the smaller is the second. In the case of the Washington teachers the correlation is: $r =$ +0.46.

This means that there is a substantial tendency for those teachers valued highly by students in 1932 to be valued highly in 1949, but that there are numerous exceptions.

Scattergrams Illustrating Various Degrees of Correlation

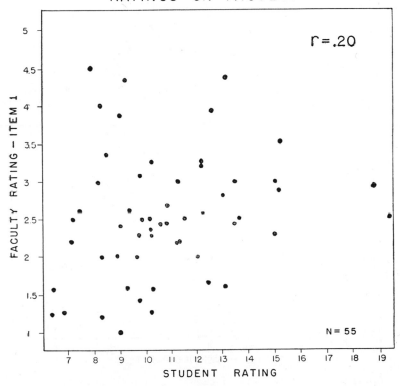

RATINGS ON FACULTY

Figure 7

This diagram shows the correlation between faculty ratings of teachers on teaching qualities and student ratings of the same teacher. This represents a very low correlation.

RELIABILITY OF FACULTY JUDGMENTS

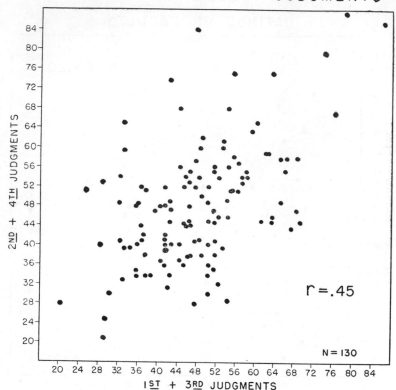

Figure 8

The diagram above shows the correlation between the combined judgments of two fellow teachers with the combined judgments of another pair on the same individual. 130 individuals are rated; the correlation ($r = 0.45$) is higher than that shown on the preceding page but lower than that on the page opposite.

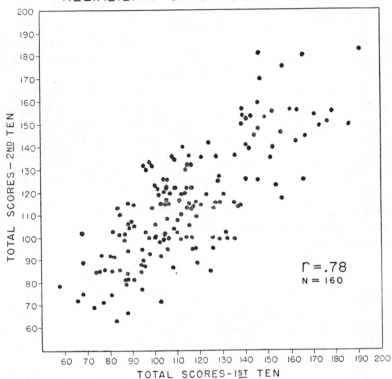

Figure 9

The above diagram represents the correlation between sum total of first and second ten opinions in each survey. It is evident that when we know the average rating the first ten students give a teacher, the average rating the next ten will give is roughly corresponding.

6. The Standard Deviation of a Difference

This is not a textbook of statistics, and the further developments of the use of statistical devices must be left to specialized texts. Only one more important statistic will here be described —the standard deviation of a difference.

In the University of Washington ratings of teachers just mentioned, we may ask: Is there a significant difference between the mean ratings of teachers in lower division (freshman and sophomore) classes and in upper division (junior and senior) classes? There is, of course, bound to be some difference between two means. Is this difference of an order that might be just due to chance (represented by the normal frequency distribution of differences)? Or is it a difference which would very rarely happen by chance even if the real means of the two groups were the same?

The standard deviation of the difference will tell the story. A difference three times its standard deviation will happen by chance 13 times in 10,000. A difference two times its standard deviation will happen by chance and where there is no real difference about two times in one hundred. When we find a difference two times its standard deviation we suspect a real difference.

The standard deviation of a difference between two means is:

$$\sigma_{m_1-m_2} = \sqrt{\sigma_{m_1}^2 + \sigma_{m_2}^2 - 2r_{12}\sigma_{m_1}\sigma_{m_2}}$$

When the two measures are not correlated, as must be true in the present case (since the measures apply to different individuals), r is zero and the standard deviation of the difference is:

$$\sigma_{m_1-m_2} = \sqrt{\sigma_{m_1}^2 + \sigma_{m_2}^2}$$

which reads: The standard deviation of the difference between two means is the square root of the sum of the squares of the standard deviations of the two means.

In these terms we can answer the question: Do Washington students rate teachers of lower division classes or teachers of upper division classes higher? The mean rating of the lower division teachers was 2.52. The mean rating of the upper division teachers was 2.36. The difference was 0.16. The standard deviation of the lower division teachers' scores was 0.58. Divided by the square root of the number of scores this gives 0.085 as the σ of the mean. The corresponding σ of the upper division teachers' scores was 0.53. Divided by the square root of the number of scores, this gives 0.073 as the σ of the mean of the upper division teachers. The σ of the difference is therefore the square root of the sum of the squares of these two quantities:

$$\sigma_{m_1 - m_2} = \sqrt{\sigma_{m_1}^2 + \sigma_{m_2}^2} = 0.11$$

The difference is 1.45 times its σ. Such a difference might occur by chance 7 times in one hundred. This makes it possible that there is no real difference between the standing of teachers in the two groups so far as student opinion is concerned. This result leaves us in some doubt about the answer to our question. If this difference could occur only once or twice in 100 times (instead of 7), we would feel certain that there is a real difference.

7. FORMULAS USED IN THIS CHAPTER

1. $M_x = \Sigma X / n$

The mean of n measures is equal to the sum of the measures divided by the number of measures.

2. $\sigma_x = \sqrt{\dfrac{\Sigma_x^2}{n}}$

The standard deviation of n measures equals the square root of the sum of the squares of their deviations from the mean divided by the number of measures.

3. $\sigma_x = \sqrt{\dfrac{\Sigma X^2}{n} - \left(\dfrac{\Sigma X}{n}\right)^2}$

The standard deviation of n measures equals the square root of the average square of the measures minus the square of the average measure.

4. $\sigma_{m_z} = \dfrac{\sigma_x}{\sqrt{n}}$

The standard deviation of the mean of n measures, X_1, X_2, X_3, $\ldots$, X_n, is the standard deviation of the measures divided by the square root of the number of measures.

5. $r_{xy} = \dfrac{\Sigma z_x z_y}{n}$

The correlation between two sets of measures of n individuals is the sum of the products of the successive pairs expressed in z scores, divided by n; or, in other words, is the average product of pairs of measures expressed as deviations from the means divided by σ.

6. $r_{xy} = \dfrac{\Sigma \dfrac{x}{\sigma_x} \cdot \dfrac{y}{\sigma_y}}{n} = \dfrac{\Sigma xy}{n \sigma_x \sigma_y}$

The correlation between two sets of measures of n individuals is the sum of the measures expressed as deviations from the mean divided by n times the product of the σ's.

7. $\sigma_{m_1 - m_2} = \sqrt{\sigma_{m_1}^2 + \sigma_{m_2}^2 - 2 r_{12} \sigma_{m_1} \sigma_{m_2}}$

The standard deviation of the difference between the means of two sets of measures is the square root of the square of the standard deviation of the mean of one set of measures plus the square of the standard deviation of the mean of the other set of measures minus the amount of correlation between the pairs of measures multiplied by the product of the standard deviation of the mean of one set of measures and the standard deviation of the means of the other set of measures.

8. $\sigma_{m_1 - m_2} = \sqrt{\sigma_{m_1}^2 + \sigma_{m_2}^2}$

Formula (7) simplifies to this when r is equal to 0; that is, when there is no correlation between the sets of measures.

QUESTIONS

1. In a normally distributed population, what per cent is above the mean?
2. What is the theoretical probability that a penny will come up heads six times in a row?
3. In Figure 5 why does the curve not quite touch the base line?
4. In a normally distributed population, what per cent have z-scores higher than 3.00?
5. If the number of measures in a distribution is decreased and the standard deviation of the distribution remains the same, what will happen to the standard deviation (or standard error) of the mean?
6. What would be the meaning of a coefficient of correlation $r=.99$?
7. Translate this formula into words: $r = \dfrac{\Sigma z_1 z_2}{n}$
8. What is the value of the Pearson coefficient of correlation r between the circumferences and the corresponding diameters of a group of circles?

Chapter 16

TRANSFER OF TRAINING

___

1. What Is Meant by Transfer?

Some Problems of Transfer.—Does knowing how to operate a typewriter aid one in learning to play the piano? Does top-notch technique in tennis carry over into skill in playing badminton? Does driving an automobile assist in learning to handle the controls of an airplane? Will knowledge of logic increase one's ability to solve abstract problems? Does honesty in one situation imply honesty in another?

Present Point of View on Transfer.—The questions in the opening paragraph are but a few of thousands that are asked daily and that must be answered. The importance of these questions lies in the fact that they put in practical form one of the most persistent and inescapable puzzles of education; namely, the problem of whether training in one function transfers to other functions, or, in other words, transfer of training. Buswell writes:

At no other point does education show its immaturity so conspicuously or suffer so much as from this failure to see that some position on transfer is the very heart of the curriculum problem or of any theory of education.[1]

According to Hendrix:

Pursuit of the problem has been kept alive by the haunting phenomena of persons who know but do not do what they know how to do. For example, persons who know that six times eight is forty-eight will often

___

[1] G. T. Buswell, "Organization and Sequence of the Curriculum," *Forty-First Yearbook*, National Society for the Study of Education, Part II, Bloomington, Ill.: Public School Publishing Co., 1942, p. 462.

count to forty-eight to find the number of chairs in a room containing six rows of eight chairs each. Any reader can supply his own list of acquaintances who know sound theory in many fields but fail to apply that theory in managing their own affairs.[2]

To believe that all skills, habits, and attitudes must be learned in nearly the situation in which they are later to be used inclines toward a job-analysis approach to curriculum building. The psychological strength of this view is that it is exact and specific. The curricular approach is to break down skills, knowledge, or attitudes into psychological components and to arrange these into courses of study. This attack has been advocated in one form or another perennially, and its persuasiveness as a method lies in the considerable experimental evidence that learning is specific in nature and that the most effective method of establishing a conditioned reaction to a novel situation is to practice the behavior in the form or under the circumstances in which it is to be used. In a recent study, Wesman worked with a group of secondary school pupils in order to measure the transfer from high school subjects to general intelligence. As a result of these studies he reached the following conclusion:

In general, the study failed to reveal superior transfer to intelligence for any one of the achievement areas measured, and indicated the desirability of direct training in mental processes rather than dependence on transfer from school subjects.[3]

The alternative approach to the problem of transfer stresses training in general modes of performance, such as attitudes, with practice in applying basic principles to given problems. To quote Mursell:

Meanings and generalized insights should be emphasized in all learnings everywhere. Learning points toward the future; it is undertaken in the hope and expectation of transfer. Nothing is ever used in the precise setting in which it was acquired. Therefore, to try to determine the course of efficient learning by specific prediction of future conditions is not only impossible in practice, but wrong in principle.

[2] *Elementary School Journal*, XLVIII (1947), 197.
[3] Alexander Wesman, "A Study of Transfer of Training from High School Subjects to Intelligence," *Teachers College Record*, XLVI (1945), p. 393.

Learning affects the future and transfers to new and unpredictable situations in so far as it is generalized.[4]

Mursell has described a form of the deductive method of which the mainstay is the body of abstractions from which the learner is expected to make inferential applications. The center of emphasis is upon generalized modes of behavior and the ability to select the proper technique to be employed from an analysis of the job to be done. The strength of the deductive approach is that much greater coverage of a wider variety of problem situations is given; its weakness is that in many instances the learner is not able to analyze the problem situation thoroughly or to make the required application. Obviously, teaching general principles and methods of applying them to the specific depends upon a high degree of transfer. Orata says on this point:

The educational significance of this notion of transfer is clear and unmistakable. If transfer is facilitated by concept formation, then education, in order to facilitate transfer, must of necessity be concept building. It is a process of equipping the individual with concepts which are rich in meanings so that he can apply them in meeting various life situations.[5]

Historical Background.—Our understanding of transfer of training is clarified by a glance at the history of the development of the theory. Transfer of training was stated in purest form by the advocates of formal discipline. These proponents accepted the faculty concept of mind, i.e., that mind is made of many separate abilities or faculties such as will, perception, memory, reasoning, and judgment. Since the primary function of education was thought to be that of *disciplining the mind,* it then followed that the discipline should be specific to the faculty trained. In other words, certain classes of subject matter—subjects or courses—would most effectively discipline or train

[4] Reprinted from *Educational Psychology* by James L. Mursell, by permission of W. W. Norton & Company, Inc. Copyright 1939 by the publishers. P. 254.
[5] Pedro Tamesis Orata, *The Theory of Identical Elements,* Columbus, O.: Ohio State University Press, 1928, p. 177.

memory. Other courses might be used to train the will power and still others the reason, etc. For each faculty there would be a separate subject. A further assumption held was that intensive training in subject matter would so improve the faculty that the learner would thereafter behave much more efficiently in a wide variety of new situations. Formal discipline techniques would, then, train the mind by specific exercise in much the same way that a boxer might increase the strength of his right arm.

William James [6] was probably the first to offer a scientific challenge to this doctrine. He set out to test whether or not his own ability to memorize poetry might be improved by previous experience in memorizing poetry. His results were a clear-cut challenge to the validity of the doctrine of formal discipline, for his performance was actually less efficient after training. The initial work of James stimulated tremendous interest in the problem and also provided a method for such investigations.

McGeoch has outlined three current and frequently used methods of measuring the results of transfer of training. Each method makes use of two groups of subjects, which ideally should be "equal" in characteristics and abilities bearing on the investigated problem. An outline of his methods follows:

Method One:

Control: Test 1 of R_1		Test 2 of R_1
Experimental: Test 1 of R_1	Training in R_2	Test 2 of R_1

Method Two:

Group 1:	Training in R_1	Test 1 of R_2
Group 2:	Training in R_2	Test 1 of R_1

Method Three:

Control:	. . . .	Test 1 of R_1
Experimental:	Training in R_2	Test 1 of R_1 [7]

---

[6] William James, *The Principles of Psychology*, Vol. I.
[7] John A. McGeoch, *The Psychology of Human Learning*, New York: Longmans, Green & Co., 1942, pp. 396-98.

A comparison of results obtained on the final tests by the two groups is then possible, and constitutes a measurement of the influence of training in one activity upon the performance of some other activity.

An interesting and possibly very useful innovation of control group design has been suggested recently by Solomon.[8] This suggestion is that two or possibly three control groups might be employed in the same investigation and given the following sequence of testing and differential experience:

	Experimental Group	Control Group I	Control Group II
Pre-test	yes	yes	no
Training, Education	yes	no	yes
Post-test	yes	yes	yes

Thorndike and Woodworth [9] became especially interested in the problem and checked on transfer of training in perceptual tasks. Among the more important conclusions derived from their research were: (1) that there are two kinds of transfer—namely, positive and negative transfer; (2) that the amount of transfer is seldom, if ever, as great as the amount of increment obtained from direct practice; and (3) that the transfer which occurs is a function of the conditions of training. *Positive* transfer refers to an improvement in performance after training on a second task. *Negative* transfer, on the other hand, refers to a decrement or decreased performance after training. The terms *associative inhibition* or *proactive inhibition* are often used to indicate negative transfer effects. Many apply the known facts regarding positive and negative transfer when they state that learning to give a familiar response to a new stimulus is quite easy to master, but learning to give a new response to a familiar stimulus is relatively difficult. In the first instance positive transfer or facilitation of learning is evident, while in the latter there is a negative transfer or an inhibition of learn-

[8] Richard L. Solomon, "An Extension of Control Group Design," *Psychological Bulletin*, XLVI (1949), 137-49.
[9] *Psychological Review*, VIII (1901), 247-61; 384-95; 553-64.

ing. The teacher might find her task made much simpler if it were possible to arrange training with a preponderance of learning old familiar responses to new stimulus patterns and fewer instances of learning new responses for old familiar stimuli.

A most elaborate transfer study was made by Thorndike. Some 8,564 high school students were given initial and final tests designed to measure selective and rational thinking. The groups were equated by means of scores made on the first test. Students in the control and experimental groups then took courses differing by one subject for the academic year. This differential training was then investigated as a cause of transfer effects revealed on the second test. Thorndike states his own conclusions in the following:

> By any reasonable interpretation of the results, the intellectual values of studies should be determined largely by the special information, habits, interests, attitudes, and ideals which they demonstrably produce. The expectation of any large differences in general improvement of the mind from one study rather than another seems doomed to disappointment. The chief reason why good thinkers seem superficially to have been made such by having taken certain school studies, is that good thinkers have taken such studies, becoming better by the inherent tendency of the good to gain more than the poor from any study. When the good thinkers studied Greek and Latin, these studies *seemed* to make good thinking. Now that the good thinkers study Physics and Trigonometry, these seem to make good thinkers. If the abler pupils should all study Physical Education and Dramatic Art, these subjects would seem to make good thinkers. . . . After positive correlation of gain with initial ability is allowed for, the balance in favor of any study is certainly not large. Disciplinary values may be real and deserve weight in the curriculum, but the weights should be reasonable.[10]

It is to be expected that once the facts of transfer had been experimentally established there would follow numerous theories attempting to explain how transfer takes place. Thorndike was, again, one of the first to offer such an explanation. In 1903, he wrote:

---

[10] *Journal of Educational Psychology*, XV (1924), 1-22; 83-89.

The answer which I shall try to defend is that a change in one function alters any other only in so far as the two functions have as factors
identical elements.[11]

He also suggested that nervous impulses might use much the
same neural pathways if two activities were sufficiently alike in
specific components. Identical elements in differing functions
might be in terms of identical motives, content, performance,
skill, ideals, techniques, or principles. In 1906 Thorndike
classified two kinds of identity, namely, identity of content and
skill and identity of procedure. Thorndike's explanation has
been referred to as the theory of identical elements.

Judd,[12] on the other hand, offered a quite different explanation in his proposal that transfer takes place to the extent that
one generalizes his experiences. His theory was deduced from
an experiment with boys shooting at a target under water. One
group was given special training in the principles of refraction
of light under water. This group exhibited a greater proficiency
in hitting the target whether it was submerged in twelve inches
or four inches of water. Those who understood the relevant
principles adjusted efficiently to changed conditions. In other
words, their training transferred by the generalization of a
principle to a variety of situations to which it was applicable.
Judd's statement which follows illustrates his viewpoint:

. . . mental development consists . . . in equipping the individual with
the power to think abstractly and to form general ideas.

When the ends thus described are attained, transfer . . . has taken
place because it is the very nature of generalization and abstraction that
they extend beyond the particular experiences in which they originate.[13]

Such, then, is the *theory of generalization.*

While both theories leave much to be desired as a complete
explanation of how transfer takes place, they have significance
from a practical point of view. One suggests that teachers

---

[11] Edward L. Thorndike, *Educational Psychology,* New York: The
Science Press, 1903, p. 80.
[12] *Educational Review,* XXXVI (1908), 28-42.
[13] Charles Hubbard Judd, *Psychology of Secondary Education,* Boston:
Ginn & Co., 1927, p. 441.

should emphasize similarities in content, skill, and procedure so that the learner would be "set" for successful transfer. The other suggests an emphasis upon general principles and basic techniques having broad application and hence great transfer value. General principles are important vehicles of transfer, but a knowledge of them does not guarantee that transfer will occur. Transfer is more likely if students are stimulated to a desire to apply principles learned and are also taught to note similarities between the familiar and the new situation.

Definition of Transfer. How, then, is transfer of training to be defined in the light of its complicated history and also of present attitudes and findings? *Transfer may be defined as a process of extending and applying behavior.* In explaining transfer, Sandiford [14] writes:

If a person studies or practices subject matter *A,* a specific improvement in *A* is expected. This is called *learning.* . . . Beyond this specific improvement there is usually a spread of the effect of study or practice which enables the person to learn *B, C,* or *D* more easily than would otherwise have been the case. This spread is called *transfer of training,* which is based on the theory that regards learning as not wholly specific in character and emphasizes the tendency for learning in one field to spill over and affect other fields.

Witherington expresses the same idea in a slightly different manner:

In any situation, the extent to which learning is facilitated or obstructed by some previous learning of a kindred but not identical nature is called transfer of training [15]

Transfer is generally of two types, of skills and of attitudes. The first is likely to be on a habit level and in response to a relatively stereotyped environment. The second is more general in nature and given in response to a more complicated stimulus

---

[14] From Monroe: *Encyclopedia of Educational Research,* p. 1306. Copyright, 1941, by the American Educational Research Association. Used by permission of The Macmillan Company.
[15] H. Carl Witherington, *Educational Psychology,* Boston: Ginn & Co., 1946, p. 371.

pattern. The dual nature of the process is expressed as follows
by Judd:

Trained intelligence is particular in its contents but general in its
methods. It is characteristic of human thinking that wherever one
encounters any phenomenon one tends to interpret it in terms of general
categories.[16]

2. Conditions and Kinds of Transfer

Factors Related to Transfer.—By definition intelligence is
very closely related to transfer, for it is most often described as
the ability to adjust to new situations by means of symbolic
processes or abstraction. Thorndike's research offers empirical
evidence of such relationship. In an investigation of the effect
of a year's training in various high school subjects upon selective and rational thinking, he found that the superior group
made an average gain of 20.5 points while the lower group made
a gain of only 1.5 points. A somewhat similar relationship was
noted by Carroll.[17] Errors made by bright pupils gave evidence
of logical transfer in that the errors usually involved one letter
and were phonetically sound. This logical tendency was not
evidenced in the errors made by duller children.

The nature of the training will determine in great measure
the likelihood and amount of transfer. An eight-year study[18]
indicated greater observable gains made by students who had
participated in an activity program. In this study 1,475
matched pairs of students from thirty high schools were compared with respect to success in college. The experimental subjects (those having previous experience in activity programs)
were notably more interested, earned slightly higher grades,
received honors more frequently, and participated more actively
in college affairs. Other differences cited were more systematic
and objective thinking, and better adjustment in choice of vocations. A recent study by DiMichael[19] indicates that transfer

[16] Charles Hubbard Judd, *op. cit.*, p. 417.
[17] *Journal of Educational Psychology*, XXI (1930), 489-99.
[18] Wilford M. Aikin, *The Story of the Eight-Year Study*, pp. 102-15.
[19] *Journal of Educational Psychology*, XXXIV (1943), 166-75

effects of methods and techniques should be judged with reference to particular students and subjects. Woodrow's [20] classical study compared the effect of practice in memorizing with the effect of practice and training. His control group spent the interval between testings in verbatim memorization of poetry and nonsense syllables. The experimental group received instruction in techniques and principles of memorizing as well as in memory drill. The trained subjects (experimental group) showed gains statistically significant at the 1 per cent level of confidence when foretests and aftertests used poetry, prose facts, dates, vocabulary, and memory-span materials.

Evidence also indicates that transfer is influenced by the amount of training. The exact nature of the influence is not so clear, for increased practice may and often does increase the amount of transfer. However, some investigators note that occasionally increased practice sets up a negative transfer.[21] Siipola and Isreal [22] found in code-learning that negative transfer appears with small amounts of practice, while with increase in practice a change to positive transfer results.

Transfer of training is conceivably also a function of the time interval between pretest and post-test. Will a learner's ability to use material he has learned in another situation decrease as his retention of the first learned material decreases? A study by Bunch [23] indicates that the amount of transfer from learning one problem to a new situation is independent of the time interval up to ninety days. A possible explanation is that transfer in this case was in terms of a mode of problem solution rather than in terms of specific identities. If so, the study supports the notion that general principles are more resistant to forgetting, and therefore should be the more emphasized in training procedures.

In the classroom situation, transfer of training may be facilitated by developing an *expectation* of transfer value. This expectation should be consciously recognized by both teacher and

[20] *Journal of Educational Psychology*, XVIII (1927), 159-72.
[21] See *Journal of Experimental Psychology*, IV (1921), 270-99.
[22] *American Journal of Psychology*, XLV (1933), 205.
[23] *Journal of Comparative Psychology*, XXII (1936), 325-37.

student. It may be largely a matter of integrating present motives with more long-term objectives. Transfer may be increased by simply stating in clear understandable language that here is a skill, an understanding, a fact, a principle, an attitude that will have future value and usefulness.

Transfer of Subject Matter.—All school subjects have some common characteristics, and what is learned in one subject may be applied in others. There are also parallel relationships in subject matter and learning which facilitate both learning and transfer of learning. These relationships are:

1. *Orientation of the pupil.* School subjects normally consist of departmentalized materials for the improved adjustment of the learner. Much can be learned by rote, however, in any subject without producing a corresponding improvement in the learner's adjustment. In all subjects there are derived principles which must be applied to a variety of specific conditions if they are to become general to the pupil. This specific applying of a principle can be initiated by either the teacher or the pupil. The teacher may make such applications either to increase the understanding of the principle itself or to facilitate the practical application to the vital situations in which the pupil is directed to use his general principle. If specific use of a principle is to be made in practical life situations, these situations must be selected for their own worth as well as for their availability. Second, the pupil must see relationships between the conditions in which the principle has been learned and other situations of his own choosing. The teacher often has time only for teaching the principle under one set of circumstances, while the pupil can gain mastery only by practice in application.

2. *Nature of subject matter organization.* All subjects provide progressive series of stimuli. The learning of a subject is, therefore, in certain respects sequential and accumulative in topical organization. What is learned at one stage is needed at a later stage. Many ineffective attempts to learn more than the rudiments of a subject are due to the inadequate mastery of the rudiments themselves. The removal of this difficulty consists not only of finding it but also of devising means for making

the rudiments significant and gripping for the beginner. The order of topics can often be changed so that pupils are not plunged at the outset into a maze of definitions.

Certain subjects are apparently more sequential and accumulative than others. A casual examination of any of the later theorems of geometry shows the learner's dependence upon the foregoing portions of this subject. This dependence is less apparent in literature, in which each topic or masterpiece may supply, through its own context, a sufficient background for the necessary understanding and aesthetic experiencing of it. The order in which *Silas Marner, Treasure Island,* and *The Courtship of Miles Standish* are read has, for example, little bearing upon the effective study of these classics.

In addition to the cumulative nature of the content of school subjects, there is a sequential character in the procedure used in the study of successive topics or materials. The advantages of this sequential treatment are fully enjoyed only in subjects which are always pursued in a certain sequence. Mathematics and foreign languages have such advantage in large measure, while history and literature have relatively less. Judd [24] has suggested four stages in teaching history at which successive demands in procedure could be required of pupils. The first stage demands only the ability to follow the story, little explanation of events being expected of pupils. The second stage demands an understanding and correlating of the physical facts, such as geographical conditions, which influence history. The third stage demands a critical study of historical evidence as found in source materials. The fourth stage demands a critical comparison of historical interpretations as given by different authorities.

If the entire sequence of courses in mathematics is considered, one finds the situation roughly conformable with the four stages in history learning described by Judd. The first stage in mathematics is devoted to simple experiences with numbers, the second to the development of principles and simple applications, the third and the fourth to the understanding and application of

---

[24] Charles Hubbard Judd, *Psychology of High-School Subjects,* pp. 456 ff.

interrelated materials and principles. Similarly increased demands at successive stages are made in all sequentially organized subjects.

The sequential and cumulative character of any year's work in a course is also common to all subjects when they are well organized. Geometry is an example of this, because this subject is always so organized. History has the same character when day-by-day or piecemeal learning of facts gives way to the continuity which is emphasized by all excellent historians. Then the unity of all human experience and an understanding of the present in the light of the past follow. Interrelationships of an analogous character can be found in any subject by anyone who is competent to teach it.

3. *Relationships as a basis for transfer.* Transfer of training is one of the simplest and also one of the most important characteristics of school subjects properly taught. It consists simply of using either content or method and their accompanying attitudes in one situation after they have already been acquired in another. Any subject that has been learned well enough to give training in useful subject matter or methods or attitudes can be applied to later situations. Transfer takes place preeminently within each subject, just as it does within each branch of an occupation, but it occurs also among various interrelated subjects and occupations.

Although the concept of the transfer of training is simple, the process by which it takes place is not. It requires the ability to see and act upon relationships. This process occurs with either subject matter or method, when one situation is known and understood well enough to admit of transfer, and when another situation is seen to have elements that are similar to the first situation. Hepner states:

Transfer of training depends upon the conscious acceptance by the learner of methods, procedures, principles, sentiments, and ideals which are common to the past subject and present interest. We make transfers whenever and wherever we sense a later experience as being similar to a previous one.[25]

[25] Harry Walker Hepner, *Psychology Applied to Life and Work,* New York: Prentice-Hall, Inc., 1941, p. 408.

To the person who is expected to make the transfer, the relationship between the situations seems simple or even obvious after it has been noted. It is not always obvious to the learner, and therefore transfer is not an automatic or necessary consequence of the mere presentation of similar situations in a sequence. One of the simplest cases of transfer is found in mathematics when, after learning how to solve a problem of a given pattern, a pupil solves additional problems of the same pattern, although the language of the successive problems is different. When the learner proceeds through problems in the four fundamental processes of arithmetic to a problem in which all these processes are involved, the transfer is more complex. When he proceeds from the logical method of geometry to a problem in history or any other subject, he may transfer the method learned in geometry. If he generalizes upon his experience in this manner, he is working upon a still higher level. Concepts then interpenetrate, as Orata [26] asserts, and by their interpenetration are applied to varying situations and enriched in content. These stages in transfer approximate the stages in history, mathematics, and other subjects as mentioned above. That transfer of this sort can take place in the laboratory as well as in the classroom was long ago demonstrated by Coover. [27] As situations are sometimes similar in certain respects and dissimilar in other essential respects, transfer, as Webb [28] showed at about the same time as Coover's experiments, may temporarily interfere with the learning of a new pattern of conduct. Such interference is increased [29] when the second situation is attempted before the first has been thoroughly learned. This may happen if a pupil attempts to proceed too rapidly in any school subject.

Whipple's summary of the pedagogical significance of the transfer of training is as clear as any before or since. The six points which follow epitomize the present discussion as well as Whipple's summary:

[26] Orata, *op. cit.*, p. 177.
[27] J. E. Coover, *Psychological Monographs*, XX, No. 3 (1916).
[28] L. W. Webb, *Psychological Monographs*, XXIV, No. 3 (1917).
[29] See Edward C. Tolman, *Psychological Monographs*, XXV, No. 1 (1917), p. 48.

1. . . . Teachers should arrange the work of pupils and their own instructional efforts in such a way as to facilitate the conscious recognition by the pupils of the methods by which efficient mental work is done.

2. . . . A skillful and "artistic" teacher will take pains to see that facts are so presented that pupils draw out the relations between these facts and utilize these relations in the handling of other sets of facts in which similar relations obtain.

3. . . . Teachers may expect bright children to surpass dull children in the amount of transfer gained from specific training; moreover, in proportion as the child's intelligence is inadequate, in that proportion must the teacher himself consciously and purposefully bring the child's attention to the relations to be educed and to the use of these relations subsequently. Even when aided by such skillful instruction, the spread of training will be decidedly less in the dull.

4. . . .The possibilities of the transfer of training should be found at their maximum in children, whose mental activities are still in the formative stage. While adults possess a much higher intrinsic capacity than do children to effect the education, the conceptualization, and the applications of relationships, this capacity is less evident in practice simply because the vast majority of these relations have already been educed, conceptualized, and applied under the stress of the extended daily experience and training they have already had.

5. . . . It is not only probable, but fairly certain, that some of the most important agencies of transfer are to be found among the higher-level relations, in generalized attitudes, moods, ideals, sets, ways of going about mental operations generally. These agencies are in the nature of the case obscure; the nature and extent of their participation has occasioned extended argument, largely futile because so little is known factually. Further study is much needed, but difficult. In the meantime the educator is not justified in resorting to any specific subject of instruction for the purpose primarily of deriving from it indirect training values, but neither is he justified in neglecting to derive from every subject all the training value that it seems to promise.

6. . . . It is particularly in the field of moral education that there has prevailed a general and uncritical acceptance of the dogma of formal discipline. While it is probably true that through the agency of the higher-level relations there may occur an important development of certain quasi-moral attitudinal traits, there has been no clear experimental demonstration of this transfer and it remains precisely in this important

field of moral education that we know least about the possibilities or the limitations of training.[30]

Transfer of Attitudes.—*Attitudes* are defined as acquired dispositions to react in certain ways to situations, objects, or persons. The transfer of an attitude from one situation to another is a common experience of everyone and is cited in many reports of investigations of transfer. Transfer of attitude may be the mere continuance of a feeling of gloom or of buoyancy through a day. Confidence in the outcome of a new project may follow the successful performance of a prior task. In the transfer of attitudes, as in that of subject matter or method, the counsel of the teacher is often needed, and as Davis [31] states:

Attitudes in children are most often patterned after example and may be influenced more by the manifestations of attitudes by the teacher than by abstract precepts.

This counsel is sometimes called inspirational, if the attitude to be transferred is one like confidence or self-reliance; but the transfer is dependent, in such cases, upon a previous successful experience. If one examines instances of the transfer or continuance of attitudes, one finds a close similarity between this transfer and the generalization involved in other transfer. In all cases, transfer is a mechanism of progressive conduct. For this reason, transfer of training in one form or another is the most frequent and the most important of the characteristics which are common in the learning of all school subjects. To quote Pressey and Robinson:

The problem of transfer may then be considered almost educationally all-pervasive. It might almost be said that if there is to be education there must be transfer, for the purpose of education is to prepare for meeting situations which must inevitably differ in many respects from the educational situation in which the preparation was acquired.[32]

---

[30] Guy M. Whipple, "The Transfer of Training," *Twenty-Seventh Year-book,* National Society for the Study of Education, Part II, pp. 203-09.

[31] By permission from *Educational Psychology,* by Robert A. Davis, pp. 126-27. Copyrighted, 1948. McGraw-Hill Book Co., Inc.

[32] Sidney L. Pressey and Francis P. Robinson, *Psychology and the New Education.* Rev. ed., New York: Harper & Bros., Publishers, 1944, p. 573.

Transfer of Training and Teaching.—The teacher's acceptance or rejection of the formal discipline theory of transfer, the identical elements or generalization explanation, will be reflected in numerous day-to-day teaching practices. The *subject-matter* teacher no doubt would give evidence of an actual, if not verbal, acceptance of the formal discipline doctrine. Exposure to the content of certain courses becomes in itself, then, the objective of education. Methods of teaching and the attempt to link content and the needs of the learner are of relatively secondary importance. The student must conform to subject matter requirements and must develop a docile, submissive role.

A challenging or questioning attitude on the part of the teacher as regards the validity of the formal discipline doctrine paves the way for educational experimentation. The teacher will ask what values, direct and indirect, are being served by pupil participation in given curricular areas. He will be willing to revise content and method as facts regarding transfer are uncovered. The child will be viewed as a growing and developing organism constantly organizing and reorganizing experiences into more or less efficient patterns of behavior. The discovery of the child's interests and wise use of effective incentives in order to motivate participation become primary tasks of instruction.

QUESTIONS

1. Explain the importance of the problem of transfer of training. Define the term.
2. Discuss the two different positions taken in solving this problem.
3. What are the two types of transfer? Give examples of each from your own experience.
4. Explain what is meant by sequential organization. How does this system aid transfer?
5. Discuss the four stages in teaching history as formulated by Judd. How can this technique be applied in your major field?
6. List Whipple's six points concerning transfer.
7. Cite some instances of transfer of attitudes from your own experience.

PART IV

IMPROVING LEARNING HABITS

Chapter 17

THE PSYCHOLOGY OF REMEDIAL PROCEDURES

---

1. WHY REMEDIAL TECHNIQUES ARE NECESSARY

Learning Never Perfect.—Golfers usually need remedial education. Why? Because the average dub golfer has learned to play the game by going out to the golf course with a bag of clubs, usually ill-assorted, and starting to bang a golf ball around. That is the reason why the majority of golfers cannot "break a hundred" honestly. It also strongly indicates one of the paramount considerations bearing on the problem of remedial education, namely, the cardinal importance of correct initial technique and the absolute necessity for accurate primary responses. In other words, the finest remedial education in the world is the prevention of any need for it. Fernald says on this point:

> In most cases in which remedial work is effective, the use of proper methods during the early stages of learning would have prevented the development of maladjustments in later life. Consequently, the application of remedial techniques before the child has failed is one of the most important phases of clinical psychology.[1]

In the same vein, Gates [2] writes:

> Prevention is, of course, better than cure. Prevention may be secured to a considerable extent by giving very diligent attention to the initial stages of learning.

---

[1] By permission from *Remedial Techniques in Basic School Subjects,* by Grace M. Fernald, p. 2. Copyrighted, 1943. McGraw-Hill Book Co., Inc.

[2] From Arthur I. Gates *et al., Educational Psychology,* pp. 349-50. Copyright, 1948 by The Macmillan Company and used with their permission.

That it will ever be possible to raise the educational system to a level of efficiency where a widespread and systematic program of remedial education will be unnecessary is too much to hope. Benson [3] points out that since guidance is not infallible and since learning is a form of trial-and-error process, there is nearly always a need for remedial work.

To begin with, not all teachers are masters of the subjects which they teach. Particularly in rural districts where surveys show it is necessary for the beginning teacher to handle anywhere from one to seven or eight subjects there is likelihood that the pupil will get an inadequate grounding in proper fundamentals. Bowen [4] claims that "there are, in fact, about 120,000 one-teacher schools in the United States." These schools, she continues, are taught by the least trained and experienced teachers in the fields. Their material is "largely of the subject-matter-set-out-to-be-learned type" with minimum requirements for each grade. The combination of these two factors makes adequate coverage of material almost impossible.

Remedial education is not a needless luxury, but the kinds and amount of remedial education needed can probably be reduced by better teacher preparation, better assignment of teachers, better supervision, and a more adequate system of checks of pupil progress through the use of scientific measurement.

All Remedial Teaching Not the Same.—There is a special point to be noted in connection with remedial education in both motor and abstract learning. When we speak of remedial procedures, the majority of teachers think of something incorrectly taught in the first place, which is natural enough since at the present time this type does constitute the bulk of the remedial work being done. It should be borne in mind, however, that efficiency is a relative term. For example, we usually term a man a master golfer because he has bested other golfers in competition. Just how close he may be to the limit of his own abso-

---

[3] Charles E. Benson et al., *Psychology for Teachers*. Rev. ed., p. 353.
[4] Genevieve Bowen, *Living and Learning in a Rural School*, p. ix. Copyright, 1944, by The Macmillan Company and used with their permission.

lute potential performance, however, is seldom known. It is a
notorious fact in the field of athletic competition that when one
man or team is much better than all the competition and win-
ning presents no problem, there is a tendency to let down. The
point of this line of reasoning and illustration is this: remedial
procedures are helpful, not only to those grossly deficient in the
lowest levels of fundamental accomplishment but also to those
at all higher levels of attainment, even the experts. Blair [5]
writes:

> Remedial teaching is essentially good teaching which takes the pupil
> at his own level and by intrinsic methods of motivation leads him to in-
> creased standards of competence.

As a matter of fact, the expert is more often than not merely
the person who has been uncommonly assiduous in improving
his technique and remedying its faults. We should avoid the
fallacy of the all-or-none theory of learning when it applies to
complex behavior. Thus we hear talk of those who can read
and those who cannot; those who can spell and those who cannot; those who appreciate music and those who do not, etc.
This tendency to regard teaching as dividing the population into
two mutually exclusive groups is psychologically pernicious in
the extreme. The real point is that the majority of those who
can read could read much better if attention were given to improving their reading habits further. Dr. Samuel Renshaw [6]
is proving the truth of this statement in his laboratories at Ohio
State University where he is teaching college students to read
four times faster than before. Therefore, it is strongly urged
upon teachers and prospective teachers that they devote some
time and attention to remedial procedures even for those whose
performance has reached a nominally satisfactory norm. Remedial work with the average and supernormal group will pay
greater dividends than with any other, since it is from these
groups that the expert performers will come. The real task in

---

[5] From Glenn Myers Blair, *Diagnostic and Remedial Teaching in Secondary Schools,* pp. 16-17. Copyright, 1946, by The Macmillan Company and
used with their permission.
[6] See David G. Wittels, "You're Not as Smart as You Could Be," *The
Saturday Evening Post,* CCXX (1948), 20-21 ff.

remedial teaching becomes one of human engineering. Each student's achievement must be judged in terms of his demonstrated as against his potential performance. Any student who, under the existing conditions, is performing below par for *him* is in need of remedial training.

The engineering approach demands a systematic procedure, or at least a clear-cut understanding of the steps a teacher may take in order to *locate* difficulties. This is basically a problem of diagnosis in order to individualize instruction. Brueckner [7] suggests the following methods of diagnosis available to the teacher:

1. Observation of the pupil at work on his daily assignments, noting his study habits and procedures, attitudes toward school and school work, interests, and motivations.
2. Supplementary analysis of various characteristics of pupil's written work.
3. Supplementary analysis of the pupil's oral responses and reactions.
4. The use of objective, analytical diagnostic devices proposed especially to bring into relief weakness in critical problems, including such devices as diagnostic charts of errors in handwriting, arithmetic and spelling and language standard progress tests, study habit inventories, and diagnostic inventories prepared by the teacher for specific units of study.
5. Interviews with the pupil, parents, and fellow pupils.
6. Laboratory procedures, including the use of such instruments as the kymograph, tachistoscope, motion picture camera, dictaphone, and records.

While standardized achievement tests are typically designed to measure information and content, some are designed to check on the child's growth in basic skills such as alphabetizing or using formulae, tables and graphs, timetables, and maps. Basic skill tests often point up the cause for poor achievement on

[7] L. J. Brueckner, "Techniques of Diagnosis," *Thirty-Fourth Yearbook,* National Society for the Study of Education, pp. 142-52.

informational tests. A testing program is not complete unless it checks on the achievement of skills as well as on informational mastery.

Very often the most helpful remedial instruction is that of training the student in *how to study*. Recently a very well-trained and capable young piano teacher expressed what to her was a personal discovery when she exclaimed, "After this, I shall spend most of each lesson period just explaining *how* to practice the assigned numbers." Making the assignment and using inspirational and motivational devices are important parts of the teacher's task, but a systematic and thorough training in the "how to do it" or the "know how" aspect must never be overlooked.

Analysis is the key to all successful remedial instruction. Students often complain of poor spelling ability. Very frequently a sense of utter hopelessness is clearly evident when the student confesses to having misspelled half the words in a theme. A systematic tallying of words misspelled and the frequency of error for each word is a first practical step. It is not uncommon to discover that a concentrated attack on the most frequently misspelled words leads to a remarkable reduction in percentage of error. The job becomes a possible one, and at least some degree of success is automatically made possible. Location of errors and clearly defined and attainable goals are often all that the student needs to set him on the right track for improved performance.

Methods courses should provide the aspiring instructor with carefully organized inventories or check lists to aid in the identification of remedial needs. In the elementary grades such a list might include the following as suggested for reading by McKee:

1. [p. 269] *Inability to work out the pronunciation of a strange word.* This deficiency may be caused by such factors as the child's lack of acquaintance with important sound elements and inability to blend the sounds of different elements, a hit-or-miss rather than a left-to-right attack on word forms, and dependence upon only one tool such as phonetic analysis. . . . [p. 330] lack of skill in using the context, and failure to use phonetic analysis, structural analysis, and the context in conjunction with one another. . . .

[p. 400] Likewise, some intermediate grade pupils are not able to work out the meanings of strange words independently. A given pupil's deficiency may be caused by inability to use verbal context, lack of skill in using pictures, or lack of ability in using the dictionary correctly. . . .

2. [p. 269] *Failure to see likenesses and differences in the forms of words and in letters to the extent that confusions are not eliminated.* The child who has this deficiency substitutes unlike words or unlike letters for one another. He substitutes for each other words that are similar or letters that are closely similar. He confuses *on* and *no, went* and *want, back* and *book, t* and *f, b* and *d, p* and *q.* In dealing with this deficiency, the first step is to discover the particular confusions made by the child. Then the distinguishing or cue differences between the confused forms should be pointed out clearly. . . . [p. 339] He reverses letters, groups of letters, and words, and he transposes letters and words. . . .

3. [p. 270] *Failure to hear differences in the sounds of letters.* . . .

4. [p. 270] *Making reversals.* . . . Those who reverse the order of letters in words need definite instruction in attacking words systematically from left to right. . . .

5. [p. 270] *Failure to keep the place.* Give the pupil who has this failing a 3 x 5 index card to use as a line marker by moving it down the page line by line as each line is read. . . .

6. [p. 270] *Failure to read persistently from left to right.* The child whose eyes move too much at random along a line rather than consistently from left to right. . . .

7. [pp. 270-71] *Saying the words to himself.* . . . Usually this vocalization is a hangover from the use of the oral approach in beginning reading and does not constitute a handicap until the child's powers of comprehension are such that he could read more rapidly with adequate understanding than his lip movement or vocalization permits. The following suggestions are concerned with the removal of the retarding and unnecessary type of lip movement and vocalization:

1. Provide the child with a large amount of simple interesting reading matter.

2. Use rapid exposure exercises with flash cards that contain sentences rather than single words.

3. Tell the child that his reading is slowed down by saying the words to himself and that he can help himself by sincerely trying to keep from saying the words.

4. Have the pupil hold a harmless object such as a pencil or an eraser between his lips as he reads.

5. Set up a problem or question which is answered somewhere in a given paragraph. Have the child read the paragraph, giving him a brief time to find the needed information. Use this type of exercise frequently.

8. [p. 271] *Failure to read with sufficient understanding.* . . . These pupils who have focused their attention almost solely upon word identification and recognition and have failed to demand meaning in their reading need special practice in comprehension. . . .

9. [p. 273] *Failure to read aloud fluently.* . . . The pupil who reads word by word has little if any eye-voice span, his eyes being no farther on in the reading than his voice. . . .

10. [p. 340] *Inability to read silently with sufficient speed.* . . .[8]

This is merely a sample of what may be provided for teachers of any subject at any level either by experts or by the teacher as her experience and understanding grow.

Remedial instruction must be based on the most careful job analysis of which both educational specialists and in-service teachers are capable. It includes a study of the movements, habits, perceptual cues, motives, incentives, and attitudes correlated with the educational activity under consideration. Many of the deficiencies just mentioned as constituting reading remedial needs may well be a function of physical disabilities. Vision and auditory tests, carefully administered, should be step number one in any remedial program. Learning is in very large measure a perceptual task, and a fundamental principle of behavior is that perception is definitely limited by the structural characteristics of the learner. Organic defects are definitely a part of the learner's reality. Moreover, personality maladjustment is often related to spelling, language, and reading disability. Such relationship is recognized with every listing of psychological causation of stuttering, functional paralysis, word-blindness, mirror-writing, and so on.

---

[8] Paul McKee, *The Teaching of Reading in the Elementary School,* Boston: Houghton Mifflin Co., 1948, pp. 269-73, 337-41, 399-407. By permission of the publishers.

2. Re-education

Difficulties of Re-education.—Let us now consider for a time the essentially psychological problem presented in remedial procedures for those pupils who are deficient in correct fundamental technique. If it is deemed necessary to change completely a behavior pattern, a stubborn problem of reconditioning is indicated. It has long been axiomatic in psychology that relearning the same act is more difficult than learning it correctly in the first place. According to Benson:

The substitution of habits probably requires a greater expenditure of effort and energy' than was necessary for the formation of the original habit. This holds true for habits of thought and attitude as well as for those which involve skill.[9]

In relearning, the pupil must be taught to substitute a second new response to a combination of stimuli to which he has already attached a conditioned response. If we may reason to human conduct by analogy from the work of Guthrie and Horton [10] on cats, which showed that animals tend to solve a problem by repeating the same series of movement-produced responses, the difficulty presents itself as formidable indeed. The more often the "incorrect" response has been given, the more likely the situation is to evoke it promptly. The remedy lies in substituting the correct response, however evoked, in the presence of the conditioning stimuli. This process must then be repeated until extinction of the first and "incorrect" response occurs. Thus, if a child develops an incorrect passage in a musical composition, it is not sufficient merely to give practice on the correct form. The part of the composition preceding must be played first, since the precursive stimuli serve as cues to the passage being redone and the whole series constitutes a succession of movements and movement-produced stimuli leading to other activity in the sequence.

---

[9] Charles E. Benson *et al.*, *Psychology for Teachers,* Rev. ed., Boston: Ginn & Co., 1933, p. 150.
[10] Edwin R. Guthrie and George P. Horton, *Cats in a Puzzle Box.*

Some college athletic coaches prefer to have on their squads boys who have had none of the sport at all in high school because so many have had a technique of performance different from that they will use in college. Furthermore, there is a tendency under conditions of emotional stress to lapse back into the original pattern, as is illustrated frequently in a fast game like basketball.

Problems of Re-education.—We come now to a consideration of some of the pupil and school conditions which underlie the need for a program of remedial education and procedures. All the following factors, either individually or in combination, enter into the situation:

1. Pupil mobility
2. Conflicts
3. Incorrect curricular gradation
4. Poor teaching
5. Low I.Q.
6. Promotion system

1. *Pupil mobility.* Mobility studies [11] both of the general population and of the school population show frequent and long shifts. Many pupils attend several elementary schools in the course of their training. The impact of a change of school situation can be pronounced. Change requires, for example, an entirely new social adjustment to new playmates, new teachers, and, not the least, a new principal. Readjustment does not necessarily harm a pupil's progress, but there is no doubt that in some cases it is definitely a cause for retardation. It is only common sense to suggest that the principal and teachers of a school pay particular attention to the newcomers in their group. Action taken to welcome the new student, to hasten his own awareness of social acceptance and of "belongingness" is an important phase of this attention. If the school is sufficiently advanced in its procedures to employ the routine check of a placement test, so much the better.

[11] See John Edward Corbally, "The Extent and Importance of Pupil Mobility as an Administrative Problem in the Public Schools of the State of Washington."

2. Conflicts. The emotional condition of the pupil bears an intimate relationship to his school progress. Any form of conflict is likely to exert a highly deleterious effect upon learning efficiency. Difficulties at home, dislike for the teacher, problems with schoolmates—these and a score of other conditions can lead to emotional conflicts of formidable proportions both to the pupil and to the school. Prescott comments as follows:

> The level of emotionality reached during learning may be of great importance. Pleasant or unpleasant feelings, mild emotion, strong emotion, and profound shock may have very different learning consequences due to differences in physiological concomitants.[12]

Gates [13] investigated 100 reading disability cases and reports the following results which suggest a relationship between learning ability and emotional stability:

10 cases of nervous tension and tics such as nail-biting, restlessness, insomnia, stuttering, finger-twisting, nose-picking, and others

14 cases of retreat reactions such as playing truant, joining out of school gangs, sullenness

18 cases of playing practical jokes, theft, cruelty, bullying

16 cases of defense reactions

26 cases of withdrawal such as mind-wandering and daydreaming

33 cases of indifference, laziness, submissiveness, and inattention

35 cases of extreme self-consciousness, blushing, inferiority feelings, and signs of being easily hurt

The precise relationship of such factors to reading disability is not easy to uncover. It is possible that reading disability is a symptom, as many tics are, and as such merely indicates an emotional disturbance. Clinical observation is necessary to discover the true cause, around which all therapy must be centered.

---

[12] Daniel Alfred Prescott, *Emotion and the Educative Process,* Washington, D. C.: American Council on Education, 1938, pp. 179-80.
[13] *Journal of the National Education Association,* XXV (1936), 205-6.

Sherman [14] supports the viewpoint that emotional factors result-ing from habitual failure inhibit the learning process.

Furthermore, since subject matter is hierarchical in nature even at the elementary level, a year of difficulty and retardation may lead to cumulative problems in the future. As Terman [15] long since pointed out in discussing the hygiene of the school child, the school situation unfortunately not only does not al-ways serve to clear up emotional problems but frequently is itself the cause of them.

3. *Incorrect curricular gradation.* A study of the determina-tion of curricula at all levels indicates too clearly that subject matter placement has often depended upon the subjective judg-ment of adult teachers rather than upon the performance of young learners. It is apparent that this type of causal factor affects entire classes rather than individuals, which accentuates the gravity of the situation. There is definite need for more and continuing study of subject matter placement.

4. *Poor teaching.* Poor teaching is always a cause of poor pupil performance. It affects both individuals and groups. Poor teaching includes poor disciplinary procedures as well as the more technical points of subject matter methodology. Prominent in the factors of poor teaching which necessitate remedial procedures is inability or lack of interest in individual-izing instruction. Griffith says: "Teachers must adjust their methods and attitudes to age, sex, and race differences." [16]

5. *Low I.Q.* A traditional reason in the mind of the average teacher for poor pupil performance is low intelligence. By design, this causal factor does not head our list, although there is no question but that insufficient mental capacity may be a serious handicap to a pupil in reaching norm performance. Monroe and Backus write:

---

[14] Mandel Sherman, "Emotional Disturbances and Reading Disability," *Recent Trends in Reading,* Supplementary Educational Monographs, No. 49, pp. 126-34.

[15] Lewis M. Terman, *The Hygiene of the School Child.*

[16] Coleman R. Griffith, *Psychology Applied to Teaching and Learning,* New York: Rinehart & Co., Inc., 1939, p. 600.

Intellectual factors affecting reading may be divided into (1) general intelligence and (2) specific intellectual abilities. . . . Sometimes children of good general intelligence show retardation in some of the specific skills which compose an intelligence test.[17]

Gates [18] concludes that children whose I.Q.'s are 80 or below make very slow progress or fail. Mental age level seems to define the upper limits of reading ability, generally speaking. The work of Bernardine Schmidt [19] is particularly interesting, since it questions the general truth of the foregoing conclusion. It may well be that present-day intelligence tests are in some sense measures reflecting a behavior complex resulting from emotional maladjustment, inferiority, reading disability, and slow development of symbolic processes.

If all the other psychological variables were equal among different students, low I.Q. would be a much more serious handicap than it actually is. Perhaps it is fortunate that interest, persistence, and other similar traits are more equitably and evenly distributed among the school population. Except in subjects which are completely beyond his grasp, a student who is less gifted mentally than the average has an opportunity to correct for this factor by increased effort, interest, and practice.

6. *Promotion system.* Promotion systems are far from uniform throughout the country. There has been considerable tendency recently, however, to advance students from grade to grade regardless of what the absolute level of their attainment may be. This is on the theory that grade retardation produces social problems and emotional disturbances which are greater than the damage done by advancing the student before he has actually reached the average performance of the group. However this may be, the fact remains that there is always the possibility of the student's falling farther and farther behind in academic attainment, and the evidence clearly shows that this happens in many cases. The least that those who hold to the

---

[17] Marion Monroe, Bertie Backus, *et al., Remedial Reading,* Boston: Houghton Mifflin Co., 1937, pp. 21-23.
[18] Arthur I. Gates, *The Improvement of Reading,* 3d ed.
[19] *Psychological Monographs,* LX, No. 5 (1946).

promotion-regardless theory can do is to provide carefully for the tutoring of students who are substandard in their performance but are advanced to the next grade. Anything less than this is a psychological injustice to the pupil.

Types of Remedial Cases.—As one might readily infer from the foregoing discussion, there are differing types of cases resulting from differing causes. It is possible to classify these types in several ways. Perhaps the simplest form of classification is the division into (1) ordinary subject matter retardation and (2) special disabilities.

The student will recall from the discussion in an earlier chapter that learning is materially affected by the efficiency of the sensory apparatus of the learner. This being the case, it is self-evident that all schools should have a system for screening out pupils with various types of sensory disability. Sensory disabilities can often be ameliorated or completely corrected. In the case of other disabilities of sufficient magnitude to interfere seriously with learning, special types of class and procedure are required. When the teacher encounters learning difficulty in a pupil, the first check in diagnosing should be on the pupil's physical equipment for learning. Jordan writes:

Teachers must ever be on the watch for signs of maladjustments, of defects in eyes and ears, of insufficient air. They must help to get parents interested in taking their children to experts and in carrying out the recommendations of these experts once they have been obtained.[20]

3. REMEDIAL TEACHING

Preparation of Teachers for Remedial Work.—The preparation of teachers for doing remedial work requires special attention. There are two general types of theory as to what this preparation should be. Some hold that remedial work, because of its specialized nature, should be carried on by a small, specially trained group of remedial specialists. The tendency in the past has run somewhat this way. Another theory holds

[20] A. M. Jordan, *Educational Psychology,* Rev. ed., New York: Henry Holt & Co., Inc., 1933, pp. 116-17.

that all teachers should have some training in remedial procedures. It is not necessary to choose between these theories. All
superior teaching involves a continuous check on the performance of the pupil in an effort to remedy inadequacies which
come to light. Blair [21] states:

> Any competent teacher who has a sympathetic attitude toward pupils
> and who carefully studies their weaknesses and problems can make
> some contribution to the remedial program of a school. For after all,
> remedial teaching is just good teaching. It is taking the pupil where he
> is and leading him on to higher levels of accomplishment and adjustment
> in the areas where he is particularly deficient.

When remedial teaching shades over into the teaching of
subnormal groups, however, special training may be required.
It would be well if the majority of teachers knew elementary
screening techniques and tests. While in the larger systems
there are elaborate devices and organizations for performing
this function, the majority of pupils are in smaller districts
where it is not possible to carry this type of specialization very
far. In remedial work the teacher should have continuously in
mind the psychological principles governing relearning and reconditioning. Then, too, the teacher who is employing remedial
procedures should remember the nature of emotional conflicts
and the manner in which they can interfere with learning.
Above all, patience is necessary, since relearning and reteaching
are tedious, time-consuming, and laborious processes both for
the pupil and for the teacher.

Remedial Work in Regular Classes.—A few suggestions on
the normal course of events in remedial classroom procedure
may be given. First, the teacher should undertake to diagnose
the exact type of problem presented and its cause. In connection with remedial reading, Monroe and Backus write:

> To be effective, remedial instruction in reading must be preceded by
> careful diagnosis. The remedial teacher must first discover the nature
> of the child's difficulty, search for causes and then set up a specific pro-

---

[21] From Blair: *Diagnostic and Remedial Teaching in Secondary Schools,*
pp. 405-6. Copyright, 1946 by The Macmillan Company and used with their
permission.

gram of treatment that will either remove the causes, or if that is impossible, will at least enable the child to read as well as his limitations permit.[22]

One pupil may suffer from two or three sorts of difficulty in the same way that a sick person may be suffering from two or three physical disorders.

When the nature, type, and extent of a learning difficulty have been determined, it should be treated in a method as nearly routine as possible at the outset. The recommended cycle of procedure is strikingly like that in medicine. Drastic alternatives are not resorted to until necessary. The beginning teacher is likely to expect results in too much of a hurry. It has been emphasized several times in this chapter that remedial work is tedious and requires patience. Therefore, do not make haste and waste. The pupil who is attempting to relearn a behavior pattern needs more than the ordinary amount of supervision and encouragement.

Obviously, some sort of measurement is highly desirable in order to check progress. In particularly puzzling cases, favorable results are often secured by calling other teachers into consultation in the same way that physicians would do in an obscure or perplexing case.

Judgment is necessary on when and when not to use remedial procedures. The novice and the faddist in all lines of work are eager to try their wares just as some surgeons are too eager to operate. Remember, remedial procedures are tedious, difficult, and time-consuming both for the pupil and for the teacher and are resorted to primarily because it is felt that definite impairment in later performance will result unless readjustment is effected.

Finally, the beginning teacher is urged to consult well and frequently the more experienced teachers, supervisors, and principals in attempting to master this intricate but vital element of methodology. There is no phase of schoolteaching in which the wisdom of the experienced technician shows more clearly, and

---

[22] Marion Monroe, Bertie Backus, *et al.*, *Remedial Reading*, Boston: Houghton Mifflin Co., 1937, p. 12.

shrewd indeed is the neophyte who avails himself of it.   Just as the beginning physician has an internship, the purpose of which is to acquaint him with the more delicate and judgment-requiring phases of medicine, so should the beginning teacher avail himself of the wealth of experience that the older teacher possesses in remedial work.

QUESTIONS

1. Define remedial education.   With what phase of learning do the majority of teachers connect this term?
2. What is the best type of remedial education?
3. Give some reasons why there will always be a need for remedial education.
4. What are some of the difficulties encountered by the remedial teacher?
5. List some of the difficulties that underlie the need for remedial procedures.
6. In what ways does the emotional health of the child affect his learning capacity?
7. Do you believe that a child should be promoted on the basis of social development alone, regardless of whether or not he has mastered the material of his particular grade?
8. What is the first step to be taken by the remedial teacher in her work with a new pupil?
9. Where are some of the places that a beginning teacher may secure information concerning remedial work?
10. What can be done to decrease the need for remedial work in the schools?

Chapter 18

TEACHING PUPILS HOW TO STUDY

1. THE NATURE OF STUDY

Psychological Definition of Study.—Study is a specialized form of learned behavior. It is not the exercise of a rare gift or mystic power. If we look up "study" in the *Dictionary of Education,*[1] we find it defined as the "application of the mind to a problem or subject." This definition does not imply passive behavior. Study is efficient only when it consists of active behavior; it is a dynamic process, although the activity need not necessarily be overt movement. According to Bird and Bird:

> Study involves the analysis of consecutive thought; it requires one to contrast and compare statements, to select important points and their supporting details, to examine the conclusions drawn, and to determine whether or not they are valid. But something more is essential, for the process thus far is nothing more than careful reading. A student *must carry away* with him what he reads.[2]

A student is one who has learned to respond in an appropriate and active manner to selected classes of stimuli. The technique of study consists essentially of learning to give selective and organized responses. The behavior which takes place is the criterion, and, regardless of the number of stimuli presented or the nature of their arrangement, no study has occurred if no response has been given or no modification of behavior has resulted. Many "students" who are not reading sit in libraries looking at books. Reading as a part of study is

---

[1] Carter V. Good, ed., *Dictionary of Education,* New York: McGraw-Hill Book Co., Inc., 1945, p. 392.

[2] Charles Bird and Dorothy M. Bird, *Learning More by Effective Study,* copyright 1945. With permission of Appleton-Century-Crofts, Inc., pp. 93-94.

not a process merely of staring at books, and students are not reading who are not reacting to what they see. The light waves from the print on the page are reaching their eyes but are not being translated into the appropriate activity which constitutes meaning. When only exposure to light stimuli occurs, we cannot say that a student is reading any more than we can say that the fly which has lit on the edge of the page is reading. The light waves reach the fly's eyes, but since they elicit no response, nothing has been learned nor has behavior been modified in any educationally significant manner.

Effective study depends upon picking stimuli to which to respond, upon attending to these stimuli closely, and upon responding. We are really reading when we are reading for a purpose such as to write an examination or to tell someone else about what we have read. *Study then may be defined as the progressive modification of behavior by the individual in the direction of selected and defined goals.*

When we say that an individual is "studying" to be a lawyer, we mean that he is selecting from his environment a pattern of stimuli, e.g., law books, etc., and learning to respond to these stimuli by behavior which is characteristic of lawyers. In the furtherance of his objective the student acquires certain typical verbal patterns of technical terminology and the other stereotypes of law such as cases. The law student learns to associate symbolic cues with the legalistic things, situations, and functions for which they stand. This learning takes place by the usual process of association. In addition, the prospective lawyer also learns to behave like a lawyer by attending court trials for purposes of observation and by putting what he sees into practice in a moot court. Thus, he learns to play a role—the role typical of lawyers.

Types of Study.—The kinds of study may be classified conveniently in terms of the purpose which the study is intended to serve. Accordingly, we discern the following:

1. Study to understand people (the social type of study)
2. Study to gain knowledge (the cultural type)
3. Study to solve problems (the practical type)

1. *Study to understand people.* It has often been remarked that the proper study of mankind is man. The Greeks said, "Know thyself." Unfortunately, Nature's gifts to man, biologically speaking, do not include the hereditary knowledge to understand his fellow man—*or himself.* We learn to understand people by studying them and their behavior. We learn to understand ourselves in the same fashion.

In study for social purposes there should be particular emphasis upon wide experience and extended opportunity for observation. It is much easier to do as the Romans do when in Rome if one has been in a number of Roman suburbs previously. Since man himself is the most complicated mechanical, chemical, and physical object known, it is merely a matter of psychological common sense to assume that the study of man is also the most complicated of all studies. When a lad going into the Army is taught to tear down and reassemble a machine gun in a dark room, he is studying and practicing the solution to a relatively simple problem in that when it recurs, factors in the situation are likely to be roughly the same in both number and arrangement. Since motor learning tends to be specific, the soldier is made to study his problem in a dark room because if he mastered the performance in daylight he could probably not repeat it in the dark—a practical contingency likely to occur. Change the make of machine gun and give the boy another of different or foreign make, and he will have some trouble, but less than a beginner. Some behavior will transfer and be appropriate to the new situation. His problems in adjusting to his new social situation, his top sergeant, and his superior officers are likely to prove more difficult and to require more study than the machine gun. The solutions are less likely to stay put because top sergeants are more variable than machine guns.

2. *Study to gain knowledge.* This is the type of study commonly stressed in schools. Its purpose is to familiarize children with the cultural heritage, national and community mores, and the factual basis underlying a social and moral behavior pattern of personal and social adjustment. Study for knowledge is intended to provide deeper understandings, mental relaxation,

and effective use of leisure time. The kind of knowledge one wishes further to acquire is in no small degree conditioned by the knowledge already acquired.

In study for cultural purposes, we find that reading emerges as a dominant form of technique to be mastered. Reading permeates all phases of our present form of social culture and the analysis of reading habits and the mastery of an adequate reading method are the cardinal points in this type of study. Both reading and thinking depend heavily upon an extensive and widely sampled vocabulary. As Witherington points out:

> Only a little introspection is needed to reveal that most of a person's thoughts revolve around words or other meaningful symbols.[3]

There is evidence that the average high school graduate could be taught many more words (with no loss in essential meaning) than he now knows when he graduates. Those who are opposed to increasing the present vocabulary spread at the secondary level base their argument almost entirely upon the contention that depth of meaning would suffer, a contention which erroneously assumes that present vocabulary learning taxes average pupil ability to the limit. Vocabulary training should be expanded at both elementary and secondary levels but particularly at the latter. As a matter of fact, from the psychological standpoint, no more profitable investment could possibly be made. The time could be found by curtailing a wide variety of superficial and pseudopractical subjects with which the curriculum is at present cluttered. Psychologically speaking, there is no more glaring omission at the present time in the hierarchical organization of subject matter than the nearly complete abandonment of systematic attention to reading and word study at the secondary level.

3. *Study to solve problems.* Problem study is directed toward a specific, utilitarian purpose. Since no two problems are exactly alike, problem-solving technique consists of deriving a group of behavior analogues which with modifications will be useful in a wide variety of similar situations. Problem solving

---

[3] H. Carl Witherington, *Educational Psychology,* Ginn & Co., 1946, p. 202.

can be reduced to a semiformulaic basis, as we shall see presently, but the study trick lies not so much in learning the formula as in how to modify it slightly to apply to new problem situations which arise.   Theorems and corollaries in geometry illustrate this idea.

Douglass and Mills point out the following uses and benefits to be derived from a problem-centered type of study:

Modern methods now have a strong and growing tendency to reorganize both content and methods of instruction on the basis of units presenting psychological challenges, called variously challenges, contracts, problems, projects, and life-units.   Goals toward which the student should work are furnished by the solution of the problems involved as well as by the standard of attainment or success.   In assignments of the nature of problems, more of the planning and oversight of the work is left to the learner and his fellow learners in the group. . . .

The problem as a unit of educational activity is probably the best adapted of all teaching situations to arouse genuine interest and purposeful, wholehearted activity on the part of the pupil. . . .[4]

Problem solving may be studied in several ways, of which one is the classic trial and error, wherein the learner blunders around until he hits the solution or near-solution to his problem, which he then tends to re-employ on the recurrence of the situation or one like it.   Historically this may be the way in which all solutions evolved.   The race is now in a position to do much better by its young than asking them to recapitulate all the previous errors in a blunder series which may have taken centuries.   Adequate solutions have been worked out to many hundreds of kinds of problems and these may be taught to pupils as generalizations which later take on more reality and meaning with experience.   The pupil, however, should understand the method employed.   Panton lists four steps in the basic formula for problem solving.   These are:

(i) The formulation and appreciation of the problem.
(ii) The collection of all relevant data by observation and by experimental work.

[4] Harl R. Douglass and Hubert H. Mills, *Teaching in High School.* Copyright, 1948, by The Ronald Press Company, p. 269.

(iii) The formulation of a conclusion as a result of a consideration of the evidence which has been collected.

(iv) The testing out of that conclusion.[5]

If a problem defines a specific difficulty which demands for solution the application of general principles, definitions, rules, or assumptions, we speak of the *deductive* type of problem solving. If, on the other hand, the problem can be solved by arriving at a generalization or principle by abstracting many particular cases, we speak of an *inductive* approach.

To those who contend that the deductive-inductive type of study in learning is superficial and devoid of depth of meaning, it may be answered that although there is partial truth in the criticism, all education is a compromise, the number of things in the world to be learned today being what they are. A strictly inductive method would be the only method for an ageless being working by the clock of eternity. But for a child to have to discover inductively all that is known about electricity before he is given the privilege of throwing a light switch is unnecessary. The majority of individuals have no notion of what happens between the switch and the light, but this knowledge if they had it would not make them throw switches any more efficiently. The point so often missed is that all problems cannot be studied inductively and need not be so studied for adequate social behavior. In a specialized world all of us must learn to do many things on a purely mechanical basis in order to conserve time for the intensive study of those things which we are expected to do well and for which we may carry some responsibility. A man who knows what happens between the switch and the light is more likely to be able to do a repair job if something goes wrong, but anyone who tries to follow this principle with his lights, his car, his plumbing, his typewriter, etc., will spend his life becoming a poor jack-of-all-trades. Whether we like it or not, the Industrial Revolution has made specialists of practically all of us and each specialist is dependent upon many others for even his everyday social conveniences and adjustments.

---

[5] J. H. Panton, *Modern Teaching Practice and Technique,* London: Longmans, Green & Co., 1947, p. 176.

2. Learning to Study

Psychological Conditions of Effective Study.—We come now to a consideration of the best conditions for efficient study. These are:

1. A clear goal
2. Mastery of fundamentals
3. Knowledge of learning phenomena
4. Concentration
5. Practice

1. *A clear goal.* From time to time one reads of startling discoveries in the field of science, not infrequently in medicine, where the searcher was looking for something quite different from what he discovered. Legend has it that this was the case with Pavlov and the conditioned salivary reflex experiment. Such things happen, but it would be a mistake to assume that accident and not a sought goal is the rule of scientific discovery. We ordinarily learn about fleas by studying fleas, tigers by studying tigers, outboard motors by studying outboard motors. Of course, the alert student is ready at all times to seize upon anything which crosses his field of observation even though it may not be strictly in the line of pursuit, but this is a corollary and not a theorem of efficient study.

In the matter of defining goals, common sense, experience, and judgment play a large role. The doctoral candidate who tackles a problem too wide in scope flounders around interminably dissipating his own energy and the patience of his faculty supervisor. On the other hand, the graduate student who picks a problem which is overlimited and overdefined correspondingly circumscribes the breadth of his own learning. There is no rule that can arbitrarily be laid down on the establishment of goals for study. Such goals must rather be adopted tentatively and modified as study proceeds. The student should understand that in our use of the word "study" we mean more here than what the little boy and girl do when they sit down in the evening to study their arithmetic lessons. All of us are forced to the study of different types of problems throughout our lives; this is the inexorable law of circumstance. Only when a child's study of his daily lesson contributes something to this greater objective can it be said to have been truly educative.

2. *Mastery of fundamentals.* From time to time in our discussions we have made reference to the basic importance of the fundamentals in education. They play their part again in connection with study. Robinson writes:

> Deficiencies in the three R's affect the success of many students in college! For instance, tests show that some college freshmen read no better than the average fourth-grader, that some cannot do a single problem in long division, and that some cannot recognize pronouns in a sentence. Difficulties such as these prevent otherwise capable students from completing their lessons, from doing physics problems correctly, or from translating a foreign language easily.[6]

Before we can do effective study in any field, we must first master the fundamentals that are involved. Obviously it is impossible to improve adjustment until one has some original adjustment; to refine behavior until there is some behavior to refine. The story of our air supremacy in the last war would have been far different if the design of new models had been in the hands of freshmen in colleges of aeronautical engineering. An engineer who is indoctrinated in one school of thought in aeronautical engineering is likely to be bound by certain prejudices and preconceptions which impede the devising of new and improved models through a study of the behavior, performance, and faults of old models. But he knows certain fundamentals upon which all heavier-than-air craft depend for operation, and without this knowledge he could not further improve designs.

3. *Knowledge of learning phenomena.* Many pupils in their study are puzzled and confused by routine occurrences which are sufficiently simple to be explained to secondary school students. For example, it is a known fact physiologically that true fatigue is relatively rare. When a student says that he is too

---

[6] Francis P. Robinson, *Effective Study,* New York: Harper & Bros., 1946, p. 103.

tired to study any more, what he usually means is that he is too bored. He should not be allowed to believe that he is actually too tired, and the fact of his boredom should be made emergent in the situation, not with the idea that it will automatically start him into studying again with furious abandon but because it will deprive him of a satisfying rationalization for ceasing his study habitually after a short time. Another common phenomenon in a learning series is the "plateau" or a period of no improvement. Such a flattening of the progress curve is likely to be taken by the uninitiated as a point beyond which it is impossible to improve, whereas in reality such a temporary cessation of progress is likely to represent only a period of consolidation and assimilation. The learning transitions that typically occur in the study of various kinds of performance are usually well known to experienced teachers. Unfortunately such factors are often so well known as to be taken for granted when in reality they should be carefully explained to the beginner.

The simple device of the learning curve, which is obtained by plotting either errors or time against trials or units of work, has provided an objective way of recording the changes in performance when learning is taking place. Such a curve certainly does not explain or describe the learning process, but it does provide a ready technique for comparing and contrasting increase in speed and efficiency of performance under variable conditions. By the use of such a comparative technique we can make some relatively useful generalizations about conditions most conducive to efficient learning. Some of these generalizations include the following:

a) Spaced or distributed practice produces higher learning efficiency and makes for better retention of learned materials than does massed practice. Space intervals may be increased progressively as mastery develops.

b) Variations in the strength of motivation (from the learner's point of view) make for more efficient learning.

c) The part method of learning, generally speaking, is less efficient than the whole method. However, in specific application the greater efficiency of one or the other of the methods depends upon the nature of the material to be learned, the

learner's past experience and familiarity with either of the two
methods, and his attitude toward the method chosen. Long
assignments or material of a complex and abstract nature may
usually be learned best by a combination of the part and whole
methods. A preview obtained by reading an entire assignment
usually provides an advantage because the meaningfulness of
each section is enhanced. A shuttling back and forth of ideas
provides many more associations and hence more complete
understanding than the simple, discrete type of chain association
resulting from a part-method mastery.

d) Overlearning retards forgetting but does not provide
equal increments for equal amounts of overlearning. For certain kinds of material, one "intuitive" experience assures permanent understanding. But, for many tasks necessarily learned
in the classroom, one correct performance is inadequate as a
criterion of learning. Skill subjects in which fundamental
operations are taught must provide for a considerable overlearning and for spacing this practice at well-chosen intervals.
Experimental investigation indicates that as much as 50 per
cent of overlearning pays worth-while dividends in retained
learning. More than 50 per cent of overlearning shows continuous increment in retention but follows the law of diminishing
returns.

e) The nature of intervening activity between original learning or concentrated study and a later test for retention or
application influences the rate of forgetting. This loss of learned
material because of intervening activity is referred to as *retroactive inhibition*. Greater loss is noted when the intervening
activity is very similar to the original learning, and there is less
loss when the learner engages in some dissimilar activity or
rests. Sleep as intervening activity very often shows an increase
in retained material. These facts should be kept in mind by the
teacher as she schedules classes and learning activities, and certainly by the student when he sets up a budget of time for study
or when he organizes his daily class schedule.

f) There is some evidence also to indicate that unfinished
tasks are remembered more efficiently than finished tasks.
Perhaps this is a simple verification of what many educators

have recognized in a slightly different way. As we associate present mastery and achievement with more distant goals and aspirations, we lay the foundation for increased transfer. The identification of the distant goal tends to enhance a feeling of incompleteness toward the newly acquired skill or understanding. This is a *set* which facilitates memory and results in greater transfer.

4. *Concentration.* Students have the superstition that only a few of their gifted fellows have a magic power of concentration which is a combination of autohypnosis and yoga. Yet these same students have not infrequently taught themselves to sit throughout a professor's lecture without hearing a word although their eyes and ears were both open. This latter is really quite an accomplishment in concentration and if applied to the study of the student's subject matter would pay fabulous dividends. Essentially, concentration is the ability to attend to selected stimuli to the exclusion of other stimuli. To quote Cole and Ferguson:

> Concentrating is a process that psychologically is a good deal like sleep. Neither will come in response to a conscious effort, but both will occur naturally when the circumstances are favorable. Sleep will come if you lie still in a dark room, close your eyes, relax, and think about something pleasant and totally unexciting. Concentration will come spontaneously if you go through the motions of working, but it will not be forced for more than a few minutes.[7]

Students do not really require quiet rooms in which to study. In fact a quiet room can be disturbing to a student who has learned to study successfully in a noisy room. Uniformity of environment is more important than quality. There is something to be said for a relatively consistent environment in which to study, because a change may be disturbing and require a new adaptation each time. Book points out the advantage of forming "a definite time and place habit" for your studying. He writes:

---

[7] Luella Cole and Jessie Mary Ferguson, *Students' Guide to Efficient Study,* 3d ed., New York: Rinehart & Co., Inc., 1946, p. 15.

When such a habit has been formed, all the surrounding stimuli will soon come to suggest or even help to elicit the particular responses which the student desires to make, such as complete concentration upon his work or continued application to his tasks until they are finished or as long as he remains in that particular place.[8]

5. *Practice.* That practice makes perfect is a deceptive truism valid only when qualified. Practice makes perfect in the sense that it builds up a pattern of more or less stereotyped reactions to situations which are roughly similar. Stimuli which have been present during a reaction will tend to call forth the reaction on future occasions, and practice becomes especially valuable when a reaction can be fixed in response to a fairly wide range of combinations of stimuli.

Teaching Pupils to Study.—How then shall we teach pupils to study and to improve their own study habits progressively? First the pupil should be led into a clear realization of the goal which he is attempting to attain and the purpose which his study will serve in attaining it. According to Burton:

Desirable assignments will give the pupil a clear understanding of:
1. What is to be done
2. How it is to be done
3. Why it is to be done [9]

Second, the pupil should begin with the fundamentals of the behavior which is being studied for mastery. Golf professionals often start beginners out with only one or two sticks, not the bagful that the self-educated dub uses.

Third, the pupil should be given practice in the type of situations in which the problem is likely to reoccur. The interaction of the two factors of drill and mastery of fundamentals is explained by Butler:

Strengthening cannot go on without initial learning, or without something already learned to be strengthened; hence, the initial responsibility in teaching is the building-up of learning to a point where drill resumes

---

[8] William F. Book, *Learning How to Study and Work Effectively,* Boston: Ginn & Co., 1926, p. 288.
[9] William H. Burton, *The Guidance of Learning Activities,* copyright 1944, with permission of Appleton-Century-Crofts, Inc., p. 317.

the activity necessary for final and satisfactory acquisition. Final and satisfactory acquisition is that degree of learning in which the associations have reached the standard desired by the instructor.[10]

Where the situations to occur are relatively unpredictable, the larger the response repertoire the better chance of solution. In other words, the old hand at the game knows more tricks to try. There is an element of enormous waste in this necessary principle of study in learning, but it is unavoidable. If human accomplishments included the ability to foretell with accuracy the future, each soldier in an army could be trained for exactly the type of problems with which he would have to deal. This would simplify and reduce the training series. Similarly with the training of physicians it would not be necessary to give a complete gamut of training to all. As a matter of fact, there is some tendency at present in the training of medical specialists to reduce the breadth and extent of the intermediate training after fundamentals have been mastered.

Some Practical Suggestions.—Smith and Tyler suggest the following comprehensive check list of work habits and study skills for a student to develop by persistent training (directly or indirectly) in how to study:

1.1 Effective Use of Study Time
    1.11 Habit of using large blocks of free time effectively
    1.12 Habit of budgeting his time
    1.13 Habit of sustained application rather than working sporadically
    1.14 Habit of meeting promptly study obligations
    1.15 Habit of carrying work through to completion

1.2 Conditions for Effective Study
    1.21 Knowledge of proper working conditions
    1.22 Habit of providing working conditions for himself
    1.23 Habit of working independently, that is, working under his own direction and initiative

1.3 Effective Planning of Study
    1.31 Habit of planning in advance
    1.32 Habit of choosing problems for investigation which have significance for him

---

[10] Frank A. Butler, *The Improvement of Teaching in Secondary Schools,* Chicago: University of Chicago Press, 1939, p. 323.

1.33 Ability to define a problem
1.34 Habit of analyzing a problem so as to sense its implications
1.35 Ability to determine data needed in an investigation

1.4 Selection of Sources
    1.41 Awareness of kinds of information which may be obtained from various sources
    1.42 Awareness of the limitations of the various sources of data
    1.43 Habit of using appropriate sources of information, including printed materials, lectures, interviews, observations, and so on

1.5 Effective Use of Various Sources of Data
    1.51 Use of library
        1.511 Knowledge of library tools
        1.512 Ability to use the card catalogue in a library
    1.52 Use of books
        1.521 Ability to use the dictionary
        1.522 Habit of using helps (such as the Index) in books
        1.523 Ability to use maps, charts and diagrams
    1.53 Reading
        1.531 Ability to read a variety of materials for a variety of purposes using a variety of reading techniques
        1.532 Power to read with discrimination
        1.533 Ability to read rapidly
        1.534 Development of a more effective reading vocabulary
    1.54 Ability to get helpful information from other persons
        1.541 Ability to understand material presented orally
        1.542 Facility in the techniques of discussion, particularly discussions which clarify the issues in controversial questions
        1.543 Ability to obtain information from interviews with people
    1.55 Ability to obtain helpful information from field trips and other excursions
    1.56 Ability to obtain information from laboratory experiments
    1.57 Habit of obtaining needed information from observations

1.6 Determining Relevancy of Data
    1.61 Ability to determine whether the data found are relevant to the particular problem

1.7 Recording and Organizing Data
    1.71 Habit of taking useful notes for various purposes from observations, lectures, interviews, and reading
    1.72 Ability to outline material for various purposes

1.73 Ability to make an effective organization so that the material may be readily recalled, as in notetaking

1.74 Ability to make an effective organization for written presentation of a topic

1.75 Ability to make an effective organization for oral presentation of a topic

1.76 Ability to write effective summaries

1.8 Presentation of Results of Study

    1.81 Ability to make an effective presentation of the results of study

        1.811 Habit of differentiating quoted material from summarized material in writing reports

        1.812 Facility in handwriting or in typing

    1.82 Ability to make an effective oral presentation of the results of study

1.9 Habit of Evaluating Each Step in an Investigation

    1.91 Habit of considering the dependability of the data obtained from various sources

    1.92 Habit of considering the relative importance of the various ideas obtained from various sources

    1.93 Habit of refraining from generalization until data are adequate

    1.94 Habit of testing his own generalizations

    1.95 Habit of criticizing his own investigations.[11]

QUESTIONS

1. Give the psychological definition of study.
2. What factor is necessary for study to become effective?
3. Name the three different types of study. How do we arrive at these classifications?
4. Why is the building of a wide vocabulary important?
5. Give the views of persons who do not stress vocabulary building in the curriculum.
6. What are the four steps in problem solving as listed by Panton?
7. What must be kept in mind when we solve problems by a set formula? Why?
8. List the conditions of effective study. Give importance of each.

---

[11] Eugene R. Smith, Ralph W. Tyler, *et al., Appraising and Recording Student Progress,* Vol. III of *Adventure in American Education,* New York: Harper & Bros., 1942, pp. 31-33. By permission of the publishers.

9. How does the establishment of a "time and place habit" help one to concentrate?

10. What are three important rules for teaching pupils to study?

11. Be able to discuss in class some of your personal problems concerning study and what you have done or would like to do about them.

PART V

PSYCHOLOGY OF SCHOOL LEVELS, CURRICULA, AND METHODS

Chapter 19

PSYCHOLOGICAL ANALYSIS OF SCHOOL LEVELS

1. Psychological Importance of Levels of School Organization

The prospective teacher should be a student not only of an area of subject matter and of teaching method but also of the many other factors which go to make up the picture of the American school system. Over a period of time, the hundreds of thousands of classroom teachers can and should exercise a potent voice along with administrators, school boards, and school patrons in the determination of organizational form and basic policies. Concerning this, Gould and Yoakam write:

> The professionally alert teacher, however, should not be satisfied with the traditional organizational and teaching practices. He should not be content to accept ready-made plans that are not appropriate for his particular group. He should be willing to engage in organizing and planning instructional activities which meet the specific needs of his pupils.[1]

One of the key factors in school organization and administration is the stratification which is found. In less technical terms, this may be described as the manner in which the school is divided into grades, how the grades are grouped, and how the curricular materials within any given grade are divided into units or courses. Administrative organization concerns the teacher intimately, because both the pupil and his learning are affected by the form as well as the spirit of the school. For

---

[1] George Gould and Gerald Alan Yoakam, *The Teacher and His Work—A First Course in Education.* Copyright, 1947, by The Ronald Press Company, p. 91.

example, many authorities on school organization and administration are inclined to view askance a building unit which is so
large that it includes very young children along with high school
juniors and seniors. Not only is the mixture of maturity, experience, and learning technique likely to be too extreme from
the learning angle under such an arrangement, but the social
factors involved can also prove complicating.

2. Varieties of School-Level Practices

Present Situations in the Organization of School Levels.—
There is a condition of decided flux in both theory and practice
in school gradation at the present time. This fluctuation is
particularly noticeable from grades six through fourteen. All
sorts of combinations are being tried, and each has its proponents and critics. For example, some school principals regard
the six-year high school, including grades seven to twelve inclusive, as a highly effective and economical type of unit; others
who are less enthusiastic about this type of organization claim
that the age spread is too wide and that the social situation is
not sound. Bolton, Cole, and Jessup [2] point out that in the use
of the 6-6 plan:

The first six grades give ample opportunity to organize the work generally assigned to the elementary schools; the last six year unit makes
it possible to enlarge the facilities for secondary education when the
students are in one center. In such instances, the equipment for manual
training and home economics, libraries, gymnasium, and auditorium,
etc., can be used in common by all of the secondary school pupils.

The 6-3-3 plan has its proponents, who feel that this spacing
of building changes affords an organizational structure which
roughly corresponds to the psychological cleavages in the child's
development. According to Douglass:

The six-three-three plan has practically national acceptance among
public-school superintendents. In contrast with the six-four-two, six-
four-four, or six-six plans, its chief advantage lies in the fact that pupils

[2] From Frederick E. Bolton, Thomas R. Cole, and John H. Jessup, *The Beginning Superintendent*, p. 139. Copyright, 1937, by The Macmillan Company and used with their permission.

are grouped more homogeneously as regards psychological and physiological development. Even so, the resulting classification of pupils into groups physiologically immature (elementary), maturing (junior high school), and mature (senior high school) is only approximate.[3]

The tendency for an increasing number of students to stay in school longer has brought into prominence the thirteenth and fourteenth grades. This program should provide for the five groups listed by the Educational Policies Commission:

1. Some students want to prepare for various technical and semi-professional occupations which require all the training that high schools can give and one or two years in addition. . . .

2. Some want advanced training beyond that which can be offered in the years of high school in the occupations for which the high schools provide the basic preparation. . . .

3. Some want to prepare for admission to professional schools and the last two years of technical and liberal arts colleges. . . .

4. Some want to round out their general education before entering employment or becoming homemakers. . . .

5. There is yet a fifth group, composed of adults and older youth, mostly employed, who no longer attend school full time, but who wish to continue their education during their free hours.[4]

Advanced work of high school grade is sometimes organized into a formal junior college, or it may be set up as a part of the common school system in the form of "extended secondary training" as in the case of the State of Washington. In this latter type of organization, the emphasis is strongly upon the retention of a larger percentage of the school population in school and upon terminal vocational work. The changes that have occurred in secondary education as a result of the development of these new types of organization are listed by Edmonson, Roemer, and Bacon[5] in their statement, "Then and Now in American Secondary Schools":

[3] Aubrey A. Douglass, *Modern Secondary Education,* Boston: Houghton Mifflin Co., 1938, p. 132.

[4] Educational Policies Commission, *Education for All American Youth,* Washington, D. C.: National Education Association, 1944, pp. 246-47.

[5] From: J. B. Edmonson, Joseph Roemer, and Francis L. Bacon: *The Administration of the Modern Secondary School* (3d ed.), pp. 22-23. Copyright, 1948, by The Macmillan Company and used with their permission.

1. *Then* the controlling objective of the high school was the preparation of pupils for the liberal arts college.

Now the high school recognizes the necessity of providing for the needs of all youth of a community—the noncollege as well as the college preparatory, the slow learners as well as the bright.

2. *Then* high school students were drawn largely from the homes of the more prosperous and more cultured social and economic groups of a community.

Now all social and economic groups are represented by students in the typical high school, and all classes of homes are represented in graduating classes.

3. *Then* the holding power of the high school was so low that only a small percentage of the entering students remained until graduation.

Now a large percentage remain in school until graduation.

4. *Then* the program of studies consisted largely of a limited number of units in the older academic fields.

Now the program of studies consists of units in a variety of academic, vocational, and avocational fields.

5. *Then* the participation of students in athletics, school journalism, school clubs, dramatics, and social life was grudgingly tolerated.

Now such participation is strongly encouraged for all students.

6. *Then* the discipline was usually characterized by teacher domination, with emphasis on repression of student interests, strict observance of rules, and severe penalties for misconduct.

Now the discipline is characterized by student-teacher cooperation, with emphasis on school citizenship, good sportsmanship, and the rewards of good conduct.

7. *Then* only a few of the students of low scholastic ability continued in high school beyond the first year.

Now it is estimated that about one fourth of the students beyond the first year should be classified as slow learners.

8. *Then* the guidance of students was not recognized as a major responsibility of the high school.

Now the guidance of students is recognized as a task of major importance, and many schools have very complete guidance programs.

9. *Then* the gulf between the eighth grade and the ninth grade was very wide.

Now the unity of the school system is emphasized through the newer types of school organization and by certain administrative policies.

10. *Then* the typical high school building consisted of one or more study halls, several classrooms of uniform size, and a small laboratory.

Now the typical building has an auditorium, a gymnasium, a library, a shop, several laboratories, many special rooms, and a variety of class-rooms.

11. *Then* the prevailing type of local school organization was the eight-year elementary school and the four-year high school.

Now a six-year secondary school, a three-year junior high school, and a three-year senior high school is a favored pattern of local school organization.

12. *Then* the demands on the high school were relatively few and easily satisfied.

Now the demands on the high school are so varied and extensive, and are multiplying so rapidly, that it is extremely difficult to satisfy them.

History of the Development of School Grades.—It would not be correct to say that the development of the graded system in the American schools has been purely fortuitous. Cubberley, in his authoritative discussion of public education in the United States, regards the growth of the graded systsm as a "natural evolution," and describes it in the following words:

The transition to the graded system came naturally and easily. For half a century the course of instruction in the evolving common or English grammar schools had been in the process of expansion, due in part to the preparation of better and longer textbooks, but largely through the addition of new subjects of study. The school term had been gradu-ally lengthened, the years of school provided had been increased in number, the school course had been differentiated into various parts or schools, the master and his assistants had from the first divided up the work in each room on a rough age-and-grade classification basis, and the entire evolution, up to about 1830 to 1840, had prepared the way for a simple reorganization of the work which would divide the schools into seven, or eight, or nine grades, and give each teacher one grade to handle. By the time of the beginnings of state and city school super-vision the school systems of the cities only awaited the touch of the or-ganizer to transform them from a series of differentiated schools into a series of graded schools that could be organized into a unified system, with a graded course of study, and unified supervision over all. The waste in maintaining two duplicate schools in the same building, each covering the same two or three years of school work, when by re-sorting the pupils the work of each teacher could be made more specialized and the pupils better taught, was certain to become obvious as soon as school supervision by teachers began to supersede school organization by laymen.[6]

It is quite apparent from an analysis of the quotation above what Cubberley means by a "natural evolution." The "naturalness" was not so much psychological as administrative. The various steps were clearly taken for reasons of convenience, expediency, economy, etc., and were seldom if ever based upon experimental and psychological study of child development, the nature of the curricular content, or the dictates of methodology. In the present postwar reorganization of American education which is adding thousands of classes and courses in the field of extension and adult education at one end of the system and kindergarten and nursery school education at the other, it is highly appropriate that attention should be given to the psychological revamping of the middle grades also. Mere adding of appendages will never effect a top-to-bottom improvement.

More and more from the standpoint of the psychologist, the curricular expert, and the methodologist, education is coming to be viewed as a continuous process which should be begun earlier than had formerly been thought and which should extend rather later. This view is held by Alberty,[7] who writes:

It would undoubtedly be a gain if we were to consider education from the kindergarten through the junior-college period as a single educational unit with a common philosophy, but with differing programs at various levels.

The tremendous expansion of day-care and nursery schools during the war taught thousands of mothers the attractive advantages (other than their personal convenience) which are to be gained from expert supervision of children at an early age. At the other end of the scale, expansion has also occurred and an increasing number of persons have come to realize that it is to their economic as well as to their cultural advantage not to

---

[6] Ellwood P. Cubberley, *Public Education in the United States,* Boston: Houghton Mifflin Co., 1919, p. 232.

[7] From Alberty: *Reorganizing the High-School Curriculum,* p. 40. Copyright, 1947, by The Macmillan Company and used with their permission.

cease an effort at serious study at the end of formal schooling. Bacon believes that these new trends present a "new potential in the growth of secondary education." He states:

It lies in the need for extending education beyond the twelfth grade. The immediate factor would appear to be the returned veteran, the non-graduate, who is too mature and too much in need of specialized adjustment for typical high school treatment. This suggests a development beyond the typical high school offerings, not only to provide an opportunity for acquiring the standardized diploma and for making up quickly any shortages in college entrance credits but also for giving occupational preparation which is more specialized and more immediately functional than is customarily offered in the secondary school.

The information now available, however, indicates that the large proportion of veterans will be high school graduates. They will include youths who have discovered new interests and abilities in the armed services with the realization that further education is necessary and those who merely wish to test the federal educational aids available to them and see what happens.

A considerable number wishing to enter college will find that they are lacking in the kind of preparation needed for the type of college specialization which they prefer. The making up of these deficiencies will be their first consideration, but this will be accompanied by a demand for as much college credit as is possible. They will not be satisfied with hastily set up, typically styled high school postgraduate courses.

At first thought, the typical curriculum of the junior college would seem to offer the solution. No doubt in many instances this will suffice but, in general, it is not likely to be desired or considered satisfactory.[8]

All the above factors influence directly the organization of school systems. The feeling is coming to be that the material to be learned is cut up into far too many small pieces and that pupils are having greater and greater difficulty in seeing the relationship between the pieces or putting them together into a meaningful whole. It is obviously desirable to try out experimentally some types of school unit which possess greater flexibility and more integration of subject matter than we have had so far, even in the integrated and core curricula. Those who

---

[8] Francis L. Bacon, "Veterans' Demands Increase Need for 13th and 14th Grades," *Nation's Schools*, XXXVII (1946), 27-28.

are dubious of such experiments take the rather natural position that the compartmentalization of homogeneous subject matter is the only way in which to preserve any semblance of curricular "purity" and that without such sectioning the curriculum would become a mass of chaotic material with all teachers teaching everything and tremendous overlapping and duplication between classes.

3. The Psychology of School-Level Organization

Need for Psychological Research in School Administration. —A curious puzzle of educational administration is that so little of it is based upon experimental findings or research data. To quote Hill:

> There is little doubt that we American educators are very much creatures of habit. We get introduced to the practices of research and evaluation in our professional training, but seldom [if] ever apply those principles and practices with any imagination or consistency. Our guidance is likely to become "putting pupils into existing courses" instead of studying pupils and modern life so we can evolve new courses to suit the discovered needs. Practical research, therefore, is a stepping stone to the possibility of change.[9]

Where an exception occurs, it is likely to be in the field of finance and not in the psychological organization of the school. The majority of school administrators have had little or no psychology—particularly the modern experimental psychology of learning. But to set up a school organization scientifically there is definite and increasing need for psychological research and experimentation. Research aplenty is to be found in the fields of learning of the school subjects and, more lately, of emotions and attitudes. Yet for the use of the administrator, charged with the organization, management, and policy-setting of the school, psychological research is available only in microscopic amounts. The old type of school administrator may even belittle

---

[9] *Bulletin of the National Association of Secondary-School Principals,* XXXII (1948), 92.

experimentation. There is no logical or practical reason why so much administrative procedure has to arise out of trial-and-error procedure. No one discounts the value of mature experience or the excellence of the results which it produces with an empirical method. Many school administrative problems, however, such as building lighting, soundproofing, etc., are still being determined subjectively, when research methods are available to solve them. For a school just to be getting along or even getting along pretty well is no evidence that a different type of organization might not produce still better results. It is time that school psychologists and school administrators cooperate and collaborate in other areas than child guidance clinics and such. Psychological research has much to offer to school administration in the fields of delinquency, student government, staff and personnel management, community relations, extracurricular activities, etc. Far from being regarded as the poles apart in departments of education, educational psychology and administration should appear much more frequently together on the major field programs of graduate students. On the contrary, the graduate student who takes educational psychology as a major field is more than likely to show up with methods, guidance, etc., as his minor fields, while the one who majors in school administration is almost sure to carry supervision, history of education, finance, or perhaps curriculum on his program. An investigation of this tendency by Altstetter shows to what a radical degree this imbalance exists. In discussing her research on the topic she says:

When administrators register in graduate schools for advanced courses they are set aside in a special compartment where their work consists in large measure of such courses as these copied from a recent catalog: School Finance, Public Relations, Problems of the Superintendency, Mental and Educational Measurements, School Surveys, Comparative Education, Pupil Accounting, Management of the Custodial Staff, School Law, Extra-Curricular Activities, Visual Aids, School Management and Organization, Curriculum Problems, Administration of Teaching Personnel and Landscaping of the School Plant. . . . In an unpublished study by the writer an investigation of the courses pursued

by one hundred forty men majoring in Administration shows that electives were chosen largely in the field of the Social Sciences, history,
geography, sociology, and economics. Not one was registered in a course
in Child Development or Mental Hygiene.[10]

Over a period of time, these stereotyped combinations produce narrow specialists, whose disagreements, based upon lack
of mutual understanding, even now rend the air in spots here
and there around the country. A few more administrators who
know scientific method, especially in psychology, and a few more
psychologists who know the problems of public school administration would bridge the gap and enormously improve school
organization. Only scientific reactionaries today believe that no
valid experimentation is possible in the mythically "intangible"
field of social science of which school administration is a part.

Unfortunately, so little has been done and so few experiments
have been conducted that the literature is not abundant in this
area, which means only that the opportunity is all the greater.
Obviously the magnitude and expense of conducting psychological experiments in the field of administration has something to
do with the paucity of studies. The average graduate student
desiring to investigate the over-all effectiveness of two types of
level organization would run into a time and expense problem
beyond his grasp. Graduate schools of education should have
more types of experimental programs in progress which extend
over several generations of graduate students and are partially
subsidized by departmental funds in exchange for control of the
data.

Psychological Problems of Level Organization.—The obstacles which are discovered when one seeks to make an objective investigation of the best type of level organization are
numerous and involved. Only by a program of continuous
experimentation will it be possible to bring these problems under
control. Some of the major subjects for study are:

1. The size of units and the number of grades to be included in
   each unit
2. The best internal organization within each grade

[10] *Peabody Journal of Education,* XXV (1948), 131.

3. Characteristic differences in organization, administration, and method between the major vertical units (elementary, high school, etc.)

1. *The size of units and the number of grades to be included in each unit.* At the present time, there is reason to think that the elementary school should not consist of as many as eight grades. Therefore, further experimentation would be in order on a controlled basis between groups of students in eight- and six-grade elementary units. Experimental work along this line has been done, but it is not conclusive. It would be interesting to try to compress the amount of material covered in a typical eight-grade school into six grades to see what results could be obtained on a comparative basis. It should be borne in mind in such an experiment that more than subject-matter mastery is involved. Previous studies have not taken sufficient cognizance of the effect upon students of undue psychological pressure and overstimulation.

2. *The best internal organization within each grade.* The way in which the grade is organized internally has a definite psychological effect upon the learning of the pupil. The role of the teacher in planning internal organization is of great importance. As Goetting points out:

The organization of the class for instructional purposes is of major concern to every teacher. Classroom activities should be planned in such form and directed according to such procedures as are psychologically sound. They should be organized and directed in keeping with those principles which govern the learning process. Teaching procedures should be conceived as ways and means of obtaining most effectively the objectives which have been set up for realization. The organization and direction of classroom instructional procedures is the test of the teacher in ability to adapt ways and means to desired ends. In effect, this is a major test of the teacher as an educational strategist.[11]

In what grades, for example, is supervised study the most effective technique? Should the typical organization within a

[11] Reprinted by permission of Prentice-Hall, Inc., from *Teaching in the Secondary School*, by M. L. Goetting. Copyright, 1942, by Prentice-Hall, Inc., p. 159.

grade provide for the student doing his studying at school or should home assignments continue to be the rule? There needs to be an extensive experiment on the basic psychological problem of whether students should study at home or not. If it can be shown that they do just as well on the average by not taking books home, this, of course, is not only an extremely challenging discovery to the school but to the parents and the community also because it poses a problem of social supervision which at the present time is handled in some measure (especially during week nights) by home study.

3. *Characteristic differences in organization, administration, and method between the major vertical units.* It is commonly held that the poorest teaching is done at the college level, the next best at the secondary level, and the best of all at the elementary level. In other words, there is a more or less direct relationship between the amount of attention that is paid to quality of teaching and the amount of good teaching that is done. Superior teaching at any level presupposes a knowledge of the psychological attributes of the school population at that level and the way in which these attributes may best be developed. Viewing education as a single and continuous process from top to bottom does not mean that there are no differences in the pupils at the various levels or that differential methods are not needed. Subtle shifts in method must be made to meet the growing maturity and development of the boys and girls. At the same time it is highly essential to preserve the continuity of development and presentation in the major content areas such as English, mathematics, and history.

A Suggested Program of Progressive Development in Organization and Administration.—A psychological attack on the problems of school organization and administration in general is an assignment far too large for any one university or school system to attempt. There is need for a coordinated experimental attack upon the problems after they have been analyzed by a composite group of experts representing psychology, administration, methodology, curriculum, and the classroom. The type of experiment would need to be long-term in nature, adequately financed, and supervised by a board of experts. It would not be necessary to build completely new buildings for some phases of the experiment. A carefully selected group of representative types of school units could be the point of departure. The main research problem would be to equate ability, method, and motivation in order that true comparability would be secured. There should also be an effort to test the social results of various programs as well as the academic.

An attack upon the difficult problem of school levels (as yet far from being solved) by the method of psychological experiment would pay rich long-term dividends. It could not be expected, however, that problems of the magnitude involved could be overcome in a short period of time; but if statistically reliable learning differences were to be established between different types of stratification, the implications for building programs, methodology, and curriculum would be enormous.

QUESTIONS

1. What is the teacher's role in planning school organization?
2. Discuss types of stratification in school organization.
3. What plan of organization did your high school have? Give the advantages and disadvantages of this type from the student's point of view.
4. Why has the present trend for prolonging the length of school attendance developed?
5. Explain Cubberley's views on the development of school grades.
6. List the factors that influence the organization of school systems.
7. Why is there such a need for research in school administration?
8. Discuss the psychological problems of level organization.
9. Give some suggestions for a program of organizational and administrative development. Give reasons underlying suggestions.

Chapter 20

PSYCHOLOGICAL INTERPRETATION
OF THE CURRICULUM

---

1. Viewpoints on the Curriculum

A functional attitude toward curricula—an attitude which maintains that curricula exist only to improve conduct—has been fundamental and dominant in every significant period of modern history. Despite wide acceptance of this attitude, it has passed through many vicissitudes, proceeding at times in only one principal direction and at other times going far astray on the ever-narrowing lanes of its numerous tangents. If pupils' attitudes toward curricula remained the same whether they held curricula useful or useless, the present topic would have no place in educational psychology. The fact is that motives control not only the quality but also the quantity of pupil effort. Motives lead to action in curricula affairs as truly as they do in crime or industry. Attitudes toward curricula determine whether or not either teachers or pupils can find sufficient motives for curricula activities. The operation of the functional attitude in contrast with other attitudes will be described in this section.

The functional attitude does not require its adherents to reject all curricula items that cannot be applied immediately to a non-academic problem. Instead, it requires that whatever is included in a curriculum be essential for such understanding of the subjects themselves as life situations may reasonably be expected to demand. For narrowly specialized demands, highly specialized curricular items may suffice. For life in general, including the marginal activities of the specialized routine worker, appropriate samplings of the essentials of many subjects are needed for profit as well as for pleasure. According to Charters:

An analysis of the important needs, activities, and interests of man outside of a professional career produces a number of areas which are well recognized as components of general education. He needs to vote intelligently on current issues as a citizen of a democracy. He should have sound health for his own sake as well as for the benefit of his friends and the financial welfare of the state. He must understand the motives and behavior of himself and his associates in order to lead a well-adjusted life and carry his share of the responsibilities of society.[1]

The broader the life of the pupil is to be, the broader his curricular experiencing must be. While excluding everything that is useless, the functional attitude includes possible contributions from every department of knowledge and does not bar general education. Faust and Frodin put the matter thus:

The present tendency of our educational system to develop amazingly able specialists without giving them a general and liberal education is a serious threat to democracy. How shall the people of the nation settle wisely their great general problems without a common knowledge of the values which men have cherished and of the way by which men have tried to secure and maintain those values? The trouble with Germany in the late 1930's was a lack not of technical skill and professional proficiency but of this kind of wisdom, the kind of wisdom which it is the purpose of general and liberal education to provide. In its absence the most expert specialists may easily become the tools of selfish and designing leaders or of leaders at least as blind and ignorant as themselves.[2]

General courses, from the nursery school through the graduate school, have been subjected to scrutiny from the functional point of view. Whatever remains in curricula simply because it has long been a favored hurdle for immature human beings stands either as a protest against the prevailing view or as a monument to bygone days when such material had significance. The adoption of the functional attitude does not necessarily exclude any subject or department of knowledge. Instead, it leads to selection of materials which are believed to be necessary for effective conduct at various levels of education and in various economic, social, and cultural pursuits. The importance of

---

[1] *School and Society*, LXVI (1947), 273.
[2] *School Review*, LVI (1948), 15.

general education in overcoming social prejudices against new developments in education is well illustrated by the following quotation from Allen's discussion of the changing nature of medical and health education in modern times:

It can be said that the level of general education determines to a certain extent the health consciousness of the people and their willingness to accept modern scientific medicine. Even in the presence of a mature educational culture some degree of ignorance in matters of health and medical service will be found. People cling stubbornly to their superstitions and prejudices and not infrequently confuse religious convictions and values with science and medical service, often to the detriment of their health. Extension of general and health education appears to be the only method by which the benefits of modern medical science can be made acceptable to these people, assuming, of course, that meanwhile fully adequate medical services are in fact made available.[3]

One of the most venerable functional attitudes toward curricula is that which separates schooling into education and training. Education consists of improvement in all types of conduct for life in general and for specialized literary, technological, or scientific pursuits, while training consists of improvement in specific skills required for a given occupational niche. This distinction has been defended by many scholars, who have usually contended that schools should be devoted to education on the ground that apprenticeship will provide training. In recent years they have asserted also that training, owing to its specific and changing character, cannot be offered except in highly specialized courses and that, even then, few schools except those of the industries concerned can provide suitable training. The amount of general education to be pursued by a given individual will depend upon his qualifications, the character of the training to be undertaken, and the nature of his future occupation. Some authorities insist that, by attempting to provide both education and training at the same time, American schools have failed in both. A suggested plan consists of doing either one or the other thoroughly at any given time and of attempting only one if facilities and time are limited.

[3] Raymond B. Allen, *Medical Education and the Changing Order,* New York: The Commonwealth Fund, 1946, pp. 26-27.

Education provides thorough knowledge of basic facts and principles which are applicable to all types of conduct. For specialized skills, further practice is necessary; the educated person is not necessarily skilful in any particular activity which requires specific skill. As it is possible to possess skill without thorough understanding, a skilled worker need not be educated. In the past, scholars valued education more than training, because of the wider applicability of education and because training fitted pupils only for routine tasks. In an age which emphasizes skilled occupations and in which skilled workers are relatively scarce, training is likely to be more highly valued. Concerning this, Bacon writes:

> Both government and business realize, as never before, the compelling necessity to have an ever larger force of highly trained technicians to support sufficiently the top experts, all of which merely increases the emphasis upon early and peculiarly specialized training.[4]

Whatever the merits of distinguishing between education and training may be, its psychological implications can be stated. Education, to measure up to the foregoing discussions, must be a means of self-realization in terms of behavior. Education for any person cannot be attempted beyond the point at which such self-realization is possible. Education must, however, proceed far enough to enable everyone to assume his responsibilities as a social individual; if such an amount of education is impossible before he begins specific training, it should be provided later. If one adopts this view, one must, therefore, be on guard especially against the assumption that education is an entity or veneer which can be taken on once and for all and which can evermore remain as an individual possession. Training will frankly neglect types of conduct which are not specifically necessary in the performance of a given task.

Many by-products of the functional attitude toward curricula have effectively blocked civilization. A study that has once had functional value has many times been continued beyond its period of usefulness. Many schools of the early modern period,

---

[4] *North Central Association Quarterly,* XXII (1948), 306.

for example, continued an exclusively classical training curriculum into an age in which science was at least equally significant. This continuance of what had been valuable during the Middle Ages proceeded to a point so far removed from functional classicism that all scholars denounced it, while pedants defended it as a means for conquering the wayward spirits of youth. The pedantic attitude was, of course, functional in the sense that otherwise useless material combined with birch rods could break the hardest spirits; the ablest boys from Erasmus to Franklin supplemented their school curricula by more significant curricula which were offered outside the school.

The tendency to glorify what has once been functional is not confined to teachers. The laity is inclined to assume that, if one generation or even an individual has risen to greatness under given curricular conditions, all other persons can rise equally to eminence if the same curricula conditions be reproduced. This notion of curricula as magic still prevents many children from following studies toward which they have strong and legitimate inclinations.

Encyclopedism, or the attempt to master all knowledge, is another by-product of the functional view. It is no longer present in its earlier sense. Comenius, an encyclopedist of the seventeenth century, would now have to content himself with all knowledge about a few divisions of thought. The tendency to regard a subject of study as important in its entirety because of the importance of certain parts of the subject still leads pedants to conclude that, if a foreign language is important for the reading of literature, all the grammar and history of the language are also significant; or that, if home economists need any basic chemistry, they should cheerfully master all basic chemistry, and so on, even to the sacrificing of what is important in favor of some variety of pedantry. Psychologically, this pedantic tendency often leads pupils to conclude that, since much of a given subject is unimportant, the entire subject can be neglected. The ensuing conflict of attitudes produces an emergent that baffles teachers and drives pupils either into rebellion or cowed compliance. Instead of leading to mastery of curricula, it leads pupils to ingenious subterfuges, such as cheating, skilful adoption of the teacher's phrases without understanding, slighting of work, and fawning praise for worthless facts. Teachers, in turn, vainly hope that their curricular materials, though without significance to learners, will correct the learners' undisciplined tendencies and some day lead to universal reverence for knowledge. The fallacies of such spurious and partial knowledge on higher educational levels are discussed by Phillips, who writes:

> While all this goes on, a somewhat significant part of the whole educational pagoda will suffer. The student, notoriously patient in the face of stupidity and contradiction, will continue to be put through his paces, will be dulled and bewildered by the failure of education to make sense. Occasionally he will rebel. He will object to being treated like some sort of corporeal building onto which ells and chimneys and balustrades have been tacked helter skelter. He will note the repetitions, the overlappings, and more than that, the omissions in his general knowledge. He will crave the "whole story"; he will want a pathway to an understanding of life instead of the honeycomb he has found. He will recall cynically the old adage "Don't let your studies interfere with your education." Occasionally he will take action. He will quit college or he will find himself one that comes closest to what he dimly feels a college should be. For the most part, however, he will resign himself philosophically to nearsightedness of his elders. He will reflect sadly that "after all it is the people you meet and not what you learn that makes college valuable." He will set about in the attempt to make his own coherence out of the miscellaneous samplings because that is all he can do.[5]

The functional attitude toward curricula breaks down the artificial division of subject matter into the cultural and the practical, and educative differences arise only in terms of the forms of conduct generated during the learning and in later life. As everyone normally engages at times in vocational conduct and in nonvocational conduct at other times, so the pupil should at times assume a vocational attitude and at other times a non-vocational attitude toward his educational activity. Teachers should strive to show pupils the ultimately practical value of the general phases of education. Adams points out that since general education deals with the "life of today and tomorrow,"

---

[5] *Journal of Education,* CXXXI (1948), 21.

administrators and teachers should keep the following points in mind when formulating a program of this nature:

a. What should be the nature of general education?
b. How may general education correlate with special education?
c. What methods and practices will facilitate general education?
d. For whom is general education to be offered?
e. What changes in school organization and administration are necessary for general education?
f. What shall be the content of general education?
g. What are the aims of general education?
h. By what criteria shall general education be evaluated?
i. How many traditionally subject matter trained teachers become teachers of general education?
j. What part may the public be expected to play in the movement to rebuild the schools' curriculum for general education?
k. What is the relation of general education to the survival of freedom?[6]

2. PSYCHOLOGICAL DETERMINERS OF CURRICULAR ORGANIZATION

The Pupil as a Curricular Determinant.—As pupil self-realization is a fundamental criterion of curriculum values, the adaptation of curricula to pupils and of pupils to curricula is necessary. First, the remoteness of a subject from the pupil is an indication of the psychological problems of this adaptation. Previous experience, present circumstances, and interests indicate the amount and nature of the background which must be provided for self-realization and therefore the distance from the pupil to curricular materials.

Second, the needs of pupils as felt by themselves affect the values derived from curricular experiences. Although the incidental felt needs of pupils form an obvious basis for many educative activities, such as stamp collecting in relation to history and geography or the doll house projects of primary grade children, there are additional needs which have to be aroused before they can be felt. The curiosity and sheer desire for

---

[6] *Bulletin of the National Association of Secondary-School Principals,* XXXII (1948), 26.

knowledge of pupils are additional bases which can be used. Such needs often arise incidentally, *i.e.,* without special effort of schools. Other equally potent needs can be aroused by teachers, and, when so aroused, these needs are as significant and dynamic as when aroused by other persons.

Third, the child's mental and physical growth seem to be achieved by both differentiation and integration. Behavior seems to progress from generalized to specific responses. Body movement in early stages is largely "mass" movement that differentiates into smaller components or more specific responses. The very young show an "all or none" responsiveness in motor, language, and emotional behavior. As time goes on, these whole-body responses tend to become more specific. Refinement of behavior is at first largely a result of differentiation. However, a parallel development may be observed. The specifics are concurrently being reorganized into new wholes so that new types of tasks may be performed. This reorganization of components of behavior into new patterns is the integrative process. Education must then proceed in much the same general manner: namely, from mass or generalized responses to the specific.

Fourth, the limitations of pupils' time, energy, and capacities restrict, perhaps unduly, their adaptation to curricula. The limits of pupils' achievements are seldom if ever reached in any of these three respects, and improved teaching yields improved curricular reactions through a better approach to materials. This improved teaching increases the pull of the learning situation and thus increases the pupils' willingness to devote their time, energy, and capacities to the learning activities required in the mastery of the materials.

The pupils' possible and probable reactions to new curriculum situations can be predicted and properly provided for only after accurate judgments have been made of their capacities. After discussion and tests, together with judgments of previous work, a suitable curriculum for each pupil needs to be planned—sufficiently rigorous for the ablest and sufficiently easy for the slowest. The difficulty here is one that has already been mentioned; that of determining the level upon which a pupil is responding. The pupil may, by dint of effort, memorize and appear by formal responses to comprehend thoroughly that which he knows only by rote. This is not self-realization, and it does not indicate proper adaptation of the curriculum to the pupil. Such a pupil's limitations require a much slower approach to abstractions— words, signs, formulae, etc.—by way of familiar, significant materials. More difficult interpretations and other abstractions will come later.

Social Demands as Curricular Determinants.—In any continuing and progressing culture, curricular values have two paradoxical but reconcilable characteristics: permanence and change. Permanence is necessary for the continuance of the culture that has been fostered through the ages, but it is necessary only so far as it holds fast to what is still good. Change is necessary for the adaptation to new conditions and the use of new data which every progressing period of history brings. Our present problem is not that of formulating criteria by which the permanent and the changing values can be judged; instead, the problem is that of examining the old and the new with reference to psychological issues involved in pupil realization of curricular values to be derived from both the old and the new.

The characteristics of old cultural materials render many of them particularly difficult for immature and inexperienced learners. The old academic culture is systematized and rationalized into abstractions, or principles and formulae which are basic, but which are difficult to grasp. The old culture tells us that there is a happy mean between extremes, that there are arithmetical and geometrical series of progressions, that there is a solar system of which the earth is a small part, that the exportation of bullion should not be prohibited, and so on. Before any of these concepts or principles can be realized by a pupil, he must be both mature and experienced. They fall into the category of the valuable but remote. Other items of the old culture are not only remote, but also valueless, save as they provide perspective: nature abhors a vacuum, meats spontaneously germinate maggots, heavy bodies fall faster than light bodies, and kings have a divine endowment of rights over their subjects.

The characteristics of new cultural materials, though largely derived from earlier conditions, render many of them readily approachable by learners. These new materials often lack systematization, rationalization, and convenient formulae by which they can be applied. English usage, grammatical nomenclature, forms of social conduct, judgments about political issues, vocational problems, and so on, are constantly changing and, in some cases, conflicting. Even though a teacher, parent, or friend may rationalize or set up principles about these matters, there is still confusion about them in the minds of pupils as well as adults. Owing to this lack of generally accepted fixity, such new materials suffer in the opinion of the older, instructed generation. As the opposition of the elders to the practices of youth is sometimes a spur to the young, this condition probably increases the popularity of these new materials when they are treated freely and with due consideration for changing practices. In other cases, new materials consist of short cuts to improved conduct. Tables of logarithms, interest tables, tables of the contents of cisterns, bins, silos, and the like render many circuitous paths of the past unnecessary. Short cuts are now used in reading, typing, modern languages, applied science, and other subjects. These short cuts, although almost invariably opposed by conservatives, have an appeal of practicality to the learner and reduce the remoteness of the subjects from him. Where correctly derived and applied, they facilitate rapid progress and, as in the case of logarithms and other devices, leave no serious gaps in the education of the learner who accepts them ready-made or with little explanation of their derivation. Youth sees in these new materials the keys to economic competence, which is important in social competence in general. Consequently, such cultural items as knowledge and skill in agriculture and industry in general yield strong motivation in learning.

In a democratic commonwealth, more persons have need for a common and a comprehensive grasp of direction of the total contemporary life of the people than in a commonwealth of sheltered persons whose views are dictated and whose actions are directed arbitrarily. For this reason culture, as the total knowledge, skill, and life of the nation, has a broader function in education than it has in a nation where almost everyone is a follower in even the details of life. The need for so broad an understanding of contemporary culture necessitates a close functional approach to this culture in order that it can be experienced and mastered in sufficient amount and quality. Studebaker lists the following information as essential for pupils who are to live in our present-day interdependent world:

. . . before they are prepared to live in an interdependent world, they must be well grounded in these "must" subjects: the geography of the British Commonwealth, the Soviet Union, Latin America, the Far East, Europe, and the United States and its neighbors; supply and demand; inflation and recession; taxation and governmental expenditures; the relation of economic freedom to civil liberties; government—Federal, state, and local, and the responsibilities each must assume for making these governments function efficiently and democratically.

This education for well-informed future citizens must not end with these essential knowledges. Because a thoroughgoing re-examination of what the high schools ought to teach is indicated, there should be a place for instruction on how public opinion is formed, how to use official reports and Government documents, how to fill in tax forms, and how to mark ballots or use a voting machine.[7]

Briefly, then, curricular values, to meet contemporary conditions, must be an outgrowth of the life needs of pupils which lead them to a recognition of both the permanence and change of cultural materials and the significance of both the old and new in our lives. To quote Michael:

Youth expect educational opportunities to meet both their common and differential needs. Young people want an understanding of their social heritage and training in preparation for their common social activities and responsibilities. In addition, they seek a wide range of opportunities for the development of their individual abilities and interests.[8]

---

[7] "Dr. Studebaker Lists 'Must' Subjects for Secondary Students," *School Management*, XVII (1948), 9. (Summary of address by Dr. Studebaker speaking before the Commission on Life-Adjustment Education for Youth.)
[8] *School Executive*, LXVII (1948), 53.

3. Psychological Objectives of the Curriculum

Integration of Behavior Through Grouping of Curricular Materials.—Curricula may be likened to a forest in which the trees must be regarded together as belonging to the forest, while the forest must be regarded as composed of trees whose peculiar characteristics distinguish the quality of the forest. The trees must not hide the forest, nor the forest the trees. In this respect, two tendencies characterize the experiencing of curricula. One leads us to put together the data of experience which belong together; the other leads us to take whole experiences apart in a search for particularized data.

What, then, is the problem? If the better course be taken, we see relationships between items which belong together and weave the items together into manageable wholes. Also, if the better course be taken, we analyze experiences which appear as wholes and search for significant items which can then be more conveniently used as separate items or understood as parts within the total experience, or within different wholes that may then be formed. As Miller points out:

> It is strictly good procedure for many of the activities of life to use that solid method based on reason called from the general to the specific. We give the uninformed first a general view of the thing and then we proceed to specific elements. The general examination lets the learners see the huge masses and how they are put together; permits them to appreciate the immensity of the whole; impresses them with the importance of their study.[9]

In actuality these two courses are pursued as parts of the same process: inductively, we seek relationships between separate items; and deductively, we seek the items which have been rightly or wrongly related.

The problem of relating our experiences—of bringing the trees back into a more clearly discerning forest—begins as soon as selfhood and other incidents of life gain their identities. Thereafter, progressive experiencing consists largely of the discovery of new identities, which, if they are ever to become

---

[9] *Education,* LXVIII (1947), 67-68.

meaningful, must be brought into relationship with one another and with other experiences. The aspect of distinguishing new identities—the trees and their characteristics—is often less acute in schools than the aspect of relating the identities—still being able to see the forest—after the identities have been found. The aspect of relating identities is so acute in the conventional elementary school that programs of unified life experiences have been devised as correctives of the tendency to keep apart the items which should be put together.

The principles which underlie the unification of experience through departmentalized curricula can now be stated:

1. Materials should be selected for their real life significance for pupils. This principle requires teachers and other curriculum-makers to select materials which can be related to pupils' past experiences and which will stimulate progressive conduct by continued use of these materials.

2. Basic materials should be selected by experts. The importance of basic controls is too great to permit dependence upon materials which have been hastily gathered and thrown together, when the supply of excellent, well-organized material is as adequate as at present.

3. Materials should be organized so that they can be mastered in natural settings. This requires actual provision for the real life significance of the materials selected according to the first principle—materials must have significance which the pupils can and do see.

4. Materials should be organized so that parts can be integrated with wholes. Curricular items are always parts of complex situations. Instead of being approached and studied in isolation in the vain hope that pupils will relate them somehow, the items should be so organized that they can be studied as related parts of a larger whole.

5. Materials should be organized to give meanings which will affect conduct. Isolated items are often meaningless; they acquire meaning when they are related or unified. Generalizations are often practically inapplicable; they acquire applicability when they are analyzed into particulars, so that the

generalizations themselves can later be modified to meet specific situations. Goodrich and Folsom write:

Long term planning is concerned largely with principles and procedures by which: the content may be balanced with respect to areas of living; subject matter learnings and study skills are put to use; the techniques of cooperative endeavor understood and practiced; the individuality of pupils developed and expressed; a fresh and interesting approach made each time the same problem is dealt with on successive maturity levels. Short term planning is concerned with choosing the actual experiences likely to have greatest value at the time they are lived and with the detail of conducting them so as to secure the maximum potential value. The greatest aid in short term planning should be the principles laid down in the long term plans. Short term planning has a much larger place in the core area than in subject courses where logical arrangement of subject matter is of greater importance. Pupils must participate in the short term planning because their reactions and their expressed interests will help to keep the activities life-centered and because they must have a part in planning in order to learn to plan.[10]

Subject-Matter Sequences.—Subject-matter sequences present psychological problems which cannot be settled by logic. Everyone knows that the use of litmus paper to discover the presence of acid or alkali is simpler than the understanding of why litmus paper can be so used, or that turning on a radio is easier than the understanding of the data of sound and electricity which are involved in the radio. It is clear also that many formulae can be used with ease, while the data as organized in deriving the formulae can be used only with difficulty; for example, any college student can readily use logarithms, but he has difficulty in understanding the data that Napier used in deriving these numbers. Likewise, one can readily employ an abstraction as an explanation in saying that masses near the earth fall because of gravity, but the data which underlie this principle, its causes and operation in the whole matter of gravitation, are very difficult. Considerations such as these lead to the conclusion that the functional value of materials, apparatus, formulae, and other abstractions can, in many cases, be learned

---

[10] *Journal of Educational Research,* XLI (1948), 358.

more readily than the particulars upon which they are based. Although a logical approach to such matters might require an understanding of data and their relationships, it must be acknowledged that few, if any, persons need such an understanding of the short cuts which they employ, and also that such an understanding can often be properly postponed in sequences.

In certain cases, however, the advanced steps taken by man can be neither understood nor applied without comprehensive knowledge of underlying data. To say to a child that economic conditions are among the most potent causes of war would seldom yield more reaction than casual verbal repetition even if the meanings of the separate words were known. The child would need data—information about living conditions, industry, commerce, unrest, and so on. This case is different from the instances cited in the preceding paragraph, because the child lacks the related background necessary for understanding or application of the principle. Therefore, the learner should proceed from the abstract to the concrete or vice versa, according to the total situation in which learning is taking place. At times, abstractions fully satisfy needs; at other times, abstractions are useless unless arrived at through laborious study of background information.

Owing to the general need for certain guides of conduct, everyone must master a common body of curricular materials. The elementary school is charged, therefore, with teaching a relatively undifferentiated body of material to heterogeneous pupils. The reasons for this period of undifferentiated study are in part psychological. As a means of gaining controls of conduct which are necessary for everyone, the elements of subjects such as language—written or oral—mathematics, science, art, social studies, and physical education must be pursued by everyone, not exhaustively, but in their fundamentals.

These elementary tools of learning are, therefore, pursued during the early period. This period is not, however, entirely undifferentiated. While all pupils pursue these studies, the manner of this pursuit is differentiated for individual pupils. All pupils in reading may, for example, read from the same basal reader, but good schools provide a rich variety of supplementary

material which is read in different amounts and for different
purposes, according to the abilities, interests, and needs of the
different pupils. This is true not only in schools which teach
the subjects separately, but also in schools which unify all the
subjects as described in the preceding section. A basal core of
material is necessary for all; beyond this comes differentiation.
A similar situation exists in arithmetic, where supplementary
work provides practice according to the individual situation.
Here lies the basic difference between the lockstep curriculum
in which everyone does the same things and the curriculum in
which everyone acquires the same fundamental controls and
supplements them according to his own abilities, interests, and
needs.

Of equal importance, psychologically, is the fact that the
curriculum must conform with the varying stages of readiness
of the learners. In many cases readiness seems to be particularly related to maturation. Exposing the learner to study
materials before he has reached a readiness stage for that particular training is wasteful of time and effort and may develop
detrimental habits of resistance or inattention in the young
learner. In the individual case the teacher should expect wide
variations in readiness in what seem to be very similar children.
Curricular materials should correlate with the emotional, intellectual, social, and experiential maturity of the learner.

As a consequence of the character of elementary school work,
as just described, the psychological problem of pupils is, in certain respects, more difficult than it is in higher levels of differentiated subjects of study. Regardless of a pupil's interest in
linguistic matters, he is expected to learn to read, write, spell,
and speak correctly. If he goes later to the high school, he will
continue these linguistic studies in the vernacular, but he may or
may not study foreign language and literature. In the elementary school he will study mathematics, but he may avoid this
subject in high school. In the elementary school, therefore,
the teacher has the problem of sufficiently differentiating the
activities of all pupils in connection with materials which are
undifferentiated in name and in basic character; while in the
high school and the college the teacher of subjects other than

English and certain social subjects has only the problem of differentiating the work of the pupils who remain in school and who elect certain curricula. The ability of one pupil may enable him quickly to connect the basic character of a unit with his previous experience and master the fundamentals of a new unit, while the ability of another pupil to see relationships and to master the new may be deficient. The rate of sequence from point to point must vary accordingly. With a given spelling vocabulary, there is need for differentiation of rate according to ability and effort and also according to individual difficulties with certain words. The interests of one pupil may drive him to concentrated persistence, while the interest of another may require much kindling from an inspiring teacher. A pupil may, for example, study geography with interest because of his stamp-collecting experiences, but another pupil may attempt to avoid geography until the teacher tells an interesting story about the people of a remote part of the earth. The needs of one pupil may press him to a study of history as a background for prospective diplomatic service, while another may see no reason for studying history until his teacher definitely shows the vital relationship of history to pressing questions of the day.

By the junior high school period, or much earlier for many pupils, the differentiation of conduct values, in accordance with aptitude shown by that time, is possible. Then, the differentiation which has been made within the subjects taken by all can be extended, as stated above, to differences in the subjects pursued. Such differentiation will normally be progressive as pupils mature and as their aptitudes become more highly specialized. Accompanying this differentiation there should be a continuation in secondary schools of curriculum offerings which are necessary for all and which are either too extensive or too exacting in demands on maturity to have been finished in the elementary school.

In the cycles of schooling provided by the different levels of training, many subjects proceed in a spiral fashion. Arithmetic may be treated first in an "elementary" way and a year or two later in an "advanced" way. History, geography, and other subjects are often treated in the same manner. One's judgment about this point should be tempered by four considerations: (1) the possibility of completing the treatment of certain topics during the first study of them and the drain upon time when they are studied in cycles year after year; (2) the need for such review as the spiral system provides, as in the fundamental processes of arithmetic; (3) the possibility that, since the work is to be repeated, pupils will not reach defensible norms of accomplishment in the lower grades; and (4) the dangers that, without a spiral treatment, pupils may not be able to grasp the possibilities of a subject until unduly late, or that they may be confused by too full treatment of the topics of a subject during the initial study of them. It is possible that, on secondary and collegiate levels, orientation courses such as general science and college freshman subjects can enable students to gain quickly a notion of a broad field which they can then pursue intelligently and fairly comprehensively.

Questions

1. Explain what is meant by a functional attitude toward curricula.
2. Differentiate between education and training.
3. What is general education?
4. Discuss the psychological problems of adapting the curricula to the pupils.
5. Explain the two necessary characteristics of curricula values.
6. Discuss the principles which underlie the unification of experience through departmentalized curricula.
7. Explain the psychological problems of subject sequence.
8. List the four points that should be given consideration in determining subject matter sequence.

Chapter 21

PSYCHOLOGY OF TEACHING METHODS

---

1. Methods in Relation to Objectives

Psychological Purpose of Teaching Methods.—The direction of teaching has the following psychological purposes:

1. *Facilitation.* The facilitation of learning is a primary psychological goal of teaching procedure. As the social heritage grows by accretion throughout the ages both in bulk and in complexity, the young learner being inducted into a new world and an intricate society is faced with an increasingly perplexing problem. Furthermore, social complexity is growing more rapidly than the slow biological evolution which may produce a compensatory increase in individual ability and capacity. Consequently, continuous shortening of the educational process with resultant effects on teaching procedures is requisite. Unfortunately, this forced abbreviation comes into conflict with certain psychological conditions, not the least of which is the necessity for an experiential background for effective learning. The life span of the individual is limited, and the portion of it which is devoted to intensive learning is correspondingly brief. Hence the necessity for facilitation of learning. If there were only one fact in the world to be mastered, a completely inductive procedure could be developed for mastering it, with all associated and concomitant learnings. Since there is a multitude of things to be learned, one of the principal objectives of all teaching procedure is to facilitate the learning of a multiplying set of facts without allowing the learning to become mechanical or meaningless.

2. *Simplification.* One of the ways in which learning is accelerated is by simplification. In this connection, the notion is erroneous that there exists an ascending hierarchy of difficulty, which begins with the concrete and ends with the abstract, and that all abstractions are difficult to master in direct proportion to their abstractness. There are hundreds of "abstractions" which can be grasped quickly by persons of moderate mental ability. Conversely, there are specific, concrete skills, such as delicate surgery involving fine motor adjustment, which are exceedingly difficult to learn.

Effective teaching procedure attempts to extract the prime factors from any conduct problem and to render them as clear and as comprehensible as possible for the learner. The objective of simplification is always the same, but the technique should be in terms of the type of problem and consist of definition, clarifying explanation, provision of experiential background, avoidance of obscure terminology, and other similar aids.

3. *Integration.* Integration in learning leads to stability and meaning. Integration is the thread upon which the beads of conduct are strung. There are two principal methodological elements in producing well-integrated and meaningful learning: first, well-planned work; and second, well-defined goals. According to Lee and Lee:

All learning should be conceived in large units, of the meaning of which each child should be aware. The large unit should be divisible into smaller units, still meaningful and having an understood connection with the larger unit. It should be made certain that all of these units or difficult portions (in terms of each individual child) are thoroughly mastered and combined into the meaningful whole. Teachers must be certain that each child sees the relationship of the parts and the unity of the whole.

When considered in perspective, all *good* teaching falls into this plan, the difficulties usually encountered being the failure to insure that the pupils are conscious of the meanings and the neglect in seeing that all difficult portions are cleared up for each individual pupil.[1]

---

[1] J. Murray Lee and Dorris May Lee, *The Child and His Curriculum,* copyright, 1940, with permission of Appleton-Century-Crofts, Inc., p. 147.

Teachers are often guilty of instruction which is so diffuse and so poorly planned that mental confusion on the part of the pupil, resulting in lack of integration, is a well-nigh guaranteed result. Even carefully planned teaching may go astray of its purpose if the significance and pertinence of what is being taught are not clear both to the teacher and to the learner.

Psychological Factors Which Determine the Teaching Method Followed.—An architect may have a perfect set of plans for the construction of a fifty-story skyscraper. The plans may be practical, feasible, and accurate. Yet architects know that a correct set of plans is only the beginning of the construction of a modern building. Excellent material must be had. Expert workmen must do the job. Skilled workmen will be handicapped by poor material, and quality material will be spoiled by clumsy workmen. Excellence of planning, material, and workmanship are all necessary.

The plans of the builder correspond to the objectives of education. The material and workmen correspond to the pupils and teachers. It is as necessary in education as in building construction to have proper plans, sound material, and skilled workmanship. Buswell points out that there are certain psychological factors which affect all methodology:

Learning is effective to the extent that it is organized and related. Psychological evidence is replete on this point. Many school people seem to have the idea that organization and relatedness are somehow akin to formality. Nothing can be farther from the truth. The main contribution which methods make to the learner is the contribution of organization. This is what scholarship has been doing with our cultural heritage from generation to generation for ages past. It is only by relating and organizing experience that significant truths can be known at all. Schools have suffered much during the past few decades from a superficial psychology which, in the name of newness and progressiveness, has substituted an incidental, unorganized body of content for a content where relationships can be seen clearly. It will take years to overcome this setback.

Furthermore, a sequence is involved in all learning activity. This sequence is determined in part by the nature of the child and his successive levels of maturation and in part by the nature of the content learned, which in itself has a necessary sequence in many cases. Some things must be learned before others because they are involved in later learning; some things must be learned before others because children's minds are not mature enough to understand the complexities of advanced learning at an earlier stage.

Again, the matter of placement of content is inherent in all problems of methodology. When should certain experiences be given? The organization of a program in terms of relationships in learning must be dealt with by administrative officers because teachers of individual subjects or specified levels do not see the whole situation as the administrator can see it.

Finally, there is a time factor which gives over-all control to methodology. How much can be taught in a given period? The entire program of education must be arranged in some sort of time relationship. Learnings are easy or difficult depending on how much time can be given to them. The amount of time that can be given for one unit or subject depends on how much time it is necessary to leave for another.[2]

The recurring factors which influence the kind of teaching procedure requisite are:

1. Pupil ability
2. Teacher personality
3. Nature of the subject
4. Educational facilities
5. Social demands and objectives of education

2. How Methods Can Be Improved

Psychological Analysis of Modern Teaching Procedures.—
1. *The recitation procedure.* The textbook-recitation method, particularly in some of its more lackadaisical forms, has of recent years rightly fallen into some disrepute. The textbook approach, along with lectures, is one form of authoritative method. Douglass and Mills have given an excellent summary of the advantages of this method as compared to the developmental method. They say:

On the basis of use, distinct advantages are claimed for both the authoritative and the developmental methods of teaching. The purported values of each method may be summarized as follows:

---

[2] *Elementary School Journal*, XLVI (September, 1945), 21-22.

Advantages of authoritative method:

1. Economy of time.
2. Presentation of subject matter in a logical manner.
3. Requires less ability and ingenuity on the part of the teacher.
4. Definite, formal presentation preferred by many students.
5. Gives students possession of a body of tangible subject matter.
6. Mastery of material presented by authoritative methods can be ascertained by accepted instruments of measurement.
7. Nature and difficulty of the material may justify the direct, authoritative method instead of more time-consuming methods.
8. Retention is facilitated by reference to textbooks or notes on the lecture.

Advantages of developmental method:

1. Concomitant learnings may be highly important outcomes such as (a) pupil initiative, (b) independent habits of study, (c) techniques of problem solving useful in meeting problems outside of school.
2. Self-activity required of learner satisfies conditions of effective learning.
3. Retention can be reinforced by the learner's repeating the developmental process.
4. More complete response of the learner in the initial learning makes it more permanent, thereby reducing need for excessive drill and repetition.
5. The reality and vividness of the pupil's experience in reaching a conclusion or solving a problem for himself contribute to greater understanding.
6. The activities involved in developmental methods make a greater appeal to active energetic adolescents than do the methods which foster passivity.
7. Method presents greater opportunity for the teacher to observe and diagnose the individual pupil's methods of study, personal qualities, and needs.

Developmental methods require more skill and background than authoritative methods. For this reason, beginning or mediocre teachers are inclined not to use such methods. After having experimented with and attained some mastery in their technique and having become conscious of their peculiar limitations, the teacher who is desirous of improving the quality and effectiveness of his teaching will make increasing use of developmental practices. Developmental methods may be employed with marked advantage if good judgment is exercised in regard to the degree to which the necessary outlay of time is not disproportionate to the educational outcomes which will probably result.[3]

Recently Alberty [4] has written:

The daily recitation procedure (1) is inconsistent with the new psychology of learning, (2) does not provide adequately for individual differences, (3) is destructive of student and teacher initiative, (4) is inadequate for purposes of achieving democratic values, (5) does not lend itself to cooperative teaching, (6) discourages the unifying of subject fields or learning experiences, (7) perpetuates the ground-to-be-covered conception of education, and (8) lends support to the slavish use of the textbook.

There can be little doubt that the textbook-recitation as it actually exists in many schools is as poor as it has been painted by its critics; but criticisms of this method are not invariably based upon psychological considerations. Rather these criticisms tend to stress the failure of the textbook-recitation method, especially when incorrectly employed, to contribute to pupil personality and character development. Some of the criticisms of the textbook-recitation method are not so much indications that the method is psychologically unsound from the standpoint of learning as that it seems to be failing to produce well-motivated learning. This type of criticism is possible of explanation in terms of teacher shortcomings as well as methodological inadequacy.

If the same care were exerted upon the refinement of the textbook-recitation method as has been spent in devising new methods, there might be marked and surprising improvement. Psychologically the textbook-recitation method has much to commend it. Gates [5] suggests the following as possible reasons for the advantages of this method:

---

[3] Harl R. Douglass and Hubert H. Mills, *Teaching in High School,* pp. 83-84. Copyright, 1948, by The Ronald Press Company.

[4] From Alberty: *Reorganizing the High-School Curriculum,* p. 222. Copyright, 1947, by The Macmillan Company and used with their permission.

[5] From Gates, *et al.: Educational Psychology* (3d ed.), p. 378. Copyright, 1948, by The Macmillan Company and used with their permission.

(1) it furnishes an immediate goal to work for; (2) it gives exact knowledge of results, leading to economical direction of effort; (3) it confirms correct responses, and induces confidence; (4) it favors an independent and aggressive attitude; (5) it favors the organization of the material into a coherent response pattern; and finally (6) it utilizes this guiding principle: *It considers the situation which life will present and so arranges the circumstances of learning that the individual will secure experiences in making those reactions which will be demanded.*

For if teaching, at least from the purely psychological standpoint, is nothing more than the scientific control of stimuli, then the recitation method measures up to psychological requirements. A well-written text takes the learner through a systematically organized body of information. In geometry, for example, with the average student, this type of training is valuable and provides the definite elements of disciplined thinking necessary in the development of individuality.

Psychologically, the following facts may be noted regarding the textbook-recitation method:

a) It is an acceptable method for beginning teachers, or for teachers who are handling subjects beyond the realm of their specialties, a practical condition found frequently. One of the objections to some of the "progressive" methods of teaching is that, although in the hands of an expert teacher they give excellent results, in the hands of beginning or inept teachers chaos may result. The project method gone wrong, for instance, is fully as distressing as a dragging recitation lesson.

b) The textbook-recitation method does not always emphasize rote memory. A subtle questioning technique, whether the questions be based upon the textbook or not, provides plenty of opportunity for practice in original thinking, training in organizing one's thoughts before a group, and in originality of expression. Because the lesson is based upon a portion of a textbook is no reason to suppose that questions must be upon only the facts treated in the textbook and that the answers must always be in the words of the textbook.

c) Motivation is not necessarily inherent in any method. There are many types of motivation. For example, it is usually assumed that the textbook-recitation method implies that the teacher asks the questions. This need not be true at all. Pupils may take turns conducting the class under this method. This technique, which has been used successfully, often provides ample training in initiative, responsibility, etc.

d) From the psychological point of view, any omnibus method is open to practical criticism. Methods of teaching as well as methods of study must be selected with several considerations in mind. Certain assumptions underlie the advocacy of any method. All methods depend upon the objective of learning. If someone offers $10,000 as a prize to the person who can quote the most lines verbatim after an hour's study of a book of 500 pages, the method of study for those competing would be different from the method if the prize were for the one who could give the best summary of the whole book. To attain certain types of educational objective, the textbook method is nearly indispensable.

2. Supervised study. Supervised study as a teaching procedure has excellent psychological foundation. For learning to be effective, it must not only be focused upon a subject continuously but must also be facilitated when the difficulties become too formidable to be surmounted by the learner unaided. The supervised study plan is of value in both instances. Unlike the old "study period," which might and frequently did result in random and aimless activity or waste of time, the correctly supervised study period furnishes unobtrusive but ever-present assistance. The style of study hall in which one teacher attempts to keep order with a group numbering hundreds and also strives to assist each pupil with his study can scarcely be regarded as a highly efficient method of directing learning.

The question arises as to whether the supervised study part of the divided period should come first or last. Psychologically there is something to be said for both placements. If the supervised study period comes first, the law of recency is likely to operate and, providing the assignment has been reasonable in length, the recitation is more apt to be a lively one. Yet the forgetting is also likely to be more rapid, since pupils, realizing that the recitation will immediately follow the study, may fall into the habit of learning material only sufficiently well to be able to recite within the hour. When the recitation follows the supervised study period, the teacher is afforded an opportunity of testing and explaining and clarifying difficulties soon after they have occurred. This prevents waste of time by the pupils and allows immediate succession of ideas. The advantage of having supervised study terminate the period is that the recitation may be used to lead up to the study and motivate it.

The psychological considerations concerning the supervised study may be summarized as follows:

a) Supervision should contribute to the facilitation of the learning process in every way possible.

b) Supervised study periods should be neither too long nor too short. Experimental evidence seems to indicate that half an hour is a desirable length for a study period.

There is evidence that a tripartite period consisting of a short review study period at the beginning in which students review what has been studied the day before in school or at home, a recitation, and a supervised study period following the recitation might be effective in promoting learning.

3. *The problem method.* One of the traits necessary, at least theoretically, for effective democratic citizenship is the ability to assume individual responsibility and to think independently. A major charge leveled against the schools on psychological grounds is that they do not so train children but rather turn out graduates who are acquiescent robots rather than keen individualists in the realm of thought.

Observation seems to show that, roughly speaking, the amount of thinking which an organism does is inversely proportionate to the ease of its existence. Thinking is most likely when conduct lines are crossed or blocked. Thought takes place when a problem is present. Therefore, the psychological organization of the school should provide vital problems. Let us examine a few of the implications in the facts noted:

a) The problem must be recognized as real by the learner. Stroud states:

The problems and goals to be of full educational value should be the pupil's own. This does not mean that he should originate them, although it is probably desirable that he have a share in their development and organization; but he must accept them as being worth while to him.[6]

The proximity and concreteness of the issues involved are vital to young learners. Teleological considerations are of small import to children on the secondary level of education. Even in colleges and universities the proximity of the problem has an important bearing on the amount of pressure which is exerted upon the learner. It is probably of more practical effect to tell a candidate for a teaching certificate that a course in methods is necessary to secure that certificate and that the certificate is necessary to teach than to attempt to describe the ultimate advantages of a course in methods in becoming a successful teacher. It is probably more effective to tell an eighth-grade boy that he must have his mathematics before he can graduate from the eighth grade and that he must graduate from the eighth grade before he can enter college to take a course in engineering than to attempt to demonstrate that the course in mathematics will be of value in some remote and distant college course. In other words, the reality of the problem is not infrequently to be judged in terms of the pupil's reaction to it regardless of abstract criteria of validity. If the problem does not seem real to the student, it is not real for pedagogical purposes.

b) The mere fact that what may be termed psychological problem-solving thinking is present in a pupil's conduct is no guarantee that the learning product is desirable socially. Concerning this, Leonard says:

The mere performance of an act of an overt nature is not of itself valuable nor is multiplicity of activities necessarily educative, even though they may be informal. They must be related to the goals established and to the abilities of the individual.[7]

---

[6] James B. Stroud, *Psychology in Education,* New York: Longmans, Green & Co., Inc., 1946, p. 461.
[7] J. Paul Leonard, *Developing the Secondary School Curriculum,* New York: Rinehart & Co., Inc., 1946, p. 107.

Psychology is not the science of social ethics. Neither is it the science of individual morals. The psychologist is primarily interested in explaining the *mechanics* of conduct. The psychological requisites of a method may be satisfied without any guarantee that the method is producing desirable social results. For example, Johnnie is late to school. He has been playing marbles. He is kept after school as punishment. Being kept after school interferes with his projected postschool activity. This is a form of blocking. It calls for some thinking. The result of the thinking is a fabrication. The next morning, Johnnie, being again late because of marble-playing, says that he is tardy because of the sickness of his mother and the fact that he was forced to stay at home for a little while to help her. This yarn produces the desired result. For a time at least, Johnnie is not kept after school, and the teacher admires the boy's manliness. He has solved his school problem. In this example there is evidence of need, not only for progressive conduct but also for progressively directed conduct. Problem-solving thinking in conduct must conform in its finality with both psychological and sociological norms in order to satisfy both psychological and social criteria of quality.

c) To attain the goal of progressive conduct by the problem method of teaching, problems must be successively interrelated. It is impossible to provide a separate motivation for every problem which confronts the learner. Artificial rewards may be effective, but they tend to become cumulative and out of proportion to the activity motivated. It is much better to have the problem present a dual aspect, one phase of which is the immediate dilemma the solution of which is merely a step toward the encompassing of the final obstacle. For example, suppose that a father believes that it is desirable to have his son each evening chop the firewood for the next day. There is no evidence that chopping firewood, except perhaps in the case of individuals who are in danger of freezing to death, is a universally satisfying phenomenon. So the father offers his son a dime the first night that the boy chops the wood. The boy's problem, of course, is to get the dime. The method is to chop the wood. But the second night, on being asked to chop the wood, the boy demurs and the father raises the inducement to twenty-five cents. This may go on and on until the reward for the solution of the problem is entirely out of proportion to its difficulty. Parents' and teachers' problems alike become less when the satisfaction resulting from tasks that are well done is inherent either in the activity itself or in hope of a greater eventual reward. All sound religious persuasion rests upon the latter principle.

The previous discussion on the nature of proximate goals or problems must not be understood to mean that an effort should be made to keep goals always proximate. Motivation through the learner's desire to overcome some problem or obstacle should rise to successively higher levels. Problem teaching in the school should do much, not only to set up proximate difficulties toward the solution of which the learner may be fired, but also to indicate as early as possible more general and remote goals of socially significant nature.

4. *The project method.* One of the chief dangers of the problem method, especially when a series of discrete and unrelated problems is considered, is the lack of continuity and relationship. The project method presents an element of progressive sequence and interrelationship which is not to be found in the ordinary discrete problem, and as such has certain advantages. According to Blackhurst:

The advantage of the project lies in the fact that if properly selected it is life-centered. It touches the concerns of the pupil without the aid of external coercion. Furthermore, it encourages him to master his abilities and apply them in ways pertinent to the problem at hand. Such attitudes and abilities as he develops in thus working are learned in the full scope of a democratic situation and, hence, are genuinely applicable to other life problems as they arise. The boy whose experience with mechanical problems is confined to the textbook and the laboratory is usually lost in the mechanical problems of the work-a-day world. When learning is done in highly abstracted situations the learner fails to perceive the connections between what is going on in the classroom and problems which face him daily about the home. Facts are learned as inert information, and, though many of them may remain as memory, they seldom if ever become applied except as directed in the classroom.

Adults are frequently startled years later in finding that they have been failing to apply principles learned in the abstract during childhood. The project reverses the learning process. The child in learning to prepare a meal as a centralizing activity must consider matters relating to health, food values, cost, aesthetics, social forms, etc. Along with scores of considerations comes the one dealing with the saving of fuel. If gas is used he learns that the flame should be reduced when the water begins to boil. Physics enters at this point as a resource in enlarging his understandings. Water, if unconfined, does not reach a temperature above 212 degrees Fahrenheit. The curiosity of the child now being aroused, he is ready to investigate further into the nature of heat. Since the principles learned grew out of a problem they will tend more than otherwise to lead to a consideration of other problems involving heat.[8]

It has sometimes been assumed that the project must involve a preponderance of overt behavior. Psychologically, a mental project may be followed through in a natural setting with but little overt behavior. This course of activity is easily seen when one bears in mind the relation between language and thought. Language is symbolical conduct. As such, it is used in the solution of problems. Psychologically the main requisite of the project which is solved through the use of symbolic conduct, language or thinking, is that such symbols are backed by and based upon actual experience.

Psychologically the project may be viewed as an elaborated type of problem teaching. With younger children whose attention span is limited, it is relatively difficult to maintain interest in conduct directed toward a distant goal. Teaching almost surely must consist of the execution of simple tasks and the exhibition of simple forms of conduct. The psychological nature of the learner requires this. As the learner matures, however, and his experiential background becomes more ramified, it is possible to expand the problem into a project. Thus the project does not differ from the problem except in extent and internal cohesion.

The following points on the psychological use of the project method should be observed:

---

[8] J. Herbert Blackhurst, *Principles of Methods,* Des Moines, Ia.: University Press, 1936, pp. 208-209.

a) The project may be either for the class as a whole or for individuals. If a project is for the class as a whole, care should be taken that all pupils have an opportunity to contribute to the solution.

b) The project may be used to develop individuality. Individuality, however, is not an unvarying accompaniment of the method. The apparently more flexible and easy-going modern methods of teaching actually require greater attention and subtlety on the part of the teacher rather than more arbitrary procedures.

c) The emphasis of the project method is psychological and not mechanical and the supervision should concentrate upon psychological and not upon mechanical points.

The psychological difference between teaching by the project method and teaching by a deadeningly routinized process is a difference in emphasis. In the project method the process of function is emphasized, whereas in a piecemeal method the structure is emphasized. No plea is here made for the easy tolerance of error; but it is possible to kill interest and initiative by overattention to routine details. When conducting a class of advanced pupils whose work is entirely project in nature, the expert teacher, in making comments upon the performance of pupils, frequently if not usually leaves until the last comments on downright inaccuracies. These latter are not omitted entirely, although when the pupils are fully aware of the faults this may be the case, but the emphasis is upon the success of the project as a whole and not upon the details. It may be contended that the success of most projects in life depends upon the accurate execution of detail as, for example, the need for sharp blocking and tackling in a football game. This contention is correct, but correction should be of such a nature both quantitatively and qualitatively as not to kill interest and initiative.

5. *Socialization.* Social competence may be defined as the ability to react intelligently to external social stimulation and to stimulate similar conduct in others. Social competence is a requisite in one's adjustment to his environment. This adjustment to one's environment is the process of socialization and

can be secured only through active participation in the social world. Discussing this, Gray writes:

> It is evident from our discussion of the basic principles of learning that the individual can acquire socialized behavior patterns only by behaving in a socialized manner. School living must be like out-of-school living. Pupils must solve school problems by co-operative endeavor if they are to learn to participate in a socialized civilization. School-work must be in the form of problems and it must be socialized. The problems must require the united efforts of many pupils. There must be division of labor, specialization, and the exchange of products. School environment must be a network of socialized relationships.[9]

The infant is egocentric or self-centered. Its training tends to accentuate rather than diminish this egocentricity. Fiske [10] has emphasized the plasticity and helplessness of the human infant. The long period of helplessness of the human infant may have its advantages in terms of learning capacity, but it likewise has its disadvantages in the possible augmenting of self-centered reactions. This is not true throughout the animal kingdom. The offspring of some animals never see their parents but take their places in the world fully responsible for their own existence from the day of birth. On the contrary, the human infant's conditioning consists largely of the acquisition of devices to secure attention and comfort. The child's genuine cry of distress becomes associated with an ensuing satisfactory state of affairs, and soon genuine cries of distress are interspersed with pseudo-distress signals. Some children never outgrow these naïve devices, particularly when they are too well protected from a socializing environment. Thus, there are children at the high school or even the college level who depend upon lachrymose or hysterical demonstrations to secure ends which could more properly be reached by somewhat more laborious and prosaic routes.

The child enters the school in an unsocial, if not an antisocial, frame of mind. The task of the school, which it begins immediately, is socialization. This socialization takes place in a

---

[9] J. Stanley Gray, *Psychological Foundations of Education,* New York: American Book Co., 1935, p. 367.
[10] John Fiske, *The Meaning of Infancy.*

number of ways. Contact with schoolmates, the classroom environment itself, the directing influence of the teacher, and the general organization of the school are all phases of the socializing process. Psychologically the recitation is an excellent place for socialization to occur. But to promote socialization the recitation must be socialized. In spite of the fact that the class is a social group, a recitation may be individualistic.

The socialized recitation should embody the following psychological elements:

a) Fairly uniform pupil reaction. As in the case of the class where the teacher is in absolute control, so also in the socialized period will certain students tend to dominate the situation. Socialization is not a passive but an active process. No student gains social competence from sitting and watching other students dominate the situation. Devices by which equality of reaction can be secured are numerous. A rotation method of assuming some responsibility in the class conduct may be used. The teacher may indirectly but effectively take care that each student is given an opportunity to react. It must be borne in mind that the main value of the socializing technique lies in the fact that, properly used, it reaches the whole group. The aggressive, "extrovert" minority will become socialized in any case. This flexibility in student participation may be arranged for in many ways. For example, the class may choose officers or chairmen for the period of the problem or project in which they are currently engaged. There can be a division of labor so that subcommittees or small groups feel that they too are contributing in a significant way. As soon as this contribution has been made, the committee disbands. Panel discussions, junior town meetings, radio interviews, reports of field trips, and other such devices will vary the method and keep interest alive. A visiting expert may discuss a live problem and be followed by a question period. Each teacher should canvass the community for sources of firsthand information.

b) Full use of the socialized recitation should be made not only to secure unanimity of participation in recitation but also to inculcate many social amenities as well. Otherwise, an opportunity has been passed to secure courtesy values fully as great as pupil autonomy in recitation periods.

c) The purpose of the socializing technique should be rationalized by the pupil or, at least, to the pupil. Socialization cannot be secured merely by turning a class loose to drift as it pleases. Even among adults the distinction between liberty and license is often not clear. It is less clear to adolescents. The lesson to be gained, namely that individual freedom of conduct carries an implication of social responsibility, can be learned by a long process of inductive experience, but the acquisition may be quite as efficient and somewhat less painful and time-consuming when the result of direct socializing training.

6. *Laboratory methods.* Education is a *doing* process; learning is active, not passive. Abstractions to be fully understood must be built up through a variety of experiences with concrete situations in detail. The learner's acquisition of knowledge depends upon his own activity rather than upon his ability to sit quietly exposed to the verbalisms of the teacher. All this has been accepted and well verified experimentally since the times of the more enlightened philosophical pedagogues.

The belief that education and progressive conduct are the result of pupil activity led naturally and soon to an emphasis upon laboratory work. In the laboratory the child actually is doing things. The fact that he makes some mistakes is not a matter of paramount concern in inductive laboratory work. Thus in the chemistry laboratory the student is working with chemicals. This direct contact with materials makes the genetics of knowledge meaningful to the learner; its primary purpose is to clarify methods, not add facts. It provides sensory background of a concrete nature upon which later generalizations and laws may be based.

Unfortunately, psychologically sound though it seems at first glance, the laboratory method has not proved as valuable in all respects as was at first hoped. Experimental observations under fairly well controlled conditions do not in all cases show advantages as against some other procedures. This failure of experimental observation to justify the laboratory method taken in conjunction with the fact that laboratory equipment is often the most expensive part of the school's plant has tended recently to diminish interest.

One reason that the laboratory method may not be as successful as would at first thought seem probable is that, in the average high school laboratory course, too many experiments are attempted and nothing can be done thoroughly. In many courses in high school physics, for instance, an effort is usually made to have the class perform practically all the classic experiments in the field. This procedure results in those inept in physics bungling through a series of experiments the meaning of which is never clear.

It would be an incorrect psychological assumption to believe that the laboratory method is the only way in which learning can be made vivid. The primary function of the laboratory method is to provide sensory data upon which general principles may be based. There are other ways in which this may be done. The teacher-demonstration method, for instance, provides sensory data through which learning is strengthened. Any provision which accords multisensory experience is valuable.

To be psychologically sound, the laboratory method should make allowances for the following:

a) Clarity: The relation of activity exercises to the general subject should be evident at all times to the learner. The laboratory should serve as a preparation for class discussions. The relationship between the material covered and theoretical discussions should be clear.

b) Simplicity: Children even at the high school level are not noted for dexterity. Some laboratory exercises require considerable manual skill. Demonstrations which are delicate or dangerous are probably better handled by the teacher-demonstration method. In this connection, it may be said that a combination of the two methods is often effective. Children often like to repeat an experiment when they have once gained an idea of how it should be done through watching the teacher.

c) Brevity: Some experiments extend over too long a period of time and require too elaborate techniques of data selection and treatment. Wherever possible, experiments should be designed to be completed within the limits of the laboratory period. This need not be true at the college level or for those who are planning to become experts in the particular laboratory technique which is being studied. Overly long laboratory exercises, however, tend to lose their pedagogical significance, which is to clarify and emphasize learning.

d) Interest: One function of the laboratory exercise is to motivate. Exercises which require a long, laborious, minute technique or data in elaborate detail do not serve this purpose. While the laboratory period is in no sense a play or recreation period and should not be allowed to result in wasted time as is sometimes the case, it should not kill the student's interest by a heavy monotony of detailed routine.

e) Cooperation: There is much opportunity for furthering social competence in laboratory periods. Many experiments are cooperative in nature. Fundamental steps in subsequent industrial cooperation can be laid at this time.

7. The drill procedure. One of the cornerstones of classroom procedure is drill. It is found in many forms. It is used in varying amounts by different teachers, but in all schools drill has its place and so established is this place in many that one might almost term them "drill schools."

Although psychologists are not universally agreed that a trial-and-error or repetitive process is necessary to discover solutions and fix the learning product in all cases, nevertheless it is generally admitted that in many cases practice through repetition must occur. Therefore, it is of advantage to examine the psychological nature of drill and the manner in which drill can most effectively be carried on.

Drill is traditionally difficult to motivate. No matter how well disguised, drill is bound to consist of more or less monotonous repetition of the same material. Interest is not the essence of monotonous repetition. Furthermore, in many schools, even in functions where drill is proper and necessary, the way in which it is used makes it doubly deadening. Even though drill contains few intrinsic elements of interest, it is possible to attach it to factors which relieve routine. An example of the way in which the monotony of drill may be relieved is the use of games in modern foreign language teaching. Many teachers consider these games frivolous, futile, and time-wasting. This is not true. For, although the class in which a game is being used may not seem to be so orderly as the routine drill class, nevertheless the gain in motivation through the use of such games more than compensates for the time lost.

Not only must drill be motivated as well as possible in view of its unexciting nature, but almost more than in any other type of method must attention to individual differences be carefully given. On the assumption that many classes are not homogeneous groups and that many schools are not able or do not wish to use homogeneous grouping, this is especially requisite. Classroom organization must be flexible enough to take cognizance of psychological differences in pupils. To feel that all students need five, ten, fifteen, or more repetitions of a given content is erroneous. There is no quicker way to raise the disciplinary problem than to keep students drilling in a monotonous fashion upon material which they feel they have already acquired. The psychology of learning teaches that practice beyond the threshold of merely being able to perform a function is valuable in fixing that function permanently. But frequently in actual practice the loss in classroom morale and individual pupil interest more than offsets this. Therefore, interest should be maintained in drill by the methods mentioned in the previous paragraph. When a pupil has mastered the activity reasonably well beyond the threshold of mere performance, routine drill upon it should be eased off. From this particular standpoint, the old monitorial system had much to commend it, because under this plan those who could learn quickly were allowed to teach others in a sort of semisocialized procedure rather than to fritter away their time waiting for slow members of the class to catch up or causing trouble to the teacher.

Drills should be systematically distributed. Some classes bunch drill periods in the way that some college students bunch their study periods during a quarter. Efficiency of practice or drill does not depend entirely upon the mere length of time which is expended. It depends likewise upon the distribution of this time. Well-written textbooks on subjects in which drill is a necessity usually have drill procedures incorporated in almost every lesson. These should be faithfully followed, although they are too often skipped. To take up new material too rapidly for too long a period of time and then to attempt to get in drill necessary on this material in a tiresome and concentrated "review" a week before the end of the semester is not good psychological procedure. An effective practice and one which it is difficult to get students to fall into the habit of following is to think about difficult points or items in odd moments. This method is not time-consuming and it pays dividends. The kind of drill or practice which is needed in mastering scales upon the piano cannot be done in this fashion, but on the other hand there are hundreds of types of learning demanding the mastery of material where such a device is possible.

Drill is most effective when it is conducted upon material which is thoroughly understood. As Butler has written:

Too often drill is depended upon, in itself, to give mind-set, meaning, and the right process. Care should be exercised in preparation of the background or foundation, otherwise drill cannot and does not function efficiently. A pupil may use the wrong process, memorize without knowing meanings, imitate blindly, or see or feel no reason for his practice. Now, before the stamping-in process aimed at in drill is begun, the needed amount of development should be completed.[11]

Everyone has probably had, at some time or other, a teacher who said, "Don't bother now about what this means. Just go ahead and learn it and I'll explain what it means later." Nothing could be less conducive to mastery. For the element of familiarity and understanding accentuates the process of learning and obviates the necessity of excessive amounts of drill.

Drill should be an attentive process if it is to be effective. The routine mumbling of verb forms or the mechanical parroting of formulae is not productive of sharp learning. Only when attention is at a reasonably high pitch can material which is being gone over and over be expected to register. The teacher

[11] Frank A. Butler, *The Improvement of Teaching in Secondary Schools,* Chicago: University of Chicago Press, 1939, p. 323.

should ask students from time to time to explain material being memorized in order to insure that what is being covered is understood and that active attention is being maintained. For this reason the practice of having students write exercises hundreds of times is not sound; interest flags, and desire to learn along with it. Indeed, the whole emphasis should not be upon any given or set number of drills but should rather be stated in terms of the amount that each pupil needs to acquire mastery of the material. Obvious as this may seem, it is unfortunately not always the case, and many teachers still follow the practice of assigning the same class drills for all pupils. Only when drill becomes an active, attentive, rationalized practice pitched in terms of individual needs will a correct place be accorded it in the learning process.

Questions

1. List the psychological aims of all teaching procedures and tell how each is fulfilled.
2. Discuss the psychological factors which influence the type of teaching procedure used.
3. What are the advantages of the recitation type of teaching procedure? the disadvantages?
4. What are the psychological factors that must be kept in mind concerning supervised study?
5. List several examples of problems that could be worked out in your major field for presentation at the secondary level. List the advantages of this method over other procedures that could be used in presenting the same material.
6. What are three psychological considerations that must be kept in mind when setting up problems?
7. What is meant by socialization? How can this best be accomplished?
8. What are the five requirements for making the laboratory method psychologically sound?
9. What factors are necessary for drill to be effective?
10. Which of the teaching methods discussed are most appropriate for use in your major field? Explain by illustration.

PART VI

SOCIAL ADJUSTMENT
THROUGH LEARNING EXPERIENCES

Chapter 22

THE PSYCHOLOGY OF SOCIAL INSTITUTIONS

1. Social Institutions and the Individual

Definition and Importance of Social Institutions.—An institution is something which has been instituted or established and which has a relatively high degree of permanence and a systematic organization. Social institutions are group establishments which have been brought into being for a definite purpose; education, government, family, and religion are examples. To quote Bowden and Melbo:[1]

. . . an institution is an idea or a set of related ideas around which are grouped individuals for the purpose of carrying out or perpetuating these ideas for a given end. Institutions are also relatively permanent group organizations.

You may be asking yourself why it is necessary to go into a discussion of social institutions in a text on educational psychology, the most basic purpose of which is to discuss the nature, mechanism, and optimum conditions for learning. The answer is simple. Learning and teaching are influenced by many things, and it is not possible to understand the complete situation with regard to learning without considering the more influential elements which impinge upon it. Judd[2] holds that social influences are powerful determinants of mental growth and conduct, for man has become civilized through community living. All persons are influenced by institutions as a phase of social environ-

---

[1] By permission from *Social Psychology of Education*, by A. O. Bowden and Irving R. Melbo, p. 13. Copyrighted, 1937. McGraw-Hill Book Co., Inc.
[2] Charles Hubbard Judd, *The Psychology of Social Institutions*, pp. v, 3.

ment, and, in order to understand people well, we must study them not only as individuals but in their group activities. Institutions, according to Judd, "cover all those accumulations of social capital which have been produced in the course of community life."

The influence of institutions upon the school is not an unmixed blessing. Society is a producer of conflict even though there seems to be something fairly deep-seated in human nature which makes human beings want to be with each other. Kinneman [3] points out that association is the dominant element in society and "As the result of this impulse to associate our institutions come to be established."

Yet we all know that the presence of large groups, particularly in relatively restricted areas, sets up a host of problems, many of which lead to disagreement, friction, and strife. Many persons want the advantages that society gives and yet object to paying the price necessary in order to make social institutions function. Organized societies have existed in an unbroken succession since the earliest times because, even though it be difficult for the individual to reconcile himself to the loss of some of his liberty, the immense advantages arising from communal living and particularly from the multiplication and division of labor are too outstanding to be ignored. Yet man has time and again rebelled against the restrictive influences of the best-managed societies and not infrequently there arise the voices of those who advocate sheer anarchy, smitten with the delusion that it is possible to gain all the advantages of group living and pay none of the price. It is the function and duty of the school to promote social understanding, adaptation, and altruism in each generation of new citizens in order to counteract these disruptive and anarchistic forces.

The ever-recurrent questions arise as to where society itself is tending and what its ultimate destiny may be. Bowden and Melbo [4] say that to secure the answer to this question man

---

[3] John A. Kinneman, *Society and Education,* New York: The Macmillan Co., 1932, pp. 164, 165.

[4] By permission from *Social Psychology of Education,* by A. O. Bowden and Irving R. Melbo, pp. 14-15. Copyrighted, 1937. McGraw-Hill Book Co., Inc.

"establishes churches and other religious organizations whose functions are to point out the path of conduct which will lead to a better life to come." Systematized thinking upon the nature and purpose of the universe produces religion as an institution. Since some machinery must be found for familiarizing the young of the group with society's mores, knowledge, and culture, education as an institution comes into being. It is probable that organized labor and organized capital should be added to the list of institutions in a modern society such as the United States, for these fulfill the basic requisites of a social institution.

Once established, social institutions exhibit persistent inertia and a marked proclivity for self-perpetuation. It has proved a well-nigh impossible task, for example, to terminate useless bureaucratic groups in government. The explanation is plain and evident. First, there is the psychological trait of selfishness and self-preservation. A person who has become well established in a paying job does not like to leave it for the hazard of securing another. Second, there is laziness. It is easier to stay in a job that one has, regardless of how unnecessary it may be socially, than to get out and look for a new one. Third, there is the psychological importance of *role*. A person becomes used to playing a certain part in the drama of life and society, and the better this part may be the less he likes to relinquish it to someone else or discontinue it altogether.

Effect of Social Institutions on Education.—There are certain advantages inherent in the nature of the social institution which indirectly affect the nature of the learning situation. These advantages are:

1. Conservation of proved and efficient techniques
2. Development of a systematic body of knowledge
3. Preservation of an orderly body of social procedures

Let us consider them separately for a moment.

1. *Conservation of proved and efficient techniques.* This is a basic social advantage so recognized even by primitive societies without anything resembling the level of social organization and

institutions found in the United States. Furthermore, the conservative function has a definite bearing on education. Education has to teach something, and unless it confines itself entirely to discussion of metaphysics and the like, what it is concerned with is teaching the young of the race ways of doing things.

2. *Development of a systematic body of knowledge.* The conservative tendency of the social institution shows itself here also as in the preservation of techniques. In fact, the massive body of social knowledge is the cultural complement of techniques and offers a rich field from which the educator can draw his materials. Out of this institutionalized body of knowledge comes the major portion of the general education program of which we hear so much today. This systematized body of knowledge is being continually screened, refined, added to, condensed, and interpreted.

3. *Preservation of an orderly body of social procedures.* These constitute the managerial aspects of social institutions. Britt writes:

The existence of the institution means that its members cannot satisfy their needs as well individually as through common routine actions with others.[5]

The continuance of the institution depends upon whether it satisfies its members in the solution of their common problems. The larger a social group becomes, the more standardization of procedure becomes necessary and the greater the degree of cooperation and conformity required. It is the task of education to teach conformity to society's orderly processes and rules such as those governing traffic. In a small country village in the horse-and-buggy days, the number of traffic rules passed by a city council was negligible. Today the problem in mechanics is entirely different. Thus in a city the size of New York there are hundreds upon hundreds of ordinances bearing exclusively upon the problem of the regulation and control of traffic. The psychological by-products are immensely significant. Notice

---

[5] Steuart Henderson Britt, *Social Psychology of Modern Life,* Rev. ed., New York: Rinehart & Co., Inc., 1949, p. 377.

what happens when even the smallest detail goes wrong in the traffic control system. Fenders are bumped, tension mounts, tempers flare, and not infrequently physical encounters occur. Even as highly institutionalized as our procedures have become, the psychic waste and loss are huge. All competent experts assure us that with present techniques tremendous gains could be made by improved use of the educational system to teach modern control methods.

In 1931 Dr. Henry Suzzallo wrote colorfully of the influence exerted by the "people" upon American schools:

> *Our folk-made schools.* Our system of public education is the most nearly folk-made of any national system of education in the world. It is the product of more than 145,000 school boards scattered throughout forty-eight States, and acting for the people of their respective communities. . . .
>
> Thus every economic and social class, and every local geographical area has, limited only by its capacity for political organization, the power to affect the purposes and the services of the public schools.[6]

All interested in education today recognize certain serious limitations arising out of this condition. The gaps in and shortcomings of education are concrete evidence that for one reason or another there is a rather widespread lack of understanding of the changing needs of education. Currently, education is faced with the monumental problem of training a greatly increased school population in an undersized school plant and with insufficient funds for personnel, equipment, and services. The immensity and complexity of the problem indicate that planning of a fundamental nature is imperative. The school of the future will probably gain a higher-level "freedom" as it realizes that such freedom is dependent upon some release of smaller-order, less basic individuality and autonomy. Just as the citizen relinquishes certain individual "freedoms" in order to gain higher-order freedom, so must the public school if it is to serve with sufficient efficiency to merit public support. The problems of war and disaster are today successfully met only by cooperative

---

[6] National Advisory Committee on Education, *Federal Relations to Education,* Part I, Washington, D. C.: The Committee, 1931, pp. 17-18.

action. So, too, must we solve the problems of peace and day-to-day emergencies.

Institutions as Limiting Conditions of Education.—It is well to know the disadvantages characteristic of social institutions and the way these disadvantages constitute conditioning and limiting factors in school organization. There are many kinds of social disadvantage to be found in a large social unit such as the institution. Mention is made particularly of those which affect the psychology of school organization. These are:

1. Retardation of progress
2. Development of fixed control groups
3. Interference with personal liberty

1. *Retardation of progress.* The standardization or institutionalization of any procedure tends toward fixation and slowing down of progress. To quote Groves and Moore:

Being conceived to protect a value held dear by a society, institutions are basically conservative. They seek to maintain the situation at the time of their creation, although changes are sometimes forced upon them.[7]

As Hightower states:

Institutions are slower to change than the material parts of our culture. The rate of change in our material culture has been so rapid in the last hundred years that our slow moving institutions have not been able to keep the pace, resulting in conflict between the two.[8]

What one gains in immediate productivity, stability, standardization, and reliability may be partially lost through the retention of an outmoded instrumentality.

2. *Development of fixed control groups.* An institution is people; it is managed by people. It has already been pointed out in this chapter that control groups tend to perpetuate themselves

[7] Ernest R. Groves and Harry Estill Moore, *An Introduction to Sociology.* New York: Longmans, Green & Co., 1941, p. 458.
[8] Howard W. Hightower, "The School—Its Social Role," *Progressive Education,* XXV (1948), 15.

in office by various kinds of devices. Even in a democracy which makes provision for the greatest possible amount of change this is true. However, a provision of the Constitution of the United States which grants educational autonomy to the several states serves to minimize this danger in the case of education.

3. *Interference with personal liberty.* This is a point that causes real trouble. Vast amounts of work need to be done in the teaching of social sciences in the schools in order to make understanding and wise citizens. As Hart points out:

The standards and judgments of the community are superior to the standards and judgments of the individuals. Education is the process by which individuals are institutionalized—until they conform to the patterns laid down by society.[9]

Many a youthful and adult delinquent is actually convinced within himself that he has been victimized by society and his liberty unnecessarily infringed and restricted. Such persons are all too likely to take the advantages of society and of institutions for granted while objecting to the sacrifice necessary in personal liberty. The nature of the child's early environment, which is definitely egocentric in nature, tends to develop a feeling that society exists to serve the individual. Psychological steps must be carefully planned by which the child progresses from this frame of mind to the stage of social altruism necessary in group living.

2. SCHOOL AND SOCIETY

Function of the School as an Institution.—What then is the psychological function of the school as a social institution? This point is highly controversial among psychologists, sociologists, social philosophers, and educators. Some believe that the primary psychological function of the school is to lead society. Others hold that the main purpose of schools is to conserve the best values of the culture and to transmit them to succeeding

---

[9] Joseph Kinmont Hart, *A Social Interpretation of Education,* New York: Henry Holt & Co., Inc., 1929, pp. 102-3.

generations. The two points of view need not be antithetical. A synthesis of these viewpoints is expressed by Moehlman:

The need for education arises from the problems involved in the continuity of society. Nature has provided for biological continuity through mating and the production of young. The experiences, inventions and habits of mankind that form the cultural patterns, have developed outside the biological area and are non-transmittable by biological means. Unless each generation is to start from scratch in its social functioning, some means must be found for the orderly transmission of social experience. This transmission of the cultural heritage, or social reproduction, has been called education. . . .

Since not even the most primitive culture is completely static, the influence of invention and discovery slowly and almost imperceptibly modifies old practices and adds new ones. If the theory of social evolution is accepted, education has a more important function than the mere transmission of the cultural heritage. It has a second purpose, enhancement or improvement. Education is thus concerned not only with social reproduction but also with the improvement of culture. . . .[10]

Well-prepared schoolteachers should certainly be in psychological rapport with the world, possess a sound general education, and know the interrelationship of their own subjects with world affairs. It is extremely doubtful, however, whether it is either sociologically or psychologically justifiable for the schoolteacher to take a position of radical leadership. Extreme progressives to the contrary, the position cannot be justified. The schools are supported, paid for, and patronized by all religious, political and economic persuasions. Therefore, there is a moral obligation upon the schoolteacher to keep his personal prejudices out of the schoolroom. Bowden and Melbo [11] maintain that not only must the teacher keep his classroom free of these prejudices and innovations but:

It is the duty of every professionally minded educator to combat any attempts to introduce into the current of our educational machinery false and selfish doctrines, whether political, commercial, or otherwise.

[10] Arthur B. Moehlman, *School Administration,* Boston: Houghton Mifflin Co., 1940, pp. 9-10.
[11] By permission from *Social Psychology of Education,* by A. O. Bowden and Irving R. Melbo, p. 208. Copyrighted, 1937. McGraw-Hill Book Co., Inc.

Indoctrination in favor of the democratic form of government is justifiable, since this is the choice of the overwhelming majority of the American people and involves the supreme national welfare. Religious prejudices, economic preferences, party politics, and the like, however, although frequently appearing in sly form, are unjustifiable ethically. The psychological purpose of the school is not to fit the pupil out with a series of prejudices and partisan viewpoints of whatever sort but to teach him how to think, how to solve problems, and how to master basic fundamental techniques of personal, social, and economic competence.

The relation of the school to other social institutions should be attended to by school administrators with the most assiduous care. Like the free press, a free public school system is one of the indispensable bulwarks of democracy. According to Bode:

There has never been a time in our history when education has had a comparable opportunity to justify our faith in liberty and democracy as a new road to peace on earth and goodwill among men.[12]

Adams, in elaborating the same point, says:

America appears to be the only power able to save freedom either for herself or for the world. The people have placed their faith in the schools to win and safeguard freedom anew with each generation. *An implication is that American education must genuinely implement the processes of freedom or be damned for perfidy.*[13]

The essence of democracy is to be found in a free system of education. When a free system of education ceases to exist, the psychological foundations of democracy are destroyed. Freedom always implies responsibility, honesty, integrity, and telling the whole truth. A teacher is the servant of all the people and enjoys public trust of the highest order. If a teacher becomes the agent of any group which is trying to use the schools for propaganda purposes, he should resign his position and promulgate his doctrine under other auspices.

---

[12] *Teachers College Record*, XLIX (1948), 285.
[13] *Bulletin of the National Association of Secondary-School Principals* XXXII (1948), 24.

Questions

1. What is an institution?
2. List some of our most important institutions.
3. Why is the study of institutions important to you as a prospective teacher?
4. What are some of the advantages and disadvantages of communal living?
5. Why does society establish government? churches? schools?
6. Give three reasons why institutions tend to perpetuate themselves?
7. List and discuss some of the advantages derived from social institutions.
8. Cite some instances of orderly bodies of social procedure that have been developed by institutions.
9. What are some of the disadvantages of social institutions? Give examples of each.
10. Discuss the psychological function of the school as a social institution.
11. Do you believe that a teacher is justified in assuming a position of religious or social leadership? Why?
12. What is the relationship of education to democracy? religion?

Chapter 23

SOCIALIZATION

—

1. SOCIALIZATION AS LEARNED BEHAVIOR

An American child has gone a long way on his road to education by the time he enters school at the age of six. At that age he is already unmistakably American in his speech and in his ways, just as a British child is British and a Spanish child is Spanish. In four years, starting from scratch, American children have acquired a facility for English, which is for them a foreign language, far beyond the facility that is gained in four years of high school or college French by most students. This is done in spite of the fact that at the age of one year we have agreed that intelligence is below the level of the brighter idiots. An adult whose intelligence is equivalent to that of the average two-year-old child is called an idiot.

At five, children not only have a great facility with speech, but they have acquired manners and many social skills. They have learned how to get information from other persons, how to make requests of other persons, how to find their way about the neighborhood. In some European countries in the terrible disruption of family life and orderly living that followed the war, occasional five-year-olds turned out to be able to find their own living with little or no help from adults.

How Children Acquire Manners and Customs.—What is the process by which children who are born just members of the species take on the characteristics of their nationality, their neighborhood, their family, their social class? How is behavior forced into social patterns so that when we know of a man the community in which he lives, his age, and his occupation, we are fairly safe in describing his opinions, his manners, his interests, in spite of the fact that we have never seen him? What is the process by which the individual becomes a social being?

When the French sociologist, Gabriel Tarde, published his book *The Laws of Imitation* in 1890, sociologists thought they had an easy answer to this question. Children are born in each generation completely without culture. They acquire it, according to Tarde, through imitation. Even as late as 1908, when William McDougall published his *Introduction to Social Psychology,* it was possible to hold that imitative action was the method by which each generation of human beings takes on the culture of the generation preceding.

This explanation turned out to be unworkable. When it was examined closely, the fact became evident that men do not imitate all they see and hear others doing. Even primitive culture demands that the individuals of the tribe learn to be very different. Some learn to command and others to follow. Some learn to cook and make clothing and others to hunt and fish. There is a division of labor in the simplest society.

We are far better equipped to explain the process of socialization if we undertake the explanation of it in terms of learning. Learning can account for differences among men as well as for likenesses. Children begin learning at birth, but it would be an exaggeration to say that children begin any elaborate socialization at birth. It is true that the very young infant begins to acquire skills beyond his first clumsy performance at nursing, but the first actual imposition on the infant of behaviors that can be properly called cultural usually has to do with toilet training. The child learns to relax the bladder sphincter only in the situation approved by the family. Not all children learn this early. When large numbers of London children were being evacuated to the country to remove them from the dangers of bombing, the country hosts discovered that many slum children had not acquired civilized toilet habits at an age when such acquisition was assumed to be universal or almost so. Children also learn early the proprieties of dress or at least the beginning of such proprieties. They learn to keep modestly covered in public.

When we ask how standards of behavior are established, the answer is not completely simple. It may involve reward, or it may involve punishment. We can, however, give an answer in very general terms. The child's behavior is forced to conform to any standard if nonconformity to this standard is sufficiently disturbing to other persons in the neighborhood.

Behavior which proves annoying to other persons tends strongly to get itself unlearned. A simple illustration of this is an experiment performed by Irvin L. Child with three monkeys.[1] The animals were confined in a cage. The bottom of the cage was a trap door which, on being released, would lower the animal sitting on it into a half-inch of hot water. Also in the cage was a high shelf on which a banana was placed. When any one of the monkeys went to the shelf to retrieve the banana, this operated the catch of the trap door and dunked the other monkeys. After a number of periods in this apparatus there were very interesting results. Notice that the animal who obtained the banana was never punished. It was the animals that did not go after the banana who got the punishment, but the effect of this punishment was to bring it about that no animal touched the banana. When any one of the three approached the shelf, the other two learned to set up such a loud outcry that the offender was distracted and frightened away from his intentions. All three learned by this method to leave the banana strictly alone, a form of primitive moral training. How does this apply to the socialization of children? The answer is that when human beings are living together in a household or neighborhood, behavior that is annoying to others leads the others to discover ways of annoying the offender until the original offense is removed. This learning is of course not perfect. There are many persons who never become completely socialized in this sense. The most civilized community has some members who are chronic annoyances to others. Our devices for punishing nonconformists should not be too severe, however. Much social progress can be traced to individuals who persisted in annoying others until important reforms were made.

---

[1] *Psychological Bulletin*, XXXV (1938), 705.

2. The Family as a Socializing Agent

Learning to Deal with Others.—It is not only annoying behavior that tends to be removed by this process. When a child is motivated by any drive or interest that requires the cooperation of others for its satisfaction, the child learns methods for getting out of the puzzle box. The successful methods will tend to be fixed as habits because they have removed the annoyance. When the annoyance is once removed, the last association with the annoyance remains the behavior that led to its removal. It is in this way that children, after they have once started to talk, quickly learn the words for the expression of their wants. These are the sounds which will activate those around them to cooperate in satisfying the want. This learning requires correct pronunciation of the word simply because an incorrect pronunciation is not understood and is not effective. Three-year-olds learn to control the individuals around them by being cajoling, or coy, or persistent, or by the more violent nuisance techniques.

The person who is learning to ride horseback, using a trained horse, must learn to give the signals to which the horse has been trained to respond. In the same way the child who is learning to make its way in the world must learn to take advantage of the habits and ways already established in those about him. He must learn to speak the language that they understand, he must learn to use the manners which they are trained to expect. The penalty for not conforming to the folkways is failure to attain his desire, gratify his interests, or satisfy his needs.

In a family in which good manners are customary, or what might be called standard operating procedure, children readily acquire these manners because they are effective. Attempts to make children use polite forms or to say "thank you," when these are not standard operating procedure in the family itself, are almost never effective. The mother who tells her child "Say 'thank you' to the lady," when this expression is almost unknown within the family itself, may by insistence or threats establish a tendency on the part of the child to say "thank you" when so commanded by the mother, but the chances that the habit will carry over in a natural situation are very remote.

Davis and Havighurst [2] suggest that parents fail to realize the extent to which their own example directs the acquisition of habits by children and overemphasize "training." This, they believe, is particularly true of middle-class mothers. Children tend to identify themselves with at least one parent and to accept the values, attitudes, and concepts of right and wrong of that parent.

Early family experience establishes a complex of behaviors centering around the use of possessive pronouns: *mine, yours, his, hers.* The early tendency of children to seize and manipulate the large variety of objects in the neighborhood and the inborn tendency for the grasping response to be intensified when an object is pulled away are the beginnings of property rights.

Property rights are first established in children toward the personal belongings of their family and associates. The extension of habits of respect toward public property comes only with later training. Even the defense of ownership will be found to depend on individual experience and so to vary from child to child.

Habits Established Toward the Father.—A number of the social patterns imposed on the growing child by the family environment show their traces in the social order. Consider the nature of the required adjustment of child to the father. In the child's early years all fathers are brighter and stronger than the child. The child must learn to get along with the family in which there is somebody indefinitely stronger than he and indefinitely more powerful. The effect of this adjustment probably never wears off entirely. The set of habits that the child forms toward this more powerful creature remains with the child long after the father's death or long after the difference in mind and body has ceased to be so great. The actual father may, as a boy grows older and stronger and brighter, no longer call out the responses which the very small boy made toward this superior creature, but the responses are there even when the father is no longer the signal for them. These responses

---

[2] W. A. Davis and R. J. Havighurst, *Father of the Man,* Boston: Houghton Mifflin Co., 1947.

explain certain political habits of men. Among the habits originally formed about the father is the strong tendency for men to
accept leadership. It may seem strange and absurd to speak of
a dictator as a father symbol, but there is little doubt that unless
the dictator served as the signal for responses formed in childhood about fathers, he would have no appeal as a leader. Minor
leaders depend for their authority on the same background of
habits. The tendency toward hero-worship varies from individual to individual because experiences with fathers differ.

Fathers differ and the types of leaders acceptable to different
men reflect the differences in fathers. The prewar German
family, particularly the prewar Prussian family, was highly
authoritarian. The father was the boss and ruler. Children
brought up in such a household have a basic habit organization
which makes them amenable to the authority of a leader.[3]

In some boys the actual authority exercised by the father has
been of a sort to encourage resistance, and resistance to the
father's authority tends to develop when that authority is not
consistently and steadily exercised and the father is by turns
insistent and severe and then indifferent. Sometimes punishing
and sometimes not punishing results in the development of habit
not in accord with the father's prejudices, and the subsequent
imposition of authority arouses strong emotional resistance.
Revolt is also favored where a boy's physical constitution offers
a good foundation for active resistance. The boy in whom in-
validism or inferior strength is present is more likely to learn
subservience or pretended compliance. When children appear in
their first classroom, behavior patterns of this kind are already
well established.

It is probably true that most of the material necessary for
understanding the nature of any present-day national government was present a generation ago in the nature of the families
of the nation in question. Eventually we may have an insight
into these childish habits and attitudes that would make it possible for us to predict the direction of change in government,
whether toward or away from increased central authority,

[3] *Character and Personality,* IV (1936), 265-93.

whether more and more organized about an all-powerful dictator. Much of the public behavior toward European dictators is like the religious worship of a sacred character. The dictator is a man-god. In the United States some of our larger cities with substantial foreign-born populations have produced political bosses who have attained authority approaching that of a dictator.

Other Habits Originating in Family Life.—In the United States the teachers of the early grades are usually women. They deal more directly than the political leader with the patterns established in the household toward the mother's authority. In households where the mother's authority is only a derived one and ultimate commands come from the father, the behavior of children towards the teacher reflects this training. The teacher finds control difficult. In some schools the school principal, particularly if he is a man, represents the more absolute authority of the father. There are, in the United States, many households where the mother exercises the authority over the children in her own right, and this is generally reflected in an equal authority possessed by the teacher.

Certain changes are taking place in American households which will ultimately make their mark upon the relation of teacher to pupils in the schools and upon the basic structure of the social order. In the present state of our knowledge, speculation concerning these changes is not yet backed by confirming studies. It is safe to say that a movement toward smaller families and toward more restricted living quarters in apartments, apartment hotels, or small suburban bungalows will cause changes in the basic habit systems on which government and industrial organization are based.

There are lacking also the systematic studies which would confirm or refute our speculation concerning the probable effects of the radio and motion picture on the habit systems built up in childhood. Both of these media reach almost the whole population. It is possible that they will alter the pattern of parental authority, although this is still a matter for speculation only.

3. Extra-Familial Factors in Socialization

Influence of Agemates.—With the onset of puberty, the adolescent is no longer regarded as a child and consequently society expects a different social behavior. The social group with which the adolescent is most intimately associated will determine in a significant way what he will be. If the group and family differ too widely in character and in expectations, the adolescent will usually favor his fellows. His place in the group, as reflected by contacts with it, will influence and mold his role. He interiorizes this role and holds it tenaciously in spite of a great deal of opposing evidence. If the role-characteristics he adopts are acceptable, he is fortunate. If they are not, his behavior will reflect the discrepancy. As he approaches the change from childish roles to the necessity for adopting some adult role, the adolescent often goes through a period in which his own conception of what and who he is (his role) is indeterminate and fluctuating and he is insecure and uncertain of himself. His behavior may appear to adults unique and outrageous when, to the adolescent himself, it is only "what is being done." His language, clothing, hair style, and mannerisms become as typical of his group as it is possible for him to make them. This conformity avoids embarrassment and self-consciousness. Identification with his group stimulates loyalty and often develops into social discrimination. Some persons he regards as his superiors, while others are his inferiors, and by his behavior he reveals that he has made this classification.

In prewar Germany and Italy the social and economic organization offered adult roles to only a portion of the youth, and Hitler and Mussolini easily enlisted the loyalty and support of the insecure portion by offering them roles and adult parts as storm troopers or as Roman legionnaires. The greatest achievement of American democracy has been the acceptance of persons of different religious faiths, different political beliefs, and different cultural origins as fellow-citizens, as neighbors. Hitler and Mussolini capitalized a strong tendency for an exclusive identification with racial group and political organization.

Indoctrination in Role.—One of the most important factors in the socialization of the individual lies in his indoctrination in the social role to be taken. The whole structure of society is built around the acceptance of roles by individuals. The division of labor that is basic to efficient operation of a social order is organized about the names of occupations and names for social status. A large number of our English family names reflect the importance of this organization of occupation about a name. When linen cloth was homespun, the bleaching of that cloth was often left to a *fuller*. If a tradesman wove the cloth, he was called a *weaver*. A man who attached the feather to an arrow which guided it in straight flight fletched the arrow and was called a *fletcher*. An old name for a wagon is *wain*. A *wainwright* was a wagonmaker, a *cartwright* made carts. Our early blacksmiths have left many *smiths* among us. *Millers* and *bakers* no longer follow their ancestral occupation. *Clarks* no longer clerk. *Taylors* no longer sew and *shoemakers* have not stuck to their lasts.

About the name for a social status or occupation were organized the ideas for appropriate behavior of that status or occupation. The rights, privileges, and duties of the role attach to the name. Knowing that the man at the door is the postman or the policeman on the beat or the Fuller brush man controls our behavior toward him. How we receive him is in large part determined by these magic words.

One of the earliest components of role to get thorough indoctrination is the designation of sex. Children learn very early that they are boys or girls. There follows immediately a mass of social compulsion. Children learn that little boys and girls dress differently. Boys are shamed out of playing with dolls at an early age and shamed out of bursting into tears and weeping. There are other cultures where grown men may weep unashamed, but they may not do so in the United States except under extraordinary stress. As children grow larger, roles become more inclusive and complex. They become aware of age, and to some extent of the behavior appropriate to an age. The celebration of birthdays helps along this temporal development of roles. The child just turned eight may be induced to break with seven-year-old habits.

Children are subjected to an impressive amount of direct propaganda aimed at establishing roles. Some of this propaganda is negative and identifies certain types of behavior with undesirable roles. The role of the naughty little boy or "common children" or, at the worst, of thief or liar is described and identified with appropriate lines of action in the hope that these will then be avoided because the role is to be avoided. On the positive side, children are urged to be good, to be nice, to live up to their age, to live up to their family traditions. Many of the private schools attempt elaborate programs for leading their pupils to identify themselves as members of the school and to behave appropriately.

A bright and amiable little girl turned out to be very proud of a grade of "D" in citizenship. The explanation was a simple one. All her other grades were the highest possible, but citizenship had been identified by the teacher with the tendency to make no trouble in the classroom and the high grade in citizenship had been accompanied by such obvious signs of approval from the teacher that it was identical with the role of "teacher's pet." This role was made almost intolerable by the teasing of other children on the playground and after school. The only obvious escape was to incur the displeasure of the teacher in some form evident to all the pupils.

Social psychologists are having some initial successes in attempts to measure and record such intangible things as interest and role. The strength of an interest can be measured by the interests which will be given up for its sake. The objective determinations by roles will be more difficult and will involve interview methods. At a large high school all the pupils were asked to state what vocation they hoped to enter. Arrangements were then made for representatives of each of the occupations which had sufficient takers to give talks on the nature of their occupation. The largest group of boys had expressed an intention to become detectives. We may well look on this apparent choice with a certain suspicion. Crime programs on the radio or screen probably explain this preference.

The evidence that a child has adopted a particular role depends on observation of behavior appropriate to that role and possible confirmation by the admission of the role in so many words. An observing teacher can often pick out among her pupils, if they are in the higher grades, certain ones who have patterned their appearance and manner on a current favorite among motion picture actresses. This can happen without any complete adoption of any appropriate role.

Fads and Fashions.—The social processes that force Americans into a pattern of behavior can be seen working at high speed and with rapid change in the behavior of school children, particularly in their clothing fads. It would require costly research to trace down the actual beginnings of most recent changes in the clothing styles of American school children. Both clothing fads and slang are probably dependent on the comics in some part for their rapid nationwide spread. All fads and fashions obey certain fundamental rules. The basic rule appears to be, astonishingly enough, that the new fashion shall be not actually new. In order to get quick recognition, it is essential that the new style be familiar to its public. This familiarity may have been won in different ways. In some cases the new fashion turns out to be merely the style of several years ago revived. Revivals of this sort are commonplace in men's and women's clothing styles. Or the new fashion may have become familiar because practical demand had forced it on public notice. In at least one large American city grade school boys developed a style of rolling up the right trouser leg. This was begun as a very practical measure. The boys who rode bicycles had to choose between a trouser guard which would keep the trousers out of the way of the bicycle chain and rolling up the trouser out of harm's way. Once the fashion had been made familiar by a sufficient number of bicycle riders, it spread to the small boys who owned no bicycles. It had become the thing to do, just as in a large city the fact that people of leisure and sufficient means can spend time in the open acquiring sunburn leads to the use of suntan makeup by the pallid folk who are confined to office or factory and have no chance to be in the sun, or leads to spending the occasional weekend at the beach in the highly uncomfortable occupation of acquiring a quick severe burn.

No new popular tune is new. If it were actually new in melody and rhythm and words, it would be too difficult to repeat. Popular tunes are popular because they are already familiar, because they are old. Twelve notes struck on the piano in random order can be repeated in that order by almost no one. Twelve notes taken from a popular song hit can be readily repeated by the majority of listeners even though they are hearing the song hit for the first time. This is because the same order and rhythm have been used in other songs. The art of writing popular songs consists in rewriting older songs which were popular in their day.

Development of "Conscience" and Social Responsibility.— It is through the process of role adoption that the standards and demands of society are implanted within the individual. Many of the prohibitions of society are more superficial. They are dependent on the presence of observers for their enforcement. There are certain things that children in the beginning of their acquisition of social norms will no longer do in the presence of parents who have corrected them. The rules of table manners and the rules of sharing alike in such desirable things as desserts or sweets depend in their beginning on the presence of the restraining elders. Only when proper behavior and fair behavior have been attached to roles and these roles accepted by the child does such behavior become a part of the individual and independent of enforcement. The child has acquired a conscience. The psychoanalysts have used the term *superego* to indicate this interiorizing of social demands. Conscience, the old-fashioned name for it, was probably a better term than superego. The behavior of American troops in foreign countries illustrated social norms which had not been successfully interiorized. Their enforcement depended on the presence of family or acquaintances or immediate threats of disclosure to persons associated with punishment and restraint. In the completely foreign environment where there were no reminders of the home town, many soldiers demonstrated the superficial nature of their home training in morals and civilized manners. Their behavior was quite analogous to the relapse into confusion and disorder that occasionally takes place in a class that appears well disciplined in the presence of the teacher.

In the process of socialization in the past, the family has undoubtedly been the most powerful determining influence. The extent to which the family's influence as a factor in the patterning of the social order has been affected by the motion picture and radio can only be guessed at. Both of them are rivals of the schools. Both of them are undoubtedly having profound effects on the selection and acceptance of roles. Occupations which a generation ago carried no disgrace are now avoided by nearly all persons because the motion picture represents them as inferior and unfortunate. It is quite possible that public manners are being radically improved by motion pictures which make polite behavior familiar. Both motion picture and radio, although they are powerful influences in socialization, have the disadvantage of being run for private profit. Both of them appeal to the largest possible audience and therefore tend not to lead and direct public taste into better channels but to cater to prevailing tastes and interests. The fortunes of a radio program depend on its "Hooper rating," which is an indication of the number of listeners. The nature of the program is controlled by this fact rather than by public interest or public welfare.

QUESTIONS

1. Why is it a poor policy to give a child favorable attention when he talks "baby talk"?
2. Why does a child's pronunciation get better as he gets older?
3. Under what conditions is resistance to a superior most likely to develop?
4. What is the principal socialization value of graduation exercises?
5. What is the main criticism of the use of the "instinct of imitation" as an explanatory concept?
6. Give an example of the imposition of a way of behaving on one child through the use of social pressure by the group.
7. Is it possible that the feeling of property rights is inborn?

PART VII

PERSONAL ADJUSTMENT
THROUGH LEARNING EXPERIENCES

Chapter 24

ORIGIN AND GROWTH OF PERSONALITY

1. Traits and their Integration

The forerunner of the word "person" was the Latin *persona*. One of the early meanings which *persona* had in Latin was as the name for a mask used on the Roman stage. This meaning gives some hint of the meaning attached to the word used by modern psychologists. A mask is not an essential part of a man, but it does determine the way he looks to others and, therefore, affects the way others will respond to him.

By personality is meant those habit responses of an individual which are judged to be relatively stable and permanent and also to be important determiners of the way in which others respond.

Names for Personal Qualities.—A man may be very tall, but his height is not a part of his personality. At the same time his height may be the cause for many of his personality characteristics. In school a child's size has a great deal to do with the way in which the child is treated by his schoolmates. This may lead the child to develop certain habit responses to his schoolmates, and these habit responses could well become features of his personality. We could give a fair account of an individual's personality if through some miracle he were made invisible to us and we could see only the way in which his playmates respond to him. The English language has many thousands of words describing personality, such as odd, shy, honest, dishonest, retiring, aggressive, dull, brilliant, grateful, ungrateful, industrious, lazy, troublesome, cooperative, vindictive, forgiving, obedient, disobedient. Allport and Odbert collected some seventeen thousand English names for personal traits.[1]

---

[1] Gordon W. Allport and Henry S. Odbert, "Trait-names: A Psycho-lexical Study," *Psychological Monographs*, XLVII, No. 1 (1936).

Many efforts have been made to simplify the description of the important personality traits by reducing them to a small number. One of the early efforts in this direction was made by the Greek physician Hippocrates. He described human beings in terms of four types. Each type was named after one of the body fluids. Excess of this particular fluid was supposed to account for the personality trait. The word *melancholy* is derived from the Greek words for "black" and "bile." A melancholy disposition was supposed to stem from an excess of black bile in the system. Choleric persons were those who had an excess of ordinary bile. Phlegmatic individuals showed the effects of an excessive amount of phlegm in the system, whereas the sanguine were sanguine because of an ample supply of blood. There have been modern efforts to describe individuals in terms of dominant secretions of the endocrine glands— the thyroid, the adrenal, the pituitary, and others. There have also been modern efforts to relate behavior traits to body build and to describe personality and temperament in terms of the relation of height to weight and other physical characteristics.

Canalization of Personality Traits.—But far more profitable strategy for understanding personality must be credited to the Viennese physician Sigmund Freud. Freud did not start by dividing people into types. He proposed to understand the individual by following his development from infancy. The natures of men and women begin to be formed in early childhood.

In the chapter on emotion and motivation it was pointed out that a well-established habit acts as a motive and tends to control behavior. This introduces a large element of what can be described only as accident into the development of personality. One boy escaped punishment from an older boy by lying down when attacked. Puppies learn a similar defense against larger dogs. This habit interferes with the development of habits of bold self-defense. On the other hand, one experience of easy victory in physical combat may serve to direct future development into channels of challenging aggression. The experience of the first day in school may set habit patterns which are difficult to eradicate.

Physical experience has so shaped the individual that it tends strongly to determine how he will react to new situations. Whether the beginning school child perceives the teacher as a friendly person or as a hostile stranger has been determined in part by the child's previous experience at home with grownups. The child who has not been punished or scolded or teased at home will not look on any stranger as a potential punisher or scold. The first days of school will be very different for three children, one of whom is habituated to an almost continuous companionship with the mother, a second used to playing with other children away from grownups, and a third habituated to finding his own amusement and being alone for long periods. It would be a great mistake to think of these early habits as fixations which will persist all through subsequent development. Children are capable of learning, and all habit patterns are subject to change. The point here is not that earlier habits remain, but that earlier habits play a part in determining the direction of the development of later habits.

The children who are gathered together in a first grade class on the first day of school represent an astonishing variety of home experiences and will therefore be capable of an astonishing variety of early reactions to the teacher and the schoolroom situation. Some have been allowed much more freedom of action than others. Some of them are used to playing with many playmates. Some of them are adjusted to a sympathetic and interested mother. Others have been supervised by an unsympathetic adult to whom the child represented just a job. Some parents have had spare energy to enjoy their children, in other parents fatigue has colored their relationship to children with undertones of impatience and bad temper.

A number of things favor the teacher at the beginning of the school year. The classroom situation is new enough and strange enough to cause a certain amount of confusion and emotional reinforcement in the children. The first day is an extremely exciting day for most of them. This excitement can serve to favor the establishment of new attitudes and new responses in place of those they bring from home. We can therefore observe in many children almost a separate schoolroom personality, a set of habits and attitudes which are practically unknown at home. At school the child is a different person. In many cases home, classroom, and playground may have compelled adjustments so different that the child could almost be described as being three persons. Children who have learned in their homes excellent English and clear diction may, if they are associating with children who speak the language of a different social stratum, quickly adopt that language with the slang and vulgarisms of the playground. Two British parents who spent some years in New York placed their children in a public school. The children continued to use at home the speech of the upper-class English, while at school they spoke a slangy and colloquial American, and in the classroom a rather stilted compromise between the two. In a sense the child develops many "selves" specific to differing situations. The same child may have a "school" self, a "home" self, a "Miss Young" self, and a "Principal Brown" self. To these different situations and persons he presents a different personality. No doubt he has discovered that a certain patterning of traits, attitudes, and wishes are satisfying in the Principal Brown situation, while a different "line" serves him best when dealing with his teacher or with his family.

The psychoanalysts, following Freud, have claimed that profound and permanent differences in personality are based on the habit adjustments of very early infancy, particularly those that center about nursing and weaning and training in the control of bladder and bowel movements. There can be no doubt whatever that early experiences organized about these situations and about the differences between the sexes leave traces which are discoverable in later life. The psychoanalytic contention that these early organizations determine patterns of adjustment in terms of which we can understand adult personalities is highly questionable. The very fact that in the psychoanalytic accounts themselves it is admitted that later experiences can have profound effects should make us cautious about attempting to explain too much in terms of infantile adjustment.

The most important habit component of personality lies in that set of habits organized around word symbols which may

be called the role. As soon as a child begins to acquire the use
of language we can observe the beginnings of role. The child
may use the word "baby" to describe himself, "Baby does this"
or "Baby does that." The infant may use its own name, "Mil-
dred likes the kitty." Children early become responsive to their
own names and descriptions. They become alert when they are
referred to by name.

Through the use by adults in his presence of words charac-
terizing him, a child may be led to incorporate these words in
his notion of himself, his role. The child frequently referred to
as a "problem child" may note the concern or displeasure or
derision that accompanies the use of the word. If he is led to
accept the role, to think of himself as a problem child, this may
have profound effects on his behavior, on what he will attempt,
on whether he will cooperate or obey. Labeling with unacceptable names carries with it potential harm. School difficulties
and failures often result from small incidents which affect role.

Defense Mechanisms.—When the role is threatened or attacked, the individual can react in a number of ways. Some of
these ways are common enough to have been given names. All
of them are to be considered normal when used within limits;
and all are frequently encountered. "Saving face" is a basic
mode of conduct. The following paragraphs describe some of
the common mechanisms by which roles tend to be defended
when disturbed.

One very common reaction is a tendency to attribute one's
own fault to others. A child points out bad manners in another
child. An accusation that another child has cheated in a test
sometimes turns out to be motivated by the tendency to get rid
of an undesirable quality by calling attention to it in another.
This tendency is called *projection*. Projection as a defense
mechanism is the act of attributing one's own faults, characteristics, attitudes, motives, or experiences to others. In a sense
it is the same mechanism of projection through which we understand and sympathize with others. The inability to project is
asserted by Cameron to be one of the outstanding characteristics
of a common form of mental disease, schizophrenia. The social
bore is a person who cannot put himself in the place of his

hearers. Extreme projection or unconscious projection is, however, an outstanding symptom of personality maladjustment, and the basis for many serious misunderstandings, quarrels, confusions, and social conflicts. Projection is often found to be the basis for the expressed suspicion of others. It enables a child to talk about the fault or sin or crime and test the reaction of other persons to it without acknowledging it as his own and having to suffer the consequences. Every clinical psychologist has had dozens of first interviews which begin with a statement that "I have a friend who . . ." This device does not amount to projection because it is conscious and soon abandoned after the ice is broken.

Very often the teacher is confused by his inability to recognize projection in his own behavior. As he looks at Henry and remarks to himself or to others, "Henry is a problem child" or "Henry is a thief," he is projecting his own evaluations of problem child and thief. Henry may not be either problem child or thief to others who know more about him or who have had some different past experiences themselves. In other words, the epithets the teacher has used tell very little about Henry but may reveal a great deal about the teacher. The teacher who sees misbehavior in every move made by certain children is often interpreting behavior in the light of his own interests and tendencies to action. The teacher who has had firsthand experience with cheating may see cheating all about him in his classroom. The child who frequently cheats may save face by projecting the same behavior upon all his classmates.

A great deal may be discovered by noting the quality of projection. This is, of course, the basic principle of the so-called projective techniques of testing personality. Ambiguous designs or pictures are shown to respondents who are requested to describe the stimulus completely. A response in such a situation can be given only by "reading into" the design some combination of experiences, motives, and attitudes that are familiar to the person making the response. Thus we learn something about the person making the response through classifying and evaluating his perceptions.

Another form of defense mechanism in daily use by practically all persons is called *rationalization*. This is a tendency to redescribe or restate some objectionable aspect of role in unobjectionable terms. When a pupil fails in a test, this could readily be interpreted either as a reflection on the pupil or on the teacher. If the pupil is asked about the failure, there is a strong tendency for the failure to be described in terms which do not do violence to the pupil's role. If he thinks of himself as without ability in the subject in which he was tested, there may be a frank admission that he failed because he was not good enough. But if the pupil's role does not include this disability, if he thinks of himself as of average ability, the explanation may take the form of a complaint of unfairness on the part of the teacher or an inability to teach, or a special prejudice or any other of the dozens of faults which pupils can find in teachers. The teacher's account will be a very different one. Few teachers are capable of admitting that they are poor teachers, because this would logically demand that they seek other employment. The failure is attributed to the stupidity of the pupil, or to laziness, or to bad home conditions. The boy or girl who is not popular at parties or who is not invited to the gatherings of schoolmates may develop elaborate rationalizations of this fact which conceal the cause of unpopularity and describe the situation in terms of a personal dislike for parties—"Parties are silly." A college graduate who had proved a conspicuous failure at teaching returned after her first year to tell her college instructors how stupid and pig-headed were the members of the school boards where she had served as a teacher, how dim-witted and backward and mannerless were the children, and how fault-finding, jealous, and hostile were the teachers.

Projection and rationalization are in many ways alike. In both there is an explaining away of faults and thereby a reduction of tension and conflict as well as a successful face-saving. Rationalization, however, is usually a matter of finding acceptable reasons rather than real reasons for one's behavior. As Shaffer puts it:

Rationalization is not a process of logical thought; it is an attempt to make conduct *appear* sensible and in conformity with custom and social expectation. The person who rationalizes gives "good" reasons for his behavior, to protect himself from the necessity of acknowledging the *real* reasons which *he* regards as inferior or blameworthy.[2]

Rationalization has constructive as well as merely protective uses. It is a resource by which self-confidence and self-respect are maintained. Cameron says of rationalization:

The public tends to hold rationalization in contempt and by implication to deny using it, little realizing that in so doing they are illustrating the technique they disclaim. But rationalizing also has positive values. If it did nothing more, its function in cutting self-analysis short would still establish it as a desirable protective device. In ordinary everyday affairs, there is neither the leisure nor the necessity for analyzing out all one's motives. As a matter of fact, the need to track down and analyze the origins and meanings of one's conduct is an outstanding compulsive symptom which has incapacitated many a patient for normal life. For routine unimportant incidents it usually does no harm to assign a socially approved but unwarranted motive, and it may make an individual happier and more self-respecting as well as more welcome to those among whom he lives. Rationalizing undoubtedly keeps down the annual crop of persons whose sense of inadequacy or guilt forces them into exaggerations of other special adjustive techniques and leaves them more vulnerable to behavior pathology.[3]

A third defense mechanism is *repression*. This may be described as a tendency to avoid all mention in thought or word of the disturbing situation which threatens role. If we listen to small boys describe their combat, we are struck with the high preponderance of victories. In the same way in which all persons tend to learn not to mention unpleasant subjects because the result is uneasiness and embarrassment, so all persons learn in some degree to avoid mentioning their own faults and humiliations. We learn to forget our humiliating and embarrassing experiences because remembering them brings distress, and dis-

[2] L. F. Shaffer, *The Psychology of Adjustment,* Boston: Houghton Mifflin Co., 1936, p. 168.

[3] Norman Cameron, *The Psychology of Behavior Disorders,* Boston: Houghton Mifflin Co., 1947, p. 164.

tress acts like any form of annoying motivation to bring about a new habit which will avoid the distress. Being in a state of embarrassment or shame is, so far as the learning process is concerned, equivalent to the confinement of the cat in the puzzle box. Under confinement the cat learns a way out. People similarly learn to avoid the signals which bring distress.

A fourth type of defense mechanism is *regression*. This consists in responding to persistent annoyance or frustration by reverting to earlier habits. The concept of regression is not a satisfactory one because it is essentially vague and ambiguous. When we are blocked or in trouble, there is nothing anyone could possibly do other than revert to habits previously formed. Every person is limited to a repertoire of reactions formed in previous experience. The psychoanalysts use the word for occasional appearances of childish or infantile behavior in mental patients. Many of these are not genuine reversions to habits from the patient's own infancy but are adoptions of a childish or infantile role which serves a present purpose.

A child's turning to toys used in solitary play after experiencing unhappiness in a group, the use of tantrums, sulking, or whining in order to secure desired objects or privileges, and the return to home and mother after disappointments in college are some of the more common reactions to which the name "regression" is rather carelessly attached. When behavior in one direction is blocked or frustrated, the individual is of necessity dependent upon his own repertoire from his own past. Regression is, like the other defense mechanisms here being described, not a mechanism in any basic sense but only a convenient term for behavior occasionally encountered. The actual basic mechanisms are habit and associative learning.

A fifth mechanism described by the psychoanalysts is *displacement*. By this is meant reacting with emotion to some situation which represents a substitution for the cause of the reaction. This rather obscure description really means little more than associative learning or conditioning. The obscurity of the notion can best be removed by giving an illustration or two. On the playground a child who has been teased or bullied by a larger child may take out the consequent resentment on some more helpless object. Or the child who has quarreled with his mother may express resentment toward the teacher.

A sixth defense mechanism is *compensation*. By this is meant a tendency to react to criticism or implied inferiority in such a way as to remove the inferiority or nullify its effect by developing excellence in some related line. The boy who is much smaller than his playmates may compensate for this inferiority (if he is made to feel inferior) in a variety of ways. One boy may learn that violent aggression will get him respectful treatment. Another may learn to win the favorable attention of his comrades by clowning. Another may learn to make himself useful and subservient. The pupil for whom school work involving verbal facility is difficult may learn to compensate by habits of industry which get there in the end, or by daily triumphs on the playground which distract companions from notice of the handicap.

A few years ago "inferiority complex" became so familiar a phrase that many a clinical psychologist was approached by patients whose complaint was that they were suffering from an inferiority complex. If no one ever felt inferior and if there were not a very natural tendency actively to compensate for inferiority, civilization might rapidly deteriorate. After all, mathematicians are persons who work hard to improve an inferiority in mathematics. Champion mile runners are made up of men whose records were inferior to the world's record and who worked until they overcame that inferiority. Any person whose feeling of competence is established beyond the possibility of feeling inferior is likely to be of little use to himself or to others.

Homeostasis.—If we look back over these defense mechanisms we can find in them something very similar to what Walter B. Cannon [4] has described in the field of physiology. The maintenance of life in a living body means the maintenance of certain constant states. Outdoors on a winter day in Minneapolis the temperature may be many degrees below zero, or in the summer time it may reach the upper 90's. The inhabitants

---

[4] Walter B. Cannon, *The Wisdom of the Body.*

of Minneapolis maintain through these radical temperature changes an almost constant temperature between 98° and 99° Fahrenheit. When the winter air tends to cool the body, the body compensates for this cooling by developing more heat. When summer weather would tend to raise the temperature of the body, there is an increased secretion of sweat and a relaxing of the surface blood vessels which bring more blood to the surface where it will be cooled. The results of these temperature defense mechanisms is to maintain the body temperature very close to 98.6° Fahrenheit. A radical departure from this temperature indicates that another regulatory mechanism, fever, has been evoked to get rid of poisons in the blood stream. Cannon applies the term "homeostasis" to this tendency of the body to maintain certain states like temperature, the concentration of mineral salts in the blood stream, the oxygen carbon dioxide balance in the blood stream, and the volume of the blood.

2. DESCRIPTION OF PERSONALITY

Difficulties in the Use of Trait Names for Describing Personality.—A personality trait may be defined as a class of actions which may be attributed to an individual. When we call a man honest, we mean that in a wide variety of circumstances we can expect him to do the honest thing. This means that we would expect him to give a reasonably accurate account of the size of the last fish he caught, that we would expect him to pay his debts, that we would expect him to carry out his promises, and that we would expect him to refrain from stealing. If we regard neatness as a trait, we would expect a person who is said to have a high degree of this trait to be neat in a large variety of situations—in the arrangement of his clothing, in the way he leaves his bedroom, in the way in which his possessions are arranged in his desk. When one man is described as more courageous than another, common sense understands this trait to cover a large variety of situations. The brave man is expected to be brave when confronted with a visit to a dentist's chair, an earthquake, a highwayman, or a dangerous path.

There are two serious troubles with describing personality in terms of these general traits. Perhaps both of these troubles are just one trouble at bottom. We know that most of the predictable behaviors that we can expect of people are acquired in the course of experience, and experience is always experience of particular situations. The background of experience that would make a child recite in the classroom without self-consciousness or embarrassment would not necessarily prepare him for visiting the dentist without fear. Contrariwise, the conditioning which some modern dentists urge with small children, which consists in having them visit the dentist on a number of occasions before there is need for doing any work on their teeth, prepares them to visit the dentist without resistance, but does not prepare them to stand bravely before the class and make a recitation. The experience that leads a child to face a dentist bravely has no connection whatever with the background of experience that would lead him to stand up to a larger boy on the playground. Habits tend to be highly specific. Fears tend to be specific. Likes and dislikes tend to be specific. It is more correct to say that we have courages rather than courage.

The first objection to describing personality in terms of general traits is, therefore, that the manner in which the personality is shaped leads to the development of specific behaviors rather than to general traits. This first objection can to some extent be overcome. It is possible to do as Gordon Allport did in developing a test of "ascendance-submission" and select a large number of situations in which an individual would have an opportunity to act aggressively or submissively and determine the proportion of the specific situations in which ascendant behavior would occur.[5] How does the subject act when someone steps ahead of him in a line waiting to buy theater tickets? Does he protest loudly to the offender and make him take his place at the rear of the line? Does he speak, with indignation over the offense, not directly to the offender, but to the two persons nearest him in the line? Or does he restrict himself to feeling injured about it and saying nothing? When a man

---

[5] *Journal of Abnormal and Social Psychology,* XXIII (1928), 118-36.

is served cold coffee in a restaurant, does he call the waitress and ask to have the cup replaced with a hot drink? Does he speak to the waitress apologetically and request the change, or does he merely brood over the incident? Allport's theory was that, by discovering as nearly as possible what a given individual would do in fifty similar situations, we could place him on a scale of ascendance-submission. The person who would react with meekness and timidity to thirty-one out of fifty sample situations might be called more submissive than the person who would react meekly to only seven out of fifty.

This approach to the measurement of general traits is a legitimate one. We might find some justification for it in such a trait as honesty. Although honest behaviors are all learned in particular situations, there are some families where children's behavior is much more supervised than in others and where we can expect the honest response to be made in a large variety of situations governed by the family training.

It was suggested that there are two difficulties with the use of general traits for describing personality, and it was further suggested that the first of these difficulties, namely the fact that learning tends to establish specific behaviors rather than general traits, can be to a certain extent overcome by our method of measurement. The second trouble is harder to deal with. This lies in the fact that when we have measured a general trait in such a way that we get consistent results there does not appear to be very much use for the measurement. The reason that there is very little use for the measurement is that it does not tell us how the person measured will behave in a special circumstance in which we are interested. Knowing that a little girl rates 30 per cent from the top among sixth grade children in industriousness or in courage would tell us very little indeed about what to expect of the girl so rated. We would not at all know what forms her bravery would take, what situations she would face without flinching. Even in the case of a trait like honesty, the actual practical use of behavior descriptions in terms of honesty is highly specific. Keeping track of businessmen's honesty is an occupation in which a large number of large firms are engaged. These credit-rating firms play a very useful part in the community. They do not attempt description in terms of general honesty, but they report a businessman's record in highly specific situations such as the time interval he takes to pay his bills. He may be classified as prompt pay, slow pay, or doubtful pay. The companies do not attempt to predict how accurate his accounts of a fishing trip will be.

Any skilled teacher knows that the understanding of the children being taught rests primarily on experience with these children in specific situations. The teacher learns how John or Harriet acts in this situation and that situation, and any experienced teacher is aware that it would be of very little help to have available at the beginning of the term, when children are unknown to her, a set of measurements on their general personality traits.

There have been published in the last two decades large numbers of tests for personality traits. There are many psychologists who do not believe that any of these tests have demonstrated their validity or their usefulness.

Human nature is highly predictable, but that predictability is not in terms of test scores or personality traits. If we wish to know how a child will behave in a specific set of circumstances, there is one item of information that will give us a reliable basis for prediction. If we can find how the child last behaved in these special circumstances, we can bet heavily on the expectation that he will repeat. The children who prove troublesome in the classroom are not troublesome because they are unpredictable. It is the very predictability of their troublesomeness that leads the teacher to seek help in dealing with them. He knows in advance what can be expected of Robert or Mabel. He knows it only too well. What he needs is not some basis for predicting but information that will enable him to interfere and change behavior in terms of learning. The teacher needs methods for establishing new habits in the place of old.

QUESTIONS

1. According to the definition of personality here used, would peevishness caused by illness be a change in personality?

2. When a child sees a teacher for the first time, what determines the way the child will respond?
3. Why should the teacher attempt to establish favorable attitudes toward the school situation *before* the child becomes accustomed to the new environment?
4. What are some of the dangers of role-playing?
5. Give some examples from everyday life of efforts to defend roles.
6. Are we usually aware of our own use of defense mechanisms?
7. If you want to know what a child will do in a given situation, what information from his past would be most useful?

Chapter 25

HOW EDUCATION AFFECTS PERSONALITY

1. DEVELOPMENT OF SOCIAL TRAITS

In the most thoughtful and comprehensive book on the subject of personality which has appeared in recent years, Gardner Murphy uses as one of his basic notions what he called *canalization.*[1] By this descriptive term he is referring to the fact that in the development of any personality one of the chief determiners of that development is the development which has already taken place. The nature of the early patterns of development can often be traced in the later personality of the individual. The psychoanalysts have not only made much of this point but have probably overemphasized it. Their studies of personality tend to end up by pointing out the direction of infantile development. However, even though there is adequate evidence for traces of this infantile development, it does not tell the whole story of adult personality.

Other psychologists have used slightly different notions to describe the same feature of developing personality. Norman Cameron[2] used the phrase "response sensitivity" to describe the fact that the responses which have been learned in a particular situation have a profound effect on the development of any new responses to that situation. Gordon Allport,[3] who is, like Gardner Murphy, the author of a comprehensive book on the subject of personality, uses the phrase "functional autonomy" to indicate that habits or bents, once they have been developed, have a strong tendency to be preserved.

---

[1] Gardner Murphy, *Personality.* See index under "Canalizations," p. 981.
[2] Norman Cameron, *Psychology of Behavior Disorders.*
[3] Gordon Allport, *Personality—a Psychological Interpretation.*

The figure of speech which is embodied in Gardner Murphy's word "canalization," refers, of course, to the effect of the wearing by a river system of the initial channels in the erosion of a plain. The path taken by the original channel will have a profound effect on the development of the valley.

In terms of canalization, it is undoubtedly true that the main lines of civilization tend to be laid down in the family. This has been pointed out in the chapter on personality. Attitudes developed towards the mother, towards the father, towards brothers and sisters, habits of sharing or of defending one's own, basic notions of property, basic attitudes toward security or the lack of security, have been established in a child by the time he starts to school. What then is left in the way of possible influence of school upon the development of personality? The answer is that school may have profound effects. The American system of education has had far-reaching effects on the development of Americans as personalities. Much of what the nation now is had its origins in the classrooms.

New Social Habits Through School Life.—It is in the classroom and the adjoining playgrounds that most children encounter for the first time numbers of strangers of their own age group and are forced into an active give-and-take with children outside the family circle. Within the family few children have any equals. The other members of the family are, except in the rare case of twins, either older or younger, stronger or weaker, brighter and more sophisticated or less bright and less sophisticated. Contests and struggles between brothers are likely to be one-sided. Families early establish what has among chickens been called the "pecking order." Schjelderup-Ebbe, a Norwegian psychologist, many years ago called attention to the fact that what he called the "pecking order" develops within a few days when a group of hens are placed in the same pen.[4] By this he meant that from their initial encounters certain attitudes developed which led to the result that hen A would peck at hen B and hen B would regularly retreat. B might in turn

---

[4] T. Schjelderup-Ebbe, "Social Life of Birds," in Carl Murchison (ed.), *Handbook of Social Psychology.*

peck at hen C, and C at D. There was established a hierarchy of precedence. In most families this is so obvious and so uniform that it is taken for granted.

At school, children find themselves confronting others of their own age and size with no antecedent pecking order established. Under these circumstances they form new habits of responding to others, new habits of getting acquainted. They encounter children who come from different economic backgrounds. They encounter those whose religious training has been radically different. In many urban schools they encounter children of a race other than their own. The fact that these encounters tend to develop tolerance and familiarity is proved by the strong efforts of many groups toward segregation of their own children from those of other religions or races.

It is only an interesting speculation that the old-fashioned ungraded school of a dozen to thirty children of different ages and different maturities tended to make for a higher degree of rugged individualism than is encouraged by a modern school. Modern schools in which classes of twenty to forty pupils associate strictly with agemates may plausibly be argued to develop a new kind of person.

It is undoubtedly true that children arrive for the first time in the schoolroom with a repertoire of habits organized by parents. On these habits will be based the response to the teacher, but it is equally true that within a fairly short period new habits and new attitudes are established towards the teacher. The schoolroom situation is in some ways radically different from the home training. At home there were no equals, and the problems of justice and equality may not yet have appeared. In large families parents may have learned by trial and error that trouble is minimized by serving equal portions of dessert, by making gifts to all the children on holidays and not to just a few, by requiring something like an equal distribution of time spent on family tasks, but in most modern families with from one to three or four children of widely distributed ages, these problems are not acute. It is at school and in the classroom that some system of just recognition must be established.

In countries where the family is strongly authoritarian, the schools sometimes reflect this by accepting an order of privilege among students, but there is a strong tendency for the school to solve such problems by rules of fairness and equality. What we really mean by fairness is that there shall be no considering of persons. No one shall be given first place because he is who he is. If there must be a first, let it be determined by lot or by a test of merit in which all have the chance to demonstrate merit.

Cooperation and Tolerance.—In one large Western city which has grown to city size almost within the span of a single lifetime, starting as a wilderness in which there were no white residents, a very wise civic leader was asked what he thought was the outstanding difference between the business leaders of thirty years ago and the present business leaders in the community. His answer was that the outstanding difference was the remarkable increase in the readiness with which the contemporary group of leaders can be interested in cooperating in activities aimed at the public welfare. The raiser of funds for public causes had a much more thorny task in this particular community thirty years ago than now. It is possible that differences of this sort may be related to differences in school background. A large number of the leaders of thirty years ago were men of little education who had worked their way up under something approaching pioneer conditions to the control of a business or an industry. They had fewer experiences of cooperation with equals.

In the United States it is usually in the public schools that children encounter and are thrown into association with children of different religious and racial backgrounds. Where that encounter is postponed by segregation, the relations between the groups concerned will be founded upon radically different attitudes and habits. The description and measurement of these attitudes is a new branch of social psychology. Full knowledge of the effects of common schooling upon children of radically different backgrounds must wait for more research. At present it is very difficult to determine the effects on race relations of racial segregation in schools because the segregation itself grows out of a background of race relations. Cities where Negroes and whites attend the same schools, for instance, are for the most part confined to communities in which one race constitutes only a small minority.

It is generally in the school environment that children are forced into what might be called a negative side of role. White children in a community where there are only whites do not think of themselves as whites. Protestant children do not think of themselves as Protestants in a community where there are few or no Catholics, nor do Catholic children think of themselves as Catholics in the communities where there are none but members of their own faith. In the public schools of the United States many children encounter for the first time hostile attitudes or ridicule or exclusion from games and parties and entertainment because of their religion or race. The lone Negro boy in a schoolroom is, in our society, acutely aware of himself as a Negro.

Self-Evaluation through School Experience.—There are many other superficial but still important components of role which depend on the school experience. One of these is the self-estimate of quality and relative ability which each person tends to carry and which is made a basis of action. Many classroom activities are in a sense competitive and establish an order of merit. Not long ago a considerable audience of school-teachers was invited to take, for demonstration purposes, an intelligence test. They were also invited, if they wished to know their own scores, to sign the test. When the test had been scored, it was discovered that the papers which bore the name of the taker averaged more than one standard deviation above the papers which remained unsigned. The only conclusion is that, in general, the teachers are aware of the relative quality of their own performance. Those who knew they were good were willing to put their names on the paper and were interested in the results.

At the University of Washington, teachers may request a survey of the opinions of their students on the quality of their teaching. In general the more than 200 members of the faculty who take advantage of this opportunity each year average far above the general average of the faculty in the quality of their teaching, indicating that teachers are for the most part well aware of the quality of their work. In the classroom children encounter evaluation from other children and from the teacher. This evaluation has in general an objectivity which is completely lacking in the evaluations of the home environment. Some of this evaluation is assimilated into each pupil's notion of his own quality. In the process of that assimilation the evaluation is often modified in the direction of the average. Children at the bottom of the class in ability tend to think of themselves as somewhat above this level, and there is some evidence that children at the top of the class often fail to realize their leading position or at least tend to be somewhat modest in their statement of it.

2. DETERMINANTS OF SOCIAL BEHAVIOR

Development of Leadership.—There is some evidence that the school environment brings out and develops leader roles in superior children. Children who are above the average in mental test scores will be found in their high school activities to be much more often represented in school offices and positions of leadership than children who are below average in mental test scores, but there is also some evidence of a striking exception to this statement. A number of children at the extreme upper limit in mental test scores do not show the strong tendency to be in positions of leadership. Their extraordinary intellectual capacity tends to remove them from the interests and occupations of other students and therefore from leadership positions. A study by Smith and Nystrom [5] showed that school leaders were taking part in an average of 6.8 activities as compared with an average of 1.75 for nonleaders. Leaders were also found to spend 15.9 per cent of their time in leisure activities as compared with 8.6 per cent for nonleaders. This experience in leadership can be predicted to continue, since Courtenay's

---

[5] *Journal of Applied Psychology,* XXI (1937), 251-59.

study [6] concluded that high school students who had experience in leadership were four times as apt to become college leaders as those without high school experience.

Influence of Family on Morals.—Very few children of unskilled laborers attend college, even in those state universities where a considerable portion of the students pay their own way. In the grade schools these children of unskilled laborers presumably were exposed to the same education as other children. We can explain the fact that they do not go on to college by the fact that the effects of primary education on personality and on interests and ambitions and the development of skills depend in a large measure on the reinforcement that education gets from the home background. In the families of unskilled laborers a higher value is likely to be put on early wage-earning. There is less appreciation of the deferred values which lie behind long preparation for a vocation or a career. Books are less conspicuously a part of the environment, and conversation at home deals less with topics of general interest and general information and more with topics of immediate practical importance. The Kinsey report on the sex histories of American white males indicates that chastity and control are closely related with the number of years to which education was limited. The behavior of men who went no farther than the grade school in education indicates that ideals of chastity and self-control tend to be restricted to those groups which are headed for more education. This does not mean that what the Kinsey report observes is in any sense the result of education. It means that it is the same families which indoctrinate children with a stricter sex morality and which encourage prolonged school attendance. The report indicates one more possible interpretation. This is to the effect that in the grade school formal education makes practically no contact with the area of the personality organized about sex and love. Self-control depends not upon the education men have had but on the amount of education they are going to have. This allows us only one conclusion, which is that school life is not a determining factor in the development

---

[6] *School Review,* XLVI (1938), 97-107.

of attitudes toward sex. These originate in the home and in associations within the social class.

Questions

1. Give an example of "pecking order" in the school situation.
2. Are teachers in general aware of the quality of their work? How would they compare with pupils in this respect?
3. Why is a given event in childhood likely to be of more importance than the same event occurring later on?
4. Does unrestricted mixing of children of different racial and religious groups usually lead to greater or less tolerance?
5. Why are evaluations made in school usually more objective than evaluations made at home?
6. Why do classes in which pupils are about the same age tend to inculcate principles of fairness and equality?
7. Why is the role "English-speaking person" so rare in our schools?

Chapter 26

MENTAL HYGIENE

___

1. How Common Is Maladjustment in Children?

Meaning of Maladjustment.—We are frequently told that "maladjustment" is not a disease like measles which a child either has or does not have. We are cautioned to remember that the school population is, in fact, continuously distributed along the adjustment dimension, some few pupils being very well adjusted and those at the other end of the curve seriously maladjusted, while the majority are found scattered between these extremes. The problem would then seem to be to discover the means of crowding the curve toward the favorable end.

This viewpoint, though valuable in indicating that maladjusted children are not a group apart, tends to divert attention from the fact that the term "maladjustment" is used in at least two very different ways. First, it refers to the lack of integration which results in indecision, inability to coordinate activity, and failure to concentrate efforts. The child is in conflict with himself, unable to reach a goal because his response patterns are not directed to a common end. The integrated child, on the other hand, is organized for efficient action.

In another and more proper sense, maladjustment refers to the conflict between an individual and the social group. In this sense, the term is entirely normative; it defines certain modes of conduct which are approved and rewards conformists by certifying them as "adjusted." Those who act contrary to the social norms are "maladjusted." We cannot facilely assume that all social maladjustment is merely the projection of integrative failure upon the world, any more than we can assume that maladjustment to the environment necessarily leads to personality disintegration, however conveniently self-evident this may appear to the conformist and disciplinarian. It is true, of course, that maladjustment in the social situation is commonly either the reflection of inadequate integration or the result simply of failure to learn socially acceptable modes of behavior. It is because these frequently go together that the term "maladjustment" is used to cover both. In some cases, however, resistance to the authority of the teacher, failure to conform to prescribed routines, and similar behavior, often considered by the teacher to be evidence of maladjustment, are really indications of refusal by the child to adopt patterns of response which, however acceptable to others, seem to him to be arbitrary and senseless. The successful imposition of meaningless conformity upon the child by insisting that he accept unquestioningly what he is told may discourage him from thinking critically and acting independently. Our society is not yet so perfect that disagreement with its values or its representatives can be confidently designated "maladjustment" in the more common sense of the term.

In the following discussion "maladjustment" will be used in its usual and somewhat vague meaning—the inability of the individual to perform in socially acceptable ways.

Need of a Mental Hygiene Program.—Since the incidence of maladjustment in the school population is dependent upon the criteria used, it is difficult to give meaningful figures. Estimates of the percentage of maladjusted school children range from 2.4 per cent to over 50 per cent. Carl R. Rogers, in a study of 1,524 pupils in Grades I to VI (Grade III omitted) reports 12 per cent to be "seriously maladjusted" and another 30 per cent "poorly adjusted." [1]

His studies, as well as most others, show that serious problems occur more frequently among boys than girls. A survey of similar reports indicates that at least 10 per cent of all elementary school children need the help of persons with professional training in mental hygiene and therapy. Probably another 40

---

[1] *Educational Research Bulletin,* XXI (March 18, 1942), 69-79.

per cent need occasional counseling and guidance beyond that ordinarily offered in the schools. And certainly all children are entitled to instruction from teachers who are themselves reasonably well adjusted and who are aware of the importance of mental hygiene.

Practically all studies are in agreement with the observation of child guidance counselors that many if not most school-age children feel that they have no one to confide in or to ask questions of. With today's overcrowded classrooms the teacher has less and less opportunity to take the remiss parents' place in this respect, and the problem of the psychologically lonely child becomes more pressing.

Most adults do not remember that first acquaintanceship with certain experiences was made under emotional stress which may have led to an entirely erroneous idea of the meaning of the experiences. The effect upon the child's adjustment may be so profound as to give the observer the impression that this must be merely the "precipitating event" for some more obscure maladjustive tendency, yet often a simple explanation will clear up the difficulty.

One eight-year-old girl who read in a Sunday supplement article by an "eminent astronomer" that the earth was about to be engulfed in a pocket of interstellar gas and destroyed was so disturbed that she was unable to do her school work for two weeks. When she finally confided her fears to an adult friend and was assured that most Sunday supplement articles contained approximately the same amount of information as the comic sheet, she was vastly relieved and had no further difficulties. She had not spoken to her parents about the matter, since they had not seen the article and she wanted their last days on earth to be spent in ignorance of the impending catastrophe.

A more serious case involved a thirteen-year-old boy who had been doing excellent work in school but suddenly became listless and preoccupied and attempted to persuade his parents to let him quit school and get a job. Not until a librarian noticed him reading a book on psychology was a clue found to his sudden change of behavior. It developed that a teacher had (very improperly!) disclosed to him the score he had made on a recent I.Q. test. She had told him "150, way above average," which he had understood as "115, way above average." Looking up the significance of this score he had become convinced that his dream of becoming a great chemist could never be fulfilled. His subsequent reading was largely devoted to searching for indication that the I.Q. could be raised. When informed that he had misunderstood the teacher's remark and that his actual ability was such that he could attain his goal, no further "therapy" was necessary.

Though in these cases the disturbance was temporary, there is reason to believe that many serious maladjustments which would otherwise not have occurred could be explained on the basis of some single but critical incident like the above. Seriousness of maladjustment is not proportional to the apparent importance of the cause. It may continue long after the original occasion for the disturbance is forgotten. Most of these incidents would have no serious consequences if children were given the opportunity to discuss such matters promptly and fully with someone in whom they had confidence. The relative values and importance of things in the world are largely arbitrary social fictions and must be learned by the child in the same way in which he learns to read or write. His accidental failure to learn an adequate response in a given situation or his assignment of a highly distorted value based upon an exceptional experience is not necessarily evidence of a personality inadequacy but is often merely a reflection of the fact that adjustment to the environment is not automatic or the result of maturation but rather a matter of learning.

It must not be supposed that all maladjustment has been as simply caused as in the examples given. If this were true, a complete mental hygiene program would consist simply in sympathetic and understanding child counseling. Many children show more basic and general maladjustive patterns which require the utmost ability of psychologists or psychiatrists either to diagnose or to treat. Our facilities for extending help to these more serious and difficult cases need considerable expansion. Society can continue to disregard the urgency of this need only at its peril.

2. Recognition and Treatment of Behavioral Problems

General Conditions Contributing to Maladjustment.—Early attempts to find the causes of maladjustment usually showed either biologic or sociologic emphasis. Studies of "defective strains" such as the Jukes and the inferior branch of the Kallikaks seemed to indicate that undesirable traits of many kinds were mainly matters of heredity and that only a thoroughgoing eugenics program would have any significant effect on the incidence of serious maladjustment. Other investigators, finding maladjustment to be frequently associated with poverty, inadequate developmental and recreational opportunities, and similar environmental circumstances, felt that these conditions were primarily responsible. Conclusions made strictly on the basis of the evidence do not justify the strong stands often taken in favor of either constitutional or environmental factors as being of exclusive importance. More recently an effort has been made to evaluate objectively all factors, including those of a psychological nature such as intrafamilial stresses and attitudes, highly emotional experiences, and the child's developing concepts. Yet, despite the large amount of careful observation and objective research, some of the principles and practices characteristic of mental hygiene programs do not have unqualified scientific standing.

It is, for example, too often tacitly assumed that the truth of the concepts of psychoanalytic theory is now well established and that the applicability of these concepts in cases of serious maladjustment is all but universal. Psychoanalytic jargon has so penetrated the entire field of mental hygiene that maladjustments having a fairly straightforward explanation are often so distorted to fit psychoanalytic concepts of causation as to obscure completely the actual problem. The teacher faced with an adjustment problem which seems to be the result of a rather obvious situation should not hesitate to risk an interpretation in simple terms. The principle of parsimony—that we should not use complicated explanations when simple ones will do as well—has not been repealed by psychoanalysis or any other ingenious but obscure systematic approach.

There are several other assumptions which have little or no real scientific evidence in their favor but which are sometimes treated as fact. Although it is well established that adult schizophrenics frequently show a history of withdrawal and introversion, it does not follow that withdrawn and introverted behavior is prognostic of psychosis (insanity). Even if this were found to be true often enough to warrant preventive therapy, we could not say confidently that prevention of such behavior would in any degree affect the onset of later psychosis, since we cannot as yet be sure what conditions are essential to the development of most of the psychoses.

Since certain psychiatric and psychological techniques are rather uniformly successful in certain kinds of maladjustment, it is sometimes taken for granted that similar techniques applied earlier, during a longer period, or by particularly competent persons will be effective in the most serious maladjustments such as the psychoses, psychopathic personality, and the like. Here again our knowledge of the causes of the conditions of serious maladjustment is insufficient to justify this assumption.

Some serious maladjustive behavior, including certain of the psychoses, has a definite constitutional or organic basis. The formerly cooperative, friendly child who has passed through a siege of encephalitis is likely to become a serious behavior problem because of organic brain damage. Epilepsy, tuberculosis, glandular imbalance, malnutrition, and many other organic conditions are sometimes responsible for maladjustive behavior which would not have developed in their absence. Behavioral disorders traceable to heritable defects are probably rare, though a few authorities believe there is evidence to indicate that schizophrenia and manic-depressive insanity, the two most common psychoses, and presumably the prepsychotic behavioral patterns that precede them, are heritable.[2] If this turns out to be true, it may be that no mental hygiene program will affect the development of these disorders or their early symptoms.

Present evidence seems to show that the vast majority of behavioral problems have no definite organic basis but are func-

---

[2] Laurence H. Snyder, *The Principles of Heredity,* 2d ed., p. 389.

tional and the result of learning. Habits of withdrawal, anxiety, tension, violence, and other patterns of behavior are learned along with speech, walking, and the more specific skills. The actual ways in which maladjustive habits have been picked up often cannot be traced, but the relationship between them and such conditions as interparental tensions cannot be doubted. Dorothy W. Baruch showed in a study of thirty-three nursery school children and their parents that occurrence of maladjustment in the children was significantly correlated with parental tensions over sex, domination of one parent by the other, lack of consideration, lack of cooperation on rearing of the child and several other conditions to a lesser degree.[3] "Rejection," extreme severity, and inconsistency of treatment of the child by the parent are other factors that establish typical maladjustive behavioral patterns. Some of these patterns have been so thoroughly learned and therefore so completely pervade the child's personality that they are often not recognized as learned responses which, in many cases at least, can be modified by a long process of re-education.

Though influences of the home on the child are usually much more profound than those arising out of any other parts of the social environment, there are other social forces, in addition to the school, which the teacher cannot afford to overlook. Among these the movies, the radio, and the comics (especially comic books) are of importance. The church, also, often has considerable influence, but where this is true it may be considered an extension of the religious training in the home. The effects of these media frequently are obvious in the classroom and cannot be disregarded by educators who recognize that schools have a far from exclusive role in the education of children.

No unequivocal answer based upon careful research can be given to the question of whether movies contribute seriously to maladjustment in children. Many individual cases have been reported in which it appeared that the maladjustive or delinquent activity observed was directly traceable to a recently seen

---

[3] *Journal of Experimental Education,* VI (1937), 187-204.

movie, but it may be that similar activity would have occurred in any event and that the movie suggested only the actual form of the activity. In other cases it can hardly be doubted that a cinematic episode was wholly responsible for severe psychic shock in otherwise well-adjusted children.[4]

Maud A. Merrill reports that delinquents attend movies frequently to a significantly greater extent than do nondelinquents (control groups) from the same neighborhood.[5] This does not necessarily mean, of course, that more frequent attendance contributes to delinquency; it may mean, as Merrill suggests, that the delinquents have less opportunity for recreation at home. Certainly the movies frequently present unsuitable models, glorify a superficial and neurotic design for living, and may foster attitudes of bigotry and provincialism, but we cannot be sure that this is a threat to the actual mental health of children even though the effects may be most undesirable in other ways.

Most children spend much more time in attentive listening to the radio than they do in watching movies. It is sometimes thought that, since radio depends upon one sense modality, it must be less effective in arousing emotional responses than are talking moving pictures. In a series of tests on 150 school-age children listening to familiar radio programs, it was found that the emotional response as indicated by blood pressure, pulse rate, respiration, and perspiration was frequently extreme; in a number of instances pulse rate rose from 80 to 130 per minute, with sharp fluctuations in blood pressure.[6]

In an investigation of the causes of bad dreams in children between the ages of one and twelve, it was found that 9 per cent were attributed to radio programs and about the same proportion to movies.[7] Again we are not justified in concluding that the causes of violent emotional states are necessarily

---

[4] An interesting case of an obsession-neurosis apparently traceable only to the viewing of a moving picture is described in the following article: Oluf Brüel, "A Moving Picture as a Psychopathogenic Factor: A Paper on Primary Psychotraumatic Neurosis," *Character and Personality,* VII (1938), 68-76.
[5] Maud A. Merrill, *Problems of Child Delinquency.*
[6] *School and Society,* L (1939), 369-73.
[7] *Child Development,* VII (1936), 77-84.

prejudicial to the child's mental health, but the possibility must not be disregarded.

In the above-mentioned investigation even "funny papers" contributed about 2 per cent to bad dreams. Since comic-book reading has recently hit an all-time high in a craze which now seems to be subsiding slightly, their effects should be of considerable interest to both parents and teachers.

Authorities differ markedly in their opinions as to the harmful consequences of comic-book and funny-paper reading. Frederic Wertham, director of mental hygiene clinics at both Bellevue and Queens hospitals in New York City, wrote in a recent article: "You cannot understand present-day juvenile delinquency if you do not take into account the pathogenic and pathoplastic influence of the comic books. . . ." [8] On the other hand, Lauretta Bender, child psychologist in the Psychiatric Division of Bellevue Hospital, has stated that ". . . the comic strip is . . . a means of helping [children] solve the individual and sociological problems appropriate to their own lives." [9] These differences in opinion may be due partly to the fact that Dr. Wertham had in mind comic books, some of which are indubitably vicious, while Dr. Bender was referring to newspaper strips which must pass a more rigorous editorial censorship.

The only really large-scale research study of the problem was one made in Brazil in 1944 by the staff of the Instituto Nacional de Estudos Pedagógicos of the Ministry of Education.[10] They found some indication of favorable influence—more initiative, inventive capacity, and intellectual curiosity about some things, with an increase in geographical and historical information. Unfavorable effects included shirking of school work, greater roughness in play, imitation of less desirable social types, and intense emotional repercussions in at least one third of the readers. The result of the study was agreement on the part of the publishers to impose a strict but voluntary self-censorship,

[8] *Saturday Review of Literature,* XXXI, 6, 7, 28, 29.
[9] *American Journal of Orthopsychiatry,* XI (1941), 540-50.
[10] Instituto Nacional de Estudos Pedagógicos, "Uma Investigação sôbre Jornais e Revistas Infantis e Juvenis III," *Revista Brasileira de Estudos Pedagógicos,* III (1945), 82-101.

and thus to minimize the unfavorable effects. A strong feeling of the investigators, which was difficult to check objectively, was that many children were learning to read faster through the increased motivation provided by comic books.

Here, again, no general indictment can be made of a recreational and entertainment medium as a threat to mental health, though there is general agreement that the worst of the comic books may be important contributors to serious emotional upset and may provide patterns for antisocial and even criminal behavior.

Although we often think of school as being the major institution which is engaged in a perpetual battle for conditions which promote improved mental hygiene among children, we should not overlook the fact that even here may be found situations which foster maladjustive behavior.   Teachers are human, too; about the same percentage of maladjustment is found among them as among other professional groups.   Correlation between frequency of maladjustment of children and their teachers is low, but significant. Most teachers have had no courses in mental hygiene, though of those who have had such a course over two thirds ranked it as the most valuable course they had taken from the standpoint of its personal value, and over two fifths ranked it first from the standpoint of its professional value.[11]

Other aspects often characteristic of school life—overcompetition between pupils, attempted forcing of slow learners, overemphasis upon grade divisions and promotions, setting of impossibly high standards for poor students—all these have been held responsible for maladjustive behavior ranging from acute inferiority feelings and complete withdrawal to overt rebellion and delinquency. Since so many factors are involved, it is hard to evaluate such charges, though even in schools in comparable neighborhoods there is sometimes found a difference in percentage of problem children which seems to be correlated with practices in the schools, "progressive" schools showing superiority in this respect.

---

[11] *Educational Administration and Supervision,* XXIV (1938), 675-86.

Recognition of Maladjustment.—The harassed teacher with several classes containing from thirty to forty students or even more has no difficulty in pointing out the problem child. He is the one whose destructiveness, disobedience, and defiance make him a greater problem than all the obedient, docile children combined. Faced with the very real task of preventing chaos in the classroom, the teacher need not apologize to the mental hygienist for differing with him in his interpretation of the term "behavior problem." When teachers are accused of over-emphasizing the importance of aggressiveness as compared to withdrawal, this fact should be borne in mind. Studies in which teachers were asked to write case reports of maladjusted children and tell why they thought the children were maladjusted indicate that teachers, at least in this case, are well aware of the danger of regressive as compared to aggressive traits when they occurred as the specific problems of actual children.[12]

The difficulty of determining the seriousness of maladjustive behavior should not, however, be underestimated. James E. Birren in a study of thirty-eight mental hospital cases for which early records were available concluded that children destined to become psychotic probably did not differ in any significant way, as far as could be told on the basis of clinical methods usually employed, from other children referred to a child study clinic for behavioral disorders.[13] Other studies show that the difficulty of distinguishing minor maladjustment from serious maladjustment as indicated by subsequent behavior is nearly as difficult, even for clinicians. Teachers, therefore, cannot expect to be able to determine with any degree of certainty the seriousness of a given behavior problem in terms of the child's future welfare and adjustment. Some suggestions might, however, be made.

As mentioned previously, it is too often forgotten that maladjustment may in a given case imply nonconformity to a somewhat arbitrary social code. What seems to the teacher to be indecent or antisocial may be the usual pattern of behavior in the child's family or perhaps in an entire community. Teachers

[12] *Journal of Educational Psychology,* XXVI (1935), 123-38.
[13] *Journal of Abnormal and Social Psychology,* XXXIX (1944), 84-96.

moving into a new school should remember that they, rather than the children, may be violating accepted standards. This fact may explain why surprised investigators sometimes naïvely report that whole classes consist of nothing but "behavior problems"; they are unaware that different modes of conduct are tolerated in different communities and different socioeconomic strata.

A given set of standards may have the formal approval of a social group or the leaders of that group but in practice be more frequently disregarded than followed. All too often a child is stigmatized as a "problem" when he has been guilty only of the same sort of conduct indulged in by his classmates who did not happen to be caught. If he is then termed a "thief" or "criminal," particularly under emotional circumstances or where such designation earns him the attention of his fellows, the term may come to represent a role into which he fits his future behavior.

The child suffering from some unnoticed physical disability such as partial deafness, impaired sight, or a similar condition is sometimes unable to engage in classwork. His inattentiveness, disobedience, or apparent defiance may be mistaken for unwillingness to cooperate and lead to his classification as a "problem child." There is little excuse for such an error, since even in circumstances where testing devices are not available the teacher can usually determine with a little patience and ingenuity whether such a defect exists to a serious degree or not. Now that physical examinations of students, particularly those showing difficulties which may be caused by sensory defects, are routine in most schools, these disabilities are seldom misinterpreted. Where the physical defect is of some more obscure variety, a superficial physical examination may not reveal it. In these cases the true cause may come to light incidentally in a medical examination or perhaps never; certainly the teacher cannot be expected to guess the cause. There is considerable evidence accumulating that vitamin deficiencies, allergies, and similar conditions may be the cause of far more cases of maladjustive behavior than has been suspected.

Inability may be mistaken for maladjustment, and in this case the converse also happens to be true. A child may be withdrawn or regressive and insure his nonparticipation in the group by feigning illness, specific inability, or even dulness, often to the point of convincing himself. The same device may be used to gain attention, but this is so common that it hardly can be called a problem unless carried to an extreme.

Efforts have been made to show that certain "types" of children are more prone to maladjustment than others. These efforts have met with as slight success as might be supposed, since it would indeed be surprising if such an inclusive and ill-defined category of behavior were closely related to any clear-cut, measurable characteristics.

Attempts to discover the effects of socioeconomic status have fared little better, although schools in poorer neighborhoods commonly show a greater proportion of "behavior problems." This actually means very little, since the "problem children" are often guilty of no more than playing in streets (where there are no playgrounds) or using language considered obscene by the teacher (where the terms used may be ubiquitous not only among the child's playmates but in his home). According to other criteria of maladjustment, children from higher socioeconomic levels have been found to contribute a greater percentage of "behavior problems." [14]

Nearly all studies show a decidedly greater frequency of maladjustment of all kinds among boys than among girls. No single reason will suffice to explain this, but in general it can be said that the classification of "behavior problem" is usually made in reference to the school situation, and the early training of girls, with strong emphasis upon docility and the advantages of conformity, probably leaves them less likely to clash with those standards of behavior which the school judges to be the criteria of adjustment.

Generally speaking, those children are least likely to be maladjusted who are most like their group. Rogers, in the study cited earlier in this chapter,[15] calls attention to the fact that in the school where the median I.Q. was 110 every child with an

---

[14] *Mental Hygiene,* XXI (1937), 452-55.
[15] Rogers, *op. cit.*

I.Q. from 76 to 85 was a problem in one way or another, but in the school where the median I.Q. was 87, children with I.Q.'s from 76 to 85 showed a lower proportion of maladjustment than those in I.Q. ranges 106-115, 116-125, 126-135, or 136-145. In each of the four last-named I.Q. ranges, the proportion of problems of mental health was greater the further the group was from the school median of 87; in this case, the brighter the group the greater the frequency of maladjustment. These figures do not represent an unusual situation but are typical of findings in other schools.

Since very bright children are likely to be in a group where they are atypical by reason of their exceptionally high intelligence, we should expect them to be rather frequently maladjusted. In the study above every child in the highest range (136-145) of the school with a median I.Q. of 87 was a "problem." We should remember, however, that the maladjustment observed was *in relation to a given situation*. By using more nearly "absolute" methods of measuring degree of maladjustment, it has been shown that in relation to these criteria very bright children are less frequently maladjusted than average children. The ambiguity in meaning of "maladjustment" has led to considerable misunderstanding on this point. It should be pointed out, however, that the devices used to determine the existence of maladjustment in very bright children are not infallible. No maladjustment inventory has yet been devised in which its purpose is sufficiently well disguised to mislead the very bright child who does not wish to answer in such a way as to disclose possible maladjustive traits. More subtle techniques are being developed but are not yet sufficiently valid to be used with confidence in this connection.

Although first recognition of maladjustment is usually made on a subjective basis, questionnaires and inventories have been used increasingly during the last twenty-five years. The first effort to apply this method to children was made by E. Mathews, who used a modification of Woodworth's Personal Data Sheet developed during the first World War. Several others have been developed since such as the Bernreuter Personality Inventory and the Bell Adjustment Inventory (student's form). Neither of these is suitable for children in the lower grades.

Because of the possibility of the subject's deceiving the tester on the above kinds of forms, some more indirect approach is often found advisable. If a child is placed in a relatively "unstructured" situation, that is, one which can be interpreted by the child in various ways, it is sometimes possible to find out things about him from what he "projects" into the situation. The testing situation may be informal, as when the child is given toys or dolls and invited to play with them. His play activity can often be interpreted reasonably as a partial representation of his attitudes and feelings toward real life problems and people. Some of these techniques have been formalized, the best known being the Rorschach Test, the responses to which can be evaluated only through an elaborate scoring procedure. Interpretation is difficult, and clinicians are not in agreement as to the value of the test. The Thematic Apperception Test (TAT), in which the subject is invited to construct a story around a series of pictures presented singly, requires even more experience to use. Projective techniques, particularly of the formal type, are of diagnostic value only in the hands of the well-trained clinician.

No rule-of-thumb procedure can be used by the teacher to determine whether a given behavior problem is serious or not. If the behavior seems to be of a kind which would be atypical or undesirable in any social environment, if it reappears in many superficially different forms, if it is persistent—these are indications that it should receive special attention. Maladjustive behavior patterns that do not call attention to themselves should be watched with particular care; aggressive behavior, because of its disruptive effects, is not so likely to be overlooked and allowed to continue. In any case, the teacher should remember that he is in a particularly strategic position for recognizing maladjustive patterns. Unlike the parents, he is able to look at the child more or less objectively and has the additional advantage of having a constant standard of comparison, namely, the behavior of other children.

Treatment of Maladjustment.—Except in a limited and informal way the teacher cannot be expected to engage in therapy or to give special attention to "problem children." Treatment of even comparatively minor difficulties in adjustment sometimes involves lengthy re-education and often the special knowledge of therapeutic techniques which only professionally trained clinicians are competent to use. The fact that treatment of this kind is usually not available would not be an excuse for turning the job over to the teacher, but rather a reason for providing more persons with specialized training in mental hygiene, guidance, counseling, and therapy.

We should be careful also to avoid overestimating the possible effects of any treatment offered in the school, no matter how excellent. No re-education can nullify the pervasive and continuing damage done by an unhealthy home atmosphere. A school situation, though providing in every respect an environment meeting the criteria of the most exacting mental hygienist, cannot always successfully undo the harm done during the two thirds of the child's waking hours when he is in another environment. Often, too, the necessary treatment is entirely impracticable in an actual situation, as unrealistic as prescribing six months of complete rest in Arizona for the unskilled laborer with five children. It is an unfortunate but inescapable fact that many cases of child maladjustment cannot be successfully dealt with or avoided without drastic changes in social customs and institutions.

Some of the diagnostic procedures mentioned previously imply obvious and direct treatment. The child showing maladjustive behavior traceable to nearsightedness clearly requires glasses. Other diagnostic procedures are closely associated with methods of treatment from which they often cannot be distinguished. Projective techniques of the informal kind, for example, combine diagnosis and treatment. The providing of play situations in which aggression may be freely released against "Daddy" and "Mommy" (and "Teacher"!) not only give an indication of the basic aim of the aggression but also help to relieve the tension.

Treatments of these kinds can be undertaken only by physicians in the case of organic disability and by clinical psychologists when special release or re-educational techniques are required. Occasionally a forward-looking school provides specially trained teachers (for example the "school mothers" of the report mentioned below) [16] who can devote their time to individual attention for less seriously maladjusted children. Some re-educational therapy is included in the regular teaching procedures of good teachers, even though it may not be specifically recognized as such. It is a significant fact that the pupils of good teachers, as judged by almost any reasonable criterion, are better adjusted than the pupils of poor teachers. Some of the educational techniques that aid in adjustment will be mentioned.

Children sometimes are plunged into a subject without sufficient previous preparation, either because of their continued absence, of moving to another school, of poor continuity of curriculum from grade to grade, or of poor planning of a course by the teacher. When a child is faced day after day with a series of problems or a type of material for which he has no response even partially adequate, he will tend to regress to an earlier type of behavior. The child who may work for hours on a fairly difficult problem which contains familiar elements may show regressive behavior such as crying, persistent looking away, and similar infantile responses if he is faced with a completely new kind of problem, no matter how simple basically.

Many otherwise intelligent older students are completely incompetent in certain fields such as algebra or foreign language because their immediate response to an algebra problem or a sentence in French is looking away with the verbal protest, "I never could get that subject." After such a response has taken place for months or years, the damage is all but irreparable; but if begun soon enough a training program going back to the simplest elements in the subject and gradually increasing in difficulty may eliminate the regressive behavior. Not only specific disabilities such as inability to read are often aided by this

---

[16] *American Journal of Orthopsychiatry*, XII (1942), 659-65.

technique, but also the general avoidance and withdrawal responses sometimes referred to as "pseudo-feeblemindedness."

The continuous fidgeting and nervous, quick glance at everything but the task; sometimes the vacant stare and relaxed body musculature; in other cases, the fixed, blank frown and tense, quivering grip on the pencil—these may be merely the repetitions of early response patterns which were the only available ones when that type of situation was first presented. Although avoidance responses thus learned are present in relation to some problems in nearly everyone, they are nevertheless essentially maladjustive, especially when generalized to any problem situation as not infrequently happens in the case of children. Every effort should be made in the classroom to see that students are not often placed in situations of such difficulty that they are forced into regressive or avoidant behavior.

Our social institutions, including our schools, openly or implicitly worship Success to a degree which can only be considered a sociopathological phenomenon. The justification for this overemphasis seems to be based on the erroneous belief that the higher the person's goal or "level of aspiration," the better for the person. The saner custom of holding up for social approval the attainment of a reasonably high level of competency in any productive field of activity could well be substituted for our neurotic insistence that "anybody can be President if he works hard enough" or that 39 A's and one B is at least one scholarship less worthy than 40 A's.

No longer do children recite in school one of a series of verses outlining a healthily realistic goal:

> When I grow up to be a man
> I'll be a bricklayer if I can.
> I'll build bridges and buildings tall
> And around the garden a strong brick wall
> If I can—
> *And I can.*

One well-adjusted, competent bricklayer coming from this school of thought is worth twenty political climbers all convinced that nothing less than the Presidency is worth working for.

The teacher can contribute immeasurably to the reduction in the number of "lives of quiet desperation" by emphasizing the importance of real if modest values rather than the fraudulent values of the social myth. He need not fear that potential greatness will be smothered by any such emphasis, since children of exceptional ability will not usually accept "phony" goals and are not socially productive or happy when they do.

In general, fears based upon lack of knowledge will tend to disappear when the knowledge is provided. Unfortunately, the kinds of knowledge which would contribute most to improved adjustment are often the very ones which are skirted or left unmentioned. Simple sex education both for children and society as a whole would help considerably in this respect. The encouragement of the spirit of free inquiry among children also has definite therapeutic effects, since the known, if feared, may at least be feared intelligently and lead to definite patterns of avoidance, while vague fears based upon lack of information more frequently create general feelings of anxiety. It must be admitted that the reckless discussion of any topic cannot be defended on the grounds that "the truth can't do any harm." Young children may as readily form groundless fears based upon inability to understand as upon misinformation. But increased competence and skill in dealing with situations with which the child is likely to come in contact is good mental hygiene.

There is much evidence to show that schools organized with the mental health of the child a matter of major attention contribute greatly to improved adjustment of pupils. The "child-centered" school really implies a fundamental reorganization of usual attitudes toward education. This type of school involves too many technical problems of administration to be dealt with here. It might be mentioned, however, that practically all studies show that any change in the direction of more informal promotion, more plasticity in curricula, and improved opportunities in vocational training for less academically inclined students leads to noticeable reduction in the percentage of "problem children."

QUESTIONS

1. Give an example of child behavior which might be termed "maladjustive" in some schools but not in others.

2. Why are more behavior problems found among boys than among girls?

3. Mention some unproved but frequently held beliefs concerning the causes and prevention of maladjustment in children.

4. Give some examples of organic defects or damage which may cause maladjustment.

5. If similar behavior problems are found in several children of the same family, may we assume that heredity is involved? Why or why not?

6. Is it possible that movies may be as a whole detrimental to a child without affecting his mental health?

7. Is there any evidence that good adjustment of teachers may affect favorably the adjustment of their pupils?

8. Would you think it likely that teachers would consider a larger proportion of the class to be "problem children" in a large class than in a small class? Why?

9. "Anybody who peeks at his neighbor's paper is a cheat." Why is this announcement to a class an example of poor psychology?

10. Name some remediable defects in our social institutions which tend to cause or aggravate maladjustment.

11. If a child is faced with a problem completely beyond his ability to solve, why would continued presentation of the problem to him be inadvisable?

12. Is a *very* high "level of aspiration" likely to be more damaging to a bright or a very dull pupil? (Careful!)

PART VIII

PSYCHOLOGICAL FACTORS IN SCHOOL ORGANIZATION AND ADMINISTRATION

Chapter 27

PSYCHOLOGY OF DISCIPLINE

1. THE GENERAL PROBLEM OF DISCIPLINE

Poor discipline is the greatest single cause of failure among high-school teachers. The percentage of failures due to this cause varies greatly because of conditions and standards. Like other forms of social weakness, it has its origin in many causes, and it is usually one of the components of a vicious circle, sometimes a cause, sometimes a symptom. And like other social phenomena, it tends to be progressive within any given group. Weakness in discipline is by far the most common apparent weakness among inexperienced teachers in training. Principals and superintendents are inclined to consider as hopeless the teacher whose classes continue to be restless, idle, or disorderly, for they know that nearly all forms of disorder are insidious, and, hence, dangerous. They are reluctant about continuing in service any teacher who is unable to maintain control.[1]

Thus wrote Pringle in 1931, and what he said at that time in all probability is more true today because of the increasing complexity of conditions and an increasing incidence of delinquency and behavior problems.

Although Pringle was speaking primarily about high school discipline, the statement could well have been made concerning teachers in general. Certainly the elementary school teachers who are not successful do not fail because of lack of subject matter—a deficiency which would obviously be less troublesome at the elementary than the secondary level. It must therefore be apparent that the control factor in teaching presents a most formidable single problem to every teacher and especially to

---

[1] Ralph W. Pringle, *The Psychology of High School Discipline,* Boston: D. C. Heath and Co., 1931, p. iii.

beginning teachers. Judd, whose writings are particularly fruit-ful in the analysis of the social processes involved in education, has the following to say:

Inexperienced teachers fail far more frequently because they do not know how to keep what is ordinarily called "order" in their classrooms than they do because of lack of knowledge of the subject matter with which they deal. Order in a classroom is a complex social product. A number of personalities with different interests and different emotional tendencies must be induced by the teacher to concentrate attention for a time on some particular line of intellectual endeavor. So delicate is the equilibrium in such a situation that the slightest distraction is likely to defeat the whole purpose of the class exercise. Sometimes the disturbing cause is external and obvious. A loud noise near the classroom or the entrance of a visitor creates a center of natural attention from which the teacher must bring the group back to the subject of the recitation if order is to prevail.[2]

Some pedagogical theorists maintain that when the school situation is ideal disciplinary problems will never arise—a condition which doubtless prevails in the schools of Utopia. Unfortunately, however, an optimum combination of circumstances is seldom present. Therefore, it is a foregone conclusion that disciplinary problems will arise, and no teacher should be allowed to enter the profession without careful training in the psychology and methods of group control, including an understanding of the nature of punishment.

There is nothing realistic about a school program which gives the child the idea that he may be casually nonconformist to the laws of nature and society; rather he must be taught that both nature and society punish transgressions. Tension and frustration will naturally arise when the child attempts to make his adjustment, and conflict is an inevitable by-product of organized society. Furthermore, the conflicting desires of individuals are bound to clash, with resultant friction and tension. The realistic pedagogical approach to teaching social adjustment comes through a knowledge of how to take calculated disciplinary risks

[2] Charles H. Judd, *Educational Psychology,* Boston: Houghton Mifflin Co., 1939, p. 539.

and how to minimize to the greatest extent possible the tensions and conflicts which inevitably occur. It is not now and never has been possible to build a school curriculum or base a methodology entirely upon the child's natural interests and desires. While self-discipline is a paramount aim of the formal educative process, the control and integrity of character which go to make up self-discipline are the product of a rigorous program of training which at times must include firm, albeit gentle, direction from parents and teachers. In different ways, from a different point of view and with a different connotation, both biology and theology deny that the nature of man is all "good." Systematic programs of general education attempt to inculcate in the learner attitudes and behavior patterns which lead toward the attainment of personal and social virtues which are defined by the group in social, theological, and legal terms. In fact, the essence of an orderly society is conformity. In order to satisfy the democratic ideal, only one further thing is needed and that is the possibility of orderly change. Such possibility should and does exist in the United States, but it definitely does not include the right of minorities to sabotage a program upon which a majority agreement has been reached. In a free society, the means should always be present for converting a minority into a majority through the shifting of marginal groups of voters. But of late years the rights of minorities, including at times the rights of the individual child in the schoolroom, have sometimes been defined in terms of license and not liberty, privilege without responsibility, and self-determination without conformity.

No one who has studied the biological nature of man and the harsh realities of social existence can be anything but amused by the statement that those who believe in any form of discipline are already embarked upon a program gratifying their own egos by brutalizing children. No one versed in genetics denies that children need affection and that a graduated program of conditioning to life's sterner realities is preferable to any other form of training. To grant this, however, is not to concede that it is never justifiable to punish a child of any age or that such punishment is invariably an admission of inadequacy on the part of the adult. Under certain circumstances punishment is the best pedagogy possible. Perhaps we can satisfy the sensitive by avoiding the term, a device not entirely unknown in educational affairs.

Psychological Definition of Discipline.—The basic difference between a mob and an army is the psychological factor of discipline. Likewise, the order found in a group in which discipline prevails distinguishes society from barbarism.

There are outer and inner aspects of discipline also. In the school, for example, the outer aspect is found in the type of conditions prevailing on the play field, in the halls, and in the classroom. The inner aspects are found in the attitudes of the pupils.

Some mention of conformity was made in the preceding section. It is considered that the point of view taken is sound, but it needs to be qualified in important ways, one of which is that mere external physical conformity does not mean that a condition of true discipline prevails. Unless proper attitudes are present, the situation is not on a self-sustaining basis. Even military discipline, which obviously must contain highly arbitrary elements, recognizes the importance of attitudinal as well as physical conformity, and an effort is always made by intelligent military leaders to develop a genuine belief in the cause for which the struggle is taking place.

We may say, therefore, that discipline should be a continuing process, should be understood by the various members of the group, and should be accepted by the individual at least in his more rational and objective moments.

Burton, after emphasizing the interrelationship of school discipline and social, economic, political, and religious factors in the environment, discusses the historical development and modern means of securing and maintaining social order. In maintaining order there have been various types of social device used which Burton classifies as follows:

a. The vindictive, in which the objective is vengeance and there is no real thought of changing the individual's attitude.

b. The retributive, which is based upon natural law and the notion that violations of natural law will be followed by automatic consequences; Burton indicates (p. 565) that ". . . the theory that natural punishment should follow misbehavior is sound."

c. The deterrent, based upon fear.

d. The remedial, in which a progressive diagnosis takes place upon which remedial measures are based.

e. The preventive, which is related in objective to the deterrent, but which is based upon positive rather than natural negative inhibitory factors.[3]

Control situations have both their negative and positive aspects. The positive usually consist of statements of the aims or objectives of the group with rationalizing data in support. The Constitution of the United States is an example. Sometimes the positive phases of the control situation are not in documentary form but exist in the shape of unwritten laws, traditions, mores, etc. The negative aspects are sometimes, although not usually, given in the basic statement of principles. Again the Constitution is an example. However, since violations are bound to occur, some machinery must exist for taking care of infractions. Otherwise morale would deteriorate and the government would collapse. In the United States, for example, there is a vast and complex system of legislation, federal, state, county, and city, the principal objective of which is the practical implementation on the individual and community level of the basic principles of the Constitution. Smith has given a clear statement of the need for both negative and positive phases of social control. He says:

Every element in this school control has both positive and negative aspects. In the best-governed states there has always been and always will be need of restrictive laws and punitive institutions. Likewise in the best-regulated school there will always be occasions for correction and punishment. The fallacy of certain sentimentalists that the child's individuality should not be curbed becomes manifest when we remember not only that each pupil has egoistic weaknesses of his own to be overcome but that one must deal with the petty prejudices, social warps, and injurious habits he has contracted in the home, on the playground, and

---

[3] William H. Burton, *The Guidance of Learning Activities,* p. 564, copyright, 1944, with permission of Appleton-Century-Crofts, Inc.

in other phases of his community surroundings. It is too much to expect of any teacher that he shall possess ingenuity enough to devise constructive appeals which will inspire all pupils to right conduct. Specific corrections, rebukes, and punishments will therefore be inevitable under the most favorably conceived circumstances.[4]

We come now to the problem of summarizing some of the foregoing thoughts in a definition of school discipline which will include the various principles stated. No better such statement can be found than that given by Douglass and Mills, who say:

Discipline in the high school seeks the development of abilities, attitudes, and habits which are essential to intelligent self-directed behavior. It is the process of guiding adolescents toward ever higher levels of rational human conduct. The ultimate objective of all forms of discipline in the high school is the pupil's growth in accepting responsibility for his actions with due recognition of the individual, social, and spiritual values involved.[5]

In elaborating upon this basic concept of discipline, Douglass and Mills state the following important related principles:

a. Rational human behavior is learned. . . .

b. Acquiring proper patterns of behavior involves self-activity on the part of the learner. . . .

c. Habits of correct behavior require practice. . . .

d. Docility, conformity, and unquestioning acceptance of authority do not in themselves constitute discipline. . . .

e. Human freedom is more than the mere removal of restraints.[6]

Causes of Disciplinary Problems.—When one undertakes to analyze the causes of disciplinary infraction within the classroom, he is at first inclined to be discouraged because the occasioning circumstances seem to be infinite in variety and innumerable in quantity. Strictly speaking, of course, there are

---

[4] Walter Robinson Smith, *Constructive School Discipline,* New York: American Book Co., 1936, p. 42.

[5] Harl R. Douglass and Hubert H. Mills, *Teaching in High School,* p. 99. Copyright, 1948, by The Ronald Press Company.

[6] *Ibid.,* pp. 99-101, *passim.*

no two control situations which are exactly the same. Several children are different from one another in their behavior at any given time, and a single child never behaves exactly the same twice. However, as cases accumulate it soon becomes apparent that, while lines of cleavage are not usually sharp and homogeneous categories of classification cannot readily be set up, the cases do group themselves into related instances in a fairly sharp manner. With this point of view as a departure, Sheviakov and Redl have made a study of discipline in both theory and practice and have contributed within a relatively few pages one of the most helpful treatises on the causes of disciplinary problems. Part of their investigation was given over to discovering what actually goes wrong most frequently in school groups. As a result of their study, six factors are described. These factors with subclassifications are as follows:

Factor I: Dissatisfactions in the Work Process. . .
  Examples: Subject matter much too easy. . .
              Subject matter much too difficult. . .
              Language of teachers too remote from the child's developmental level. . .
              Load of assignments too heavy. . .
              Load of assignments too light. . .
              Assignments badly planned, poorly explained, unfairly judged. . .
              Type of work or way of presentation too advanced. . .
              Type of work and presentation too infantile. . .
              Activities too much on a merely verbal level. . .
              Work badly scheduled as to sequences of different types. . .

Factor II: Emotional Unrest in Inter-Personal Relations. . .
  Examples: Individual friendships and tensions. . .
              Cliques and sub-group formations. . .
              Disorganization in group roles. . .
              Pupil-teacher frictions. . .

Factor III: Disturbances in Group Climate. . .
  Examples: The punitive climate. . .
              The emotional blackmail climate. . .
              The hostile competition climate. . .
              The group pride climate. . .

Factor IV: Mistakes in Organization and Group Leadership. . .

   Examples: Organizational mistakes. . .

            Too much autocratic pressure. . .
            Too little security. . .
            Too high or too low standards for group behavior. . .
            Too much organization. . .
            Too little organization. . .
            Group organization out of focus. . .
            Personal mistakes. . .
            Lack of tact. . .
            Indulgence in personal sensitivities and allergies. . .
            Over-reaction to dignity violations. . .
            Plan for revenge instead of educational change. . .
            Inconsistency in promise and threat. . .
            Stupidity in carrying out promises or threats. . .
            Wrong use. . .
            Wrong arguments. . .
            Mistakes in emotional distance and proximity. . .

Factor V: Emotional Strain and Sudden Change. . .

   . . . Examples: The stage of anxiety in which many school groups
find themselves for weeks during "examination period" and after-
wards, waiting for the results, is a frequent type of group strain. In
the same way, *sudden effects,* which may sweep classrooms at times,
are productive of problem behavior beyond expectation. Excitement
about contemporary events (community riots), extreme fury, enthusiasm, unusual hilarity, as well as depression and fear, are among
the prime dangers to stable morale. Needless to say, the constantly
whipped up excitement and *aggression* in times of war works as a
chronic irritant on the discipline of many school groups and adds
unnoticeably but considerably to the problems of the teacher as group
leader. . .

Factor VI: The Composition of the Group. . .[7]

   A glance over the preceding points indicates that emphasis
is laid upon the group and the group process. While it is the
individual who gets out of line in a disciplinary infraction, it is
often the group climate which causes trouble. True, children

---

[7] George V. Sheviakov and Fritz Redl, *Discipline for Today's Children and
Youth,* Washington, D.C.: Department of Supervision and Curriculum Development, National Education Association, 1944, pp. 44-55.

are very different in their individual emotional patterns and they come to school under varying degrees of tension from home, but if the group climate is highly favorable and is not itself charged with tension, conflict, and strain, difficulty is not so likely to ensue.

Conflicting Theories of Disciplinary Technique.—It has been stated in this discussion that self-discipline through self-development is the ideal of disciplinary techniques. Promoting the growth of self-discipline in the child requires pedagogical skill of the highest order and much more patience and subtlety of technique than the mere maintenance of superficial order and regularity. Since we all learn what we do, the obvious principle governing such self-development is that the child be placed in circumstances where he must make choices of alternate courses of action and follow those which are in accord with standards with which he has become familiar. This process will inevitably lead to some sacrifice of regimented order, but the price is well worth paying provided the goal is attained. Attention is called to the fact, however, that the mild disruption of absolute regularity resulting from an effort to make children think and act for themselves is a calculated risk and not at all to be confused with the air of perpetual bedlam found in some classrooms where no particular objective is being sought and no planned program is being carried out.

2. EFFECTIVE METHODS OF DISCIPLINE

Criteria of Sound Disciplinary Procedures.—There are two basic criteria of the effectiveness of the disciplinary control of any school, one being the efficiency of the learning as judged by objective measurement and the other being the number of going activities which necessitate some self-control on the part of the pupil.

Many long lists of the aims and objectives of education have been drawn up. But when all is said and done, if pupils are learning their subjects and control of themselves, any statement of aims has been largely met.

A dead silence may not be necessary for the successful mastery of school subjects, the learning of which constitutes one of the aims of education, but one thing is certain and that is that these subjects cannot be properly learned in a continual air of bustle and pandemonium. In children the threshold of reaction to distraction is fairly low, and until they have learned the art of concentration there is much to be gained by reducing distraction during study periods to a minimum. On the other hand, in order to provide variety and a different form of self-expression, definite provision should always be made not only for free play periods but a wide variety of extracurricular activities in which there is opportunity for development of leadership, self-initiative, etc.

When disruptions and wilful violations of the established pattern occur, there are certain general principles of sound disciplinary action which should be observed. The following quotation from one of the most profound thinkers on biological, educational, intellectual, and moral problems who ever lived, Herbert Spencer, gives a fundamental point of view on the general principles involved in the philosophy and psychology of punishment:

Observe, in the first place, that in bodily injuries and their penalties we have misconduct and its consequences reduced to their simplest forms. Though according to their popular acceptations, *right* and *wrong* are words scarcely applicable to actions that have none but direct bodily effects; yet whoever considers the matter will see that such actions must be as much classifiable under these heads as any other actions. From whatever basis they start, all theories of morality agree in considering that conduct whose total results, immediate and remote, are beneficial, is good conduct; while conduct whose total results, immediate and remote, are injurious, is bad conduct. The happiness or misery caused by it are the *ultimate* standards by which all men judge of behavior. We consider drunkenness wrong because of the physical degeneracy and accompanying moral evils entailed on the transgressor and his dependents. Did theft uniformly give pleasure both to taker and loser, we should not find it in our catalogue of sins. Were it conceivable that benevolent actions multiplied human pains, we should condemn them—should not consider them benevolent. It needs but to read the first newspaper leader, or listen to any conversation touching social affairs, to see that acts of parliament, political movements, philanthropic agitations, in common with the doings of individuals, are judged by their anticipated results in multiplying the pleasures or pains of men. And if on looking on all secondary superinduced ideas, we find these to be our ultimate tests of right and wrong, we cannot refuse to class purely physical actions as right or wrong according to the beneficial or detrimental results they produce.

Note, in the second place, the character of the punishments by which these physical transgressions are prevented. Punishments, we call them, in the absence of a better word; for they are not punishments in the literal sense. They are not artificial and unnecessary inflictions of pain; but are simply the beneficent checks to actions that are essentially at variance with bodily welfare—checks in the absence of which life would quickly be destroyed by bodily injuries. It is the peculiarity of these penalties, if we must so call them, that they are nothing more than the *unavoidable consequences* of the deeds which they follow: they are nothing more than the *inevitable reactions* entailed by the child's actions.

Let it be further borne in mind that these painful reactions are proportionate to the degree in which the organic laws have been transgressed. A slight accident brings a slight pain, a more serious one, a greater pain. When a child tumbles over the door-step, it is not ordained that it shall suffer in excess of the amount necessary, with the view of making it still more cautious than the necessary suffering will make it. But from its daily experience it is left to learn the greater or less penalties of greater or less errors; and to behave accordingly.

And then mark, lastly, that these natural reactions which follow the child's wrong actions, are constant, direct, unhesitating, and not to be escaped. No threats: but a silent, rigorous performance. If a child runs a pin into its finger, pain follows. If it does it again, there is again the same result: and so on perpetually. In all its dealings with surrounding inorganic nature it finds this unswerving persistence, which listens to no excuse, and from which there is no appeal; and very soon recognising this stern though beneficent discipline, it becomes extremely careful not to transgress.[8]

A more recent but similar statement of the criteria for disciplinary action has been given by Cutts and Moseley, who say:

---

[8] Herbert Spencer, *Education*. Copyright 1860. With permission of Appleton-Century-Crofts, Inc., New York, pp. 183-85.

Our criteria for a good disciplinary action are briefly these. It should be both safe and effective, safe for the physical and mental health of the child and effective in restraining him from undesirable behavior. It should be immediate. It should be related to the offense and the relation should be clearly understood, as, for example, in the case of the boy who had his ball taken away from him when he broke the rule—and a window —by playing catch in the room before school. It should be just and consistent with experience and pronouncements. It should be administered calmly and objectively, and the child, while made aware of the teacher's disapproval of what he has done, should be allowed to feel sure of her kindly interest in himself. Conversely, a disciplinary action is likely to be dangerous to physical and mental health and in the long run ineffective if it is much delayed, if the child does not understand the reason why it is taken or how it is related to the occurrence, if it is oversevere or unjust, if it is charged with ill feeling, if it by any chance aggravates the cause of the trouble, for example, by interfering with rest and exercise, or if it is emotionally upsetting to the child, causing him fear, worry, shame, humiliation, or feelings of insecurity, failure, and inadequacy.

We feel that though some occurrences are properly ignored, generally the steps in discipline which seem best by our criteria are, first, simple control, followed if necessary by an individual or group conference and then, if a penalty seems required, by some form of removal from the situation, by sending to the principal, or by deprivation. In special circumstances, rectification and reparation may be substituted as a penalty. Other desirable actions—specifically those which we have grouped in the appendix under "indirect action"—are likely to be a result of more consideration than is possible in a minor crisis, or to be more in the nature of prevention. Here we pause only to point out that a kind action in place of a scolding or penalty may pay big dividends. The cases of pupils who have reformed when they were given special help instead of being punished for copying are to the point, as are those of pupils who have been kept out of trouble by being sent on errands when they showed signs of restlessness. Of immediate use is praise of past good actions or of pupils who are doing what is expected of everyone. Such praise can be sincere and may secure better cooperation than criticism or a negative approach. A good rule of thumb is to try to treat a child who makes a mistake as kindly as one would treat a friend and equal.[9]

---

[9] Norma E. Cutts and Nicholas Moseley, *Practical School Discipline and Mental Hygiene,* Boston: Houghton Mifflin Co., 1941, pp. 37-39.

Interest, Success, and Discipline.—Psychologists are far from being in agreement as to the exact role which interest and success play in producing socially well-disciplined and acceptable citizens. There is considerable evidence that the person who is interested in his work is likely to achieve a considerable measure of success in it, principally because the interest leads to the effort and perseverance which are usually requisite elements to achievement. Although in any rigorous academic discipline a considerable amount of application and self-control are necessary, it cannot be said that, from the social standpoint, all successful persons are well-disciplined social beings. Sometimes the academically successful pupil is just as antisocial, just as much a trouble to his teachers now and to the police later, as the unsuccessful child, although the latter is supposed to be the problem type. Possibly the explanation lies in the fact hinted at in some of the readings which have been cited that in a school situation, which of necessity must be pitched at the level of the average child, some children are successful too easily and have time left for becoming disciplinary problems.

The problem arises of how best to handle the "unsuccessful" child or the child who thinks he is a failure. The hypothesis is herewith advanced that proper use of the tendency of human beings to play a psychological role offers great possibilities. The contention is based upon the following line of reasoning: it is demonstrable psychologically that the majority, if indeed not all individuals, fancy themselves in some sort of role which need not necessarily be and very often is not the role which they play superficially. For example, a banker may fancy himself as a champion golfer, and a champion golfer may fancy himself as an authority on banking. Sometimes these covert roles are socially acceptable and sometimes they are not. For example, the boy who fancies himself as a modern Jesse James is playing a secret role which if made overt would be highly unacceptable socially. When, however, the role that the child is playing is socially acceptable, every effort should be made to discover what that role is and to make the child feel that he is successful in it. This device seems simple enough on the surface, but there is much more in it than meets the eye. For if an individual feels that he is successful in the role that is truly close to his heart, he can accept gracefully many a setback and rebuff that would otherwise be much more painful. In this way, many of life's unavoidable failures and shocks are cushioned. Conversely, a child may be successful at academic achievement and yet constitute a serious problem case if he feels that he is very unsuccessful in the role of his own choosing that he is trying to play. It is not too difficult, especially in dealing with children and preadolescents, to discover the roles which they are more or less secretly playing for themselves; when these are known to the teacher, it is possible to make many kinds of use of them.

3. Environmental Factors Affecting Discipline

Home Life and School Behavior.—One of the paradoxes of human existence is that we are all living one life, but, at the same time, many lives. As one reads psychiatry and abnormal psychology, he is impressed at one time with the almost unbelievable compartmentalization that can take place psychologically within a human being and at another time with the fact that there seems to be almost no compartmentalization at all and that the slightest touch on the edge of the spider web of the organism seems to be transmitted to every other part. Possibly this paradoxical situation is one of the many kinds of difficulty we get into in trying to verbalize everything; it may be just a matter of words.

Each child at a fairly early age evolves a psychological pattern or frame of reference based partly on his biological nature and partly upon his experiences up to that time. This pattern exhibits an increasing degree of perseveration and is changed in its fundamental structure only with considerable difficulty. In this basic pattern, however, there are phases in which action one way or the other is fairly closely balanced, so that any strong stimulus may pull response in either direction. Such a situation is the relation between home life and school life. Both occupy a large portion of the child's existence in varying proportions at varying times. Since the child reacts quickly and intensely to emotional tension, the worst thing that can possibly happen is for home life and school life to be pulling in opposite directions, because this condition produces basic conflicts and tensions in the fundamental pattern. Obviously, therefore, one of the prime psychological objectives of the school is to ascertain as much as possible about the home life and home background of each child in order to adjust in so far as it is possible to the pattern already established. Parents on their part would do well not to side with the child in his difficulties with the school without a thorough and objective investigation of what the facts are. Since the child must deal with the school for a considerable number of years, blind emotional defense of the child by parents in any problem that he encounters can only serve to make him feel that he is right and encourage him in other disciplinary infractions.

The Whole School Environment as a Factor in Discipline.— All higher organisms, including man, have the ability to make differential responses. On the other hand, there are many situations in which we probably respond primarily to the whole pattern of stimuli, although doubtless, if the reaction could be completely analyzed, it would be found that certain stimuli were emergent.

A disciplinary situation is an illustration of reaction to an over-all pattern as well as to its parts. The environment of the school as a whole does much to determine what the behavior of the child is going to be. If this environment is one of confusion, inconsistency, and trouble, then woe unto the teacher who attempts to run an orderly classroom in which learning proceeds on an efficient basis. Conversely, if the school is well ordered and well run, the chances of any classroom being disorderly are minimized and the individual teacher has less difficulty.

Admittedly, life is not a completely consistent experience and society is not a completely consistent process, but the majority of mature, normal individuals have worked out something which passes for consistency and in the aggregate the same may be said for society. To subject the child to all the inconsistencies with their attendant shocks that the adult realizes do exist is like putting a young boxer into the ring with a hardened professional to absorb the hardest blows before he has learned the defenses. The school environment should be patterned upon the social environment closely enough so that the transition from the one to the other can be made easily and naturally. Having been so patterned, it should present the aspect of consistency to the pupil. Its program, both of training and control, should be known and understood by all teachers and parents. Furthermore, the administration has not only the opportunity but the duty of seeing to it that reasonable conformity to the program is forthcoming on the part of the staff. Intellectual and academic freedom do not consist of breaking down the operating routines of the organization. Disciplinary infractions are far less frequent and much more easily handled when the entire staff is cooperating in putting over a program which was planned together.

4. The Disciplinary Problem from the Teacher's Viewpoint

Teacher Personality in Discipline.—The venerable axiom that "He who would rule others must first learn to rule himself" is a paramount guiding principle in considering the personality and character requisites of the teacher which best fit him to handle disciplinary problems. Children are extremely quick to sense and detect certain kinds of inconsistency, and inconsistency is the justification to the child for disciplinary infractions of his own. The teacher must reasonably well exemplify the main premises upon which his disciplinary procedure is built. For example, the teacher who preaches self-control to the class but periodically loses his temper is not laying a sound foundation for control of the class. The transmutability of tension is high, which makes the mental hygiene of the teacher important. It is probably fortunate that common schools are usually in session only about nine months a year. Considering the nervous tensions which the teacher undergoes, it is doubtful whether the average individual could stand the strain on a twelve-months basis. The general public, or for that matter the other professions, are not aware of what teaching exacts in nervous energy. Those who are distracted and made nervous by two or three of their own children may speculate on the tension when there are thirty to forty to a class five periods per day.

Many efforts have been made, as indicated by citations given in other chapters, to describe the type of personality best fitted for teaching. So far as this search relates to the problem of discipline, the needs can be stated fairly simply. The teacher should be a person who likes children and enjoys working with them; who has better than average nerves and social poise; and who is highly adaptable to a variety of social situations.

A Suggested Program of Disciplinary Methods.—An excellent point of departure for a discussion of a program of general disciplinary principles may be had by again referring to Burton, who has given a comprehensive statement of these principles. He says:

1. The teacher's general aim in the maintenance of order with special reference to the group should be the development within the group of a social conscience and group cooperation. . . .

2. The teacher's general aim in the maintenance of order with special reference to the individual should be the achievement by the individual of social ideals, attitudes, and habits which make possible self-control and responsibility.

3. Public opinion within the group is, in the last analysis, the determiner of the level of behavior.

4. Group and individual standards are far more effective than imposed rules and regulations.

5. The development of group and individual standards should be recognized as a long slow process of social growth.

6. The standards already operative in the group must be recognized and taken into account.

7. The personality of the pupil must be respected, whether the situation is a simple one of redirecting activity or a serious one of formal punishment. . . .

8. The personality of the teacher is an important factor which must be used with care. . . .

9. The clinical view should dominate at all times. . . .

10. Punishment and authoritarian control will be necessary in a limited number of cases. . . .

11. The final outcome desired is always understanding and responsibility resulting in changed behavior. The desired outcome is not outward conformity with and control by rules.[10]

In addition to the principles as stated by Burton, emphasis should be laid upon the importance of keeping all pupils busy. On the lowest level this means busy work; on the highest level it means activity in which pupils are interested and which will produce educational results.

The establishment of routines to which pupils are expected to conform is also a valuable control technique. The secret of the successful establishment of routines lies in practice or drill and the prevention of exceptions. Routine properly used is a prime source of efficiency in learning.

First impressions are important. A class of high school students sizes the teacher up in a hurry, and certain members at least come to some tentative conclusions immediately as to how much lax behavior will be tolerated. See to it that the first impression that you make is not an accidental one or an incorrect one; it often takes a long time to undo an incorrect or false first impression.

Analysis of the real nature of a disciplinary infraction is vital to proper control measures. Very often the disciplinary breach itself is a symptom and not a cause. Like the physician, disciplinarians should treat causes and not symptoms.

When it is necessary to use punishment, be sure that it is rationalized to the pupil. He should understand why he is being punished, even though he does not agree. If the rationalization is sincere and honest, the pupil on his part cannot conscientiously react to it with a blind rage which is reserved for punishment which is purely vindictive in nature. We repeat for the benefit of those who recoil from any system of punishment that society has never yet in groups of any size found it possible to order its affairs without a system of penalties.

[10] William H. Burton, *The Guidance of Learning Activities,* pp. 573-75, copyright, 1944, with permission of Appleton-Century-Crofts, Inc.

There are always those who are late with their taxes, who exceed speed laws, who damage theater seats, and, yes, who commit felonies and murders. Many grave offenses could have been prevented if children had been introduced early to the fact that society does have a system of penalties.

Finally, the teacher should do everything possible to prevent the appearance of disciplinary problems. Commenting upon this point, Schorling[11] in a discussion of preventive discipline gives the following helpful ways of minimizing disciplinary infractions:

1. *Learn the names of pupils quickly.* . . .

2. *Study carefully the seating of the students.* . . .

3. *Learn to "ride your eye" through the eyes of your students.* . . .

4. *Learn to call upon those pupils whose attention is wavering.* . . .

5. *Be businesslike.* . . .

6. *Make every effort to avoid all suggestions of criticism, disorganization, or anger before the group.* . . .

7. *When a member of the group obstructs the work, the treatment of the case should be calm, dignified, and firm.*

8. *Use special occasions to carry over to the pupils the idea that you are interested in them as human beings.* . . .

9. *Stop the little things.* . . .

The homely suggestions listed above constitute, as Schorling himself points out, devices rather than fundamental principles. Knowledge and use of a thousand such devices, however, is characteristic of the teacher who handles disciplinary situations smoothly and well.

Questions

1. How do you account for the fact that discipline is the greatest single cause for failure among teachers?

2. Define discipline from the psychological point of view. How does this differ from your personal definition?

---

[11] By permission from *Student Teaching,* by Raleigh Schorling. Copyrighted, 1940. New York: McGraw-Hill Book Co., Inc., pp. 59-60.

3. Discuss the reasons why discipline is so important in the school situation.

4. Give examples of the types of disciplinary devices listed by Burton.

5. Construct a list of possible situations in the classroom that would lead to disciplinary action on the part of the teacher. Give suggestions for dealing with each.

6. Analyze the criteria listed by the author for sound disciplinary procedures.

7. Compare Spencer's philosophy of discipline with that formulated by Cutts and Moseley.

8. Do interest, success, and home conditions play a major or minor part in the school behavior of the student? Explain.

9. List the characteristics of a school that would be conducive to positive behavior on the part of the students.

10. Is teacher personality a salient factor in school discipline? Give reasons for your answer.

11. Summarize the author's suggested program for disciplinary methods. What suggestions can you add to this list?

Chapter 28

PSYCHOLOGY OF THE GUIDANCE PROGRAM

1. EVALUATION AND SOCIAL GENESIS OF GUIDANCE

Historical Development of Guidance.—From the earliest days of formal school systems it has been recognized that the school must furnish guidance to pupils. As Brewer points out:

So insistent down the ages has been the ever-recurring question, "What shall I do?" that it was inevitable that thinkers and writers should grapple with the problem suggested.[1]

Various devices have been tried, some of which have made their appearance, have completely disappeared, and have reappeared again in the guise of new programs. For example, considerable use is now being made in many school systems of excursional education and trips to industrial plants for purposes of acquainting pupils, especially boys, with the business world in which many of them later will secure jobs. Such vocational tours are an excellent and commendable form of education, but they are not new. In the early days of the Roman Empire the value of a practical introduction to the market place was recognized, and Roman boys often accompanied their fathers on the daily round of business. Psychologically the function served was the same as it is now. The arrangement was somewhat more informal, but the idea was assuredly the same as at present. Today our effort is directed at giving the young boy a sampling of several kinds of business and industrial experience rather than a systematic indoctrination in any particular one, at least until later.

---

[1] John M. Brewer, *et al.*, *History of Vocational Guidance*, New York: Harper & Bros., 1942, p. 13.

The apprenticeship system is a form of vocational guidance which is of remarkable antiquity. The realization that it is difficult for the learner to transfer sharply from the field of theory into the field of application and practice underlies this program.

Industrial schools and technical institutes attempt to combine theory and practice in one type of organization in which there is continuous opportunity to practice and at the same time to acquire a concurrent grounding in the theory being applied.

In early American schools, the need for academic guidance was at a minimum because the tendency was for the curricula to be stereotyped and fixed. The guidance function, therefore, was largely served in the moral field and consisted of maxims, preachments, and moral exhortation in various forms. According to Chisholm,[2] the modern trend in guidance began about 1900 when changes in the needs of schools, society, and individuals necessitated an extensive expansion in guidance facilities.

One difficulty with guidance efforts through the schools up until comparatively recently has been the subjective nature of the counseling. Of the two main phases of any extensive guidance program—survey of possible choices and prediction of possible success—the first may be set up without a too elaborate foundation of experiment. It is quite possible, for example, in the field of vocational guidance to present descriptively in the schoolroom and graphically by visits and excursions the major divisions of industry in any given community so that the pupil may, either by observation or participation or both, determine for himself the one which he prefers. At Dobbs Ferry High School, New York, seniors are given experience in choosing an occupation, in evaluating their characteristics in relation to their choice, in conducting research into its advantages and disadvantages, and lastly in methods of job-hunting. Heuss, Wood, and Kurilecz write that this plan has been most successful and list the three main parts of the project outline as follows:

---

[2] Leslie L. Chisholm, *Guiding Youth in the Secondary Schools,* pp. 15-28.

  I. Choosing a Vocation

   A. The students are asked to write a biographical and character sketch of themselves, and to read one book of character molding.

 II. Outline for the Study of an Occupation

   A. Write a composition telling all you know and can find out about an occupation that you are interested in at present.

   B. Spend a day and a half actually working at the occupation selected for your occupational study.

   C. Make a vocational ladder showing future possibilities of your chosen occupation.

   D. Write a letter of application.

   E. Visit an employment office.

III. Where Can I Get My Training?

   A. If you plan to go to college, select three colleges and send for catalogues. Answer the questions given concerning one college.

   B. If you plan to go to a business school or a trade school, select a school that trains specifically for your field. Obtain a catalogue and answer given questions.

   C. If you plan to go directly to work after graduation, read thoroughly one of the books listed on obtaining a job and write a 500-1,000 word composition giving the steps of a planned campaign in job-getting.[3]

Some guidance programs consist primarily of survey techniques and minimize the second or predictive effort, which is much more difficult and requires more thorough training and technical knowledge. The rationale of an emphasis on the observational type of program is that in the long run the pupil must make his own decision and that the main function of the guidance program is to show him the various choices or alternatives which may be a solution to his occupational desires and preference.

A complete guidance program must include a program of measurement, particularly the measurement of aptitudes, and those who aspire to be expert in the field of guidance must be familiar with methods of handling data derived from measurement, including the statistics of prediction. Darley says:

---

[3] *Occupations,* XXVI (1948), 291.

To use tests, one must know something about the rates of growth of various kinds of behavior in individuals to determine whether testing will yield intelligible results. To select tests, one must be aware of the importance of available norms, in order to see students not only *as they now are* relative to others like them, but also *as they may be* relative to others whom they want to be like, or with whom they want to compete.[4]

It requires a high correlation between two variables in order to predict one from the other in individual cases. Therefore, in the guidance of the individual pupil, the best that it is possible to do is to give the statistical odds for or against success in any chosen line of work. When we consider the compensatory effect of drive and similar factors, the certainty of the prediction becomes less.

Influence of Social Tradition on Guidance Procedures.— Social tradition exerts a profound influence on all kinds of guidance; this is noticeable particularly in the vocational field. For many centuries and in many countries it was customary for the cobbler's son to become a cobbler, the lawyer's son to become a lawyer, and so on. There is still no country in the world where this type of influence is not exerted and where a considerable tendency does not exist for parental guidance to be determinative. Germane and Germane write:

> Certain parents insist on choosing a vocation for their son or daughter. They may even be so stubborn as to refuse to finance preparation for any other. Family tradition says that Johnny must be a doctor, so a mediocre and unhappy doctor he becomes, when he might have been a happy and expert auto mechanic. Many parents so plan a son's career from early childhood that he comes to believe it is his own choice.[5]

Anyone who has had experience in guidance work either at the secondary or a higher level knows that one of the typical kinds of case encountered is the victim of incorrect family guidance not based upon objective and impersonal data on aptitude but upon wishful parental thinking. Children do not always

---

[4] John G. Darley, *Testing and Counseling in the High-School Guidance Program,* Chicago: Science Research Associates, 1943, p. 62.
[5] Charles E. Germane and Edith G. Germane, *Personnel Work in High School,* New York: Silver Burdett Co., 1941, p. 379.

desire to follow in their parents' footsteps and, even when they do, are not always endowed with the same biological gifts required to tread the same path successfully.

One of the most difficult cases that the writer ever had in the guidance field was the son of a brilliant engineer whose father was determined that his son should become an engineer also. The boy's intelligence test score was low, and his grades in mathematics in both elementary and secondary school were also low. His performance in general engineering courses was what one would expect from the test result pattern and previous grades. The boy was on the verge of a nervous breakdown because of his father's inexorable and inflexible determination that he should become an engineer. The father alternated between punishing the boy and blaming the professors. The case was solved when the father was finally convinced that his son had neither the aptitude nor the interest to succeed as an engineer. The case is typical of thousands still occurring every day at all levels of the school system, particularly in colleges. It illustrates the fact so frequently found that often the problem is not with the pupil being guided but with some member of his family or his teacher. Such cases call forcibly to our attention the point that guidance psychologically is a highly complicated procedure involving much more than one child, the results on one test, and one guidance officer. To quote Traxler:

> In the practice of guidance, the whole process is as unitary as the lives of the individuals with which it deals. No school can successfully conduct a few selected functions of guidance, for the reason that the personalities of individuals cannot be divided into compartments. Hence no school should attempt a guidance program unless it is willing ultimately to undertake all phases of it.[6]

An expert in guidance needs to be just as sophisticated in the analysis of his case and the interpretation of his laboratory data as does the physician. He must take into account the history, the preceding circumstances, and all of the environmental factors which have gone to produce the pattern of behavior with which

---

[6] Arthur E. Traxler, *Techniques of Guidance,* New York: Harper & Bros., 1945, p. 3.

he is dealing. This strongly implies the value and necessity of cumulative record-keeping in school systems, a problem which has not until recently received anything like adequate attention. There are numerous behavior trends, some abnormal and difficult to measure within a brief period of time, which are revealed eventually by complete, carefully kept cumulative records.

The influence of social and family tradition on the guidance of the young is not necessarily always harmful. In many cases parental solicitude starts the child early on the path which he would have followed in any case and produces under optimum circumstances a highly trained product at a precocious period. On the other hand, when social tradition influences the child's curriculum at an early age in a direction which he later cannot or will not follow, much time and effort are wasted.

2. Psychological Analysis of the Guidance Process

Types of Guidance.—One classification of types of guidance is into three groups :

1. Toward cultural and general education
2. Toward earning competence
3. Toward character and citizenship

Guidance toward cultural and general education is, as the name indicates, that type of guidance which assists the pupil in his choice of school subjects and in the problems which he encounters in following these subjects. In schools which employ a relatively fixed curriculum, cultural guidance is ordinarily internal within the subjects. Concerning this, Cox and Duff state :

When high-school curricula consist largely of subject-matter-to-be-taught, curriculum guidance must be a compromise. There is sometimes little room for choice in the menu we offer our customers—it is equivalent to asking them, How will you have your spinach ? [7]

In schools which allow a wide range of electives, guidance toward general education tends to take the form of assisting the

[7] Philip W. L. Cox and John Carr Duff, *Guidance by the Classroom Teacher,* New York: Prentice-Hall, Inc., 1938, p. 96.

pupil in picking those elected subjects which he will need for his best cultural development.

Guidance toward earning competence, when the pupil is allowed to exercise free choice, consists primarily in pointing out possibilities and in furnishing the pupil with information bearing on the possibility of success in the various choices which he might make.

Guidance toward character and citizenship is a large, important, and as yet not thoroughly developed area. It includes assisting the pupil to make his personal adjustment to social problems. Mental hygiene and social philosophy are involved as well as sex education. Manners, morals, and social ethics play their part. The importance of this phase of guidance is being recognized by more and more educators. Erickson lists the following as an example of this trend:

The recent meetings of the Central States Association of Colleges and Secondary Schools established guidance as one of the nine criteria for the accreditation of secondary schools. They passed the following recommendation: "Each school should have organized a coordinated guidance service to aid people in meeting educational, moral, health, civic, and personal problems. . . .[8]

The great range of guidance service in the junior high school is clearly illustrated by the following suggestions by Detjen and Detjen for grades 7, 8, and 9:

Seven B. *Orientation*
1. Organization of Home Room
2. Rules and Regulations of the School
3. Student Organizations of the School
4. Our School Building
5. Care of Personal Property
6. History of Our School
7. Elementary Principles of Parliamentary Law
8. Effects of Absence and Tardiness
9. Program of Studies Offered in Our School
10. Use of the Library
11. Health
12. Self-Improvement

[8] *North Central Association Quarterly*, XXII (1948), 285-88.

13. Improvement of Our School
14. Résumé of Semester's Work

Seven A. *Social, Moral, and Ethical Guidance*
1. Organization of Home Room
2. Thrift
3. Safety
4. Good Citizenship in the Community
5. Good Citizenship in School
6. Sportsmanship
7. Good Manners in the Home
8. Good Manners in School
9. Good Manners in Public Places
10. Good Manners in Business
11. Valuable Personality Traits
12. Character Traits
13. Other Valuable Traits
14. Résumé of Semester's Work

Eight B. *Recreational and Cultural Guidance*
1. Organization of Home Room
2. How to Study
3. Everyday Culture
4. Music
5. Art
6. Literature
7. Plays and Photoplays
8. Travel
9. Sports
10. Hobbies
11. Avocations
12. Value of Participation in Extracurricular Activities
13. Americanism
14. Résumé of Semester's Work

Eight A. *General Educational Guidance*
1. Organization of Home Room
2. The Responsibilities of a Junior High School Citizen
3. The Junior High School
4. Our Public School System
5. Local Educational Institutions
6. Advantages of an Education
7. Advantages of Punctuality and Regular Attendance

  8. Occupations Open to Junior and to Senior High School Graduates
  9. High School or Work
  10. Choosing High School Subjects According to Interests
  11. Choosing High School Subjects According to Abilities
  12. Courses Offered in Senior High School
  13. Choice of Ninth Grade Course
  14. Résumé of Semester's Work

Nine B. *Vocational Guidance*
  1. Organization of Home Room
  2. Planning for the Future
  3. Causes of Vocational Failure
  4. The Importance of Self-Analysis in Choosing a Vocation
  5. Important Facts One Should Know in Making a Vocational Choice
  6. A Brief Study of Occupations in the Field of Agriculture
  7. A Brief Study of Occupations in the Field of Industry
  8. A Brief Study of Occupations in the Field of Commerce
  9. A Brief Study of Occupations in the Professional and Public Service Fields
  10. A Brief Study of Occupations in the Fields of Homemaking and Personal Service
  11. 12. 13. Intensive Individual Study of a Few Occupations
  14. Applying for a Position

Nine A. *Educational Guidance*
  1. Organization of Home Room
  2. Making the Best Use of One's Time
  3. Educational Careers of Famous Americans
  4. Educational Careers of Local Citizens
  5. The Advantage of Working Toward a Goal
  6. Educational Requirements in Occupations of Special Interest to Students
  7. Colleges and Universities
  8. Requirements for Graduation from Senior High School
  9. Planning a High School Career
  10. 11. Preparing a Complete Tentative Schedule for Senior High School
  12. Individual Problems in High School Schedules
  13. History and Traditions of Local Senior High Schools
  14. Class Day [9]

---

[9] Mary E. Ford Detjen and Ervin W. Detjen, *Home Room Guidance Programs for the Junior High School Years,* Boston: Houghton Mifflin Co., 1940, pp. xiii-xvi. By permission of the publishers.

Psychological Aspects of the School Guidance Program.—
There are certain psychological considerations which need to be
borne in mind by the administrator, particularly the principal,
in setting up a guidance program. The first one has been implied by the statement that guidance is a generalized procedure.
We do not organize one room for guidance, or one teacher, or
one child. We organize entire schools for guidance. Information collected by Erickson and Happ [10] from the "statements
made by school people about the purposes of their guidance
programs" led them to write in conclusion:

> These definitions exhibit the variety of approach of different indi-
> viduals, schools, and organizations in attempting to define guidance.
> They show clearly that guidance permeates almost every activity of the
> school. There is ample evidence of the extent to which guidance is
> concerned with the *total development* of pupils. These statements of the
> guidance concept refute the criticism made by some that guidance is
> narrow or concerned only with the vocational development of pupils.
> It is evident that these school staffs are attempting through guidance
> to find better ways to serve their pupils.

The atmosphere which permeates the school building—the
attitudes of the teachers toward the pupils and the attitudes of
pupils toward the teachers—are more important as guidance
factors than any single mechanical or technical device. When
the morale of the teaching staff is high and when all teachers
are collaborating and pursuing a clearly understood educational
objective, that one factor alone constitutes a guidance force in
the school which is of immeasurable value. When the principal
is at outs with his staff or the staff is bickering among itself,
it is virtually impossible to set up a psychologically sound guidance program. Faculty morale is a weighty factor in the correct
psychological organization of a school guidance program.

Equal in importance to morale within the school is the interpretation of the school program to the community and especially
to the parents. Guidance personnel know that part of their

---

[10] By permission from *Guidance Practices at Work,* by Clifford E. Erickson and Marion Crosley Happ, p. 9. Copyrighted, 1946. McGraw-Hill Book
Co., Inc.

problem lies in the home. A school program cannot be interpreted to the community by the intermittent attendance of
parents at infrequent parent-teacher functions, however desirable and enjoyable these may be. School-community relations to be functional must be a continuous, dynamic process.
One effort to make the relationship more real is the new type of
report card which attempts to give a picture to the parent of the
personal and social performance of the child in the school. These
new-type cards have been satisfactory as far as they go, but
they serve only a limited purpose. Parents need to see the
school actually at work, and any form of effort to get parents
into the school helps to gain that objective. The more frequently teachers and principal can visit parents, the better the
mutual understanding. By way of illustration Hamrin and
Erickson summarize the report of a workable guidance program
which includes the following statement:

. . . it is clear that the guidance program will be much more effective
if a spirit of understanding and cooperation is fostered through many
informal contacts between advisers and parents.[11]

Some schools have attempted to secure a picture of the home
problem of each child by little essays about home incidents.
This device, while possessing an element of psychological clever-
ness, has backfired in some instances and led to results which
were both embarrassing and amusing. It is not too strongly
advised.

In addition to maintaining morale and interpreting the school
program to parents, it is wise to have the technical services of
the guidance program clearly understood by the entire teaching
staff, particularly in a large school system. Some teachers,
particularly of the old-fashioned variety, are inclined to be suspicious of the child research and guidance divisions or similar
services. To quote Fensch:

Some schools will also have older teachers and parents who lived
through the days in which rash statements were made concerning I.Q.'s

---

[11] Shirley A. Hamrin and Clifford E. Erickson, *Guidance in the Secondary
School*, p. 26, copyright 1939, with permission of Appleton-Century-Crofts, Inc.

and Mental Ages, statements that had to be modified at later dates. Unfortunately, some of these older teachers and parents were no longer on the scene when the modifications came or have not kept abreast of the latest findings of psychologists and specialists. These individuals are sometimes "hard customers" to deal with in beginning a guidance program.[12]

Fensch believes that in order to get a guidance program off on the right foot it is necessary to start a program of public relations that will acquaint the family and the teachers with its aims and procedures. Unfortunately, the personnel of the technical services by their attitude sometimes make situations worse instead of better. These technical services should never adopt a patronizing or condescending attitude toward the work of the rest of the staff. It should be clearly understood both by them and by the teaching staff that all are a part of a program of giving service to children.

Guidance can be most effectively given in any classroom and by any teacher. In a sense, all master teachers render their most important service in this way. Threlkeld offers the following practical suggestions for teachers in meeting cases:

1. The best attitude is one of cheerful, thoughtful objectivity, avoiding pronounced sympathizing, condemnation, or an air of easy optimism or slap-'em-on-the-back.

2. Remember the whole child. While you work for one character objective, take care lest you get undesirable by-products in other character objectives.

3. The child with extreme withdrawing, recessive characteristics is as much a problem in need of individual help as is the child with extreme aggressive characteristics. Too great shyness may mean more potential trouble than too great forwardness.

4. Utilize all readily accessible data, such as those relating to health, school progress, and home conditions. Cumulative pupil records already available in most schools furnish a large amount of valuable information.

5. Avoid treating symptoms. Try to find out why the child acts as he does, and then fit the treatment to the cause of the difficulty.

6. In some cases, the counselee should be kept informed of the pur-

---

[12] *School Executive,* LXVII, (1947), 37.

pose of the counselor, and should be appealed to consciously to aid in solving the problem. In other cases the counselee may be kept in partial or complete ignorance of the changes desired in him. . . .

7. Single experiences do not afford ground for generalization. Vivid incidents are particularly to be distrusted. Habitual and recurring behavior is the significant source of data.

8. Do not offer authoritative explanations. By the use of other cases and of questions, build up in the counselee his own reasonable interpretation of his behavior.

9. Expect patterns. Among the more common are dependence, fear of the new, avoidance of people, breakdowns, running away from a situation, projecting the blame onto an individual of a given type, and displacement, making a mountain out of a given molehill.

10. Do not give advice. Give the experience of yourself and others as far as it is useful, taking particular care to emphasize the differences in the situation faced by the counselee. No two persons have faced exactly the same situation. What the counselee needs is ability to handle situations himself, not advice to follow.

11. Emphasize success rather than failure. Seek to arrange situations that will give the child a taste of success.

12. It is sometimes necessary to study other persons than the one immediately involved. A problem child means at least one and probably two problem parents.

13. It is seldom possible to depend exclusively upon the readjustment of persons and objects in the environment, or upon the new insight and attitude of the person being advised. Both are usually in need of some readjustment.

14. Keep confidences inviolate.

15. Avoid letting the plans focus on too distant goals without adequate attention to immediate steps. Help the counselee plan on improving adjustment this week, not console himself with phantasy. The past and future exist to enrich the present.

16. Learn to identify early the cases which require a specialist, and be willing to refer them to him.[13]

Finally should be mentioned the enormous effect of the behavior of the teachers, parents, and administrators upon chil-

---

[13] A. L. Threlkeld, "Character Education," *Tenth Yearbook*, Department of Superintendence, National Education Association, (1932), pp. 251-52.

dren. A "do as I say and not as I do" program of education cannot succeed because it is on an unsound psychological basis. Pupils cannot take seriously lectures on sportsmanship from a teacher who they know is a cheat and a poor sport; they do not take well to discussions of temperance from a teacher who smokes three packages of cigarettes a day; and they take a very dim view of sermons on the evils of overindulgence from parents who weave home from taverns or a social hour at the neighbor's. In the last analysis we are all judged by our fellowmen more on the basis of what we do than what we say and there are no more observing or sharp judges of behavior than children.

QUESTIONS

1. Why has some type of guidance been necessary throughout the ages?
2. Give an example of guidance as it was practiced in the days of the Romans. How did this arrangement differ from the type we have today?
3. What psychological purpose does the system of apprenticeship serve?
4. What two forms does guidance take in most schools? Explain each.
5. How do social traditions influence guidance procedures?
6. What do we mean when we say that guidance is a generalized process?
7. List the three types of guidance.
8. How does curricular guidance differ in the large and small school?
9. Define vocational guidance. Relate your experiences along this line.
10. Why do some parents and teachers object to the introduction of a guidance program? How can this objection be overcome?
11. What is the role of the parent in the guidance program?

Chapter 29

PSYCHOLOGY OF
EXTRACURRICULAR ACTIVITIES

1. ANALYSIS OF EXTRACURRICULAR ACTIVITIES

Definition of Extracurricular Activities.—As McKown [1] has pointed out in an excellent discussion of the topic, it is difficult at present to define extracurricular activities with exactness. Actually the term as commonly used refers to those activities which are outside the organized classroom activity of the school. For this reason, some authorities prefer to speak of extraclass and intramural activities. In our discussion, "extracurricular activities" will have reference to any of those activities which are in addition to the planned subject matter course offering of the school. The number and type of these activities are different in each school, but there is an underlying pattern which all schools seem to follow. Concerning this Eugene S. Farley writes:

The usual extra-curricular activities consist of clubs; athletics; assemblies; musical organizations such as orchestras, glee clubs, bands, and choruses; publications, such as yearbooks, newspapers, handbooks, magazines, student council; homeroom organizations; dramatics; and honorary societies. In a well-planned school they furnish an organized environment which supplements the regular curricular program in an effective manner. [2]

Changing Viewpoints on Extracurricular Activities.—For many years the typical attitude of the school administration

---

[1] Harry C. McKown, *Extra-Curricular Activities*, p. 4.
[2] See Frank G. Davis (ed.), *Pupil Personnel Service*, Scranton, Pa.: International Textbook Co., 1948, p. 233.

toward extracurricular activities was one of tolerance, with occasionally a little mild supervision thrown in. Administrators and teachers in the school were primarily held responsible for teaching school subjects, and in public opinion anything reputable above and beyond that was permissible so far as the students were concerned but not a duty so far as the faculty was concerned. To quote McKown: [3]

In the beginning these activities were ignored. The teacher considered his job that of classroom instruction and this usually meant lecturing. He recognized and accepted no responsibility for what the students did outside of his own narrow subject. He simply ignored their social and physical lives.

Early exceptions were athletic coaching, supervision of school plays, and school papers. Thoughtful administrators and teachers came gradually to realize that extracurricular activities were actually an intrinsic part of the school program and should be provided for accordingly. In discussing the modern trend in extracurricular activities Carter states:

More and more attention is being paid by educators to social activities as a means of developing well rounded and integrated adolescent personalities. Time is allotted to such activities in the regular morning or afternoon hours, some schools even granting credits toward graduation. Trained faculty advisers and coaches are provided and pupil participation is encouraged.[4]

It took many years, however, for the recognition of the value of extracurricular activities to reach a point where proper compensation both in time allowance and money was available to those teachers who were willing and competent to supervise them. Many teachers are still not completely satisfied with administrative provisions, especially load allowances. At the present time the situation is improved, but there are still backward communities that expect the teacher to superimpose a heavy load of extracurricular supervision upon a full program of class

---

[3] From Harry C. McKown, *Extra-Curricular Activities*, p. 2. Copyright, 1937, by The Macmillan Company and used with their permission.
[4] *Nation's Schools*, XL (1947), 32.

teaching. This is particularly true in the small high school, where according to Bowlby:

. . . the problem of extracurricular duties is really enough to take your time, your health, and your breath away. Every teacher is expected to serve as a class adviser as well as sponsor two or more activities, plus a little coaching or dramatic work on the side. Three-in-one oil is modest in its numerical claims when compared to the small-high-school teacher who is expected to be a seven-in-one paragon—guidance expert, adviser, teacher, clerk, and assistant janitor, plus football and basketball coach! [5]

Educational and Psychological Value of Extracurricular Activities.—Extracurricular activities are the methods by which the schools project themselves into all phases of the student's life. Rich in writing of the value of these activities says:

But the real educator knows that what people learn to *do* with things, not what they hear about them, constitutes real learning. . . . Education comes to students when they are helping to make melody themselves, working the do-dads and seeing the effect, leading the gang, getting out of the tight place, exposing the error, joining with others in putting something big and worthwhile across.

Naturally those who have been converted to this dynamic theory of education, have come to see in activities outside the curriculum subjects opportunities for leadership, initiative, and creation, greater than in the old line curricular studies. The school scout troop, for instance, under good leadership might contribute more to information and character than any scholastic subject on the program. Progressive educators, in an attempt to supply as many kinds of experience as are available for the welfare and improvement of students, have taken on a more or less elaborate organization of extra-curricular activities. In some schools, an extra period a day is devoted to home-room guidance, assembly projects, pupil government responsibilities, club work, thrift, athletics, school publications, scouting, dramatics, honor societies, library work, commencements, excursions and musical and literary societies. [6]

These values are recognized by Americans and Europeans alike. Boone gives the viewpoint of a German officer in a recent article in which he says:

---

[5] *Clearing House*, XXII (1947), 21.
[6] *Journal of Education*, CXXVII (1944), 161.

Before the beginning of the recent war, a former captain of the German navy said to several American educators: "Perhaps there are some things in European education that are superior to those you have in the United States, but if we had the activities in those European schools that you have here I do not believe that dictators could arise or wars start." [7]

In summing up his own opinion concerning their value, Boone states further:

In conclusion, we may also add that, in giving a student an opportunity to participate in some activity, we do much to prepare him for later life. There is also provided a stance for college, if he is one of those who will attend some institution of higher learning. Whether for college or not, it will prepare him for an avocation, an occupied mind, and a stimulating interest with an appreciation for the better parts of life. Without the experience of school activities, the individual is far more susceptible to *isms,* unrest, dissatisfaction, and an unsettled condition of mind.[8]

The human organism is active in varying degrees twenty-four hours a day. Some of this activity, such as that which takes place during sleeping, is on a reflex and unplanned basis. The greater portion of the child's activity during his waking hours, however, is of such a nature that it can and should have educational significance. One of the reasons that the general public is dissatisfied at times with the products of our educational institutions is that graduates, while passably well trained in the routine phases of subject matter, are likely to lack the social and character values necessary to proper adjustment to a complex society. Walsh and Johnson show that the increase in student activities is the "outgrowth of a philosophy of education based upon the need for the development of the whole child." [9]

We must bear in mind that these plus values as they may be called are not a casual by-product of the academic classroom work. Morality, social responsibility, worthy citizenship, and

[7] *Bulletin of the National Association of Secondary-School Principals,* XXXII (1948), 117.
[8] *Ibid.,* 122.
[9] *Nation's Schools,* XL (1947), 30.

durable character traits depend upon the formation of habits and are the result of a planned program. Extracurricular activities make a widespread and extensive contribution to this phase of the child's education.

Objectives of Extracurricular Activities.—In order to be socially and educationally effective, the extracurricular activities program needs to be aiming toward nonacademic objectives which are understood and recognized by both teachers and pupils. Aims such as health, good sportsmanship, community service, and the like are in some ways more readily understood by pupils than academic goals. The psychological contribution of extracurricular activities lies in the values which they offer in the activity phases of the less formally organized areas of school life. According to Barr, Burton, and Brueckner:

The modern school with its greater understanding of the nature of the learner, of the learning activities, and of the integration of experience recognized that the so-called "extracurricular" activities were in fact excellent experiences. The extra activities have been moving over steadily into the curriculum. The extra activities are in fact based upon a principle basic to modern education; pupil participation in selecting, planning, and carrying on learning activities.

[These authors suggest that:]

While examining programs for co-curricular activities we may ask:

1. Is an extensive program of student participation in the government of the school indicated?
    a. Student councils and policy-forming committees
    b. Participation in management of school functions: registration, commencement, dances and other parties, assembly programs, special drives and campaigns
    c. Participation in minor routines of traffic control, classroom management, record keeping
2. Is a home-room program outlined with educational as well as administrative objectives?
3. Is there a wide variety of club activities indicated?
    a. Literary and debating
    b. Vocational and avocational (hobbies)
    c. Dramatic, musical, artistic.

4. Is there an adequate list of school publications?
   a. Newspaper
   b. Yearbook
   c. Student Handbook
   d. Literary magazine
   e. Humorous magazine

5. Is there provision for activities giving training in the management of money?
   a. School banks and thrift programs
   b. Handling money for school activities

6. Is a varied program of school excursions and trips included?

7. Is there an extensive program of intramural sports and games, with reasonable interscholastic contacts? [10]

McKown has done a superior job of stating clearly the objectives of extracurricular activities in the modern school program. Note in the items as they are given the intimate relationship to democratic life, self-criticism and adjustment, motivation, etc. McKown [11] gives the objectives of extracurricular activities as follows:

To capitalize, for educational profit, important fundamental drives. . . .
To prepare the student for active life in a democracy. . . .
To make him increasingly self-directive. . . .
To teach social co-operation. . . .
To increase the interest of the student in the school. . . .
To develop school morale. . . .
To foster sentiments of law and order. . . .
To discover and develop special qualities and abilities. . . .

The following diagram from Douglass provides another interesting comparison of the relationships between the contributions of the extracurricular program to the objectives of education:

---

[10] A. S. Barr, William H. Burton, and Leo J. Brueckner, *Supervision,* 2d ed., copyright 1947, with permission of Appleton-Century-Crofts, Inc., pp. 436, 437.
[11] From Harry C. McKown, *Extra-Curricular Activities,* pp. 12-16. Copyright, 1937, by The Macmillan Company and used with their permission.

CONTRIBUTIONS OF EXTRA-CURRICULAR ACTIVITIES TO THE OBJECTIVES
OF EDUCATION [12]

Objective	Type of Outcome	Contributing Activity
Health and Safety	Information about sports, games, animals, flowers, plants, scientific basis of health and sanitation, first aid, fire and accident prevention Habits and skills in games, sports, outdoor activities, dancing, first aid, avoiding accident, and general bodily skill and strength Ideals of sound, healthy bodies and proficiency in physical activities Tastes and interests in outdoor sports and health	Athletic teams of all sorts, hiking, outdoor clubs, biology, clubs, nursing club, dancing, Junior Red Cross
Vocation	Information concerning occupations (nature of work, rewards, chance for advancement, etc.) and concerning pupils' abilities in different pursuits —information underlying choice of vocation Habits and skills: those general habits (honesty, industry, and ambition) that make for vocational success; skills in one or more vocations or activities common to several vocations (salesmanship, accounting, writing) Ideals: of success, influence, independence, fair dealing, cooperation, and service Tastes and interests: explorations of such as a basis for vocational choice	Sports and games, musical and other fine arts clubs, journalistic and forensic clubs, household arts clubs, semi-scientific clubs (radio, photography, automotive, aeronautic); semi-vocational clubs (printing, millinery, cartooning, agricultural and commercial clubs)
Worthy Use of Leisure	Information about things of culture: art, music, drama, current and classical literature, and authors: about current social problems and events; about games and sports, and reading Habits and skills: in fine arts, games and sports, and reading Ideals: of culture, dignity, and self-respect, of approval of others in such matters. Tastes and interests in fine arts, sports, games, hobbies of various sorts	Athletic and other sports; chess, checkers, and other games; musical and other fine arts clubs; foreign language clubs; mathematical clubs; dramatic clubs; reading clubs; history clubs; sewing and basketry clubs; short story clubs
Command of Fundamental Processes	Information—how to read, to study, to write, to speak, to solve problems Habits and skills in the application of computation, study methods, skills in written and oral communication, getting on with other people Ideals, tastes, and interests: continuation of desirable types begun in the elementary school	Practically every activity, particularly those involving the reading of books, the writing of reports, and the keeping of accounts, giving oral reports or participating in discussions (journalistic and forensic activity)

[12] Harl R. Douglass, *Organization and Administration of Secondary Schools,* Boston: Ginn & Co., 1945, pp. 210-11.

CONTRIBUTIONS OF EXTRA-CURRICULAR ACTIVITIES TO THE OBJECTIVES
OF EDUCATION — *Continued*

Objective	Type of Outcome	Contributing Activity
Worthy Home Membership	Information about things of culture, human nature and character, biology, sanitation, household decoration, purchasing, budgeting, diet and nursing, preparation of foods, the construction and repair of clothing, household machines, children's reading. Habits and skills in fields mentioned above Ideals: culture, monogamy, fair play, courtesy, happiness to others, happy and beautiful homes Tastes and interests in fields named above, in artistic things, and in games and sports	All sorts of fine arts clubs, household arts clubs, and semi-scientific clubs All clubs in so far as they develop an understanding of human nature and psychology and how to get on in close contact with others
Citizenship	Information about government (national, state, and local), public utilities, community organizations, results of unsocial acts or neglect Habits and skills: in getting along in group activities as followers and as leaders respecting feelings and rights of others, repressing unsocial impulses, thinking through consequences of behavior Ideals: 'the group above the individual,' fair play, service, patriotism Tastes and interests: in local and other social institutions, in justice and fair play, in the welfare of others; antagonism toward unsocial ideas and acts	All organizations involving group efforts, student government, teams, civic clubs, letter clubs, traditions clubs or committees, Girl Reserves, Girl Scouts and Boy Scouts, Hi-Y clubs, service clubs
Ethical Character	Information about ethical ideals and practices and philosophies underlying them Habits and skills in carrying such ideals into automatic and effective practice Ideals of an ethical nature, of right behavior to self and to others Tastes and interests: in service, in religious activities and philosophies, in human beings as creatures of God	Hi-Y clubs; Catholic, Hebrew, or other denominational clubs; service clubs; and practically all activities mentioned under citizenship

2. EVALUATING EXTRACURRICULAR PROGRAMS

Psychological Criteria of a Sound Extracurricular Program.
—1. *Planning and Organization.* Extracurricular activities
require fully as much planning as classroom work. Not long
ago, the author was visiting a school of which the principal is
proud and from many angles most properly so. One particular

point of pride with this principal is the orderliness, cleanliness, and beautiful appearance of the school. Naturally this is the result of care, planning, and organization. When we came to examine his extracurricular activities, the same meticulous precision was in clear evidence. Each activity was proceeding smoothly under unobtrusive but vigilant supervision and with hearty pupil cooperation, but there was one noticeable omission. The extracurricular activities, carefully planned and organized as each one individually was, were small in number and represented the personal bias of the principal rather than the group planning of his staff and pupils. Specifically, the extracurricular program was mostly athletic in nature because the principal was an enthusiast on high-school athletics.

2. *Relation to pupil interest.* As a general rule it may be said that pupils should be allowed to select their own extracurricular activities. The one qualification on this is that some variety be required. If pupil interest were the governing psychological criterion by which programs of extracurricular activities were organized, there would doubtless be more types of program than there are at present. Only recently have such things as fly-tying been regarded as sufficiently reputable to be recognized as an extracurricular activity. The author is familiar with one high school where the fishing club is the most popular extracurricular activity of all, thanks to the personality and interest of one man. Citizenship, character education, and the like can be taught in many more ways than through the class play, the athletic field, and the activity period, excellent as all of these are.

3. *Articulation with the regular school program.* The extracurricular activity program should be part of a meaningful whole of which the regular school classroom is a part. According to Fretwell:

. . . whenever possible the extra-curricular activities grow out of the curricular activities and return to them to enrich them. In accordance with this idea, the school newspaper would be all or a part of a course in English; intramural and inter-scholastic athletics would grow out of and be a part of a real program of health and physical education; assemblies and commencements, rather than being specially contrived for the occasion, would grow out of the real life of the school.[13]

Normally motivation is easier in the extracurricular program than in the regular school program. Therefore the former should be used to assist the latter. When the principal and his staff view both as part of an over-all program of educating children, the best results are obtained.

4. *Proper supervision.* If there is any art in teaching, much of it must surely be found in supervision. To supervise correctly means to watch, to help, and at times to direct and control. All should be done as unobtrusively as possible, particularly the directing and controlling. Instead of recognizing these functions of the supervision of extracurricular activities, however, a few teachers tend to dominate the situation by too much direction and control, thus destroying the essential spirit of the extracurricular program, while others go to the opposite extreme, which results in a mild form of educational anarchy. Meyer maintains that: "A complete co-operation is needed. TEACHER INTEREST and STUDENT CONFIDENCE can make the school a happy place in which to grow." [14]

Supervision in any school properly starts with the principal. In a program which is soundly organized psychologically, it is his duty to evince a lively and keen interest in all the principal phases of the school's activities. When the principal is on the job and showing sincere and genuine interest in the program, this attitude is quickly caught up by the teachers and it is easy for the students to understand that the extracurricular activities in which they are engaged are regarded by those in control of the system as a part of the program. Unfortunately, many a principal who is proud of the fact that he is on the bench sitting beside the coach during every game of the football season is blissfully unaware of what is going on in the Spanish Club, the

---

[13] Elbert K. Fretwell, *Extra-Curricular Activities in Secondary Schools,* Boston: Houghton Mifflin Co., 1931, p. 4.

[14] From *A Handbook of Extra-Curricular Activities in the High School* by Harold D. Meyer, published by A. S. Barnes and Company, Incorporated, New York, 1926, p. 8.

stamp-collecting group, the junior play, and elsewhere in the school.

QUESTIONS

1. Give a definition of extracurricular activities and list those types that are most frequently found.
2. Discuss the changing viewpoints on extracurricular activities.
3. What steps can be taken to remedy the conditions prevailing in many of our small high schools with regard to these activities?
4. Explain the educational and psychological value of extracurricular activities and give examples of how these values are transmitted to the pupil.
5. What are the objectives of extracurricular activities?
6. Give examples of activities that would aid in securing each of the objectives listed by McKown.
7. List and discuss each of the psychological criteria of a sound extracurricular program.

Chapter 30

PSYCHOLOGY OF SCHOOL LEADERSHIP

1. Meanings and General Conditions of Leadership

The word "leadership" is applied to so many very different social relationships that it would be a serious error to treat it as a single quality or social phenomenon or to pretend that the conditions of leadership in one situation are necessarily applicable to another situation. We should also be careful in making evaluative judgments as to its social desirability, since this depends upon what sort of leadership we are talking about.

Leadership is frequently treated as if it had a more or less necessary connection with social progress. We often attribute the static or moribund condition of a social system to "lack of leadership"; we picture a social group without leaders as milling around in helpless confusion, without direction or purpose. Actually an objective survey of history or of present society indicates that the amount of leadership found in a given society is no dependable measure of the progress of that society or of the happiness of the individuals in it. Indeed, the demand for decisive, dictatorial leadership is a sociopathological symptom; a society may look for leaders most desperately when its internal structure or the qualities of its members are insufficient to guarantee its continued existence. More than one great nation has turned to the *Führerprinzip* too trustingly, only to find that complex social problems are not thus easily solved. Political parties, social movements, and even business firms have found that dependence upon a single dominant personality for a long period, though it may lead to temporary advantages, often results in later collapse with the death or disability of the dominant figure. Leadership of this kind is more highly thought of and more typical of our society than we may be willing to admit. The special connotation of "leader" in our culture is so evident that the word, changed to *líder,* was taken over into Spanish (and Portuguese) as having an urgent flavor not found in *caudillo* or *jefe.* Let us hope that "leader" does not become a term with the present meaning of "Führer." Leaders of the driving, domineering type are exactly what we do not want in a democracy.[1]

Even in the most democratic groups there are, of course, *primi inter pares*—first among equals who, though arrogating to themselves no special rights of decision or command, are nevertheless recognized as leaders in some sense. What are the special qualities or characteristics which these persons have?

First of all, the leader of a group is able to see things from the group viewpoint. He must genuinely share group enthusiasms and values. The Machiavellian leader who pretends a strong interest in group aspirations merely to forward his private and quite different ambitions is rarer in the adult world than is generally supposed, and this type is practically unknown in school groups. The ball-team captain elected by popular acclaim is often not the star player but the one who has shown the most intense interest in the welfare and success of the team.

Since the leader shares the group viewpoint, he cannot be too original, as this characteristic tends to alienate its possessor from the group. The supposed originality of the leader usually consists in his ability to put into words or action a group attitude or tendency which already exists. He maintains his position by watching which way the group is about to go and putting himself in front just before it starts moving. The really original person, no matter how sound his reasoning or brilliant his proposed plan of action, can seldom gain an audience, much less a following. An original plan or suggestion may as well fall upon deaf ears, since it is suggesting action patterns which have not been previously learned. The successful leader, whether political figure, publicist, or teacher, suggests at most

---

[1] For a discussion of domination as the antithesis of leadership, see Paul Pigors, *Leadership or Domination,* Boston: Houghton Mifflin Co., 1935.

only slight variations of activities and attitudes which have already been well learned. Sometimes, indeed, even slight variations cannot be elicited, and the leader must watch for new action patterns to occur more or less accidentally, at which time he can label them and point out their value, fooling not only others but himself into thinking that he created them as well.

The successful leader knows how to express what the group wants or feels in terms of a simple formula. He uses slogans, battle cries, and clichés with the confident knowledge that predictable behavior will result. He is either too uncritical or too careful to complicate issues by mentioning embarrassing exceptions and paralyzing doubts, since these may lead to ways of behaving for which the leader is unprepared. There is also the possibility that a group confused by one leader will depose him in favor of another who offers an alternative and simpler solution.

Maintaining a position of leadership requires in almost all groups a considerable expenditure of energy. Leadership often is the reward for willingness to do a great deal of work in return for the position. In many organizations the titular leader, at least, is merely one of the few persons willing to accept the onerous duties of the office with only a title as compensation. Many a teacher has relieved himself of unpleasant jobs by assigning them to a Playground Captain, Hall Officer, or some other dignitary. Such ways of attaining leadership are too frequently overlooked, since the group has not done the selecting; nevertheless the leader often gets his start this way, as persons who get things done are thus discovered by the group.

In other words, leaders learn to lead by experience in leading. The school situation offers a large range of activities which present opportunities to delegate responsibility, to recognize special talents, and to provide for legitimate training in leadership. Almost any desirable skill developed beyond average competence can be made use of. Leadership and the perfection of some special skill are, in many instances, interdependent. The skill often serves as a ticket of admission to group membership, which in turn is the only framework within which leadership can develop. There are always present differences in skill and talents, and always situations which demand direction and cooperation. With moderate alertness and imagination the teacher can combine situations demanding cooperation or direction with the use of the more skilled pupils to give some training in leadership every day.

In general, leaders in school groups of all kinds tend to be above average in desirable characteristics. In a study of 409 pupils from Grade III to junior high school it was found that the best-liked and most popular students were, as a group, above average in school achievement, intelligence, health, attractiveness, adjustment, physical achievement, and home rating.[2] Leaders in high school tend to be slightly older than their group, are above average in scholarship and intelligence,[3] and more often are following a college-preparatory rather than a vocational curriculum.[4] A comparison between thirty-seven high-school leaders and a carefully matched group of thirty-seven nonleaders showed the former had a better record in school attendance and health, were rated as higher in general appearance, and participated to a greater extent in extramural activities.[5] The cause-and-effect relationship is obscure. For example, high scholarship does not insure success in leadership. Scholastic superiority, when coupled with habits of cooperation, skill in teamwork, and identification with group aims, is an asset. School leaders tend to share the interests and enthusiasms of the group. We are not justified in concluding that superiority in these various items such as attendance, health, and identification with group aims make leadership easier to obtain; it may be that leaders are, because of their position, more careful of their appearance and school record, and make a greater effort to maintain their status in other ways.

---

[2] *Journal of Social Psychology,* VIII (1937), 365-84.

[3] If the leadership is in athletics, the scholarship is usually slightly below the average. See, for example, L. Ruth Nutting, "Some Characteristics of Leadership," *School and Society,* XVIII (1923), 387-90.

[4] For an attempt to isolate the qualities basic to leadership by factor analysis, see "A Factor Analysis of the Personality of High School Leaders," *Journal of Applied Psychology,* XIX (1935), 596-605.

[5] *School Review,* XLVI (1938), 523-31.

It might be inferred from the preceding remarks that only a relatively few pupils can hope to become leaders. Since it is generally recognized that the experience of leadership of some kind should be part of the education of as many children as possible, it should be emphasized that we have been concerned with "all-round" leadership of the kind found in those "big men on campus" who take prominent part in many different activities. A well-planned school program provides opportunities for every student to have some special recognition. Practically every child has some interest or ability which makes him a potential leader in some field. The pupil who has no chance of making the honor roll may be excellent yell-king material; the little girl too candid and artless in politics to become class secretary may have a positive advantage in tryouts for the school-play ingénue. This fact is completely disregarded in many schools where every new position of leadership is given to one of the élite who already has too many offices and duties. Since being in a position of leadership is the only training for leadership, it is not surprising that after a few semesters of this policy the failure of a "nonleader" accidentally chosen for such a position seems to support the fallacy that a leader is born, not made. Teachers who have gone to the trouble of developing leaders know that nearly any pupil can be trained to lead in a field where he has some particular competence.

In a society where leadership is so highly regarded as here, it is not surprising that the child who has had no chance to be a leader in any situation is likely to develop an inferiority feeling which may be a serious drawback to his personal success as well as result in a loss to society. Many competent men have not received the attention they deserved while their less able associates have been put into positions of authority and influence simply because the latter had confidence in their ability to lead.

Some attention has been paid recently to the importance of "followership"; it is contended that we need more people who know how to follow. It is not, however, so much a matter of *how* to follow but rather of *what* and *whom* to follow. Since the leader is usually a sort of personification of the resultant of group tendencies, "followership" is often merely an uncritical drifting in whatever direction the group is going. There is quite enough of that in the world already; it seems more desirable that our educational system emphasize rather the development of a critical and even skeptical attitude toward leaders in those fields in which leadership consists mainly in an understanding of mass psychology.

In some situations a given person is so clearly entitled to a position of leadership that no one but a complete anarchist would think of challenging the situation. When children play "work-up" baseball or when adults play bridge, leadership changes hands in a previously established systematic way which is accepted by all participants. Conventional leadership of this kind is necessary in a smoothly functioning social group and is wholly desirable so long as the conventions are acceptable to all members of the group and do not confer unfair advantages on some. The individual who insists that others follow the conventions when he is benefited but refuses to do so in other cases is socially immature. This attitude is often found in children who come from homes in which no principles of fairness or equity are recognized, each incident being "settled" by whatever method seems most effective, perhaps violently repressive discipline, perhaps indulgent yielding to the child's dictatorial demands. In the latter case the "spoiled" child quickly establishes his unchallenged leadership in the home group and naturally uses the successful technique in school, continuing to do so as long as it works. Failure to impose this leadership upon school companions may lead to the abandonment of overt efforts to do so, but usually the basic attitude of the child remains the same. Sulkiness, pouting, aggressiveness, jealousy, lack of cooperation, and similar types of behavior are often protests against the unaccustomed leadership of others. Through a policy of strict fairness in distributing opportunities for conventional leadership and by frequently showing the impossibility of genuine social cooperation in a situation continually dominated by a few, the teacher can gradually build up a willingness to relinquish leadership when the rules of the game

require it. This is the principal ingredient of good sportsmanship and the reason why games organized and played fairly can
be a very important contribution to social maturation. It
should be mentioned that great champions are notoriously "poor
sports" in this respect, although of course there are notable
exceptions. Where the will to win becomes an obsession, grace-
ful relinquishment of leadership is hardly to be expected. The
average teacher, however, is more interested in turning out
socially mature citizens than in training temperamental champion athletes. Modern society is risking social stability as well
as the social adjustment of its members if it fails to teach its
future citizens that the price of driving in comparative safety
on an arterial highway is obeying stop signs; that the showing
of our clever home movies to friends commits us to a dull evening of listening to their stuffy classical recordings; that the
free expressing of one's opinion today implies the readiness to
permit another to speak as freely tomorrow; that the denial of
another's rights inevitably puts our own in jeopardy.

2. Determining Group Structure

An interesting technique for analyzing social structure and
for the identification of leaders, isolated persons, or the more
popular members of any classroom society has been developed
by Moreno.[6] Simple questions regarding preferences of a child
for a seating partner, a theater guest, and so on reveal many
interesting facts in human relationships. Such data may be
skilfully used in committee selection to make for a friendly total
group. Isolates are located, and their preferences become valuable data. Other sociometric techniques used by Bogardus [7]
suggest interesting procedures for classroom use. The teacher
can through these techniques view the class objectively as a
social pattern. Objectivity in describing the social pattern of
the class is a necessary tool for helping individuals find their
places in the group.

[6] J. L. Moreno, *Who Shall Survive? A New Approach to the Problem of
Human Inter-Relations.*
[7] *Sociology and Social Research,* XVII (1933), 265-71.

3. The Teacher as Leader

It was once assumed that the teacher should establish his position of leadership with a show of force and authority—"let 'em know who's boss." The slave-pupils were to learn their lessons under the figurative or even literal whip of the "master," as the teacher was appropriately called. The usual result, as might be expected, was a hatred of the material studied—a hatred which often extended to all intellectual activity. In a reaction against the traditional methods the opposite extreme of complete lack of discipline and leadership was sometimes attempted. It was maintained by the advocates of this procedure that children are naturally curious and that if the necessary pencils, books, and other instructional materials are made available the pupil will "pick up" an education without the active help of a teacher. Where this method was actually tried it was, of course, found to be highly inefficient. The number of ways to do a thing wrong is so much greater than the number of ways to do it right that a great deal of time can be wasted in random behavior that is far from the activity to be learned. It is the duty of the teacher to limit the activities of the pupil to the extent that the desired activity will have a good chance of occurring frequently. To do this unobtrusively but effectively is the object of class leadership. How best to establish and exploit for the benefit of the pupils the recognition of the teacher's leadership is one of the principal concerns of the successful teacher.[8]

A study by Lewin, Lippitt, and White [9] on the nature of group response to authoritarian, democratic, and laissez faire leaders has attracted considerable attention. In one group conducted as an authoritarian society all policy was determined by the teacher. The boys were told what project would be used, were assigned tasks, and were given step-by-step directions as

---

[8] For an interesting and informative report on an experiment in the re-training of leaders see Alex Bavelas, "Morale and the Training of Leaders," chap. 8 in Goodwin Watson (ed.), *Civilian Morale,* Boston: Houghton Mifflin Co., 1942, pp. 143-65.

[9] *Journal of Social Psychology, S.P.S.S.I. Bulletin,* X (1939), 271-99.

they worked each day. Future steps were left uncertain, and the leader (teacher) was "personal" in his praise or criticism. "Permissiveness" was absent, for students were hemmed in by directions, restrictions, and orders. In a test situation when the leader was absent or arrived late, the members showed their hostility. Members of the group tended to be either submissive or attention-demanding toward the leader. One boy destroyed his work at the end of the final meeting.

By contrast, the democratic leader permitted group choice of the project to be carried out and encouraged group discussion of procedure and progress. The members were free to choose partners and tasks. The leader remained objective in his praise or criticism. He tried to act as a member of the group without doing too much of the actual work. If he arrived late or was absent from the classroom, activity went on in much the same way as during his presence. There was less competition among members of the group, and more appreciation of the results was in evidence. Relations with the leader were on a more friendly basis than in the authoritarian group.

As suggested previously, the laissez faire group accomplished little and failed to become an effective working unit. These results with groups organized on authoritarian, democratic, and laissez faire lines, do not, of course, do much more than illustrate the general remarks made about the three methods. It is very difficult to set up an experiment in this field without prejudicing the results by the manner in which the different groups are managed. The results of the experiment are suggestive only.

When the teacher first walks into the classroom, he is largely an unknown quantity. His pupils are in a state of tension, sizing him up, ready with a number of possible responses learned in similar situations in the past. In our culture leaders act in certain ways which are already recognized by the elementary school child. The stereotype is easily described. He appears confident, competent, cooperative, and friendly, but can be reserved and aloof if the occasion demands. He has something to say, and says it in a firm but quiet voice. He is well groomed and carries himself with dignity. He has no distracting mannerisms or peculiarities. To this stereotype practically any class will respond with respectful attention, for a short while at least. Those teachers who feel that conscious imitation of a stereotype is a technique beneath their dignity, if not actually dishonest, should remember that if no effort is made to impress pupils favorably *some* impression will nevertheless be made, and a response, desirable or not, will be elicited. It is not suggested that the teacher cultivate a "front" which misrepresents his true personality. Unlike the salesman who need "turn on the charm" only until his product is sold, the successful teacher must actually have the qualities which will insure his continued favorable acceptance. Pupils in daily contact with the teacher will discover the absence of these qualities in a surprisingly short time no matter how convincingly the leadership role be enacted. The whole point is that pupils as well as adults accept leaders partly on the basis of superficial, stereotyped cues. It is the duty of the teacher to act the part until his real qualifications for class leadership have been recognized. No incompetent teacher has succeeded in maintaining leadership on the basis of a pose, but very many competent ones have never given themselves a chance to be accepted because of failure to establish a beachhead in the classroom.

If we admit the evidence of common sense and experience without demanding statistical verification, a number of additional characteristics of successful leadership in teaching can be mentioned:

1. Pride in the profession and active participation in professional organizations. Association with leaders in the profession and with colleagues helps to establish the sense of belonging to an important group doing important work.

2. An interest in people and particularly in children. This interest should extend beyond the school and include the larger community, state, nation, and world.

3. Willingness to fit into the administrative scheme of the school system and to carry out one's individual responsibility in the school program. A clear realization that the school system as a whole will function only as well as reasonable compliance and cooperative action of individuals will allow

is one mark of a good teacher. Schoolteaching is a co-operative enterprise.

4. A persistent recognition of pupils as individuals and as persons differing from other persons.

5. The ability to profit from mistakes and from criticism which depends on a readiness to face objective facts even when they are disturbing.

6. Attention to conditions that make for physical and mental health. Teaching is strenuous. Teachers should accordingly permit themselves time for relaxation and stimulating change, time for the cultivation of friendships among persons with whom one can be at ease.

QUESTIONS

1. Why does the successful leader usually present his program as a very simple formula?

2. After the names of several students have appeared in the school paper as "leaders," what changes in their behavior would you expect?

3. In a certain small school it was possible to organize so many activity groups that every pupil in school had some position of "leadership." Would you expect the pupils to disregard their titles and duties because all others had titles and duties as well?

4. Why should pupils be encouraged to require leaders to answer questions concerning proposed plans?

5. If "we learn what we do," why isn't hard study under sternly repressive discipline a good idea?

6. How would one go about making a "leader" of a pupil with no outstanding talents or abilities?

7. Some children never learn the importance of relinquishing conventional leadership to others according to the "rules of the game." Mention some adult situations where this would lead to considerable trouble.

Chapter 31

THE IMPROVEMENT OF TEACHING

1. THE TEACHER'S ROLE IN PUPIL LEARNING

Place of the Teacher in the Learning Process.—Adaptive orientation can and would take place without the benefit of teachers, but it would be a lengthy and wasteful process. Because of the enormous increase in the social heritage and the accumulated stock of human knowledge which must be transmitted to each succeeding generation, it has become increasingly necessary to shorten the process of learning. Consequently, even in inductive teaching which aims to lead the learner through the essential elements of experience preliminary to reaching a final generalization, the process must be shortened.

In the psychological analysis of the total teaching situation, it must be recognized that the teacher is only one factor in the highly complex environment to which the learner responds. There is sometimes a temptation to think that the child is in rapport with the environment solely through the medium of the teacher and that, were the teacher removed, the child's learning progress would be retarded. It is commonly assumed that the teacher's contribution to the child's progress in learning is represented by his fund of knowledge at the end of the year minus the amount at the beginning of the year. Experimental work with groups of children under teachers of various degrees of competence or no teachers at all does not bear out this assumption.

As one talks with teachers, principals, supervisors, board members, parents, etc., it becomes evident that unanimity as to the place of the teacher in the educative process does not exist. The following points of view are encountered:

1. *That the teacher should concentrate effort principally upon providing content.* Those who hold that content mastery by the pupil is the paramount objective of the teacher's efforts maintain that there is a tremendous amount of factual content material which must be acquired by the child in order to make him socially and vocationally competent. This content, as such, is valuable above all else. The teacher need think little about method except in its disciplinary phases. The facts are presented; the children learn them. Pupils who do not attain mastery are punished. Education is inherent in the material itself.

2. *That the teacher should provide content and instruct.* This theory differs from the foregoing one in that it throws a somewhat heavier emphasis upon method. More organization of material is required. Somewhat less emphasis is laid upon the intrinsic value of subject matter.

3. *That the teacher should provide content and motivate the learner's mastery of it.* This view of the function of the teacher is more in accord with psychological principles because learning is viewed as a moving, active process and not a passive, receptive one. Impression will be gained through expression. The teacher is not a taskmaster but rather one who, by a series of subtle devices, arouses and maintains interest.

4. *That the teacher should provide content, motivate activity, and direct progress.* The motivating and directive view of the functions of the teacher reflects sound psychological theory. Guidance is a process of counseling and suggestion; motivation is grounded in the psychological nature of the child. Content is viewed not as an end in itself or as possessing any intrinsic merit, but merely as the medium by which the child passes from one level of adaptive experience to another.

In analyzing the place of the teacher in the educative process, the following points should be borne in mind:

a) The teacher is only one of several factors which influence child development.

b) The results of teaching cannot be measured by the difference in the total amount of knowledge at the beginning and total amount of knowledge at the end of any given period of time. Natural development will account for some of the progress. An extreme statement of the influence of natural development in learning is given by Courtis:

It is true, and will always be true throughout the world, that when any test appropriate for the children tested is given, individuals will differ widely in raw scores because a test measures the resultant of *all* the factors operating—age, sex, capacity, experience, training, conditions, motives, purposes, and a thousand and one other factors which cannot possibly be the same for all.

When a class made a lower score than other classes in the same grade, it was similarly "natural" to assume that "poor teaching" was the cause. Careful experimentation, however, has shown that the more precisely the effects of teaching are determined under single variable controlled conditions, the less can any effect of teaching as such be discovered. The school offers such an enormous excess of opportunities and does so little in assisting children to make use of them that all teachers, by and large, obtain nearly the same results. Rate of maturation is a more influential factor than teaching.[1]

c) Unguided development will not produce an individual adequately prepared to cope with the problems of modern society.

d) The teacher who is most likely to be successful in furthering conduct development of a desirable sort among pupils is the one who not only provides content but motivates activity and directs progress.

2. The Successful Teacher

Ways of Judging Teaching Efficiency.—"Teaching success" is a relative term usually defined in subjective ways. Some authorities prefer to omit mention of "teaching success" and, in studying the problem, confine themselves entirely to objectively defined results. For example, instead of making studies of "teaching success," it is possible to conduct surveys of the reasons given by superintendents why teachers are dismissed.

---

[1] *National Elementary Principal,* XXV (1946), 21.

Status studies make little effort to define teaching success but are concerned with factors upon which permanence of tenure depends. The difficulty is that only the superficialities of teaching may be involved. Any definitive judgment which is passed upon a teacher's effectiveness should be rendered upon more fundamental considerations than tenure.

Several tenable opinions may be held concerning what constitutes teaching efficiency. The more important of these may be described briefly:

1. *Administrative.* In terms of practical expediency the administrative criterion of teaching effectiveness commands consideration. Administrative and supervisory officers have occasionally devised rating scales for the measurement of teaching effectiveness, and the itemizing of qualities to be considered has undoubtedly contributed to an increased reliability of administrative evaluation. According to Cocking:

> An acceptable merit program must be developed cooperatively. Regardless of the excellence of the scheme, it cannot well succeed if it has been prepared only by the superintendent or his class advisers. Joint participation of administrators, teachers, and selected representatives of the public would seem wise and necessary.[2]

2. *Economic.* The economic criterion of teaching effectiveness need not be considered at length. The assumption is that the teacher who is receiving the highest salary is the best one. Such a criterion is closely allied to the administrative, since higher-level salaries are usually determined by administrative judgment.

3. *Ethical.* The ethical criterion minimizes administrative judgment, salary of the teacher, and even extent of the pupil's mastery of content and holds that the social conduct and conformity of the pupil when he has been graduated are the best evidence of the value of teaching which he has had. Practice based upon this theory has been carried far in some schools. For example, the old type of report card has been abandoned altogether in places and a new type adopted which tells parents

---

[2] *School Executive,* LXVII (1947), 5.

about the social conduct of the child as well as about his progress
in subject matter acquisition.

4. *Academic.* Conservatively speaking, it may be said that
the academic judgment of a teacher's effectiveness is one which
should always be given. For, after all, are not teachers employed primarily for the purpose of imparting knowledge to
children, and if one wishes to estimate how well a teacher has
done his work, is it not logical to measure pupil's knowledge?
The accepted method of making such measurements is to use
standardized tests, compare the results with norms, and judge
the teacher accordingly. This method of teacher evaluation has
strong proponents who maintain that our school systems have
expanded too much, have become defined in too wide terms, and
contain too many extracurricular ramifications. It is held that
the curriculum should be restricted to more narrow academic
channels and teaching success judged accordingly. The operation of this theory can be seen in an economic depression when
its exponents were among the first to suggest the abolition
of the so-called "fads and frills" and to demand a return to the
"fundamentals" in education. The teacher is then judged on
the extent to which the pupils have mastered these fundamentals. A more naïve expression of the same thought is to judge
teaching effectiveness by pupil marks. Thus one hears of so-
and-so being a "good teacher" because no pupils fail in her
classes. Brownell points out the fallacy of such a criterion
when he writes:

Where a teacher is rated on the basis of the number of pupils who
pass examinations or who make high marks on examinations, the prudent
teacher will see that by hook or crook her pupils *pass the examinations*
even though other considerations are badly neglected. Such a plan for
recognition of merit, furthermore, fails to consider that good teachers
may do an excellent job for pupils who have limited ability but, because
of their limited ability, these pupils cannot make good examination
marks.[3]

The fact of the matter is that teachers' marks, if corrected
sufficiently for the operation of a number of variables, do give

---

[3] *Nation's Schools,* XL (1947), 20.

a reasonably accurate index of the extent to which teaching has been effective on narrowly defined academic lines. On the whole, the academic criterion of teaching success is valid but partial.

5. *Psychological.* Success according to the psychological criterion may be defined in terms of improved pupil adjustment to life situations and problems. The psychological criterion of teacher success emphasizes what the pupil does and not what the teacher does; stresses the end and not the means; and employs a functional and not a structural criterion. The extent to which the pupil has been made familiar with the relationship existing between the material which has been learned and life problems is a determinative criterion as Savulak points out:

He is not educated who holds a large number of facts for which he can find no use except to store them in his mind. Facts and skills, and all knowledge in general, have value only in so far as they enable a person to live the life he ought to live both here and hereafter. No subject, regardless of the importance given it in the school curriculum, has any value at all if it does not enable boys and girls, men and women, to be more human or to live better lives.[4]

This procedure for evaluating teacher success would require a series of observations of students in action. Test situations might be devised and check-lists used in evaluating the conduct of the class as it meets the situation. Such situations would provide the stimulus for the behavior from which implications and inferences regarding teaching success would be drawn. Not only mental development but physical, social, and emotional growth would be noted in such an analysis.

Teaching Aptitude.—It has for some time been realized that the intelligence and content mastery of the teacher are by no means the only factors which make for success in teaching, but no one has yet succeeded in making a practical statement of the combination of traits which one must have to be a successful teacher. Beautiful teachers succeed and fail; homely teachers succeed and fail; bright teachers succeed and fail; not so bright teachers likewise, etc.

[4] *Education,* LXVIII (1947), 195-200.

Boyce [5] early observed that teachers are too often rated by their administrative or supervisory officers on an unanalytical basis of general impression. Following the lead of Elliott and others, Boyce worked on score cards which would make ratings more objective. There followed many investigations of teacher rating, and these later studies attempted to penetrate more deeply into the personal aptitude of the teacher than do administrative ratings. Morris,[6] for example, after discussing at length a "Trait Index" and considering the predictive value of various measures of temperament for teaching success, came to the conclusion that in weighing personality traits and their relation to teaching, the whole personality must be always in the forefront. Recent studies have tended to bear out the findings of previous work but have gone further, as shown by Barr:

There has been a relatively great amount of activity in the measurement and prediction of teaching ability during the three-year period covered by this summary. The main trends and emphases for this period may be briefly summarized as follows:

1. There appeared to be a growing interest in the qualities that characterized the good teacher at the college level.

2. Very few studies of teacher rating scales as instruments for the evaluation of teaching efficiency were reported.

3. Attention seemed to have shifted to more objective tests and inventories; Rostker and La Duke reported studies wherein different combinations of these were combined into composite measures of teaching ability.

4. Interests in the prediction of teaching efficiency continued; studies by Martin and Seagoe are typical of this area.

5. Troyer and others found measurements extensively used in all areas of teacher selection, guidance, education, placement, and follow-up.

6. While no new statistical devices were developed during the period, correlation technics and factor analyses were fairly systematically applied in several instances.[7]

---

[5] Arthur Clifton Boyce, "Methods for Measuring Teachers' Efficiency," *Fourteenth Yearbook*, National Society for the Study of Education, Part II, p. 77.
[6] Elizabeth Hunt Morris, *Personal Traits and Success in Teaching*, p. 2.
[7] *Review of Educational Research*, XVI (1946), 207.

Even with a list of general traits of demonstrated significance, the problem of what makes a master teacher is not too well advanced toward a solution, because traits or qualities, however carefully they may be defined and isolated, are significant in a performance so complex as a teaching situation only when observed as a functioning pattern which can and does change from one person to another. The effect of the teacher upon pupil conduct must be determined in terms of the total teaching situation or teacher-pupil relationship, and this effect cannot be accurately predicted by a consideration of separate teacher or pupil personality traits, however accurately measured they may be. To provide an empirical test in teacher training, practice teaching experience is offered. Practice teaching is rich in situations which are valuable not only to the prospective teacher for trying himself out but also to supervisors for judging the total effectiveness of each trainee under classroom conditions, although even here the correlation between performance as judged by marks and superintendents' ratings is woefully low (0.18), as Martin [8] has shown.

Methods of Rating Teachers.—In actual practice, teachers may be rated in several ways. The following are in common use:

1. *Teacher rating by the pupil.* Numerous schools, both secondary and higher, in attempting to improve teaching, have resorted to the technique of asking students to rate defined phases of teacher activity. The student evaluation method usually takes the form of a questionnaire which the pupils fill out evaluating textbooks, teaching in general, teacher personality, etc. Pupil ratings of teacher traits often serve as aids to the teacher in his own self-improvement program. Typical of information derived from pupil investigations are the following traits listed by students as necessary to teaching success:

1. Seemed sincerely interested in progress of students and not personal gains.

---

[8] Lycia O. Martin, *The Prediction of Success for Students in Teacher Education,* p. 93.

2. Was intensely interested in subject taught.

3. Gave endless time, over what was expected, to students individually and to student activities.

4. Expected a great deal of students.

5. Inspired students to harder work, better living, better philosophy.

6. Neat, well dressed and well groomed personally.

7. Willing to give time to any student in solving individual problems connected with his course or not.

8. Often gave stirring, dramatic talks on philosophy, current affairs, life, personal ambition, occupational choices, self-discipline, etc.

9. Interested in extracurricular activities, such as parties, picnics.

10. Formal enough in class.

11. An inspiring teacher and helpful.[9]

2. *Rating by standardized test batteries.* Fairly accurate batteries of tests which will measure widely different functions and products of the teaching process have been devised and are in use. Test batteries should contain at least three elements:

a) Checkup on the educational progress of the pupil

b) Evaluation of increased social competence

c) Measurement of emotional stability and adjustment

3. *Opinion of parents.* Parents are the clients and patrons of the school and able to judge the quality of its product. If parent opinion is used as an index of teacher success, it should be widely sampled. The expressions of only those parents who pay office calls when some teacher-pupil problem is being handled represent a very biased sampling. Parent opinion may certainly serve as *another* pointer-reading on a success scale, but it must always be used in conjunction with other indices. Parents see and hear at first hand the results of the child's time spent in school. Thus they are able to react keenly. Only recently, however, have systematic attempts been made to get parents to cooperate in determining objectively the effect which teaching is having upon the child's behavior.

---

[9] Harl R. Douglass and Hubert H. Mills, *Teaching in High School,* p. 571. Copyright, 1948, by The Ronald Press Company.

Prediction of Teaching Success.—Palmer, in an early discussion of the ideal teacher, attempted to analyze the factors which would be of value in predicting success in teaching. He derived the following:

1. An aptitude for vicariousness
2. An already accumulated wealth of knowledge
3. An ability to invigorate life through knowledge
4. A readiness to be forgotten [10]

Later semisubjective studies produced similar interesting but inconclusive itemizations of the preteaching aptitude and experience necessary for success. Characteristic of the better attempts to predict teaching success was the work of Kriner,[11] who, after considerable experimentation on the problem, came to the following conclusions concerning the factors upon which teacher success depends:

1. Stamina or persistence is a valuable asset in teaching. Students who persistently and successfully pursue the study of subjects such as Latin and mathematics are more apt to succeed later in their teaching efforts.

2. Early and continued interest in teaching is highly indicative, because interest leads to effort and effort is likely to lead to success. Although interest is not necessarily based upon ability, it frequently arises from success in an early trial and serves as a powerful motivating force. Since the evidence to date does not indicate that teaching success depends upon any extremely high level of technical aptitude, the importance of the role of interest is augmented.

3. Participation of the future teacher in extracurricular programs which are conducted during the period of secondary education contains some predictive value for teacher success.

4. Individuals who lack a persistent and rather long-time interest in teaching or who are planning to use it as an intermediate step to some other line of work should be barred from training to become teachers.

---

[10] George Herbert Palmer, *The Ideal Teacher,* Boston: Houghton Mifflin Co., 1910, p. 8.
[11] Harry Luther Kriner, *Pre-Training Factors Predictive of Teacher Success,* State College, Pa.: Pennsylvania State College, 1931, p. 79.

5. There is no great difference between the traits or characteristics necessary for success in the elementary school and the high school.

Recently some progress has been made in the field of selection of candidates for teacher training. Syracuse University has pushed the development of screening devices. Smith writes of the system employed:

The chairman attempts to formulate an appraisal of the candidate's voice, physical appearance, grooming, speaking ability, initiative, social intelligence, and emotional balance.

No attempt is made to derive a numerical index on the basis of data obtained from the cumulative-record folder. It is believed that such procedure is impracticable because one factor, such as poor scholarship, extreme speech defect, or emotional maladjustment, may be considered important enough to bar admission, even though ratings on other factors are extremely high.[12]

Crowley has devised a detailed list of qualifications for the selection of teaching candidates. His breakdown is as follows:

The candidate who expects to satisfy the requirements of a selection program should have the following traits:

1. Intelligence and ability to use it in reasoning and solving problems

2. Scholarship as demonstrated by a satisfactory high school or college record

3. General culture as typified by a lively and lasting interest in wide reading

4. Health as expressed in vigor and poise of posture

5. Emotional stability as reflected in the ability to face reality and to direct the mental growth of the students properly

6. Facility in oral and written expression characterized by clarity of thought and in conformity with the speech standards of cultured people

7. Personality as evidenced by a proper integration of effective traits

8. Character as displayed in a life governed by principle

9. Interest in the profession as a lifework

---

[12] *School and Society,* LXV (1947), 170.

10. Ability to understand and willingness to employ the basic psychological, philosophical, and social principles governing educational programs.[13]

An excellent study of the prediction of teaching success has been made by Martin at Teachers College, Columbia University. In discussing the selective elimination of candidates for prospective teaching, Martin stresses the oft-encountered fact that no single variable can be used by itself to predict teaching success. She says:

A prediction formula is needed at the end of the first semester, when advice has to be given regarding students' chances for success in the college. The variables in the regression equation that were used for prediction of success at the end of the first semester included the nine entrance requirements and four variables from the first semester data. The multiple correlation between the thirteen variables and the success criterion was .86. Because two of the variables from the first semester data were not available for a check on the 1937 class, a new regression equation was computed, omitting the two variables. The multiple correlation coefficient was lowered from .86 to .84 by this omission. . . .

The recommendation for prediction at the end of the first semester is that a new regression equation be computed from eight variables. These variables that contribute most to the prediction of four years' marks are: first semester marks, written English, objective English, science, high school personality rating, history, high school rank, and mathematics. Until such time as a new regression equation is computed, the one including the nine entrance requirements, the American Council Psychological Examination scores, the first semester marks may be used. . . .[14]

Martin further feels that in the guidance of prospective teachers it is important that they know their own scores on the measurements which are being used to predict their success. She remarks on this point:

One suggestion, therefore, is that students be given the opportunity to know their own entrance test scores. It is important that the students

---

[13] *Phi Delta Kappan*, XXIV (1942), 348.
[14] Lycia O. Martin, *The Prediction of Success for Students in Teacher Education*, New York: Teachers College, Columbia University, 1944, pp. 91-92.

be told their test results by faculty members who know the correct interpretations of the derived scores and the implications of the scores in the future plans of the students. The eight most important factors of success about which the student should be informed are: first semester marks, written English, objective English, science, high school personality rating, history, high school standing, and mathematics.[15]

Improvement of Teaching.—The improvement of teaching is of two kinds: (1) improvement in the conditions and environment in which teaching and learning take place and (2) the self-improvement of the teacher.

1. *Improvement in the conditions and environment in which teaching and learning take place.* Modern psychology stresses the environmental factors in the learning process and that the effectiveness of a learning series is conditioned by the medium in which the practice occurs. Certain features of environment exert a pronounced effect upon the behavior of the child in school, including his learning performance. These conditioning factors in the environment are as follows:

   a) School morale and discipline
   b) Community support
   c) Adequate plant and maintenance
   d) Extracurricular organization
   e) Guidance program

a) School morale and discipline: Much attention has been given in recent years in the field of experimental psychology to the influence of the total situation upon learning. In general it may be said that the experimental evidence is to the effect that the general environment or psychological climate, so to speak, exerts a profound influence upon learning effectiveness. This psychological climate may be called school morale. Pupils, teachers, and administrators all have a share in the building of school morale. So also does the school board and the community. Probably the administrative staff, however, which makes the rules by which the school is governed and by which

[15] Lycia O. Martin, *The Prediction of Success for Students in Teacher Education,* New York: Teachers College, Columbia University, p. 94.

the discipline is set, has more to do with the psychological atmosphere of the school than any other single group. Considerable attention, therefore, should be given by school administrative officers to building in pupils a pride in their school and its accomplishments.

b) Community support: Sociological studies of delinquency are showing with increasing clarity that one of the etiological factors in the wave of misconduct among the young which is sweeping the country at the present time is lack of interest on the part of parents in the activities of their own children. Nowhere can this lack of interest be more detrimental than as it affects the work of the child in school. Parents owe to the child a great deal more than a glance at his report card once a month. An active, sincere, and dynamic attention is vital. Both the administration of the school and the parents themselves owe it to children to promote community support and interest in the school in every way possible, for these are prime psychological factors in the maintenance of school morale. Every school should supplement its curricular materials with discussions, reports, demonstrations, entertainment, and the like furnished by the successful and outstanding adult members of the community. School personnel who are interested and active in the community and who invite community interest in the school are laying excellent foundations for continued appreciation and support of public schools. P.-T. A. organizations are at their best when they offer parents an opportunity to contact the school staff in a friendly and professional way. School patrons furnish (1) the taxes that pay for school needs and (2) the children that create the demand for professional services. Both are vital contributions. Frequent contact between teacher and parent offers benefits to both, to say nothing of the advantages resulting for the children.

c) Adequate plant and maintenance: Learning efficiency is determined by the physical conditions under which the learning takes place. The quality and care of the school plant are basic determining factors in the kind of learning which occurs. Progressively more attention should be given to school buildings from the standpoint of the efficiency and hygiene of learning. School architecture and construction are being revolutionized with special attention to lighting, sound treatment, multiple room usage, etc. The modern, thoroughly functional school plant, in addition to its effectiveness as a learning environment, offers an excellent opportunity for training in neatness, pride of possession, consideration for the property of others, etc.

d) Extracurricular organization: To fulfill its true social function the school must go further in its activities than the classroom. When teaching came to be defined as the direction of the pupil in all phases of his development instead of in subject matter mastery only, a long step forward psychologically was taken. Extracurricular activities make a fundamental contribution to this development and should be regarded as just as much a part of the teaching process as work in subject matter. Progress has been made, but there still remains something to be done in the way of making extracurricular activities an integral part of the school program.

e) Guidance program: The guidance plan may be regarded as the connective tissue of the school organism. To be psychologically effective, guidance activities should permeate every phase of the school's work. When one finds a school which has an adequate academic program but whose pupils are exhibiting a high incidence of behavior problems, the trouble is almost always to be found in the guidance program. Experienced school supervisors and instructors are more than likely to start with a guidance program in evaluating a school because they know that, if it is strong and well organized, the school will be superior throughout and that, if it is weak and faulty, the school is likely to show the deteriorative results as a natural consequence.

2. *Self-improvement of the teacher.* The average beginning teacher is a young college graduate, sometimes with fifth-year work, who, like the beginner in any other line of work, has crudities of technique, inadequacies of knowledge, and lack of experience. Furthermore, the teaching profession is faced with the problem of a continuous turnover and the depletion of its

ranks through marriage. Relaxation of the rules against married teachers eased this latter problem somewhat in the face of a teacher shortage following the second World War, but in varying degrees it will always present difficulty.

It is the professional duty of every teacher, however, whether he expects to stay in the profession a short or a long time, to do his utmost to improve his teaching. As Kriner [16] has properly pointed out, those who do not expect to put in at least a reasonable time in the profession should be barred from starting training if they can be located. The very considerable number of persons who intend to make teaching their permanent vocation should pay particular attention to their own self-improvement professionally. The following points are suggested as well worth the consideration of any teacher in his program of self-improvement:

   a) Interest in individual pupils
   b) High personal attainment
   c) Continuous follow-up work
   d) Progressive scholarship
   e) Worthy example

a) Interest in individual pupils: It is almost impossible to conceive of a teacher's being successful who does not like children. The pupil is the material with which the teacher artisan works. No artisan in any line can be truly successful who is not attentive to his raw material. A violin maker concentrates closely on the wood from which he molds his instrument; a watchmaker is tremendously concerned with the steel from which he fabricates parts; the printer cannot help but be something of an expert on paper, etc. Entirely apart from the human angle, the teacher in order to be a successful artisan must exhibit an avid interest in the material with which he works and a profound knowledge of that material.

b) High personal attainment: School children are devotees of action. They admire expert performance and are able to

---

[16] Harry Luther Kriner, *op. cit.*, p. 79.

judge it competently. High school boys enthusiastic about football are more likely to follow a coach who has been an All-American than one who has not. True, there have been instances of successful coaches who had little or no personal competence in football. Such cases, however, are the exception and not the rule. The teacher who can perform as well as theorize is spared a multitude of difficulties and embarrassment. Therefore, it is a practical point of competence for the teacher to keep in first-rate performing fettle and to strive continually to improve his own personal technique.

c) Continuous follow-up work: Teaching is no different from other skilled acts in that many of its superlatively admirable results depend upon unexciting routine and drudgery. Follow-up work with pupils frequently comes under this heading. But there is no single spot where the teacher may improve his technique any more successfully than in follow-up work. Follow-up work is needed because few pupils learn anything the first time. A world-famous piano virtuoso once remarked that fifteen hundred times was the minimum number that a piece had to be practiced before it began to assume the semblance of a smooth performance. Fifteen hundred repetitions of an error would be the fixation of that error. Only by patient, assiduous, and unrelenting follow-up to initial teaching can pupil attainment reach a high level through the location and elimination of errors and the fixing of the correct pattern.

d) Progressive scholarship: Professional people owe it to themselves and to society to keep up to date in their own profession through progressive scholarship. The physician, however busy, who neglects to read the journals describing advances in medicine may be responsible for the loss of a patient's life through his ignorance. A lawyer who has been a little easygoing in keeping track of his cases and decisions may easily lose a suit for his client thereby. Losses in schoolteaching are not always so spectacular and apparent, but they are there all the same. There are many ways in which progressive scholarship may be advanced—by journals, by institutes, by summer school, by travel, and by writing. It does not matter so much which one of these is pursued at any given time, although the master teachers are more than likely to have had a hand at all of them. But it is a very poor teacher indeed who has done nothing along any of these lines of professional advancement.

e) Worthy example: Teachers cannot escape the responsibility of serving as models for their pupils. Although pupils sometimes seem to have been doing nothing but making fun of both their parents and their teachers, the actual fact is that a tremendous amount of imitation takes place. The teacher cannot be expected to be a social paragon, perfect in all ways. However, society has a right to expect and does expect that the teacher set a worthy example in citizenship and character. There is no way in which the beginning teacher can improve his teaching better than by seeing to it that he is a worthy example to his pupils.

The modern educator is engaged in a task similar to that of the modern physicist, for he is attempting to unleash the mighty forces of potential intelligence in the same way that the physicist is attempting to release the hidden forces in the material world. Intelligence, however profound, will be of no social value unless it gains sufficient momentum to approximate its possibilities. It may be that master intellects have lived and died without making any substantial contribution to the betterment of the race or the improvement of civilization. Just as a physical mass may be said to increase with momentum, so also may the mental potentialities of the brain be said to accrue in force through function. The best method at present known to activate potential intellects is the stimulation provided by well-motivated learning directed and guided by superior teachers.

Questions

1. Is the teacher necessary in order that learning take place?
2. Why is it necessary to shorten the process of learning?
3. Discuss the teacher's task in the elementary schools; in the higher grades.
4. Discuss several of the views held concerning the teacher's place in the educative process.

5. List some of the more important ways of judging teaching efficiency and their drawbacks.
6. Discuss the criteria for judging teaching success.
7. What are some of the things that we must keep in mind when considering the teacher's place in education?
8. List some of the methods used in rating teachers and evaluate their effectiveness.
9. What are some of the characteristics which make for successful teaching?
10. How can teaching be improved?

SELECTED REFERENCES

CHAPTER 1

THE CHALLENGE OF MODERN EDUCATION TO THE PSYCHOLOGIST

BEAUMONT, HENRY, and MACOMBER, F. G. *Psychological Factors in Education.* New York: McGraw-Hill Book Co., Inc., 1949.

BENSON, CHARLES E., *et al. Psychology for Teachers.* Rev. ed. Boston: Ginn & Co., 1933.

BOBBITT, FRANKLIN. *Curriculum of Modern Education.* New York: McGraw-Hill Book Co., Inc., 1941.

BODE, BOYD H. *Modern Educational Theories.* New York: The Macmillan Co., 1927.

BURTON, WILLIAM H. *The Guidance of Learning Activities.* New York: Appleton-Century-Crofts, Inc., 1944.

CONANT, JAMES B. *On Understanding Science.* New Haven, Conn.: Yale University Press, 1947.

DEWEY, JOHN. *Democracy and Education.* New York: The Macmillan Co., 1916.

EDUCATIONAL POLICIES COMMISSION. *Education for All American Youth.* Washington, D. C.: National Education Association, 1944.

————. *The Purposes of Education in American Democracy.* Washington, D. C.: National Education Association, 1938.

Establishing the Goals. Vol. I of *Higher Education for American Democracy.* Washington, D. C.: U. S. Government Printing Office, 1947.

FISKE, JOHN. *The Meaning of Infancy.* Boston: Houghton Mifflin Co., 1911.

GARTH, THOMAS R. *Educational Psychology.* New York: Prentice-Hall, Inc., 1937.

GATES, ARTHUR I., *et al. Educational Psychology.* New York: The Macmillan Co., 1948.

GUTHRIE, E. R. *The Psychology of Learning.* New York: Harper & Bros., 1935.

MELTON, A. W. "Learning," *Encyclopedia of Educational Research.* New York: The Macmillan Co., 1941.

PEARSON, KARL. *Grammar of Science.* London: Adam and Charles Black, 1900.

"Sex in the Schoolroom," *Time,* LI (1948), 71-72.

SKINNER, CHARLES E. (ed.). *Educational Psychology.* Rev. ed. New York: Prentice-Hall, Inc., 1945.

SKINNER, CHARLES E. (ed.). *Elementary Educational Psychology.* New York: Prentice-Hall, Inc., 1945.

―――― (ed.). *Readings in Educational Psychology.* New York: Rinehart & Co., Inc., 1937.

STARCH, DANIEL, STANTON, HAZEL M., and KOERTH, WILHELMINE. *Psychology in Education.* New York: Appleton-Century-Crofts, Inc., 1941.

SYMONDS, PERCIVAL M. "Education and Psychotherapy," *Journal of Educational Psychology,* XL (1949), 1-32.

TRABUE, M. R. "The Fundamental Purpose in Public Education," *School and Society,* LXVI (1947), 416-18.

CHAPTER 2

THE DEFINITION AND MEANING OF EDUCATIONAL PSYCHOLOGY

ARISTOTLE. *Parva Naturalia.* (*The Works of Aristotle,* ed. W. D. Ross, Vol. III.) Oxford: Clarendon Press, 1931.

BENSON, CHARLES E., *et al. Psychology for Teachers.* Rev. ed. Boston: Ginn & Co., 1933.

BRENNAN, ROBERT EDWARD. *Thomistic Psychology.* New York: The Macmillan Co., 1941.

BRETT, GEORGE SIDNEY. "History of Psychology." *Encyclopaedia Britannica* (14th ed.), XVIII, 706-20.

CRUZE, WENDELL W. *Educational Psychology.* New York: The Ronald Press Co., 1942.

GARTH, THOMAS R. *Educational Psychology.* New York: Prentice-Hall, Inc., 1937.

GATES, ARTHUR I., *et al. Educational Psychology.* New York: The Macmillan Co., 1948.

HARTMANN, GEORGE W. *Educational Psychology.* New York: American Book Co., 1941.

JORDAN, A. M. *Educational Psychology.* Rev. ed. New York: Henry Holt & Co., Inc., 1933.

JUDD, CHARLES H. *Educational Psychology.* Boston: Houghton Mifflin Co., 1939.

SANDIFORD, PETER. *Foundations of Educational Psychology.* New York: Longmans, Green & Co., 1938.

SARGENT, S. STANSFELD. *The Basic Teachings of the Great Psychologists.* New York: The New Home Library, 1944.

STROUD, JAMES B. *Psychology in Education.* New York: Longmans, Green & Co., 1946.

TRIGGS, FRANCES O. "The Diagnosis of Reading Deficiencies as an Aid to Remedial Work," *Educational and Psychological Measurement,* VII (1947), 638-46.

WITHERINGTON, H. CARL. *Educational Psychology.* Boston: Ginn & Co., 1946.

CHAPTER 3

BRIGHTNESS AND DULNESS

CATTELL, J. McKEEN, and FARRAND, LIVINGSTON. "Physical and Mental Measurements of the Students of Columbia University." *Psychological Review.* III (1896), 618-48.

DOUGLASS, HARL R., and MILLS, H. H. *Teaching in High School.* New York: The Ronald Press Co., 1948, ch. 19.

GALTON, FRANCIS. *Inquiries into Human Faculty and Its Development.* London, Macmillan & Co., Ltd., 1883.

GODDARD, H. H. "What Is Intelligence?" *Journal of Social Psychology,* XXIV (1946), 51-69.

MURSELL, JAMES L. *Psychological Testing.* New York, Longmans, Green & Co., 1947.

REICHARD, SUZANNE. "Mental Organization and Age Level." *Archives of Psychology,* XLI (1944), No. 295.

REMMERS, H. H., and GAGE, N. L. *Educational Measurement and Evaluation.* New York: Harper & Bros., 1943.

ROSS, C. C. *Measurement in Today's Schools.* New York: Prentice-Hall, Inc., 1941.

SPEARMAN, CHARLES EDWARD. *The Abilities of Man.* New York: The Macmillan Co., 1927.

STODDARD, GEORGE D. *The Meaning of Intelligence.* New York: The Macmillan Co., 1945.

THOMAS, LAWRENCE G. "Mental Tests as Instruments of Science." *Psychological Monographs,* No. 54 (1942).

THURSTONE, L. L. *The Nature of Intelligence.* New York: Harcourt, Brace & Co., 1924.

———. *Primary Mental Abilities.* Chicago: University of Chicago Press, 1937.

———. *Multiple-Factor Analysis.* Chicago: University of Chicago Press, 1947.

WEBB, L. W., and SHOTWELL, ANNA MARKT. *Testing in the Elementary School,* 2d ed. New York: Farrar & Rinehart, Inc., 1939.

WELLMAN, BETH L. "Iowa Studies on the Effect of Schooling," *Thirty-Ninth Yearbook,* National Society for the Study of Education (1940), Vol. II.

CHAPTER 4

PERCEPTION AND ATTENTION

ADRIAN, EDGAR DOUGLAS. *The Physical Background of Perception.* Oxford: Clarendon Press, 1947.

BARTLETT, F. C. *Remembering.* Cambridge: Cambridge University Press, 1932.

CARMICHAEL, L., HOGAN, H. P., and WALTER, A. A. "An Experimental Study of the Effect of Language on the Reproduction of Visually Perceived Form." *Journal of Experimental Psychology,* XIV (1932), 73-86.

HARTMANN, G. W. *Gestalt Psychology.* New York: Liveright Publishing Corp., 1947.

HERTZ, MARGUERITE R., ELLIS, ALBERT, and SYMONDS, PERCIVAL M. "Rorschach Methods and Other Projective Technics." *Review of Educational Research,* XVII (1947), 78-100.

KATONA, G. *Organizing and Memorizing.* New York: Columbia University Press, 1940.

KINGSLEY, H. L. *The Nature and Conditions of Learning.* New York: Prentice-Hall, Inc., 1946.

KÖHLER, WOLFGANG. *Dynamics in Psychology.* New York: Liveright Publishing Corp., 1940.

————. *Gestalt Psychology.* New York: Liveright Publishing Corp., 1947.

KOFFKA, K. *Principles of Gestalt Psychology.* New York: Harcourt, Brace & Co., Inc., 1935.

LASHLEY, K. S., and WADE, M. "The Pavlovian Theory of Generalization," *Psychological Review,* LIII (1946), 72-87.

LEWIN, K. "Field Theory and Learning," *Forty-First Yearbook,* National Society for the Study of Education (1942). Part II, pp. 215-42.

————. *Principles of Topological Psychology.* New York: McGraw-Hill Book Co., Inc., 1936.

PIAGET, J. *The Language and Thought of the Child.* New York: Harcourt, Brace & Co., Inc., 1935.

PROSHANSKY, H., and MURPHY, G. "The Effects of Reward and Punishment on Perception," *Journal of Psychology,* XIII (1942), 295-305.

CHAPTER 5

EMOTION AND MOTIVATION

BALDWIN, JAMES MARK. *Social and Ethical Interpretations in Mental Development.* New York: The Macmillan Co., 1902.

BENDER, I. E., IMUS, H. A., ROTHNEY, J. W. M., KEMPLE, C., and ENGLAND, M. R. *Motivation and Visual Factors.* Hanover, N. H.: Dartmouth College Publications, 1942.

DORING, E. G., LANGFELD, H. S., and WELD, H. P. *Foundations of Psychology.* New York: John Wiley & Sons, Inc., 1948.

CANNON, W. B., and WASHBURN, A. L. "An Explanation of Hunger," *American Journal of Physiology,* XXXI (1912), 441-54.

DASHIELL, J. F. *Fundamentals of General Psychology.* Boston: Houghton Mifflin Co., 1949.

DOCKERAY, FLOYD C. *Psychology.* New York: Prentice-Hall, Inc., 1942.

FRANK, J. D. "Recent Studies of the Level of Aspiration," *Psychological Bulletin,* XXXVIII (1941), 218-26.

GILES, H. H. *Teacher-Pupil Planning.* New York: Harper & Bros., 1941.

GUTHRIE, E. R., and EDWARDS, A. L. *Psychology.* New York: Harper & Bros., 1949.

HILGARD, E. R. "Human Motives and the Concept of the Self," *American Psychologist,* IV (1949), 374-82.
HUNT, W. A. "Recent Developments in the Field of Emotion," *Psychological Bulletin,* XXXVIII (1941), 249-76.
JERSILD, ARTHUR T., MARKEY, FRANCES V., and JERSILD, CATHERINE L. *Children's Fears, Dreams, Wishes, Daydreams, Likes, Dislikes, Pleasant and Unpleasant Memories.* New York: Teachers College, Columbia University, 1933.
LANCELOT, W. H. *Permanent Learning.* New York: John Wiley & Sons, Inc., 1944.
LEWIN, K., DEMBO, T., FESTINGER, L., and SEARS, P. S. "Level of Aspiration," *In Personality and the Behavior Disorders,* ed. J. McV. Hunt. New York: The Ronald Press Co., 1944.
LUND, FREDERICK H. *Emotions.* New York: The Ronald Press Co., 1939.
McDOUGALL, WILLIAM. *An Introduction to Social Psychology.* London: Methuen & Co., Ltd., 1908.
MURPHY, LOIS BARCLAY, and LADD, HENRY. *Emotional Factors in Learning.* New York: Columbia University Press, 1944.
RAPAPORT, D. *Emotions and Memory.* Baltimore: The Williams & Wilkins Co., 1942.
RUCH, F. L. *Psychology and Life.* Chicago: Scott, Foresman & Co., 1948.
TEAGARDEN, FLORENCE M. *Child Psychology for Professional Workers.* New York: Prentice-Hall, Inc., 1946.
WATSON, J. B., and RAYNOR, R. "Conditioned Emotional Reactions." *Journal of Experimental Psychology,* III (1920), 1-4.
YOUNG, PAUL THOMAS. *Emotion in Man and Animal.* New York: John Wiley & Sons, Inc., 1943.
———. *Motivation of Behavior.* New York: John Wiley & Sons, Inc., 1936.
ZACHRY, C. B. *Emotion and Conduct in Adolescence.* New York: Appleton-Century-Crofts, Inc., 1940.

CHAPTER 6

PHYSICAL BASIS OF BEHAVIOR AND LEARNING

HALSTEAD, W. C. *Brain and Intelligence.* Chicago: University of Chicago Press, 1947.
HATHAWAY, S. R. *Physiological Psychology.* New York: Appleton-Century-Crofts, Inc., 1942.
KANTOR, J. R. *Problems of Physiological Psychology.* Bloomington, Ind.: Principia Press, 1947.
LASHLEY, K. S. "Learning: I. Nervous Mechanisms in Learning." In *The Foundations of Experimental Psychology,* ed. Carl A. Murchison. Worcester, Mass.: Clark University Press, 1929.
———. "Basic Neural Mechanisms in Behavior." *Psychological Review,* XXXVII (1930), 1-24.
MAIER, N. R. F. "The Specific Processes Constituting the Learning Function," *Psychological Review,* XLVI (1939), 241-52.

MARQUIS, D. G. "The Neurology of Learning," In *Comparative Psychology,* ed. F. A. Moss. New York: Prentice-Hall, Inc., 1942.

MORGAN, C. T. *Physiological Psychology.* New York: McGraw-Hill Book Co., Inc., 1943.

MORGAN, J. J. B. *Psychology.* New York: Farrar & Rinehart, Inc., 1941.

MUNN, N. L. *Psychology.* New York: Houghton Mifflin Co., 1946.

PAVLOV, I. P. *Conditioned Reflexes.* London: Oxford University Press, 1927.

PRESSEY, SIDNEY L., and ROBINSON, FRANCIS P. *Psychology and the New Education.* New York: Harper & Bros., 1944, chs. 2 and 3.

CHAPTER 7

LEARNING AS A PROCESS

EBBINGHAUS, H. *Memory.* Trans. H. A. Ruger and C. E. Bussenius. New York: Teachers College, 1913 (original publication 1885).

FLETCHER, JOHN MADISON, *Psychology in Education.* New York. Doubleday, Doran & Co., Inc., 1934.

GATES, A. I. "Connectionism: Present Concepts and Interpretations," *Forty-First Yearbook,* National Society for the Study of Education (1942). Part II pp. 141-64.

GUTHRIE, E. R., and HORTON, G. P. *Cats in a Puzzle Box.* New York: Rinehart & Co., Inc., 1946.

HARTMANN, G. W. "The Field Theory of Learning and Its Educational Consequences," *Forty-First Yearbook,* National Society for the Study of Education (1942). Part II, 165-214.

HARTSHORNE, H., and MAY, M. A. *Studies in Deceit.* New York: The Macmillan Co., 1928.

HILGARD, E. R. *Theories of Learning.* New York: Appleton-Century-Crofts, Inc., 1948.

HULL, C. L. *Principles of Behavior.* New York: Appleton-Century-Crofts, Inc., 1943.

KINGSLEY, HOWARD L..*The Nature and Conditions of Learning.* New York: Prentice-Hall, Inc., 1946.

McGEOCH, JOHN A. *The Psychology of Human Learning.* New York: Longmans, Green & Co., 1942.

PAVLOV, I. P. *Lectures on Conditioned Reflexes.* Trans. W. Horsley Gantt and G. Volborth. New York: International Publishers Co., Inc., 1928.

SANDIFORD, P. "Connectionism: Its Origins and Major Features," *Forty-First Yearbook,* National Society for the Study of Education (1942). Part II, pp. 97-140.

WATSON, J. B. *Behaviorism.* New York: W. W. Norton & Co., Inc., 1925.

CHAPTER 8

VIEWPOINTS ON THE LEARNING PROCESS

ALLPORT, G. W. "Effect: A Secondary Principle of Learning." *Psychological Review,* LIII (1946), 335-47.
DUNLAP, K. *Habits: Their Making and Unmaking.* New York: Liveright Publishing Corp., 1932.
GUTHRIE, E. R. *The Psychology of Learning.* New York: Harper & Bros., 1935.
———. "Conditioning: A Theory of Learning in Terms of Stimulus, Response, and Association," *Forty-First Yearbook,* National Society for the Study of Education (1942). Part II, pp. 17-60.
HARTMANN, G. W. "The Field Theory of Learning and Its Educational Consequences," *Forty-First Yearbook,* National Society for the Study of Education (1942). Part II, pp. 165-214.
HILGARD, ERNEST R., and MARQUIS, DONALD G. *Conditioning and Learning.* New York: Appleton-Century-Crofts, Inc., 1943.
HILGARD, ERNEST R. *Theories of Learning.* New York: Appleton-Century-Crofts, Inc., 1948.
HULL, CLARK L. "Conditioning: Outline of a Systematic Theory of Learning," *Forty-First Yearbook,* National Society for the Study of Education (1942). Part II, pp. 61-95.
———. *Principles of Behavior.* New York: Appleton-Century-Crofts, Inc., 1943.
KÖHLER, W. *The Mentality of Apes.* New York: Harcourt, Brace & Co., Inc., 1925.
———. *Gestalt Psychology.* New York: Liveright Publishing Corp., 1947.
LEWIN, KURT. "Field Theory and Learning." *Forty-First Yearbook,* National Society for the Study of Education (1942). Part II, pp. 215-42.
McCONNELL, T. R. "Reconciliation of Learning Theories." *Forty-First Yearbook,* National Society for the Study of Education (1942). Part II, pp. 243-86.
McGEOCH, J. A. *The Psychology of Human Learning—An Introduction.* New York: Longmans, Green & Co., 1942.
ROCK, R. T., JR. "Thorndike's Contributions to the Psychology of Learning," *Teachers College Record,* XLI (1940), 751-61.
THORNDIKE, EDWARD L. *Human Learning.* New York: Appleton-Century-Crofts, Inc., 1931.
TOLMAN, EDWARD C. *Purposive Behavior in Animals and Men.* New York: Appleton-Century-Crofts, Inc., 1932.
WHITE, R. K. "The Case for the Tolman-Lewin Interpretation of Learning," *Psychological Review,* L (1943), 157-86.

CHAPTER 9

HOW CHILDREN LEARN

BAKER, E. *Children's Questions and Their Implications for Planning the Curriculum.* New York: Bureau of Publications, Teachers College, Columbia University, 1945.

BURTT, H. E. "An Experimental Study of Early Childhood Memory," *Journal of Genetic Psychology,* XL (1932), 287-95.

CARMICHAEL, LEONARD, et al. *Manual of Child Psychology.* New York: John Wiley & Sons, Inc., 1946, ch. 8.

DAVIS, W. ALLISON, and HAVIGHURST, R. J. *Father of the Man.* Boston: Houghton Mifflin Co., 1947, chs. 4, 14.

DUNLAP, KNIGHT. *Habits, Their Making and Unmaking.* New York: Liveright Publishing Corp., 1932.

GATES, A. I. "Recitation as a Factor in Memorizing," *Archives of Psychology,* No. 40 (1917).

GOODENOUGH, F. L., and BRIAN, C. R. "Certain Factors Underlying the Acquisition of Motor Skill in Pre-School Children," *Journal of Experimental Psychology,* XII (1929), 127-55.

HURLOCK, E. B. *Child Development.* New York: McGraw-Hill Book Co., Inc., 1942.

JERSILD, A. T. *Child Psychology.* New York: Prentice-Hall, Inc., 1947.

MORGAN, J. J. B. *Child Psychology.* New York: Farrar & Rinehart, Inc., 1942.

MUNN, N. L. *An Introduction to Animal Psychology.* Boston: Houghton Mifflin Co., 1933.

———. "Learning in Children." In *Manual of Child Psychology,* ed. L. Carmichael. New York: John Wiley & Sons, Inc., 1946.

MUSE, M. S. *Efficient Study Habits.* Philadelphia: W. B. Saunders Co., 1929.

RUCH, F. L. "The Differentiative Effects of Age upon Human Learning," *Journal of General Psychology,* XI (1934), 261-86.

CHAPTERS 10 AND 11

HOW TEACHING GUIDES LEARNING

BILLS, A. G. *The Psychology of Efficiency.* New York: Harper & Bros., 1943.

BURTON, WILLIAM H. *The Guidance of Learning Activities.* New York: Appleton-Century-Crofts, Inc., 1944.

CARR, H. "Teaching and Learning," *Journal of Genetic Psychology,* XXXVII (1930), 187-219.

COOK, T. W. "Distribution of Practice and Size of Maze Pattern," *British Journal of Psychology,* XXVII (1937), 303-12.

DOUGLASS, HARL R., and MILLS, HUBERT H. *Teaching in High School.* New York: The Ronald Press Co., 1948.

FREDERICK, R. W., RAGSDALE, C. E., and SALISBURY, R. *Directing Learning.* New York: Appleton-Century-Crofts, Inc., 1938.

GATES, A. I. "Recitation as a Factor in Memorizing," *Archives of Psychology,* No. 40 (1917).

GESELL, ARNOLD L., *et al. Infant and Child in the Culture of Today.* New York: Harper & Bros., 1943.

HALL, W. E., and CUSHING, J. R. "The Relative Value of Three Methods of Presenting Learning Material," *Journal of Psychology,* XXIV (1947), 57-62.

JOHNSON, WENDELL L. *People in Quandaries.* New York: Harper & Bros., 1946.

McGEOCH, JOHN A. *The Psychology of Human Learning.* New York: Longmans, Green & Co., 1942.

MORGAN, J. J. B. "Following the Path of Least Resistance in Thinking," *Journal of Educational Psychology,* XXV (1944), 27-38.

MUENZINGER, KARL F. *Psychology: The Science of Behavior.* New York: Harper & Bros., 1942.

SNYGG, D., and COMBS, A. W. *Individual Behavior.* New York: Harper & Bros., 1949.

THORNDIKE, E. L. *Human Learning.* New York: Appleton-Century-Crofts, Inc., 1931.

WERTHEIMER, M. *Productive Thinking.* New York: Harper & Bros., 1945.

WOODRUFF, A. D. *The Psychology of Teaching.* New York: Longmans, Green & Co., 1948.

CHAPTER 12

CREATIVE ACTIVITY IN THE SCHOOL

ALSCHULER, ROSE H., and HATTWICK, LABERTA WEISS. *Painting and Personality: A Study of Young Children.* Chicago: University of Chicago Press, 1947.

BENSON, CHARLES E., *et al. Psychology For Teachers.* Rev. ed. Boston: Ginn & Co., 1933.

BLACKHURST, J. HERBERT. *Principles of Methods.* De Moines, Ia.: University Press, 1936.

BURTON, WILLIAM H. *The Guidance of Learning Activities.* New York: Appleton-Century-Crofts, Inc., 1944.

BUSWELL, GUY T. *Visual Outline of Educational Psychology.* New York: Longmans, Green & Co., 1939.

BUTLER, FRANK A. *The Improvement of Teaching in Secondary Schools.* Rev. ed. Chicago: University of Chicago Press, 1946.

CUNNINGHAM, WILLIAM F. *The Pivotal Problems of Education.* New York: The Macmillan Co., 1940.

FLETCHER, JOHN M. *Psychology in Education.* New York: Doubleday, Doran & Co., Inc., 1934, chap. 11.

GARTH, THOMAS R. *Educational Psychology.* New York: Prentice-Hall, Inc., 1937.

HARTMANN, GEORGE W. *Educational Psychology.* New York: American Book Co., 1941.

JOHNSON, ROBERT E. "Fine Arts as a Means of Personality Integration," *School Review,* LVI (1948), 223-28.

LOWENFELD, VIKTOR. "Self-Confidence Through Creative Work," *Progressive Education,* XXVI, 1949, 75-77.

———. *Creative and Mental Growth.* New York: The Macmillan Co., 1947.

LUNDQUIST, JOHN A. "Learning By Doing," *Childhood Education,* XXV (1949), 317-19.

PANTON, J. H. *Modern Teaching Practice and Technique.* London: Longmans, Green & Co., 1947.

PATRICK, CATHERINE. "Creative Thought in Poets." *Archives of Psychology,* No. 178. New York: Columbia University, 1935.

———. "Creative Thought in Artists," *Journal of Psychology,* IV (1937), 35-73.

SANDIFORD, PETER. *Foundations of Educational Psychology.* New York: Longmans, Green & Co., 1938.

SKINNER, CHARLES E., ed. *Elementary Educational Psychology.* New York: Prentice-Hall, Inc., 1945.

STRAYER, GEORGE DRAYTON, *et al. Principles of Teaching.* New York: American Book Co., 1936.

STRUCK, F. THEODORE. *Creative Teaching.* New York: John Wiley & Sons, Inc., 1938.

WITHERINGTON, H. CARL. *Educational Psychology.* Boston: Ginn & Co., 1946.

CHAPTER 13

PSYCHOLOGY OF AUDIO-VISUAL LEARNING AND TEACHING

AHL, FRANCES NORENE. *Audio-Visual Materials in the High School.* Boston: The Christopher Publishing House, 1946.

BRODERICK, GERTRUDE G. *Catalog of Radio Recordings.* Washington, D. C.: Federal Radio Education Committee, 1946.

CHANCELLOR, PAUL G. "The Care and Feeding of an Audio-Visual Program," *Independent School Bulletin* (May, 1948), p. 15.

COOK, DOROTHY E., and HOLDEN, KATHARINE M. *Educational Film Guide.* New York: The H. W. Wilson Co., 1948.

DALE, EDGAR. *Audio-Visual Methods in Teaching.* New York: The Dryden Press, Inc., 1946.

DENT, ELLSWORTH C. *The Audio-Visual Handbook.* Chicago: Society for Visual Education, Inc., 1942.

DORRIS, ANNA V. *Visual Instruction in the Public Schools.* Boston: Ginn & Co., 1928.

EXTON, WILLIAM, JR. *Audiovisual Aids to Instruction.* 1st ed. New York: McGraw-Hill Book Co., Inc., 1947.

FALCONER, VERA M. *Filmstrips: A Descriptive Index and User's Guide.* New York: McGraw-Hill Book Co., Inc., 1947.

FERN, GEORGE H., and ROBBINS, ELDON. *Teaching with Films.* Milwaukee: Bruce Publishing Co., 1946.

FOWLKES, JOHN G., and MORGAN, DONALD A. *Elementary Teachers Guide to Free Curriculum Materials.* 4th ed. Randolph, Wis.: Educators Progress Service, 1947.

HAAS, KENNETH B., and PACKER, HARRY Q., *Preparation and Use of Visual Aids.* New York: Prentice-Hall, Inc., 1946.

HARTLEY, WILLIAM H. (ed.), *Audio-Visual Materials and Methods in the Social Studies. Eighteenth Yearbook,* National Council for the Social Studies. Washington, D. C.: National Education Association, 1947.

HOBAN, CHARLES F., JR. *Focus on Learning.* Washington, D. C.: American Council on Education, 1942.

HOBAN, CHARLES F., HOBAN, CHARLES F. JR., and ZISMAN, SAMUEL B. *Visualizing the Curriculum.* New York: The Cordon Co., Inc., 1937.

HORKHEIMER, MARY F., and DIFFOR, JOHN W. *Educators Guide to Free Films.* Rev. ed. Randolph, Wis.: Educators Progress Service, 1947.

INGLIS, RUTH A. *Freedom of the Movies.* Chicago: University of Chicago Press, 1947.

LEVENSON, WILLIAM B. *Teaching Through Radio.* New York: Farrar & Rinehart, Inc., 1945.

McKOWN, HARRY C., and ROBERTS, ALVIN B. *Audio-Visual Aids to Instruction.* 1st ed. New York: McGraw-Hill Book Co., Inc., 1940.

Multi-Sensory Aids in the Teaching of Mathematics. Eighteenth Yearbook, National Council of Teachers of Mathematics. New York: Teachers College, Columbia University, 1945.

OLSEN, EDWARD G. *School and Community.* New York: Prentice-Hall, Inc., 1945.

PARKER, CECIL. "Experiences to Meet Goals," *Educational Leadership,* VI (January 1949), 199-203.

PHILLIPS, BROSE. *Index of Free Teaching Aids.* Harrisburg, Ill.: Free Teaching Aids Co., 1945.

ROBERTS, ALVIN B. "An Introduction to Visual Aids," *School Activities,* X (1939), 212-214, 221.

STANLEY, JULIAN C., JR. "Induction and Early Learning," *Peabody Journal of Education,* XXXVI (January 1949), 220-25.

WEINMAN, CONSTANCE. *Bibliography on Audio-Visual Instructional Materials for Teachers in the Elementary School.* New York: Teachers College, Columbia University, 1947.

WILLEY, ROY D., and YOUNG, HELEN A. *Radio in Elementary Education.* Boston: D. C. Heath and Co., 1948.

CHAPTER 14

INDIVIDUAL DIFFERENCES

CRUZE, WENDELL W. *Educational Psychology.* New York: The Ronald Press Co., 1942.

FOLEY, LOUIS. "Passing All Pupils—and the Buck," *School and Society,* LIX (1944), 353-56.

GRAY, J. STANLEY. *Psychological Foundations of Education.* New York: American Book Co., 1935.

GRIFFITH, COLEMAN R. *Psychology Applied to Teaching and Learning.* New York: Farrar & Rinehart, Inc., 1939.

JAGGERS, CRADDOCK H. "Teaching Children According to Their Individual Needs," *Peabody Journal of Education,* XXIV (1947), 323-26.

JORDAN, A. M. *Educational Psychology,* rev. ed. New York: Henry Holt & Co., Inc., 1933.

KANDEL, I. L. "Individual Differences," *School and Society,* LXIV (1946) 374-75.

————. *Professional Aptitude Tests in Medicine, Law, and Engineering.* New York: Teachers College, Columbia University, 1940.

KRUG, EDWARD, and ANDERSON, G. LESTER (eds.). "Adapting Instruction in the Social Studies to Individual Differences," *Fifteenth Yearbook,* National Council for Social Studies. Washington, D. C.: National Education Association, 1944.

McQUITTY, LOUIS. "Diversity of Self-Endorsements as a Measure of Individual Differences in Personality," *Educational and Psychological Measurement.* IX (1949), No. 1, 3-14.

PAULU, EMANUEL MARION. *Diagnostic Testing and Remedial Teaching.* Boston: D. C. Heath and Co., 1924.

PRESCOTT, DANIEL ALFRED. *Emotion and the Educative Process.* Washington, D. C.: American Council on Education, 1938.

PRESSEY, SIDNEY L., and ROBINSON, FRANCIS P. *Psychology and the New Education.* Rev. ed. New York: Harper & Bros., 1944.

Ross, C. C. *Measurement in Today's Schools.* 2d ed. New York: Prentice-Hall, Inc., 1947.

RUNKE, RUTH J. "Meeting the Individual Needs of Children in the Intermediate Grades," *Indiana University School of Education Bulletin.* XXV (January 1949), 19-23.

SCOTT, M. GLADYS, and FRENCH, ESTHER. *Better Teaching Through Testing.* New York: A. S. Barnes & Co., Inc., 1945.

STROUD, JAMES B. *Psychology in Education.* New York: Longmans, Green & Co., 1946.

THURSTONE, L. L. *The Vectors of Mind.* Chicago: University of Chicago Press, 1935.

TROW, WILLIAM CLARK. *Introduction to Educational Psychology.* Boston: Houghton Mifflin Co., 1937.

WITHERINGTON, H. CARL. *Educational Psychology.* Boston: Ginn & Co., 1946.

CHAPTER 15

EVALUATING LEARNING: MEASUREMENT AND STATISTICAL METHODS

I. MEASUREMENT

BERNARD, WILLIAM, and LEOPOLD, JULES. *Test Yourself!* New York: Hellman, Williams and Co., 1947.

BINGHAM, WALTER V. "Walter V. Bingham Reports on the Army Testing Program," *School and Society,* (1944). LX (1944), 276.

BROOM, M. E. *Educational Measurements in the Elementary School.* New York: McGraw-Hill Book Co., Inc., 1939.

BROWNELL, WILLIAM A. "The Measurement of Understanding," *Forty-Fifth Yearbook,* National Society for the Study of Education, Part I. Chicago: University of Chicago Press, 1946.

BUROS, OSCAR K. (ed). *The Nineteen Forty Mental Measurements Yearbook.* Highland Park, N. J.: The Mental Measurements Yearbook, 1941.

GREENE, EDWARD B. *Measurements of Human Behavior.* New York: Odyssey Press, Inc., 1941.

GREENE, HARRY A., JORGENSEN, ALBERT N., and GERBERICH, J. RAYMOND. *Measurement and Evaluation in the Elementary School.* New York: Longmans, Green & Co., 1942.

———. *Measurement and Evaluation in the Secondary School.* New York: Longmans, Green & Co., 1943.

Journal of Educational Research, 39 (1946), 321-400.

MCCALL, WILLIAM A. *Measurement.* New York: The Macmillan Co., 1939.

MCKOWN, HARRY C. *How to Pass a Written Examination.* 1st ed. New York: McGraw-Hill Book Co., Inc., 1943.

1944 Fall Testing Program in Independent Schools and Supplementary Studies. New York: Educational Records Bureau, 1945.

OSS ASSESSMENT STAFF. *Assessment of Men.* New York: Rinehart & Co., Inc., 1948.

REMMERS, H. H., and GAGE, N. L. *Educational Measurement and Evaluation.* New York: Harper & Bros., 1943.

ROSS, C. C. *Measurement in Today's Schools.* New York: Prentice-Hall, Inc., 1947.

SIMS, VERNER. "Achievement Testing," *Educational Digest,* XIV (1949), 29-31.

STEWART, JOHN ARTHUR. "A Study of the Army Testing Program During World War II at the Induction Station and Reception Center, Fort Lewis, Washington," Unpublished Master's thesis, University of Washington, Seattle, 1946.

STODDARD, GEORGE D. *The Meaning of Intelligence.* New York: The Macmillan Co., 1943.

TROYER, MAURICE E. *Accuracy and Validity in Evaluation Are Not Enough.* The J. Richard Street Lectures for 1947. Syracuse, N. Y.: Syracuse University, 1947.

WECHSLER, DAVID. *The Measurement of Adult Intelligence.* 3d ed. Baltimore: The Williams & Wilkins Co., 1944.

WESMAN, ALEXANDER G. *A Study of Transfer of Training from High School Subjects to Intelligence.* New York: Teachers College, Columbia University, 1945.

WRIGHTSTONE, WAYNE. "New Emphasis and Broader Scope for Tests and Measurements," *Nation's Schools,* XLIII (March, 1949), 39-41.

WRINKLE, WILLIAM L. *Improving Marking and Reporting Practices in Elementary and Secondary Schools.* New York: Rinehart & Co., Inc., 1947.

II. STATISTICAL METHODS

BUTSCH, R. L. C. *How to Read Statistics.* Milwaukee: Bruce Publishing Co., 1946.

EDWARDS, A. L. *Experimental Design in Psychological Research.* New York: Rinehart & Co., Inc., 1950.

EDWARDS, A. L. *Statistical Analysis.* New York: Rinehart & Co., Inc., 1946.

GREENE, E. B. *Measurements of Human Behavior.* New York: Odyssey Press, Inc., 1941.

GREENE, H. A., JORGENSEN, A. N., and GERBERICH, J. R. *Measurement and Evaluation in the Secondary School.* New York: Longmans, Greene & Co., 1943.

GUILFORD, J. P. *Fundamental Statistics in Psychology and Education.* New York: McGraw-Hill Book Co., Inc., 1942.

LEVY, H., and PREIDEL, E. E. *Elementary Statistics.* New York: The Ronald Press Co., 1945.

McNEMAR, Q. *Psychological Statistics.* New York: John Wiley & Sons, Inc., 1949.

SMITH, G. M. *A Simplified Guide to Statistics.* New York: Rinehart & Co., Inc., 1946.

WALKER, H. M. *Elementary Statistical Methods.* New York: Henry Holt & Co., Inc., 1943.

CHAPTER 16

TRANSFER OF TRAINING

AIKIN, WILFORD M. *The Story of the Eight-Year Study.* New York: Harper & Bros., 1942.

BUNCHE, MARION E. "Amount of Transfer in Rational Learning as a Function of Time," *Journal of Comparative Psychology,* XXII (1936), 325-37.

BUSWELL, G. T. "Organization and Sequence of the Curriculum," *Forty-first Yearbook,* National Society for the Study of Education, Part II. Bloomington, Illinois: Public School Publishing Co., 1942. Pp. 445-63.

CARROLL, HERBERT A. "Generalization of Bright and Dull Children, A Comparative Study with Special Reference to Spelling," *Journal of Educational Psychology,* XXI (1930), 489-99.

COOVER, J. E. "Formal Discipline from the Standpoint of Experimental Psychology." *Psychological Monographs,* XX, No. 3 (1916).

CRUZE, WENDELL W. *Educational Psychology.* New York: The Ronald Press Co., 1942.

DAVIS, ROBERT A. *Educational Psychology.* New York: McGraw-Hill Book Co., Inc., 1948.

DIMICHAEL, SALVATORE G. "The Transfer Effects of a How-to-study Course upon Different I.Q. Levels and Various Academic Subjects," *Journal of Educational Psychology,* XXXIV (1943), 166-75.

HENDRIX, GERTRUDE. "A New Clue to Transfer of Training," *Elementary School Journal,* XLVIII (1947), 197-208.

HEPNER, HARRY WALKER. *Psychology Applied to Life and Work.* New York: Prentice-Hall, Inc., 1941.

JAMES, WILLIAM. *The Principles of Psychology.* New York: Henry Holt & Co., Inc., 1896, vol. I.

JUDD, CHARLES HUBBARD. *Psychology of High-School Subjects.* Boston: Ginn & Co., 1915.

Judd, Charles Hubbard. *Psychology of Secondary Education*. Boston: Ginn & Co., 1927.

———. "The Relation of Special Training to General Intelligence," *Educational Review*, XXXVI (1908), 28-42.

Kline, Linus W. "An Experimental Study of Associative Inhibition," *Journal of Experimental Psychology*, IV (1921), 270-99.

McGeoch, John A. *The Psychology of Human Learning*. New York: Longmans, Green & Co., 1942.

Mursell, James L. *Educational Psychology*. New York: W. W. Norton & Co., Inc., 1939.

Orata, Pedro Tamesis. *The Theory of Identical Elements*. Columbus, O.: Ohio State University Press, 1928.

Pressey, Sidney L., and Robinson, Francis P. *Psychology and the New Education*. Rev. ed. New York: Harper & Bros., 1944.

Rosenbaum, Eric. "Application of Transfer Between Foreign Languages," *Modern Language Journal*, XXXIII (1949), 287-94.

Sandiford, Peter. "Transfer of Training." *Encyclopedia of Educational Research*. New York: The Macmillan Co., 1941.

Siipola, E. M., and Isreal, H. E. "Habit Interference as Dependent upon Stage of Training," *American Journal of Psychology*, XL (1933), 205.

Solomon, Richard L. "An Extension of Control Group Design," *Psychological Bulletin*, XLVI (1949), 137-49.

Stroud, James B. *Psychology in Education*. New York: Longmans, Green & Co., 1946.

Thorndike, Edward L. *Educational Psychology*. New York: The Science Press, 1903.

———. "Mental Discipline in High School Subjects," *Journal of Educational Psychology*, XV (1924), 1-22; 83-89.

———, and Woodworth, R. S. "The Influence of Improvement in One Mental Function upon the Efficiency of Other Functions," *Psychological Review*, VIII (1901), 247-61; 384-95; 553-64.

Tolman, Edward C. "Retroactive Inhibition as Affected by Conditions of Learning." *Psychological Monographs*, XXV, No. 1 (1917).

Webb, L. W. "Transfer of Training and Retroaction." *Psychological Monographs*, XXIV, No. 3 (1917).

Wesman, Alexander. "A Study of Transfer of Training from High School Subjects to Intelligence." *Teachers College Record*, XLVI (1945), 391-93.

Whipple, Guy M. "The Transfer of Training." *Twenty-Seventh Yearbook*, National Society for the Study of Education. Bloomington, Ill.: Public School Publishing Co., 1928. Part II.

Witherington, H. Carl. *Educational Psychology*. Boston: Ginn & Co., 1946.

Woodrow, Herbert. "The Effect of Type of Training upon Transference," *Journal of Educational Psychology*, XVIII (1927), 159-72.

CHAPTER 17

THE PSYCHOLOGY OF REMEDIAL PROCEDURES

BENSON, CHARLES E., *et al. Psychology for Teachers,* rev. ed. Boston: Ginn & Co., 1933.

BLAIR, GLENN MYERS. *Diagnostic and Remedial Teaching in Secondary Schools.* New York: The Macmillan Co., 1946.

BOND, GUY L., and BOND, EVA. *Developmental Reading in High School.* New York: The Macmillan Co., 1941.

BOWEN, GENEVIEVE. *Living and Learning in a Rural School.* New York: The Macmillan Co., 1944.

BRUECKNER, L. T. "Techniques of Diagnosis," *Thirty-Fourth Yearbook,* National Society for the Study of Education. Bloomington, Ill.: Public School Publishing Co., 1935.

BUSWELL, GUY THOMAS. "Developmental, Remedial, Counseling Programs," *Elementary School Journal,* XL (1949), 309-10.

CORRALLY, JOHN E. "The Extent and Importance of Pupil Mobility as an Administrative Problem in the Public Schools of the State of Washington." Unpublished Ph.D. thesis, University of Washington, Seattle, 1929.

DOUGLASS, HARL R., and MILLS, HUBERT H. *Teaching in High School.* New York: The Ronald Press Co., 1948.

FERNALD, GRACE M. *Remedial Techniques in Basic School Subjects.* New York: McGraw-Hill Book Co., Inc., 1943.

GATES, ARTHUR I. "Failure in Reading and Social Maladjustment," *Journal of the National Education Association,* XXV (1936), 205-6.

——. *The Improvement of Reading.* 3d ed. New York: The Macmillan Co., 1947.

——. *et al. Educational Psychology.* New York: The Macmillan Co., 1942.

GRIFFITH, COLEMAN R. *Psychology Applied to Teaching and Learning.* New York: Farrar & Rinehart, Inc., 1939.

GUTHRIE, EDWIN R., and HORTON, GEORGE P. *Cats in a Puzzle Box.* New York: Rinehart and Co., Inc., 1946.

HILDRETH, GERTRUDE. "Speech Defects and Reading Disabilities," *Elementary School Journal,* XLVI (1946), pp. 326-32.

JORDAN, A. M. *Educational Psychology,* rev. ed. New York: Henry Holt & Co., Inc., 1933.

KIRK, S. A. *Teaching Reading to Slow Learning Children.* Boston: Houghton Mifflin Co., 1940.

McKEE, PAUL. *The Teaching of Reading in the Elementary School.* Boston: Houghton Mifflin Co., 1948.

MONROE, MARION, BACKUS, BERTIE, *et al. Remedial Reading.* Boston: Houghton Mifflin Co., 1937.

PRESCOTT, DANIEL ALFRED. *Emotion and the Educative Process.* Washington, D. C.: American Council on Education, 1938.

SANDIN, ADOLPH A. *Social and Emotional Adjustments of Regularly Promoted and Non-Promoted Pupils.* New York: Teachers College, Columbia University, 1944.

SCHMIDT, BERNARDINE G. "Changes in Personal, Social, and Intellectual

Behavior of Children Originally Classified as Feebleminded." *Psychological Monographs,* LX, No. 5.

SHERMAN, MANDEL. "Emotional Disturbances and Reading Disability," *Recent Trends in Reading.* . . . Supplementary Educational Monographs, No. 49, ed. William S. Gray. Chicago: University of Chicago Press, 1939, pp. 126-34.

SIMPSON, ROBERT G. *Fundamentals of Educational Psychology.* Philadelphia: J. B. Lippincott Co., 1949.

SUMMERS, LILLIAN A., and WALDEN, ADELE C. "Adjusting Disabled Readers," *Chicago School Journal,* XXX (1949), 145-50.

TERMAN, LEWIS M. *The Hygiene of the School Child.* Boston: Houghton Mifflin Co., 1914.

UMSTATTD, JAMES G. *Secondary School Teaching.* Boston: Ginn & Co., 1937.

WITTELS, DAVID G. "You're Not as Smart as You Could Be," *The Saturday Evening Post,* CCXX (1948), 20-21f.

CHAPTER 18

TEACHING PUPILS HOW TO STUDY

BIRD, CHARLES, and BIRD, DOROTHY M. *Learning More by Effective Study.* New York: Appleton-Century-Crofts, Inc., 1945.

BOOK, WILLIAM F. *Learning How to Study and Work Effectively.* Boston: Ginn & Co., 1926.

BURTON, WILLIAM H. *The Guidance of Learning Activities.* New York: Appleton-Century-Crofts, Inc., 1944.

BUTLER, FRANK A. *The Improvement of Teaching in Secondary Schools.* Chicago: University of Chicago Press, 1939.

COLE, LUELLA, and FERGUSON, JESSIE MARY. *Students' Guide to Efficient Study.* 3d ed. New York: Rinehart & Co., Inc., 1946.

DOUGLASS, HARL R., and MILLS, HUBERT, H. *Teaching in High School.* New York: The Ronald Press Co., 1948.

GOOD, CARTER V. (ed.). *Dictionary of Education.* New York: McGraw-Hill Book Co., Inc., 1945.

MUENZINGER, KARL F. *Psychology: The Science of Behavior.* New York: Harper & Bros., 1942, appendix I.

PANTON, J. H. *Modern Teaching Practice and Technique.* London: Longmans, Green & Co., 1947.

ROBINSON, FRANCIS P. *Effective Study.* New York: Harper & Bros., 1946.

SMITH, EUGENE R., TYLER, RALPH W. *et al., Appraising and Recording Student Progress, Adventure in American Education,* Vol. III. New York: Harper & Bros., 1942.

STEPHENSON, O. W. "Preparation and Use of Study Guides," *Social Studies,* XL (1949), 167-71.

"Study Habits," *Phi Delta Kappan,* XXX (1949), 273.

WITHERINGTON, H. CARL. *Educational Psychology.* Boston: Ginn & Co., 1946.

CHAPTER 19

PSYCHOLOGICAL ANALYSIS OF SCHOOL LEVELS

ALBERTY, HAROLD. *Reorganizing the High-School Curriculum.* New York: The Macmillan Co., 1947.

ALTSTETTER, MABEL F. "On the Training of Administrators," *Peabody Journal of Education,* XXV (1948), 131-32.

BACON, FRANCIS L. "Veterans' Demands Increase Need for 13th and 14th Grades," *Nation's Schools,* XXXVII (1946), 27-29.

BOLTON, FREDERICK E., COLE, THOMAS R., and JESSUP, JOHN H. *The Beginning Superintendent.* New York: The Macmillan Co., 1939.

CUBBERLEY, ELLWOOD P. *Public Education in the United States.* Boston: Houghton Mifflin Co., 1919.

DOUGLASS, AUBREY A. *Modern Secondary Education.* Boston: Houghton Mifflin Co., 1938.

EDMONSON, J. B., ROEMER, JOSEPH, and BACON FRANCIS L. *The Administration of the Modern Secondary School.* 3d ed. New York: The Macmillan Co., 1948.

EDUCATIONAL POLICIES COMMISSION. *Education for All American Youth.* Washington, D. C.: National Education Association, 1944.

GOETTING, M. L. *Teaching in the Secondary School.* New York: Prentice-Hall, Inc., 1942.

GOULD, GEORGE, and YOAKAM, GERALD ALAN. *The Teacher and His Work—A First Course in Education.* New York: The Ronald Press Co., 1947.

HILL, ANDREW P. "How the High School Principal Develops a More Functional Program of Education," *Bulletin of the National Association of Secondary-School Principals,* XXXII (1948), 92-100.

LAUGHLIN, BUTLER. "Wanted, New Pattern for Secondary Education," *Bulletin of the National Association of Secondary-School Principals,* XXXIII (1949), 6-9.

"Opportunities for the Thirteenth and Fourteenth Grades," *Nation's Schools,* XLI (1948), 46-49.

PANTON, J. H. *Modern Teaching Practice and Technique.* London: Longmans, Green & Co., 1947.

PINCKEY, PAUL W. "Organization for Improved Learning," *Educational Leadership,* VI (1949), 385-91.

WESLEY, EDGAR BRUCE. *Teaching the Social Studies.* 2d ed. Boston: D. C. Heath and Co., 1942.

WHITE, ROBERT I. "Toward an Understanding of the 6-4-4 Plan," *School and Society,* LXVII (1948), 113-16.

CHAPTER 20

PSYCHOLOGICAL INTERPRETATION OF THE CURRICULUM

ADAMS, CARL. "Are You 'Old Fashioned'?" *Peabody Journal of Education,* XXV (1948), 132-34.

ADAMS, J. HARRY. "Keeping Faith with the People," *Bulletin of the National Association of Secondary-School Principals,* XXXII (1948), 24-30.

ALBERTY, HAROLD. "Should the Modern Secondary-School Curriculum Be Experience Centered?" *Bulletin of the National Association of Secondary-School Principals,* XXXIII (1949), 115-24.

ALLEN, RAYMOND B. *Medical Education and the Changing Order.* New York: The Commonwealth Fund, 1946.

BACON, FRANCIS L. "How Should the High School React to the Increasing Pressures to Predetermine Talent for Specialized Fields?" *North Central Association Quarterly,* XXII (1948), 306-7.

CHARTERS, W. W. "General Education and Vocational Guidance," *School and Society,* LXVI (1947), 273-75.

DOUGLASS, HARL R., *et al. The High School Curriculum.* New York: The Ronald Press Co., 1947, ch. 3.

"Dr. Studebaker Lists 'Must' Subjects for Secondary Students," *School Management,* XVII (1948), 9.

FAUST, CLARENCE H., and FRODIN, REUBEN. "Notes on a Secondary-School Curriculum," *School Review,* LVI (1948), 12-25.

GOODRICH, T. V., and FOLSOM, A. E. "School Subjects and Life Activities," *Journal of Educational Research,* XLI (1948), 348-62.

"The Horace Mann-Lincoln Institute of School Experimentation," *Teachers College Record,* XLIX (1948), 305-62.

HUNNICUTT, C. W. "Curriculum Research," *Educational Leadership,* VI (1949), 472-73.

JERSILD, ARTHUR T., *et al. Child Development and the Curriculum.* New York: Teachers College, Columbia University, 1946.

LEONARD, J. PAUL. *Developing the Secondary School Curriculum.* New York: Rinehart & Co., Inc., 1946.

MICHAEL, L. S. "The High School of Tomorrow," *School Executive,* LXVII (1948), 53-54.

MILLER, CARL G. "More About General Education," *Education,* LXVIII (1947), 67-68.

PHILLIPS, A. G. "The Fallacy of Divided Knowledge," *Journal of Education,* CXXXI (1948), 20-21.

CHAPTER 21

PSYCHOLOGY OF TEACHING METHODS

ALBERTY, HAROLD. *Reorganizing the High-School Curriculum.* New York: The Macmillan Co., 1947.

BLACKHURST, J. HERBERT. *Principles of Methods.* Des Moines, Ia.: University Press, 1936.

BUSWELL, G. T. "Psychology of the Newer Methods of Teaching," *Elementary School Journal,* XLVI (1945), 14-22.

BUTLER, FRANK A. *The Improvement of Teaching in Secondary Schools.* Chicago: University of Chicago Press, 1939.

CARRINGTON, J. W., et al. "How One Laboratory School System Attacks Its Problems," *Peabody Journal of Education,* 24:327-31 (1947).

DOUGLASS, HARL R., and MILLS, HUBERT H. *Teaching in High School.* New York: The Ronald Press Co., 1948.

FISKE, JOHN. *The Meaning of Infancy.* Boston: Houghton Mifflin Co., 1909.

GATES, ARTHUR I., et al. *Educational Psychology.* New York: The Macmillan Co., 1948.

GRAY, J. STANLEY. *Psychological Foundations of Education.* New York: American Book Co., 1935.

LEE, J. MURRAY, and LEE, DORRIS MAY. *The Child and His Curriculum.* New York: Appleton-Century-Crofts, Inc., 1940.

LEONARD, J. PAUL. *Developing the Secondary School Curriculum.* New York: Rinehart & Co., Inc., 1946.

MONTGOMERY, GRAY. "Effective Supervised Study," *Journal of Education,* CXXXI (1948), 15-16.

PANTON, J. H. *Modern Teaching Practice and Technique.* London: Longmans, Green & Co., 1947.

RISK, THOMAS M. *Principles and Practices of Teaching in Secondary Schools.* New York: American Book Co., 1941.

SCHNEIDEMAN, ROSE. "Begin Early to Teach Social Living," *Nation's Schools,* XL (1947), 25-26.

SIEGEL, HENRY. "The Art of Teaching," *High Points,* XXXI (1949), 55-57.

STROUD, JAMES B. *Psychology in Education.* New York: Longmans, Green & Co., 1946.

THELEN, HERBERT A. "Group Dynamics in Instruction: Principle of Least Group Size," *School Review,* LVII (1949), 139-48.

VAN TIL, WILLIAM A. "Fable of Textbook Strategy," *Educational Leadership,* V (1948), 215-20.

CHAPTER 22

THE PSYCHOLOGY OF SOCIAL INSTITUTIONS

ADAMS, J. HARRY. "Keeping Faith With the People," *Bulletin of the National Association of Secondary-School Principals,* XXXII (1948), 24-30.

BERNARD, L. L. *An Introduction to Sociology.* New York: The Thomas Y. Crowell Co., 1942.

BODE, BOYD H. "Education for Freedom," *Teachers College Record,* XLIX (1948), 276-85.

BOWDEN, A. O., and MELBO, IRVING R. *Social Psychology of Education.* New York: McGraw-Hill Book Co., Inc., 1937.

BRITT, STEUART HENDERSON. *Social Psychology of Modern Life.* Rev. ed. New York: Farrar & Rinehart, Inc., 1949.

DOUGLASS, HARL R. "Place of Education in Social Evolution," *Secondary Education,* XIII (1947), 11-14.

EMBREE, EDWIN R. "Democracy Through the Schools," *High School Journal,* XXXI (1948), 17.

GROVES, ERNEST R., and MOORE, HARRY ESTILL. *An Introduction to Sociology.* New York: Longmans, Green & Co., 1941.

HART, JOSEPH KINMONT. *A Social Interpretation of Education.* New York: Henry Holt & Co., Inc., 1929.

HERTZLER, J. O. *Social Institutions.* Rev. ed. Lincoln, Neb.: University of Nebraska Press, 1946.

HIGHTOWER, HOWARD W. "The School—Its Social Role," *Progressive Education,* XXV (1948), 15-18.

JUDD, CHARLES HUBBARD. *The Psychology of Social Institutions.* New York: The Macmillan Co., 1926.

KINNEMAN, JOHN A. *Society and Education.* New York: The Macmillan Co., 1932.

LASKI, HAROLD J. *Liberty in the Modern State.* New York: Harper & Bros., 1930.

MOEHLMAN, ARTHUR B. *School Administration.* Boston: Houghton Mifflin Co., 1940.

NATIONAL ADVISORY COMMITTEE ON EDUCATION. *Federal Relations to Education.* Washington, D. C.: The Committee, 1931, Part I.

NORTON, JOHN. "Church, State, and Education," *Journal of the National Education Association,* XXXVIII (1949), 21-24.

NUNN, SIR T. PERCY. "Educational Theory," *Encyclopaedia Britannica* 14th ed., Vol. VII, 964-67.

PEELER, HELEN E. "Some Psychological Aspects of Family Relationships," *Pittsburg Schools,* XXIII (1948), 63-65.

CHAPTER 23

SOCIALIZATION

BROWN, FRANCIS J. *The Sociology of Childhood.* New York: Prentice-Hall, Inc., 1939.

CHILD, IRVIN L. Abstract of paper "An Experimental Investigation of 'Taboo' Formation in a Group of Monkeys," *Psychological Bulletin,* XXXV (1938), 705.

CLARK, W. R. "Radio Listening Habits of Children," *Journal of Social Psychology,* XII (1940), 131-49.

DAVIS, W. ALLISON, and HAVIGHURST, ROBERT J. *Father of the Man.* Boston: Houghton Mifflin Co., 1947.

FRANK, L. K. "Adolescence as a Period of Transition," *Forty-Third Yearbook,* National Society for the Study of Education (1944), chap. 1.

HOLLINGSHEAD, A. B. *Elmtown's Youth.* New York: John Wiley & Sons, Inc., 1949.

HURLOCK, ELIZABETH B. *Adolescent Development.* New York: McGraw-Hill Book Co., Inc., 1949.

JERSILD, A. T. "Radio and Motion Pictures," *Thirty-Eighth Yearbook,* National Society for the Study of Education (1939), 153-73.

JONES, H. E. *Development in Adolescence.* New York: Appleton-Century-Crofts, Inc., 1943.

Jones, M. C. "A Functional Analysis of Colloquial Speech Among Adolescents," *American Psychologist*, I (1946), 252-53.

Katz, D., and Braly, K. W. "Racial Prejudice and Racial Stereotypes," *Journal of Abnormal and Social Psychology*, XXX (1935), 175-93.

Lehman, H. C., and Wetty, P. A. "The Compensatory Function of the Movies," *Journal of Applied Psychology*, XI (1927a), 33-41.

Lewin, Kurt. "Some Social-psychological Differences Between the United States and Germany," *Character and Personality*, IV (1936), 265-93.

Moreno, J. L. "Who Shall Survive?" *Nervous and Mental Disease Monograph Series*, No. 58 (1934).

Preston, M. I. "Children's Reactions to Movie Horror and Radio Crime," *Journal of Pediatrics*, XIX (1941), 147-68.

Zachry, C. B. *Emotion and Conduct in Adolescence*. New York: Appleton-Century-Crofts, Inc., 1940.

CHAPTER 24

ORIGIN AND GROWTH OF PERSONALITY

Allport, Gordon W. "A Test for Ascendance-Submission," *Journal of Abnormal and Social Psychology*, XXIII (1928), 118-36.

Allport, Gordon W., and Odbert, Henry S. "Trait-names: A Psycho-lexical Study," *Psychological Monographs*, XLVII, No. 1 (1936).

Axline, Virginia M. *Play Therapy: The Inner Dynamics of Childhood*. Boston: Houghton, Mifflin Co., 1947.

Barker, R., Dembo, T., and Lewin, K. "Frustration and Regression: An Experiment with Young Children." *University of Iowa Studies in Child Welfare*, XVIII, No. 1 (1941).

Beverly, Bert I., M.D. *In Defense of Children*. New York: John Day Co., Inc., 1941.

Breckenridge, M. E., and Vincent, E. Lee. *Child Development: Physical and Psychological Growth through the School Years*. Philadelphia: W. B. Saunders Co., 1943.

Cameron, Norman. *The Psychology of Behavior Disorders*. Boston: Houghton Mifflin Co., 1947.

Cannon, W. R. *The Wisdom of the Body*. New York: W. W. Norton & Co., Inc., 1932.

Murphy, Gardner. *Personality*. New York: Harper & Bros., 1947.

Piaget, Jean. *The Language and Thought of the Child*. New York: Harcourt, Brace & Co., Inc., 1926.

Shaffer, L. F. *The Psychology of Behavior Disorders*. Boston: Houghton Mifflin Co., 1947.

Stroud, James B. *Psychology in Education*. New York: Longmans, Green & Co., Inc., 1946.

CHAPTER 25

HOW EDUCATION AFFECTS PERSONALITY

BLANCHARD, B. E. "Recreation and Delinquency," *School Review*, LIV (1946), 360-63.

BRATTON, DOROTHY. "Classroom Guidance of Pupils Exhibiting Behavior Problems," *Elementary School Journal*, XLV (1945), 286-92.

COURTENAY, M. E. "The Persistence of Leadership," *School Review*, XLVI (1938), 97-107.

DREIKURS, RUDOLPH. *The Challenge of Parenthood*. New York: Duell, Sloan & Pearce, Inc., 1948.

ENGLISH, H. B., and RAIMY, VICTOR. *Studying the Individual School Child*. New York: Henry Holt & Co., Inc., 1941.

HAVIGHURST, R. J., and TABA, H. *Adolescent Character and Personality*. New York: John Wiley & Sons, Inc., 1949.

HOLLINGSHEAD, A. B. *Elmtown's Youth*. New York: John Wiley & Sons, Inc., 1949.

HURLOCK, ELIZABETH B. *Adolescent Development*. New York: McGraw-Hill Book Co., Inc., 1949.

KELLOGG, RHODA. *Nursery School Guide*. Boston: Houghton Mifflin Co., 1949.

KLEIN, D. B. *Mental Hygiene*. New York: Henry Holt & Co., Inc., 1944.

MURPHY, GARDNER. *Personality*. New York: Harper & Bros., 1947.

ROGERS, CARL R. *The Clinical Treatment of the Problem Child*. Boston: Houghton Mifflin Co., 1939.

SCHJELDERUP-EBBE, T. *Social Life of Birds*. In *Handbook of Social Psychology*, ed. Carl Murchison. Worcester, Mass.: Clark University Press, 1935.

SMITH, M., and NYSTROM, W. C. "A Study of Social Participation and of Leisure Time of Leaders and Non-leaders," *Journal of Applied Psychology*, XXI (1937), 251-59.

CHAPTER 26

MENTAL HYGIENE

BARUCH, DOROTHY W. "Incorporation of Therapeutic Procedures as Part of the Educative Process," *American Journal of Orthopsychiatry*, XII (1942), 659-65.

——. "A Study of Reported Tension in the Interparental Relationships as Co-existent with Behavior Adjustment in Young Children," *Journal of Experimental Education*, VI (1937), 187-204.

BENDER, LAURETTA, and LOURIE, REGINALD S. "The Effect of Comic Books on the Ideology of Children," *American Journal of Orthopsychiatry*, XI (1941), 540-50.

BIRREN, JAMES E. "Psychological Examinations of Children Who Later Became Psychotic," *Journal of Abnormal and Social Psychology,* XXXIX (1944), 84-96.

BRÜEL, OLUF. "A Moving Picture as a Psychopathogenic Factor: A Paper on Primary Psychotraumatic Neurosis," *Character and Personality,* VII (1938), 68-76.

DEBOER, JOHN J. "Radio and Children's Emotions," *School and Society,* L (1939), 369-73.

FOSTER, JOSEPHINE C., and ANDERSON, JOHN E. "Unpleasant Dreams in Childhood," *Child Development,* VII (1936), 77-84.

INSTITUTO NACIONAL DE ESTUDOS PEDAGÓGICOS. "Uma Investigação sôbre Jornais e Revistas Infantis e Juvenis III," *Revista Brasileira de Estudos Pedagógicos,* III (1945), 82-101.

MERRILL, MAUD A. *Problems of Child Delinquency.* Boston: Houghton Mifflin Co., 1947.

PECK, LEIGH. "Teachers' Reports of the Problems of Unadjusted School Children," *Journal of Educational Psychology,* XXVI (1935), 123-38.

PISULA, CECILIA. "Behavior Problems of Children from High and Low Socio-Economic Groups," *Mental Hygiene,* XXI (1937), 452-55.

ROGERS, CARL R. "Mental Health Findings in Three Elementary Schools," *Educational Research Bulletin,* XXI (March 18, 1942), 69-79.

SHOOBS, NAHUM E., and GOLDBERG, GEORGE. *Corrective Treatment for Unadjusted Children.* New York: Harper & Bros., 1942.

SNYDER, LAURENCE H. *The Principles of Heredity.* 2d ed. Boston: D. C. Heath & Co., 1940.

TIEGS, ERNEST W., and KATZ, BARNEY. *Mental Hygiene in Education.* New York: The Ronald Press Co., 1941.

TRAVIS, LEE EDWARD. *Personal Problems of Everyday Life.* New York: Appleton-Century-Crofts, Inc., 1941.

WALLIN, J. E. WALLACE. "What Teachers Think about the Value of Mental Hygiene Courses," *Educational Administration and Supervision,* XXIV (1938), 675-86.

WERTHAM, FREDERIC. "The Comics ... Very Funny," *Saturday Review of Literature,* XXXI (1948), 6, 7, 28, 29.

WITTY, PAUL, Chairman, The Committee for the Thirteenth Yearbook. *Mental Health in the Classroom.* Department of Supervisors and Directors of Instruction of the National Education Association, 1940.

WITTY, PAUL, and SKINNER, CHARLES E. *Mental Hygiene in Modern Education.* Rahway, N. J.: Quinn and Boden, 1939.

CHAPTER 27

PSYCHOLOGY OF DISCIPLINE

BLACK, HAROLD GARNET. "Discipline, a Virtue and a Necessity," *Journal of Education,* CXXIX (1946), 304-6.

BOSSING, NELSON L. *Progressive Methods of Teaching in Secondary Schools.* Rev. ed. Boston: Houghton Mifflin Co., 1942.

BURTON, WILLIAM H. *The Guidance of Learning Activities.* New York: Appleton-Century-Crofts, Inc., 1944.

BUTLER, FRANK A. *The Improvement of Teaching in Secondary Schools.* Rev. ed. Chicago: University of Chicago Press, 1946.

CHAPMAN, PAUL E. "Sarcasm: Pedagogical Poison," *Clearing House,* XXIII (1948), 219-20.

CRUZE, WENDELL W. *Educational Psychology.* New York: The Ronald Press Co., 1942.

CUTTS, NORMA E., and MOSELEY, NICHOLAS. *Practical School Discipline and Mental Hygiene.* Boston: Houghton Mifflin Co., 1941.

DOUGLASS, HARL R., and MILLS, HUBERT H. *Teaching in High School.* New York: The Ronald Press Co., 1948.

FENSCH, EDWIN A. "Discipline: Not the Act, but the Cause," *Clearing House,* XXI (1947), 483-84.

FINLEY, JOHN W. "A Student Personnel System Recommended," *California Journal of Secondary Education,* XXI (1946), 21-23.

FOLEY, JOHN D. "Discipline: A Student Counseling Approach," *Educational and Psychological Measurement,* VII, No. 3 (1947), 569-82.

FREEMAN, FRANK N. "Education, Training, and Discipline," *School and Society,* LXI (1945), 321-4.

HUGHEY, A. H. "Discipline and the Spirit of the School," *Journal of Education,* CXXVIII (1945), 310-12.

JUDD, CHARLES H. *Educational Psychology.* Boston: Houghton Mifflin Co., 1939.

NEUMANN, BERTHA G. "What Discipline *Really* Means," *Journal of the National Education Association,* XXXIII (1944), 169-70.

OHLSEN, MERLE M. "Guidance and School Discipline," *Bulletin of the National Association of Secondary-School Principals,* XXXI (1947), 108-12.

PRINGLE, RALPH W. *The Psychology of High-School Discipline.* Boston: D. C. Heath and Co., 1931.

PULLIAS, E. V. "Discipline and Mental Hygiene," *Education,* LXVI (1946), 569-72.

RISK, THOMAS M. *Principles and Practices of Teaching in Secondary Schools.* New York: American Book Co., 1941.

RIVLIN, HARRY N. *Teaching Adolescents in Secondary Schools.* New York: Appleton-Century-Crofts, Inc., 1948.

SCHORLING, RALEIGH. *Student Teaching.* New York: McGraw-Hill Book Co., Inc., 1940.

SHEVIAKOV, GEORGE V., and REDL, FRITZ. *Discipline for Today's Children and Youth.* Department of Supervision and Curriculum Development, National Education Association, Washington, D. C.: 1944.

SMITH, WALTER ROBINSON. *Constructive School Discipline.* New York: American Book Co., 1936.

SPENCER, HERBERT. *Education.* New York: Appleton-Century-Crofts, Inc., 1860.

TORGERSON, THEODORE L. *Studying Children.* New York: The Dryden Press, Inc., 1947.

CHAPTER 28

PSYCHOLOGY OF THE GUIDANCE PROGRAM

BACON, FRANCIS L. "What is Expected of the Counselor?" *School Review,* LVII (1949), 37-41.
BAXTER, E. D. "What is Guidance?" *Childhood Education,* XXV (1949), 202-5.
BENSON, CHARLES E., *et al. Psychology for Teachers.* Rev. ed. Boston: Ginn & Co., 1933.
BREWER, JOHN M., *et al. History of Vocational Guidance.* New York: Harper & Bros., 1942.
CHISHOLM, LESLIE L. *Guiding Youth in the Secondary Schools.* New York: American Book Co., 1945.
COX, PHILLIP W. L., and DUFF, JOHN CARR. *Guidance by the Classroom Teacher.* New York: Prentice-Hall, Inc., 1938.
CRUZE, WENDELL W. *Educational Psychology.* New York: The Ronald Press Co., 1942.
DARLEY, JOHN G. *Testing and Counseling in the High-School Guidance Program.* Chicago: Science Research Associates, 1943.
DETJEN, MARY E. FORD, and DETJEN, ERVIN W. *Home Room Guidance Programs for the Junior High School Years.* Boston: Houghton Mifflin Co., 1940.
ERICKSON, CLIFFORD E. "Promoting World Citizenship in School and College Through Effective Guidance Practices," *North Central Association Quarterly,* XXII (1948), 285-88.
———, and HAPP, MARION CROSLEY. *Guidance Practices at Work.* New York: McGraw-Hill Book Co., Inc., 1946.
FENSCH, EDWIN A. "A Neglected Factor in Guidance," *School Executive,* LXVII (1947), 36-37.
GERMANE, CHARLES E., and GERMANE, EDITH G. *Personnel Work in High School.* New York: Silver Burdett Co., 1941.
GOETTING, M. L. *Teaching in the Secondary School.* New York: Prentice-Hall, Inc., 1942.
HAMRIN, SHIRLEY A., and ERICKSON, CLIFFORD E. *Guidance in the Secondary School.* New York: Appleton-Century-Crofts, Inc., 1939.
HEUSS, CHARLOTTE A., WOOD, F. MARION, and KURILECZ, MARGARET. "High School Seniors Study Occupations," *Occupations,* XXVI (1948), 290-93.
POWERS, FRANCIS F. *Character Training.* New York: A. S. Barnes & Co., Inc., 1932.
———, *et al. Psychology in Everyday Living.* Boston: D. C. Heath and Co., 1938.
THRELKELD, A. L. "Character Education," *Tenth Yearbook,* Department of Superintendence, National Education Association (1932), pp. 251-52.
TRAXLER, ARTHUR E. *Techniques of Guidance.* New York: Harper & Bros., 1945.
UHL, WILLIS L., and POWERS, FRANCIS F. *Personal and Social Adjustment.* New York: The Macmillan Co., 1938.

CHAPTER 29

PSYCHOLOGY OF EXTRACURRICULAR ACTIVITIES

BARR, A. S., BURTON, WILLIAM H., and BRUECKNER, LEO J. *Supervision,* 2d ed. New York: Appleton-Century-Crofts, Inc., 1947.

BOONE, WILLIAM R. "Student Activities That Count," *Bulletin of the National Association of Secondary-School Principals,* XXXII (1948), 117-23.

BOWLBY, CHARLES L. "A Little 'Extra' for Those Extracurricular Duties," *Clearing House,* XXII (1947), 20-22.

CARTER, JOSEPH C. "Co-Curricular News in Best School Papers," *Nation's Schools,* XL (1947), 32.

DAVIS, FRANK G. (ed.). *Pupil Personnel Service.* Scranton, Pa.: International Textbook Co., 1948.

DIXON, FRED B. "Not More but Better Activities," *School Activities,* XVII (1946), 243-44f.

DOUGLASS, HARL R. *Organization and Administration of Secondary Schools.* Boston: Ginn & Co., 1945.

FRETWELL, ELBERT K. *Extra-Curricular Activities in the Secondary Schools.* Boston: Houghton Mifflin Co., 1931.

LINDEL, ALBERT L. "Personal Growth Through Extracurricular Activities," *School Activities,* XVII (1945), 123-24f.

MCKOWN, HARRY C. *Extra-Curricular Activities.* Rev. ed. New York: The Macmillan Co., 1943.

MEYER, HAROLD D. *A Handbook of Extra-Curricular Activities in the High School.* New York: A. S. Barnes & Co., Inc., 1926.

PATTY, WILLARD W. "To Complement or to Supplement?" *School Activities,* XVI (1945), 203-4.

RICH, FRANK M. "What is Good Extra-Curricular Work?" *Journal of Education,* CXXVII (1944), 161-62.

WALSH, J. HARTT, and JOHNSON, LOWELL M. "Courts Favor Student Activities," *Nation's Schools,* XL (1947), 30-31.

CHAPTER 30

PSYCHOLOGY OF SCHOOL LEADERSHIP

"A Factor Analysis of the Personality of High School Leaders," *Journal of Applied Psychology,* XIX (1935), 596-605.

BAVELAS, ALEX. "Morale and the Training of Leaders." In G. Watson (ed.), *Civilian Morale.* Boston: Houghton Mifflin Co., 1942.

BAXTER, BERNICE, and CASSIDY, ROSALIND. *Group Experience.* New York: Harper & Bros., 1943.

BOGARDUS, E. S. "A Social Distance Scale," *Sociology and Social Research,* XVII (1933), 265-71.

CARR, WILLIAM G. *Educational Leadership in This Emergency.* Stanford University, Calif.: Stanford University Press, 1941.

DOUGLASS, HARL R., and MILLS, HUBERT H. *Teaching in High School.* New York: The Ronald Press Co., 1948.

GIBB, CECIL A. "The Principles and Traits of Leadership," *Journal of Abnormal and Social Psychology*, XLII (1947), 267-84.

HARDY, MARTHA CRUMPTON. "Social Recognition at the Elementary School Age," *Journal of Social Psychology*, VIII (1937), 365-84.

JENNINGS, HELEN HALL. *Leadership and Isolation.* New York: Longmans, Green & Co., 1943.

KOTSCHNIG, WALTER M. *Slaves Need No Leaders.* New York: Oxford University Press, 1943.

LEWIN, KURT, LIPPITT, RONALD, and WHITE, RALPH K. "Patterns of Aggressive Behavior in Experimentally Created 'Social Climates'," *Journal of Social Psychology*, *S.P.S.S.I. Bulletin*, X (1939), 271-99.

MORENO, J. L. "Who Shall Survive? A New Approach to the Problem of Human Inter-relations." Washington, D. C. Nervous and Mental Diseases Publishing Co., 1934.

NUTTING, L. RUTH. "Some Characteristics of Leadership," *School and Society*, XVIII (1923), 387-90.

PIGORS, PAUL. *Leadership or Domination.* Boston: Houghton Mifflin Co., 1935.

REALS, WILLIS H. "Leadership in the High School," *School Review*, XLVI (1938), 523-31.

WOODWORTH, A. D. *Psychology of Teaching.* New York: Longmans, Green & Co., 1946.

CHAPTER 31

THE IMPROVEMENT OF TEACHING

BALDWIN, BIRD T., and STECHER, LORLE I. *The Psychology of the Preschool Child.* New York: Appleton-Century-Crofts, Inc., 1925.

BARR, ARVIL S. "The Measurement and Prediction of Teaching Efficiency," *Review of Educational Research*, XVI (1946), 207 f.

BOYCE, ARTHUR CLIFTON. "Methods for Measuring Teachers' Efficiency," *Fourteenth Yearbook*, National Society for the Study of Education, Part II. Chicago: University of Chicago Press, 1915.

BROWNELL, S. M. "A Workable Plan for Recognition of Merit," *Nation's Schools*, XL (1947), 20-22.

BURTON, WILLIAM H. *The Guidance of Learning Activities.* New York: Appleton-Century-Crofts, Inc., 1944.

COCKING, WALTER D. "As I See It," *School Executive*, LXVII (1947), 5.

COURTIS, S. A. "Forty Years of Educational Measurement," *National Elementary Principal*, XXV (1946), 19-22.

CROWLEY, FRANCIS M. "Selection by Training Agencies," *Phi Delta Kappan*, XXIV (1942), 347-49, 368.

DOUGLASS, HARL R., and MILLS, HUBERT H. *Teaching in High School.* New York: The Ronald Press Co., 1948.

GREENE, JAMES E., and FINDLEY, W. G. "Evaluative Procedures for the Improvement of Instruction," *Educational Record,* XXX (1949), 33-44.

HALL, G. STANLEY. *Adolescence.* Vol. I. New York: Appleton-Century-Crofts, Inc., 1904.

HARMS, HARM. "Indices of Good Teaching," *Journal of Business Education,* XXIV (1949), 25-26.

HORST, PAUL. *The Prediction of Personal Adjustment.* New York: Social Science Research Council, 1941.

KRINER, HARRY LUTHER. *Pre-Training Factors Predictive of Teacher Success.* State College, Pa.: Pennsylvania State College, 1931.

MARTIN, LYCIA O. *The Prediction of Success for Students in Teacher Education.* New York: Teachers College, Columbia University, 1944.

MORRIS, ELIZABETH HUNT. *Personal Traits and Success in Teaching.* New York: Teachers College, Columbia University, 1929.

PALMER, GEORGE HERBERT. *The Ideal Teacher.* Boston: Houghton Mifflin Co., 1910.

RICHEY, ROBERT W., and FOX, WILLIAM H. "An Analysis of Various Factors Associated with the Selection of Teaching as a Vocation," *Indiana University School of Education Bulletin,* XXIV (May 1948), 1-59.

SAVULAK, JOHN H. "The Teacher in the Atomic Age," *Education,* LXVIII (1947), 195-200.

SMITH, HENRY P. "The Selection of Students for the Profession of Teaching," *School and Society,* LXV (1947), 169-71.

STODDARD, GEORGE D., and WELLMAN, BETH L. *Child Psychology.* New York: The Macmillan Co., 1934.

INDEX

Acquisition and retention, 114
Adjustment as learned behavior, 401, 403, 404
Administrators, training of, 300-302
Adrenalin, 56
Aesthetics, 165-68
Aggressive behavior, 408
and discipline, 428
"Aha" phenomenon, 45
Ambivalence, 64
Anxiety, 55, 428
Appreciation, education for, 160-62
Apprenticeship system, 442
Aptitudes, 37
Art, value of, 164
Ascendance-submission, 386-87
Association, 97, 106
by contiguity, 88
principle of, 87-89
theories of, 100-107
Astigmatism, 74
Attention, 40-41, 43-44, 48-50
definition of, 48
voluntary and involuntary, 49
Attention-getting, 66-67
Attitudes, 46-47, 146, 156-57
measurement of, 64
and social understanding, 13-14
Audio-visual education, 170-86
classification of materials used in, 171-72
psychological values in, 186
Authoritarianism
in family, 363-65
and leadership, 466-67, 473-74
in schools, 393
Average deviation, 219-20

Barriers to goal objects, 114
Behavior, physical basis of, 70-80
Belonging, law of, 105-106
Blackboard, utilization of, 180-82
Blood pressure, 80, 405
Brain damage, organic, 403
Breathing rate, 54, 405

Canalization, 58, 68, 390-91

of personality traits, 376-79
Central tendency, 218-21
Cheating, 60
Children, "exceptional," 195
Classroom contact, importance of, for evaluation of student adjustment, 198
Clinics, child research, 197
Closure, 44
law of, 109
Comic books, effect of, on children, 406-407
Compensation, 384
Competitiveness, 62
Conditioning, 92
Conferences with students, educational value of, 198
Conflict, 140
Connectors, 76-79
Conscience, development of, 370-71
Cooperation, 393
Correlation, 230-35
formula for coefficient of, 231, 232, 238
use of z-score in, 231-32
Counseling, of children, 399-401
Creative activity, 162-65
Curriculum,
grouping of materials for, 317-79
psychological objectives of, 317-23
psychological problems of, 5-6
pupil as determiner of, 312-14
sequence of subject matter in, 319-23
social demands as determinants of, 314-16
"spiral" planning of, 322-23
viewpoints on, 306-12

Deafness, 73
Defense mechanisms, 379-84
Depression, 54-55
Difference, standard deviation (error) of a, 236-37
Disciplinary methods, 437-39
Disciplinary problems, causes of, 426-29

Discipline, 433-34
  definition of, 424-29
  and environmental factors, 434-36
  interest and, 433-34
  methods of, 429-34
  preventive, 439
  psychology of, 421-39
  school as factor in, 435-36
  success and, 433-34
  teacher personality in, 436-37
  theories of, 427-29
Dispersion of scores, 218-21
Displacement, 383-84
"Docility" in learning, 112
Drill,
  and discipline, 438
  efficient use of, 342-45
Drive, 101-102

Ear, 72-73
Education,
  aesthetics in, 167-68
  definition of, 4
  intercultural, 14
  philosophy of, 6-10
  psychological aims of, 11-15
  and scientific attitude, 12
  sex, 12
  vs. training, 308-10
Educational psychology, definition
    and meaning of, 16-21
Effect, law of, 104-105
Effectors, 79-80
Emotion, 52-69
  in the classroom, 61-63
  definition of, 53
  discipline problems and, 428
  and habits, 157
Emotions, education of the, 160
Encyclopedism, 310-11
Epilepsy, 403
Excitement, 54-56
Exhibits, use of, 182
Exteroceptors, 73-74
Extracurricular activities, 455-65,
    491
  changing viewpoints on, 455-57
  definition of, 455
  evaluation of, 462-65
  objectives of, 459-62
  and pupil interest, 463
  supervision of, 464-65
  value of, 457-59
Eye, 72

Factor analysis, 34
Fads, 369-70

Failure, effect of, on pupils, 131
Farsightedness, 74
Fashions, 369-70
Fatigue,
  muscular, 77, 80, 86
  nerve, 77
Fear,
  nature of, 62
  effect of, on pupils, 62-63
Fixation, 68
Fibers, motor, 77-79
Field trips, planning of, 185-86
Figure and ground, 43, 45, 46, 49
Filmstrips,
  projection of, 175
  selection of, 176
Forgetting, 92-93, 114
Freedom of action, 129-30
Frustration, 56, 422
Functional autonomy, 390
Fundamentals, mastery of, 282, 286-
    87

g, 33
Gambling, 140
General education, 306-309
Generalization, 63
Genius, 26, 32, 36, 162
Gestalt, 43-46, 49, 107-16
Glands, 79
Glandular imbalance, 403
Good continuation, law of, 109
Good figure, law of, 45-46
Grading systems, comparison of, 227-
    28
Guidance, 491
  effect of, on character and citizen-
    ship, 447
  historical development of, 441-44
  influence of social tradition on,
    444-46
  parental, 444-46
  practical suggestions on, 452-54
  types of, 446-49
  vocational, 37, 442-44

Habits, 97-99, 145-46, 151-55
  making and breaking of, 154-55
  and motivation, 67-68
Homeostasis, 384-85
Honesty, general and specific, 387-
    88
Hostility and social understanding,
    13-14
Hunger as drive, 53

Ideals, 146

Imagery, visual and auditory, 26
Imitation, 66
    as explanatory concept, 360
Incentives, 60-61
Individual differences, 188-200
    automatic promotion and, 199, 200
    classification of, 192-94
    differential teaching and, 199, 200
    importance of, 188-89
    methods of dealing with, 196-200
    problem of, 189
    remedial education and, 199, 200
    specific provisions for, 198-200
    track systems and, 199, 200
    ways of approaching problem of,
        190-92
Insanity, 403
Insight, 107-109, 163
Instinct, 66, 68
Instructional aids, 172-86
    auditory, 182-85
        evaluation of, 183
        preparation for use of, 183-85
        types of, 182, 184
    blackboard, 180-82
    exhibits, 182
    mock-ups, 182
    models, 182
    nonpictorial, 180-82
    psychological values of, 186
    selection of, 183
    tests as, 213-16
    visual, 172-82
Intelligence, 26, 27
    cultural and racial differences in,
        38-39
    definition of, 36-37
    feeble-mindedness and, 32
    levels of, 32
    maturation of, 135-36
    nature of, 32-36
    normal, 32
    as performance, 28
    and poor pupil performance, 269-
        70
    precautions in testing of, 31
    quotient (I. Q.), 29-32, 37-39, 269-
        70
    sex differences in, 38
    testing of, 28-32, 196, 203-204
Interest, definition of, 57
Interoceptors, 73-74
Intolerance, 13, 393

Language as an aid in learning, 122
Leaders, characteristics of, 467-72,
    473-77

Leadership,
    authoritarianism and, 466-67, 473-
        74
    development of, 395-96
    meaning of, 466-67
    mistakes in, 428
    psychology of, 466-76
Learning,
    as an adaptive process, 95-99
    concentration and, 285-86
    curves of, 283
    definition of, 3, 85
    efficiency in, 147-51, 283
    and emotional stability, 268-69
    environmental factors in, 489-91
    facilitation of, 324
    as improvement, 85
    integration in, 325-26
    law of diminishing returns in, 284
    meaning of, 85-87
    overlearning, 284
    part method of, 147-48, 283-84
    physical basis of, 70-80
    plateaus in, 283
    practice and, 286
    principle of association in, 87-89
    pupil understanding of process of,
        282-85
    reward in, 89-91
    role of teacher in, 477-79
    simplification of, 325
    theories of, 100-16
    theory and practice in, 10-11
    use of language in, 141-44
    whole method of, 147-48, 283-84
    whole versus part, 147-48
Least effort, law of, 132
Level of aspiration, 415-17
Life space, 41-42
Loyalties to the group, 131-32

Maladjustment,
    comic books and, 405-407
    conditions contributing to, 402-11
    and conformity, 398-99, 408-11
    incidence of, 398-401
    and intelligence level, 410-11
    and interparental tensions, 404
    motion pictures and, 404-406
    meaning of, 398-99
    as normative concept, 398-99
    and physical disability, 409
    radio and, 405
    recognition of, 408-12
    school situation and, 407, 414-15
    seriousness of, 408

Maladjustment (*Continued*)
sex differences in, 399, 410
and social pressure, 415-16
and socioeconomic status, 410
treatment of, 413-16
Malnutrition, 403
Manic-depressive psychosis, 403
Manners, acquirement of, 359-61
Mean, standard deviation (error) of,
225-26, 238
Mean (arithmetic), 216, 218-19, 237
formula for, 237
Means-objects, 111-12
Measurement, concept of, 217
Median, 216
Mental age, 29
Mental hygiene, 398-416
need of program of, 399-401
Methods of teaching,
authoritative, 328
developmental, 328-29
drill, 342-45
improvement of, 327-45
problem, 332-33
project, 335
psychological factors and, 326-27
psychological purpose of, 324-26
Mobility of pupils, 267
Mock-ups, use of, 182
Mode, 216
Models, use of, 182
Morals, influence of family on, 396-
97
Moron, 32
Motion pictures, 173, 175-80
effect of, on children, 404-406
frequency of attendance at, 405
value of, in education, 179-80
Motivation, 52-69
secondary, 61
strength of, 283
Motives, classification of, 65-69
Muscles, 79-80

Nearness, law of, 109
Nearsightedness, 74; *see also* Short-
sightedness
Negative adaptation, 50
Negativism, 138-41
Nerve cell, 76-77
Nerves, 72-79
motor, 77-79
Nervous impulse, 76-78
Nervous system, 71-79
Nonsense syllables, 88, 146-47, 149-
50
Normal curve, 221-25, 230

probability and, 222-24
table of, 229

Obedience, 50, 75; *see also* Disci-
pline
Objectives, educational, 7-10
Obscene language, 410
Overprotection, 12

Parsimony, principle of, 402
Perception, 40-50
delayed, 45
and inner attitudes, 46-47
and language, 45-46
and law of *Prägnanz,* 109
of meanings of words, 47-48
and past experience, 47-50
Personality, 34
description of, 385-88
effect of education upon, 390-97
effects of primary education on,
396
psychopathic, 403
of teacher, 436-37
Physical disability, 73, 271, 409
Pictures,
flat, 174
motion; *see* Motion pictures
projection of, 174-76
still, 173-74
Play, motivation of, 64-65
Power tests, 212
Practice, 94-95, 153, 286
distributed, 147-48, 283
law of, 106
massed, 147-48
negative, 125-26
spaced, 283
Prägnanz, law of, 109
"Problem child," 379
Problem solving, 13, 279-80
deductive and inductive approaches
to, 280
Project method, 60-61
Projection, 379-82
Projective techniques, 46-47, 411-13
Promotion systems, nonuniformity
of, 270-71
Proprioceptors, 73-75
Proximity, law of, 109
Psychoanalysis, 68, 378, 402
Psychologists,
contributions of, to education, 6
school, 20
Psychology,
child, 20
comparative, 19

definition of, 18
nature of, 16-19
Psychosis, 403, 408
Pulse rate, 54, 55, 80, 405
Punishment, 57, 60, 90, 140, 150-51, 423-24, 438-39
    Herbert Spencer on, 430-31
Puzzle-box experiments, 90-91, 106-107

Radio, effect of, on children, 405
Range of scores, 216
Rationalization, 381-82
Readiness, law of, 105
Reading, learning of, 45, 58, 263-65
Reading disability, 268
Recall, 88, 105
Receptors, 72-79
Recitation, 149-50
    procedure, criticism of, 329-31
    value of, 150
Recognition, 88
Redintegration, 88
Re-education, 266-71
    difficulties of, 266-67
    limitations of, 413
    problems of, 267-71
Reflex, psychogalvanic, 54-55
Regressive behavior, 408, 414-15
Reinforcement,
    emotional, 61, 68
    in learning, 89-92, 100-103
Rejection, 404
Remedial teaching, 259-74
    courses in methods and, 263-65
    determining need for, 262, 272
    and learning to read, 263-65
    and physical disabilities, 265
    in regular classes, 272
    training for, 271-72
    value of, 259-60
    various kinds of, 260-65
Repetition in learning, 93-95, 115-16
Response sensitivity, 390
Responses,
    of avoidance, 414-15
    conditioned, 35, 62-63, 79, 88-89
    latency of, 102-103
    minimal, 138
Retention, 88, 114
Retraining, 63
Retroactive inhibition, 148-49, 284
Reward,
    in learning, 89-92, 100-103, 112, 150-51
    secondary, 102
    as teaching device, 334-35

Ritual, 120-21
Role, 130-32, 367-69, 394, 433-34

Schizophrenia, 403
School levels,
    analysis of, 293-305
    history of development of, 297-300
    psychological importance of, 293-94
    psychology of organization of, 300-305
    and teaching effectiveness, 304
    varieties of practices in, 294-97
Schooling as a selective agent, 26
Schools, changes in, 295-97
Scientific method, 14
Segregation in schools, 392-94
Self-discipline, 423, 429
Self-expression, 165
Sense-organ adaption, 86
Sense organs, 72-80
Sensory disability, 73, 271, 409
Sex education, 416
Shortsightedness, 74
Similarity, law of, 88, 109
Skills, 95, 145-46, 151-53
    motor, 152-53
Smoking, 154
Social behavior, determinants of, 395-97
Social institutions,
    conservative tendency of, 352
    and the individual, 349-55
    influence of, upon education, 350-54
    as limiting factors, 354-55
    managerial aspects of, 352-54
    and personal liberty, 355
    psychology of, 349-57
Socialization,
    extra-familial factors in, 366-71
    influence of family on, 362-65
    as learned behavior, 359-61
    role as factor in, 367-69
Sociometric techniques, 472
Specialization and general education, 307-308
Speed tests, 212
Standard deviation, 220-21, 227
    formula for, 221, 237
Standard deviation (error) of mean, formula for, 238
Standard deviation (error) of difference between means, formula for, 238
Standard error, 226
Stereograph, 173-74, 186

Stereoscope, 174
Stimulus, 52-53, 55, 78-79, 89
Study,
  as behavior, 275-76
  conditions for efficient, 281-86
  definition of, 275
  nature of, 275-80
  practical suggestions for, 287-89
  practice as a condition of, 286-87
  supervised, 331-32
  types of, 276-80
Success, 61, 106-107, 130-31, 415
Survey of community as instructional
    device, 186

Tasks, finished and unfinished, 284-85
Teacher ratings, by students, 394-95
Teaching, 477-94
  aptitude for, 482-84
  factors in successful, 479-84
  judging efficiency of, 479-82, 484-85
  prediction of success in, 486-89
  self-improvement and, 491-94
Temper tantrums, 75
Tension, 54
Testing,
  in industry, 205
  limitations of 37-39
  in second World War, 205
Tests,
  classification of, 207-208
  comparable forms of, 214
  construction of, 211-14
  early development of, 27-31
  how to use, 208-11
  ink-blot, 8
  as instructional aids, 213-16
  interpretation of, 214-16
  objectivity of 210
  power, 212
  reliability of, 31-32, 209-10, 211
  Rorschach, 18
  selection of items for, 212
  speed, 212
  student evaluation of, 213
  Thematic   Apperception   Test
    (TAT), 412

usability of, 211
uses of, 205-207
  administrative, 206-207
  in remedial instruction, 196-97
  by students, 207
  by teachers, 207
validity of, 208-10
Thinking, 34-35
Thought, creative, 162-63
Tics, 125-26
Tolerance, 13, 393
Tonus, 54
Training,
  of animals, 127-29
  vocational, 13
Traits,
  integration of, 375-85
  psychological measurement of, 26
Transfer,
  of attitudes, 255
  of subject matter, 250-55
  of training, 116, 133, 240-56
  definition of, 247-48
  and expectation, 249-50
  as function of time interval between
    tests, 249
  history of, 242-47
  identical elements in, 246
  kinds of, 248-56
  relationships as a basis for, 252
  teaching and, 133, 256
  theories of, 245-47
Trial and error, 35, 106-107, 118-22,
    124-25, 279
Trial and success, 118

Validity,
  curricular, 209
  statistical, 31-32, 208-11
Vector, 113
Vision, 74
Vocabulary, increase of, 278

Writing, learning of, 118-19

z-score, 228-30
  use of, in correlation, 231-32